DIOGENES (c.404–c.323 .... Sinope on the Black Sea coast as the son of a banker, but later settled in Athens, where he became acquainted with Socratic moral thought, supposedly from Antisthenes, a disciple of Socrates who advocated an ascetic way of life. Taking such ideas to an extreme, Diogenes cast aside whatever he may have owned to live as a beggar in the streets. He thought that we should anticipate the worst that fate can bring by living a life of hardship, and be contented to satisfy our basic needs in the simplest way possible. Casting scorn not only on luxury but on civilized life and culture in general, he tried to shock others into changing their lives by behaving in a provocative and shameless manner, and by subjecting people to his acerbic wit. He thus came to be known as the Dog, and his philosophy and way of life as Cynic, meaning dog-like. Our knowledge of him is derived almost entirely from anecdotes and from sayings ascribed to him. His most notable follower was Crates of Thebes, a man of more conciliatory character who had Zeno, the founder of Stoicism, as one of his pupils. Although Cynicism left its mark on the Stoic movement, it was not widely adopted in its own right until the Roman period, when the Cynic street-preacher would become a familiar figure.

Aristippos of Cyrene (c.435–c.360 BC), the disciple of Socrates who became the founder of the Cyrenaic school of philosophy, is known to us mainly through anecdotes as in the case of Diogenes; but his view of life could hardly have been more different, since he thought that happiness is to be sought in the pleasure of the moment, and so introduced a hedonistic strain into the Socratic succession.

ROBIN HARD has translated Apollodorus' *Library of Greek Mythology* and Marcus Aurelius' *Meditations* for Oxford World's Classics. He is the author of the Routledge *Handbook of Greek Mythology*.

OXFORD WORLD'S CLASSICS

For over 100 years Oxford World's Classics have brought
readers closer to the world's great literature. Now with over 700
titles—from the 4,000-year-old myths of Mesopotamia to the
twentieth century's greatest novels—the series makes available
lesser-known as well as celebrated writing.

The pocket-sized hardbacks of the early years contained
introductions by Virginia Woolf, T. S. Eliot, Graham Greene,
and other literary figures which enriched the experience of reading.
Today the series is recognized for its fine scholarship and
reliability in texts that span world literature, drama and poetry,
religion, philosophy, and politics. Each edition includes perceptive
commentary and essential background information to meet the
changing needs of readers.

OXFORD WORLD'S CLASSICS

DIOGENES THE CYNIC

Sayings and Anecdotes

with Other Popular Moralists

Translated with an Introduction and Notes by
ROBIN HARD

OXFORD
UNIVERSITY PRESS

OXFORD

UNIVERSITY PRESS

Great Clarendon Street, Oxford OX2 6DP

Oxford University Press is a department of the University of Oxford.
It furthers the University's objective of excellence in research, scholarship,
and education by publishing worldwide in

Oxford New York

Auckland Cape Town Dar es Salaam Hong Kong Karachi
Kuala Lumpur Madrid Melbourne Mexico City Nairobi
New Delhi Shanghai Taipei Toronto

With offices in

Argentina Austria Brazil Chile Czech Republic France Greece
Guatemala Hungary Italy Japan Poland Portugal Singapore
South Korea Switzerland Thailand Turkey Ukraine Vietnam

Oxford is a registered trade mark of Oxford University Press
in the UK and in certain other countries

Published in the United States
by Oxford University Press Inc., New York

British Library Cataloguing in Publication Data

Data available

Library of Congress Cataloging in Publication Data

Library of Congress Control Number: 2012930317

Typeset by Cenveo, Bangalore, India
Printed in Great Britain
on acid-free paper by
Clays Ltd, Elcograf S.p.A.

ISBN 978-0-19-958924-1

15

CONTENTS

Introduction   vii

The Cynic Succession   xxvii

The Cyrenaic Succession   xxviii

Note on the Texts   xxix

Note on the Ancient Sources   xxxi

Select Bibliography   xxxv

SAYINGS AND ANECDOTES

PART 1 · DIOGENES AND THE EARLY CYNICS

I   A Humorous Portrait of Diogenes and Aristippos   3

II   Diogenes' Conversion to the Ascetic Life   6

III   The Sage as Beggar   12

IV   Self-characterization   19

V   A Short Cut to Philosophy and Virtue   26

VI   The World of Illusion   36

VII   Religion and Superstition   44

VIII   Politicians and Rulers   50

IX   The Enslavement of Diogenes   57

X   Moralistic and Traditional   62

XI   Diogenes as Wit   72

XII   Old Age and Death   79

XIII   Immediate Followers of Diogenes   84

XIV   Sayings, Anecdotes, and Verses of Crates   88

XV   The Followers of Crates and Later Cynics   99

XVI   Postscript: Bion of Borysthenes   105

XVII   Antisthenes as Forerunner of Cynicism   117

PART 2 · ARISTIPPOS AND THE CYRENAICS

XVIII　Aristippos of Cyrene　　　　　　　　　　　123

XIX　The Cyrenaic School under the Younger Aristippos　　143

XX　The Other Cyrenaics　　　　　　　　　　　150

PART 3 · APOCRYPHAL LETTERS

XXI　Selections from the Cynic Letters　　　　　　159

XXII　Correspondence of Aristippos　　　　　　175

Explanatory Notes　　　　　　　　　　　　181

Index of Names　　　　　　　　　　　　　261

Index of Themes　　　　　　　　　　　　　265

INTRODUCTION

DIOGENES the Cynic remains a widely familiar figure, even if very little is remembered about him among people who have no special interest in the ancient world. He is popularly known for having lived in a barrel or tub and for his barbed utterances. But Diogenes was more than a picturesque eccentric, and it is only when such stories are considered in their wider context, as part of the very full surviving record of what Diogenes was supposed to have said and done, that it becomes apparent that he was trying to convey a serious message through his disconcerting behaviour and caustic wit.

Diogenes' makeshift home was more accurately a very large ceramic jar, of a kind that was used for storing grain or water. Since he had deliberately chosen to live as a beggar in the streets of Athens, he had no house to return to, and would have taken shelter at night wherever he could, in doorways, temples, or public arcades. It need not be thought that he used a particular jar as his regular home, this is merely one form of shelter that was mentioned among others, even if it became especially memorable for its emblematic value. It is not in fact as highly stressed in ancient sources as one might suppose—more emphasis was placed on Diogenes' Cynic uniform and accoutrements. To be prepared for any kind of weather, he would wear a rough cloak folded double, which would enable him to keep warm in winter and cool in summer; and since he owned no more than what he could lug around with him, he would carry a knapsack (*pera*) for his provisions and scanty possessions. Perhaps there was even room in it for a few books and for writing materials.

It was a commonplace of Socratic thought that one can be rich by being satisfied with little, and so achieve a measure of invulnerability to fortune. Diogenes radicalized this idea, taking it to the utmost extreme. If one takes into account only one's most basic needs and desires, putting everything else aside as mere fancy and illusion, and is content to satisfy those needs in the simplest and most direct way possible, one needs hardly anything at all; and if one divests oneself of all that one possesses to live as a vagrant, one can anticipate the very worst and become inured to any hardship, and so achieve complete invulnerability to fortune. Dismissing almost everything that people value and pursue, not only luxury and pleasure but also civic and cultural endeavour, as being utterly worthless, one can achieve assured contentment, so Diogenes thought, by living like an animal in the streets, without any concern for the future. According to an anecdote recorded by a younger contemporary of his, he claimed to have drawn this lesson by observing the behaviour of a mouse (see **9a**[1]).

Someone who lives in the open in this way has to do everything in public; Diogenes would eat such food as he could gain out in the streets, and the story even went that he would masturbate in public (for what easier way could there be to satisfy his sexual desires). The Cynic life was thus of necessity a shameful one, and far from playing that down, Diogenes deliberately behaved in a shocking manner to show his contempt for conventional social attitudes. This brings us to the meaning of the Cynic name, which was derived from a nickname bestowed on Diogenes because of the shameless manner of his life. He came to be called the Dog (*Kuōn*; Aristotle could refer to him by that name without need for further specification, see **189**), and those who followed his example by choosing to live like dogs came to be known accordingly as Cynics (*kunikos* being the corresponding adjective). Diogenes is presented in anecdotes as having welcomed the name with glee, putting his own constructions on it to make points of his own.

The name could also be interpreted as referring to the way in which he accosted people to force his ideas on them, through cutting wit and acerbic humour. He yapped like a dog and had a biting tongue. In taking his philosophy into the streets, he adopted a very different procedure from that of Socrates, and instead of causing people to reflect on their moral assumptions by questioning them and engaging in reasoned discussion, he resorted to shock tactics both in the manner of his speech and in his behaviour. It does him no discredit to say that he put on a constant performance, playing his chosen role as dog and mad Socratic. His approach is summed up in two anecdotes in which he provokes a response by assuming a contrary path to the crowd. He walked into a theatre against the flow of the emerging crowd, and when asked why, said that he spent his entire life doing that; he walked backwards in a public arcade, and when people laughed at him, retorted that it was they who should be ashamed for taking the wrong direction in life.

---

[1] Bold numbers refer to the numbered anecdotes in the text.

To become a true individual and proper human being, so he thought, one must turn aside from conventional society and reject all its values, to live in accordance with nature, and nature at a very basic level; otherwise one will simply remain a member of the crowd. It is this thought that is expressed in what is perhaps his best-known anecdote. He lit a lamp in daylight and walked through the streets of Athens with it; and when asked why, replied that he was looking for a man. Since lighting a lamp in daylight was a proverbial expression for a futile exercise, this was a symbolic action which was designed to suggest that it is pointless to expect to be able to find a man in Athens. An honest man? A good one? No, the thought is more radical than that. The mass of people, who accept conventional social values, not knowing what human nature is and what it means to live in accordance with nature, are not really proper human beings at all, but anonymous members of the crowd, or slaves, or scum (to use the expressions that Diogenes applies to such people in anecdotes in Section IV).

A man who could suggest such a thing was not remotely cynical in the modern sense of the word, but in deadly earnest. He was convinced that people should utterly change their lives, just as he had done, if they were to fulfil their nature as human beings and so become fully human. The shift in meaning in the word 'cynicism' reflected the way in which Diogenes came to be perceived after he was rediscovered during the Renaissance, from translations of Diogenes Laertius and other writings. As he became a familiar figure in the wider culture, people seem to have been particularly struck by the biting tone of his humour, and thus to have interpreted his sallies as being purely negative in intent. 'It cannot be helped that dogs bark and vomit their foul stomachs', wrote William Harvey in the seventeenth century, 'and that Cynics should be numbered among philosophers.' If Cynicism could be seen in this way as the expression of a bilious and misanthropic spirit, it is understandable that the term should have come to describe the attitude of those who are disaffected with the world, and are thus determined always to put the worst construction on human motives. But one has to put such thoughts aside in approaching Diogenes; he attacked conventional attitudes because he wanted to restamp the currency, replacing false values with those which would (according to his conception) enable human beings to fulfil their true nature.

The Socratic Succession

Diogenes was, then, a man who took everything to extremes, with regard not only to the arduous and (according to conventional standards) shameful manner of his life, but also to the provocative way in which he set out to advance his ideas. Plato is supposed to have remarked, when asked about Diogenes, that he was Socrates gone mad. If this saying points to the way in which he flouted normal rules of behaviour, it acknowledges at the same time that his ideas and mode of action represented an extreme development of certain Socratic ideas, and could be interpreted as meaningful in that light. He was perceived as being something more than a mere eccentric.

If the Cynic life was to be practicable, it was in fact necessary that its practitioners should be able to rely on the understanding and complicity of the public. For a paradox lay at the very heart of Diogenes' enterprise. Although the Cynic may have claimed to achieve complete independence by reducing his needs to a minimum and living in the streets, it was nonetheless true that by dispossessing himself in such a way, he was depriving himself of all means of support in the environment in which he was living. Cynicism was an urban phenomenon. Its practitioners would not withdraw from human society, like some later Christian ascetics, to support themselves in the countryside or wilderness by their own labour. They had to rely instead on alms from people who valued them for providing a moral example or performing a beneficial service as moral preachers. Their activities had to be perceived accordingly as having some relevance to the moral lives of ordinary people, even if few would choose to adopt the Cynic life. According to the anecdotal tradition, Diogenes had no compunction about begging because he was confident that he was offering something far more valuable in return; he was thus said to have refused an invitation to a meal because the man who was offering the invitation had not been properly grateful to him on a previous occasion.

To appreciate how Diogenes fitted into the Socratic tradition, we must consider the chronology. He lived long enough into the fourth century for it to be plausible that he should have met Alexander as king. The two came to be associated in the apophthegmatic tradition as symbolic opposites, Alexander being a man possessed by such insatiable desires that he could barely find satisfaction in the conquest of much of the known world, while Diogenes could find contentment in what nature offered in any particular moment, a contrast expressed in the famous story in which he could find nothing else to ask of Alexander than that he should stand out of his sun. Although the notion that he died on the same day as Alexander, in June 323, was surely an idea inspired by this symbolic connection, he does seem to have died in that general period. If he was old in the 113th Olympiad, i.e. 328–325, as is reported, and lived to an advanced age, seventy or eighty in different accounts, he would have been born at or near the end of the fifth century, not long before the death of Socrates in 399. He might thus have been able to meet immediate followers of Socrates, even if not the master himself, and he died at the threshold of the Hellenistic age, during which Stoicism would become the dominant moral philosophy in the Socratic tradition. The dates to keep in mind, then, are 399, when Socrates died, and 301, when Zeno of Citium, the founder of Stoicism, began teaching his philosophy in the Stoa Poikile at Athens.

Cynicism and Stoicism were interrelated. Although Zeno studied with masters from a number of schools, having broader interests and greater speculative ambitions than could be satisfied by any Cynic, it was above all by becoming acquainted with Cynic ideas through Crates, the foremost follower of Diogenes, that he was inspired to develop the austere ethical doctrines that would be central to his system; and early Stoicism had a distinctly Cynic flavour, even if later Stoics generally sought to disown the more scandalous and anti-social features of Cynicism. Diogenes was highly regarded among the Stoics, not only as a predecessor but also as a link in the succession that led back to Socrates. As has been noted, he was separated from Socrates by a generation, just as he was from Zeno. If he arrived at Athens before he was much beyond the threshold of middle age, he could have learned about Socrates and his ideas from men who had known him. There are many anecdotes that show him jousting with Plato (died 349), but we have to look to a less familiar figure, Antisthenes, to find a friend of Socrates with whom he would have had some affinity. For it was Antisthenes who took the lead in developing the ascetic strain in Socratic thought; and it was he who, rightly or wrongly, came to be regarded as having been the master of Diogenes, so forming the first link in the chain that led from Socrates to the Stoics: Socrates–Antisthenes–Diogenes–Crates–Zeno.

The moral thought of Socrates is too subtle and elusive to be open to brief discussion. The essential point for present purposes is that he introduced a revolution in moral ideas by questioning traditionally accepted values, suggesting that our highest and essential good lies in the good of the soul, as our moral centre and best self, and that all external goods, such as bodily pleasure, health, and social reputation, are correspondingly of subordinate value. If Socrates truly believed in this way that our essential good is to be sought within rather than in externals, it might be expected that he would have set no store on luxury or appearances, and he was in fact famous for the simplicity of his way of life. He would walk around bare-footed and his shabby cloak was something of a joke. In Xenophon's *Memorabilia*, a critic accuses him of living a life that no slave would put up with: 'Your food and drink are of the cheapest sort, your cloak is only a wretched one, but you wear one and the same winter and summer, without ever donning shoes or a tunic. . . . You should consider yourself to be a professor of wretchedness.' But one gains the impression that this was as much an expression of idiosyncrasy as a deliberately chosen course of action; Socrates seems to have been absent-minded with regard to matters which were of subordinate interest to him. It was Antisthenes who developed this asceticism into a deliberate programme, and made it central to his endeavour.

One can conveniently gain an impression of Antisthenes' general outlook from a speech that is put into his mouth by his contemporary Xenophon (see 534). He declares that he prides himself on his wealth even though he does not have a penny in the world. For while many who own a fortune remain unsatisfied and desire ever more, someone like himself, who is satisfied with a bare sufficiency, and recognizes that true wealth lies in one's soul, cannot discover the bounds of his riches. What is more, he can pass on the wealth of his soul to anyone who desires it, and finds his greatest pleasure in conversing at leisure with like-minded people. This accords with sayings in which Antisthenes praises frugality and self-control, and pours scorn on physical enjoyment ('I'd rather be mad than feel pleasure'; see further under 533).

After becoming acquainted with such ideas from the Socratic tradition, Diogenes radicalized them in such a way as to transform their very nature. For someone like Antisthenes, poverty meant nothing more than being satisfied to live modestly on limited private means, while Diogenes thought that one should anticipate the very worst that fate can bring by plunging into a life of complete destitution. He came to believe, furthermore, that a positive value can be put on hardship, because it not only serves as a form of training which enables a person to rise above any suffering, but also makes it possible for him to find a positive pleasure in self-abnegation. 'For in fact the very despising of pleasure is itself a very great source of pleasure provided that one has exercised oneself in that beforehand; and just as those who have become habituated to a life of pleasure find it most disagreeable to cross over to a contrary form of life, so those who have undertaken the opposite course of training find greater pleasure in scorning pleasure than in the pleasures themselves' (from 105).

In the second place, Diogenes' course entailed a complete rejection of ordinary civilized life. He had nothing but contempt for civic society and almost every aspect of Greek culture. To him literature, music, mathematics, science, and philosophical investigation and discussion were a distraction and a waste of time. By comparison to more conventional Socratics, he had an uncomplicated, naturalistic, and (one might say) diminished view of human nature. We have to put aside the illusions that are propagated within the social order, so he thought, to live a simple animal life, being contented to satisfy our basic needs in the simplest way possible. How far this takes us from the views of Antisthenes as presented in Xenophon's discourse, as a man who wanted to suppress any excessive desires for external goods to be able to concentrate on his inner wealth, and so enjoy a cultivated life of leisure centring around discussion and shared pursuits with his friends. Diogenes was a great simplifier who lost sight of an entire dimension of human life by scorning it as a tissue of illusion.

While it is meaningful and illuminating to view the ideas of Diogenes in relation to those of Socrates and Antisthenes, it is far from certain that he was really a pupil of Antisthenes as the tradition suggested. In view of the importance that came to be attached to philosophical pedigrees, the idea of a formal pupil–master relationship could well have been a figment of Hellenistic authors who wrote about the philosophical successions. This is a matter which we must consider in relation to the biographical tradition.

Diogenes came from a city that was very much at the fringes of the Greek world, the Milesian colony of Sinope about half-way along the southern coast of the Black Sea. This was a prosperous merchant-city which lay at the end of a caravan route from the upper Euphrates valley, and traded in a wide variety of goods including salt-fish, timber for ship-building, and the ochre known as Sinopean red earth. We may assume that Diogenes was a fairly well-educated man who would not have been born into poverty, and tradition stated that he belonged to a family of some importance, as the son of a banker called Hicesias, who was responsible for the issuing and supervision of the Sinopean currency. As it happens the inscription 'HIKESIO' can be found on the Sinopean coins issued between about 360 and 320 BC; and although it is hardly likely that these marks refer to Diogenes' father, since the coins date to the latter part of Diogenes' own lifetime, they do serve to confirm the biographical tradition if it can be assumed that their issuer belonged to the same family, perhaps as a cousin or nephew of his.

If he really was born into such high circles in his home city, it is all the more surprising that he should have ended up in exile in Athens. Legend suggested that this came about precisely because his father occupied the position that he did, since it furnished a tempting opportunity for fraud. While supervising the mint on his father's behalf, so the story went, Diogenes adulterated the coinage, or else Hicesias himself did, but the malpractice was discovered and he had to flee into exile, either on his own or along with his father. As confirmation of the truth of this story, it was pointed out that Diogenes himself had admitted to adulterating the currency in a book that was attributed to him. Whether or not the book was genuinely written by him, he really does seem to have spoken in such terms, but applying the words in a figurative rather than a literal sense; he was setting out to 'restamp the currency' by rejecting conventional values to embrace those more in accord with nature, at its most basic level. In all probability, the idea that he had been exiled for altering the currency arose because this metaphorical expression came to be interpreted in a literal sense.

It is true that numismatic evidence has been put forward in support of the historicity of the tale, but to provide independent corroboration it would have to be shown that the coinage had been altered with fraudulent intent. Although coins were apparently defaced in unusually high proportion in the 340s, the cancellations would have served the beneficial purpose of putting bad coinage out of circulation, and they could only account for the exile of Diogenes and discrediting of his father if enemies had exploited them as a pretext for unfounded accusations. Since this is a mere hypothesis which would never have been suggested if it had not been for the prior existence of the biographical legend, the argument is a circular one. It provides the sole basis for the common assumption than Diogenes did not arrive in Athens until he was over fifty (and well after the death of Antisthenes). The only other specific suggestion that can be offered is that his departure from Sinope was connected with a major upheaval in 370 or somewhat earlier, when the Persian satrap Datames seized control of the city. But it is quite possible that he initially travelled to Athens for reasons of his own, out of cultural curiosity or for commercial reasons.

If Diogenes' exile was explained by the story of the coinage, his conversion to philosophy, and more specifically an ascetic way of life, was explained through an encounter with Antisthenes. There was doubtless an element of truth in this, in so far as he would have been inspired to set out on his peculiar path by becoming acquainted in Athens with the moral thought of Socrates, and especially the ascetic strain of it that was expounded above all by Antisthenes, both in person and in his writings; but whether he really became a pupil of Antisthenes in a formal and direct sense is more doubtful.

In late Hellenistic and later sources Antisthenes is sometimes imagined as initiating Diogenes directly into the Cynic life. Thus in an apocryphal letter of Diogenes (see **641**), Antisthenes shows him the short cut to virtue (see below) and prepares him for that arduous path by fitting him out with the standard Cynic accoutrements, dressing him in a doubled cloak and hanging a knapsack around his shoulders. After Antisthenes came to be regarded by many as the founder of Cynicism as a result of the place assigned to him in the succession, some people did in fact come to believe that he himself had worn a rough cloak of that kind and perhaps even carried a knapsack (see under **533** and note); but what use would they have been to a married man who owned a house, however modest, in Athens? The notion that Antisthenes initiated Diogenes into specifically Cynic ideas and practices, and was thus the founder of Cynicism, can safely be discounted.

It is among the anecdotes that one can generally find the best evidence for the early legend of Diogenes. Remarkably enough there are only two in which he appears in the company of Antisthenes. One presents him as vainly suggesting suicide to an ailing Antisthenes,

xvi   *Introduction*

who is plainly regarded as being of relatively weak character, while the other purports to explain how he initially managed to become a pupil of Antisthenes. Antisthenes tried to drive him away at first, so we are told, because he was generally unwilling to accept pupils, but when Diogenes persisted and refused to be intimidated when threatened with a blow from his stick, he was so impressed that he relented and accepted him as a pupil (see **6**). There is no reason to think that the historical Antisthenes was in any way surly or unsociable. Xenophon portrays him as an urbane character who is happy to engage in discussion with like-minded people; after having been generously endowed with spiritual wealth by Socrates he in his turn (so he is presented as saying, p. 121) is not mean or grudging with anyone, but passes on the wealth that he has in his soul to anyone who would like to share it. He is recorded as having had followers, furthermore, who were known as Antistheneians (not Cynics!). Our anecdote reflects a problem that arose when Antisthenes came to be regarded as the original founder of Cynicism. If that was the case, why did Diogenes stand at the head of the entire subsequent succession, as the only Cynic to be recorded from the generation after Antisthenes? It was surely this consideration that prompted the invention of a story in which Antisthenes is imagined as being so cantankerous (a familiar Cynic trait) that only Diogenes has sufficient strength of mind to force his way into his company. The anecdote itself is not even original but simply a reworking of a well-known story that was recounted about Themistocles, as explained in a note to **6**.

The lack of tales connecting the two figures suggests that they were not associated in any special way when the anecdotal tradition first crystallized during Diogenes' lifetime and shortly afterwards, especially as the main story was plainly of relatively late fabrication. How Diogenes first became acquainted with the currents of thought in Athens, and through what circumstances he came to devise and adopt the full Cynic way of life, are matters that are fated to remain a mystery to us. Biographical tales of another kind which portray him as learning from the example of animals or children probably do go back to the early tradition.

The Ancient Sources

Our best single source for Diogenes, and indeed the only one to provide a comprehensive account of the early Cynics and Cyrenaics, is Diogenes Laertius' *Lives and Opinions of the Ancient Philosophers*, dating from the third century AD. This is an uncritical compilation by an author whose intellectual resources were plainly limited; but in the case of sages like Diogenes and Aristippos, whose messages were conveyed mainly through records of their actions and sayings, his limitations became a virtue, since he liked nothing better than a good story or witty saying, and was happy to accumulate any number of them without alteration or elaboration.

It may be useful to examine how he constructed his account of Diogenes, because it will give an idea of the nature of the material from which we have to form our understanding of him, and of the relative richness and value of the different kinds of material.

Our author begins with a summary of his earlier life-history, which is our main source for the matter summarized above. Since such biographies tend to concentrate on the main turning-points that are relevant to a philosopher's calling, one would not expect to find much about the accidents of his life, but this history of Diogenes is thin and schematic even by normal standards, covering only his exile and conversion. His life then assumed an unchanging pattern, and his activities are indicated through a multitude of apophthegms, which are set at no specific point in time and do not form part of the biography proper. At some stage in the latter part of his life, however, he was supposed to have been captured by pirates and sold into slavery, to serve in Corinth as a masterful slave; although this was almost certainly a fiction invented in the third century BC (see Section IX and notes), it was adopted into his biography to form the concluding part of it, along with the stories of his death, which was sometimes placed in Corinth. Rightly or wrongly, Corinth came to be regarded as having been something of a second home for him. He may not have spent his whole time in Athens in any case, and there are stories that show him as travelling abroad, especially to the games, where he could have found a large audience for his moral preaching.

In accordance with his usual practice, Diogenes Laertius passes without break from the beginning of this life-history to a collection of sayings and anecdotes. Although these are of course biographical in a sense, in so far as they show Diogenes living the life that he has chosen and trying to convince others of its virtues, the material belongs to a distinctive genre, that of the apophthegm, consisting either of pithy sayings or of brief anecdotes centred around such a saying, often delivered as repartee. The nature of this material will be considered further below. Our author had a special love for it, always trying to gather together a good selection for his philosophers, and one can sense the delight that he felt in having such a gold-mine to draw on in the case of Diogenes, for whom it was all-important. He recounts one short anecdote after another, page after page, piling them together higgledy-piggledy in no sort of order. And it is here that Diogenes comes to life, and the meaning of his message becomes apparent, rather than through teachings and arguments and a body of ideas, as with any ordinary philosopher.

Although primarily a biographer, Diogenes Laertius did also try to offer an account of the opinions and doctrines, *doxai*, of his philosophers in the form of a doxography. This was a more demanding task than cobbling together life-histories or collecting anecdotes, and the results were not always very satisfactory; but he could provide clear and useful summaries, as for the Cyrenaics. When it came to Diogenes and the Cynics, however, he plainly had real difficulty, and could come up with nothing better than a rag-bag of ill-assorted material, not so much as a result of his own incapacity as of the fact that Cynic teaching was not conveyed through abstract ideas. The centre of gravity lay elsewhere.

There are two Cynic doxographies to consider, one specifically Diogenean and the other relating to the teaching of the early school as a whole. We will cast an eye on the latter (96) because it raises some basic points about the nature of Cynicism, indicating at the start that there was dispute as to whether it was really a philosophy at all or just a way of life. If it was accepted as being a philosophy, it had to be acknowledged that the Cynics did not attempt to provide any thorough or elaborate theoretical foundation for their moral teachings. By contrast to the Stoics, they devoted no attention to 'logic' and 'physics', thinking it a waste of time to develop a theory of knowledge and discourse, or to try to establish the place of man in the order of nature and the world as a whole.

If they resembled Socrates in concentrating on the moral issues alone, the Cynics differed from him in thinking that it was equally a waste of time to engage in subtle and extensive moral investigation and discussion. Action of a very simple kind was what was demanded: to plunge into a life of deprivation and hardship. To live in accordance with virtue was the end and chief good for them as for the Stoics, but they had adopted their own special route to that end, which could be described as a short cut to virtue. This notion has an interesting background. Prodicos, a contemporary of Socrates, had devised a little allegory in which Heracles was made to choose between two paths in life, the easy one that leads to a life of pleasure and self-indulgence, or the difficult one that leads to virtue; the path to virtue may be hard at first, but nothing worthwhile can be achieved without toil and effort, and that is the sole route to true happiness. This idea and image, which was taken up by Antisthenes, was altered in the Cynic context, so that the choice now had to be made between an easier or harder route to the same destination, namely to virtue and the happiness that is grounded in it. In this form the image summarized very neatly how Cynicism came to be viewed, especially in relation to Stoicism, and became so familiar that authors writing for a general audience could refer to 'the short cut' without need for further explanation. If understood in such a way, Cynicism could be regarded as representing an alternative route to the same goal as the Stoics were aiming to reach, a strenuous and unintellectual route which might be appropriate for some and not for others.

Sayings and Anecdotes

We must now pass on to the all-important sayings and anecdotes. These belonged to a specific genre of literature, that of the apophthegm, which formed part of the wisdom literature along with proverbs, fables, and the like. Apophthegms depended on their brevity for their expressive power. They could consist just of a pithy saying, 'the roots of education are bitter but their fruit is sweet'; the Greek term for this was a *gnomē* (hence our word 'gnomic'). Or a saying could be presented as an answer to a question. 'When asked how the educated differ from the uneducated, Aristotle replied, "As do the living from the dead."' Although the answer is put into the mouth of Aristotle, one senses at once that the thought originated as anonymous wisdom in the oral tradition, as in the case of the preceding saying, which was also ascribed to Aristotle. A question and answer could be simply a different way of presenting gnomic wisdom; indeed the response could already be fully implicit in the question (see e.g. 314). In many cases, however, the response would be set in a

more definite context, within a brief anecdote; and this could help to
bring out the idiosyncrasies of the speaker, or to set his character or
outlook in contrast with the questioner who appears with him in the
anecdote. The pre-Socratic philosopher Anaxagoras, for instance, devoted himself to the study of nature and the universe, and so gained
a reputation for otherworldliness, as expressed in the following anecdote: 'When someone asked, "Have you no concern for your native
land?", he replied, "Hush now, I have the very greatest concern for
it", pointing up to the sky.'

The basic unit of currency within this genre was, then, the *gnomē*
or the apophthegm (in the narrow sense). Although many of these
were enjoyed simply for their wit and lacked any serious content,
they could also serve a useful purpose by expressing moral ideas in a
pungent form and helping to propagate them. The word *chreia*, effectively meaning a 'useful' saying or anecdote, thus came to be employed
as a collective term for them, especially in regard to their usefulness.
First recorded in the title of a work by the early Cynic Metrocles (see
188), this usage may actually have originated within Cynic circles,
and it reflects the value that was attached to the apophthegm as a
mode of expression within that tradition. If the *chreiai* of Diogenes
are sometimes regarded nowadays as being no more than a collection
of funny stories, that was in no way the ancient view of the matter.

Originating for the most part in the oral tradition (although they
could also make their first appearance in written works as variants or
original inventions), such sayings and apophthegms came to be set
down in writing in anthologies, which could either be general in
scope or more specialized. In addition to sayings of philosophers and
sages, those of a wide range of other people were also collected, as can
be seen in Plutarch's anthologies of the sayings of kings and com-
manders and of the laconic wit of the Spartans. These collections
were partly designed to furnish immediate enjoyment or edification,
and partly to provide a resource for those who might want to make
use of *chreiai* in their own compositions, such as speeches or moral
treatises. When putting apophthegms to use in such a context,
authors would often present them in an elaborated form, as can be
seen in examples from Aelian and Plutarch below (e.g. **70a** and **236**);
but the core would remain unchanged, and nothing essential would
be added in the process.

Even if Diogenes Laertius did not confine his attention to the *chreiai* of his philosophers, he devoted a section of his biographies to them, in so far as they were available. In doing so, he acted essentially as an anthologist, making no attempt to elaborate them or order them into a coherent narrative. On the whole they are of marginal interest for those who would wish to gain a better understanding of the character or thought of the philosopher in question. As can be seen from the examples cited for Aristotle above, the ascriptions tend to be arbitrary and the thoughts expressed tend to be too commonplace to reveal anything about the specific ideas of the supposed speaker. Anecdotes which are more personal in nature, like the one about Anaxagoras, are usually of interest primarily for what they reveal about later attitudes to the thinkers in question. To form a conception of their own ideas, one has to turn to what is recorded of their teachings and arguments. In the case of Diogenes, however, the situation is very different, because he himself set out to communicate his message through his wit and odd behaviour, rather than through a body of argument, and the stories that came to circulate about him in the oral tradition, whether true or happily invented, were creations or reflections of his own propaganda. Terse wit and repartee were his main medium of expression. His *chreiai* came to be collected in writing, moreover, at a very early period, especially in Cynic and Stoic circles, because people who attached value to his teaching were aware that these were his main legacy, and thus needed to be preserved if it was to be conveyed to future generations. Metrocles, the brother-in-law of Diogenes' main follower Crates, compiled the first recorded collection of *chreiai*, which presumably concentrated on Cynic material with Diogenes to the fore.

From the more typical anecdotes and sayings, as collected in Sections III–VIII, one can form a remarkably clear and definite picture of the man, and of his way of life, and of the ideas on which it was founded. And since this picture almost certainly crystallized within a century of his own lifetime, by the time of the early Stoics, it is reasonable to assume that it does reflect, without undue distortion, the true nature of the historical Diogenes.

The *chreiai* preserved under his name are of varied nature and origin, however, and have to be approached with some discrimination. It is always a problem with apophthegms that all too many of them are only loosely attached to the person to whom they are attributed. Anonymous material from the oral tradition would be arbitrarily ascribed to well-known people, and material would be transferred from lesser-known people to more familiar ones; and a figure like Diogenes, as a special hero of the genre, acted like a magnet in this regard, attracting all kinds of foreign matter. Even if some of it may be sufficiently appropriate to be scarcely distinguishable from what was originally Diogenean, much is devoid of any Cynic character or is even positively unsuitable. Since he was noted for his wit, any number of jokes with no moral content at all, either of anonymous origin or properly connected with wags like the musician Stratonicos (see e.g. 346 and note), were put into his mouth; and as with other moralists, moral commonplaces of indefinite origin came to be ascribed to him, and even hoary proverbial wisdom of the kind associated with the Seven Sages. Although this material can be interesting or entertaining, and has to be taken into account if one is to understand how Diogenes came to be popularly regarded in antiquity, it has no proper connection with him or his teaching, and is liable to confuse our idea of him. All the more definitely foreign material has therefore been placed separately in Sections X and XI. That does not mean, of course, that all the other *chreiai* originally belonged to Diogenes, but they are at least appropriate and can be interpreted in a Cynic light.

A second point that needs to be stressed is that among the *chreiai* that are typically Diogenean, there are many that are surely fictional. It is hardly likely, for instance, that Diogenes would ever have met Alexander, or that the king would have been either interested in him or impressed by him. One can go further and say that most or all of the anecdotes that place Diogenes in confrontation with a named individual, whether a ruler, orator, or philosopher, would have been invented by others to convey an idea of the contrasting attitudes of the two figures. That does not mean that they cannot reveal anything worthwhile about Diogenes. We have to rely quite as much on anecdotes of this nature, which convey other people's interpretation of him, as we do on those which could possibly have a historical basis.

The Cynic and Cyrenaic Successions

As can be seen from the diagram on p. xxvii, the Cynic succession can be traced for only three generations, with the last named successor of Diogenes living no later than the end of the third century BC.

Cynicism then disappeared from sight and was perhaps even extinct in the second and first centuries BC (except as a strain within Stoicism). It came back to life, however, in a most remarkable way by the first century AD, and the Cynic street-preacher would remain a familiar if not always welcome sight through much of the Roman Empire until the fifth century.

The Cynicism of Diogenes could all too easily have turned out to be a dead end. Not only did it demand exceptional fortitude and nerve to cast everything aside to live in destitution, but since the Cynic way of life was so closely associated with Diogenes, anyone who adopted it must have run the risk of appearing to be no more than a pale imitation of him. One such imitator was indeed known as Dog-collar. Diogenes was said to have remarked that even if people praised the Dog, none dared to accompany him on the hunt. Seven disciples are recorded by name, however, of whom Crates of Thebes was by far the most important. A man of gentler and more conciliatory character than Diogenes, he gave the creed a more human stamp and helped to ensure its survival. All the subsequent early Cynics who are named in the succession were either immediate followers of his or pupils of those followers; and most crucially, it was he who set Zeno on his Stoic path (see 463–6). Cynic ideals would then be transmitted as a strain within Stoicism, to be available for revival in their pure form. Of the Cynic followers of Crates, Hipparchia, who became his wife, was the most noteworthy.

Among the early Socratics, there is another founder of a school apart from Diogenes who is known to us primarily through sayings and anecdotes, namely Aristippos of Cyrene, and the second part of the book is devoted to him and his school. He belonged to an earlier generation than Diogenes, having been born in about 435, and was a friend and immediate associate of Socrates. His attitude to life could hardly have been more different from that of Diogenes and Antisthenes, since he regarded pleasure, in the form of immediate sensual gratification above all, as being our chief end, and so introduced a hedonistic strain into the Socratic tradition.

In his understanding of the end of human life and his basic conception of human nature, Antisthenes evidently followed Socrates quite closely, while Aristippos had ideas of his own. If Aristippos is to be counted as a Socratic nonetheless, the influence of the master is to be sought elsewhere, in his notion of the spirit in which one should seek for pleasure. He believed that one should not allow oneself to become enslaved by it or ever lose one's self-control, but should, on the contrary, maintain a sort of ironic detachment, enjoying pleasure on the wing in so far as it is available, but not being distressed if it should cease to be available. It should then be possible to grasp such pleasure as one can without sacrificing one's inner freedom, and to maintain one's cheerfulness and poise in all circumstances. For an appreciation of his character and the art of life that he cultivated, we have to rely largely on the anecdotes. Whether or not they give a reliable impression of the historical figure, which is more doubtful than in the case of Diogenes, a personality of distinctive and memorable character is revealed in them, and one who has evoked contrasting responses. W. K. C. Guthrie remarks in distaste that the anecdotes 'show that mixture of a kind of cockney wit with sheer boorish rudeness which also characterized Diogenes the Cynic'.[2] Others are disarmed by his humour and raffish charm. When asked what philosopher was most to his taste, Demonax, a Cynic of the Roman period, replied, 'I admire them all: Socrates I revere, Diogenes I admire, Aristippos I love.'

Although Aristippos spent much of his time abroad, notably at the court of Dionysios I of Syracuse, it seems likely that he finally returned to his native city of Cyrene in North Africa, where his Cyrenaic school would be mainly centred. In all probability he did not attempt to establish a theoretical basis for his ideas, and such doctrines as are recorded for the school, for instance those that relate pleasure to different kinds of movement, were formulated at a later period in any case. Aristippos transmitted his philosophy to his grandson of the same name through his daughter Arete ('Virtue'), and it was apparently Aristippos 'the Mother-taught' who developed the standard doctrines of the school, while Hegesias and Anniceris, two Cyrenaics who belonged to another line (see the diagram on p. xxviii), formed somewhat different ideas. The basic ideas of all three are clearly summarized in doxographies compiled by Diogenes Laertius (see 619, 625, and 630 respectively). Hegesias is of interest for the way in which his hedonistic premises led him into the direst pessimism; concluding that a predominance of pleasure cannot generally be assured, he came to believe that suicide can often be the best

---

[2] W. K. C. Guthrie, *Socrates* (Cambridge, 1971), 173.

option in life, and so came to be known as 'the Death-persuader'.
The Cyrenaics were sceptical in their epistemological outlook, argu-
ing that sense-impressions provide no reliable information about
anything that lies beyond our immediate sense-experience (see 621–
4). Our survey of the school concludes with Theodoros the Atheist,
who studied under Anniceris but was more eclectic in his views.

The book concludes with a selection from the apocryphal letters of
the Cynics and of Aristippos, in Part 3. The Cynic letters cannot be
dated with any certainty, but it is generally believed that most were
written in around the first century BC or AD, or somewhat later in the
case of those ascribed to Crates (which are of poorer quality than
those of Diogenes, and are partly dependent on them). This was an
unsophisticated form of literature, in which familiar stories and
themes were dramatized without any attempt at originality. This
mediocrity of ambition is an advantage for present purposes, since
the letters remain true to the early tradition, and do not present an
amended or idealized image of Diogenes as is the case with authors
like Epictetus or Dio Chrysostom. The letters addressed to
Hipparchia, which combine to build up a narrative, provide a welcome supplement to the little that is recorded about her elsewhere;
but the picture of her life that emerges from them should not be
regarded as being in any way authentic.

The correspondence of Aristippos from 667 onward is drawn from
another collection, the Letters of Socrates and the Socratics; it probably dates to the third century BC or thereabouts. In 667 he expresses
his final wishes to his daughter Arete, while the following group
presents him as crossing swords with sages who belonged to the
ascetic wing of the Socratic movement. Although he generally gains
the advantage over his opponents, with the help of liberal doses of
irony and sarcasm, the author of the letters was probably more interested in the portrayal of character than in the relative value of the
moral ideas of the two parties.

About this Edition

The selection of material included in the following translations begins with Lucian's humorous portraits of Diogenes and Aristippos.
That of Diogenes remains quite faithful to the tradition, even if the
matter is presented in an exaggerated and satirical form; but that of

Aristippos has to be taken with a heavy dose of salt—he may have thought that our happiness is to be found in pleasure but he was not a dissolute drunkard.

The *chreiai* and biographical matter collected in Sections II and III describe how Diogenes came to adopt his distinctive way of life, and show the basic nature of his everyday life, while the anecdotes and sayings in IV indicate the various ways in which he presented himself, as a true man as opposed to a member of the crowd, as a true victor who had gained mastery over himself, as a contrarian, and of course as a dog. The attitude that he assumed toward philosophy and culture is indicated in the testimonies and anecdotes in Section V. Sections VI to VIII are devoted to what might be described as his campaigns, against self-indulgence, illusion, and false values. The remaining biographical material, relating to the legend of his enslavement and to his old age and death, is collected in Sections IX and XII respectively, while sayings and anecdotes which have no proper Cynic content, and cannot be regarded for the most part as having been originally connected with Diogenes, have been segregated into Sections X and XI. Reports about the writings ascribed to Diogenes can be found in the latter part of Section VII.

Sections XIII to XV are devoted to the other early Cynics. By way of a postscript, most of the anecdotes and sayings of Bion of Borysthenes (*c*.325–250) have been translated in Section XVI. Although Bion studied under masters from a variety of schools and did not adopt the Cynic way of life, except perhaps temporarily, the ideas expressed in his *chreiai* have a distinctly Cynic flavour, as does his mode of expression. Passing backwards in time, part of Diogenes Laertius' account of Antisthenes is translated in Section XVII, along with the discourse from Xenophon mentioned above, to give some idea of his moral outlook for comparison with that of Diogenes.

Sections XVIII to XX cover Aristippos and other Cyrenaics, including Hegesias and Theodoros, with a selection from the apocryphal letters of Diogenes, Crates, and Aristippos in Sections XXI–XXII.

THE CYNIC SUCCESSION

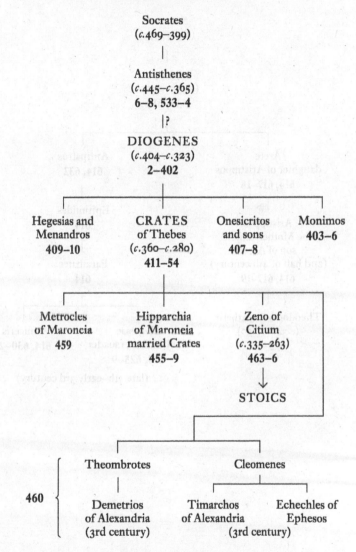

Socrates
(c.469–399)

|

Antisthenes
(c.445–c.365)
6–8, 533–4

|?

DIOGENES
(c.404–c.323)
2–402

Hegesias and
Menandros
409–10

CRATES
of Thebes
(c.360–c.280)
411–54

Onesicritos
and sons
407–8

Monimos
403–6

Metrocles
of Maroncia
459

Hipparchia
of Maroneia
married Crates
455–9

Zeno of
Citium
(c.335–263)
463–6

↓

STOICS

Theombrotes

|

Cleomenes

460

Demetrios
of Alexandria
(3rd century)

Timarchos
of Alexandria

Echechles of
Ephesos

(3rd century)

The numbers in bold refer to the anecdotes and testimonies in this edition. All dates are BC.

THE CYRENAIC SUCCESSION

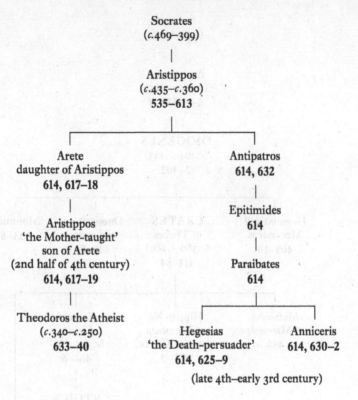

Socrates
(*c.*469–399)

Aristippos
(*c.*435–*c.*360)
535–613

Arete
daughter of Aristippos
614, 617–18

Antipatros
614, 632

Aristippos
'the Mother-taught'
son of Arete
(2nd half of 4th century)
614, 617–19

Epitimides
614

Paraibates
614

Theodoros the Atheist
(*c.*340–*c.*250)
633–40

Hegesias
'the Death-persuader'
614, 625–9

Anniceris
614, 630–2

(late 4th–early 3rd century)

NOTE ON THE TEXTS

THE Greek and Latin texts for Diogenes and the early Cynics, and for Aristippos and the Cyrenaics, have been collected by G. Giannantoni in his *Socratis et Socraticorum Reliquiae* (Naples, 1990), and I have used the texts in that collection as the main basis for the translations in this volume. For Bion of Borysthenes in Section XVI, I have relied on J. F. Kindstrand's collection of his fragments and testimonies (*Bion of Borysthenes*, Uppsala, 1976). For the apocryphal letters in Part 3, I have followed the texts in E. Museler, *Die Kyniker-briefe* (Paderborn, 1994), and Jacopo Bolzan, *Socratis et Socraticorum Epistolae* (Padua, diss., 2009); but texts for these can also be found in Giannantoni's collection.

Although the present collection does not aim at completeness, it is something more than a mere anthology. The great majority of the sayings and anecdotes of Diogenes have been included, and with regard to the apophthegmatic material more generally, the selection is a very full one, embracing, I hope, everything that is of any real interest (apart from a few apophthegms in which the humour rests on the untranslatable word-play). Sayings and anecdotes form the main focus of the book however, and only a more limited selection has been made from the later testimonies, often repetitive in character, about the philosophy and way of life of Diogenes and others.

It will be noted that anecdotes are sometimes repeated in varied forms. Except in the case of a few stories which are central to the biographical tradition about Diogenes, I have generally included variants only where the differences are sufficiently great to make some real difference to the story, or when an anecdote is recorded both in its basic form (as it would have been recorded in a collection of apophthegms) and in a more elaborate version in the work of an author like Plutarch.

References to the sources are included in brackets after each item, beginning with the ancient source and followed by the number in Giannantoni's collection. With regard to the latter, the reference is given simply as G (e.g. G 133) in the case of the most important figures, that is to say Diogenes, Crates, and Aristippos, and in full for the rest; for Diogenes, Crates, and Aristippos, the full references would be G VB, G VH, and G IVA respectively. Since Giannantoni's collection is organized in a different way from the present one, some items which are placed separately here are included by him under the same reference, and some material which is presented here as a continuous passage is broken up by him into separate items. For that reason it is occasionally not possible to give a meaningful 'G' reference; and in a few cases, there is no such reference because the item was not included by him. For the material relating to Bion of Borysthenes, the second reference, e.g. K30, refers to the item's number in Kindstrand's collection. For the apocryphal letters, I have included the standard number for that letter in the heading at the beginning, e.g. 'Diogenes 44, to Metrocles', and there are accordingly no references afterwards.

Where the same item is recorded in the same or closely similar form in several ancient sources (e.g. various gnomologia), it would have served no purpose to enumerate all of them here, and the modern collections may be consulted for further detail.

NOTE ON THE ANCIENT SOURCES

THE original source for everything included in this book is indicated after each item. Sayings and anecdotes are quite often taken from manuscript collections of unknown authorship, in which case the reference will refer to the manuscript volume from which it is taken, followed by the number of the specific item (e.g. *Codex Vaticanus Graecus* 409. n.116). In some cases the relevant collection may be referred to as a Gnomologium, i.e. collection of sayings and apophthegms; the most important of these is a large Byzantine collection of apophthegms, the *Gnomologium Vaticanum*, contained in *Codex Vaticanus Graecus* 743. The *Suda* (i.e. Fortress, also referred to as Suidas as though this were a personal name) was a large lexicon or encyclopaedia from the tenth century AD. Otherwise the items are drawn from the works of identifiable authors, of whom the following are the most significant:

AELIAN, Claudius Aelianus, *c.* AD 175–235, a Roman author who wrote in Greek, author of compilations, including a historical miscellany which contains anecdotes of Diogenes and Aristippos, presented in elaborated form.

ANTONIUS, 11th–12th century AD, compiler of a compendium of apophthegms and extracts on religious and moral themes; sometimes known as Melissa (Bee), doubtless after the title of his work.

APULEIUS of Madaurus, *c.* AD 125–75, Latin prose-writer whose *Florida*, a collection of extracts from his discourses, contains some relevant material.

ARISTOCLES of Messene, 1st century AD, Peripatetic philosopher; Eusebius records some valuable reports of his about the Cyrenaic school.

ARISTOTLE, 384–322 BC, the great philosopher, a contemporary of Diogenes.

ATHENAEUS of Naucratis, 2nd–3rd century AD, author of the *Deipnosophistae*, philosophers of the dinner-table, a huge compilation containing material relating directly or indirectly to food, drink, and banqueting.

AULUS GELLIUS, *c.* AD 123–*c.*165, Latin author of a miscellany, the *Attic Nights*, which ranges over a wide range of subjects.

CICERO, 106–43 BC, Roman orator, politician, and author, who wrote about philosophical matters among much else.

CLEMENT OF ALEXANDRIA, 1st–2nd century AD, Christian author of works on religious matters, in which he often refers to, and quotes from, Greek philosophers.

DIO CHRYSOSTOM, *c.* AD 40–after 112, orator and popular philosopher who showed some sympathy for Cynicism, author of some eighty surviving speeches.

DIOGENES LAERTIUS, 3rd century AD, compiler of a work about the lives and opinions of the Greek philosophers, a prime source for the early Cynics and Cyrenaics. See Introduction.

EPICTETUS, AD 55–135, Stoic philosopher whose discourses were recorded by a pupil of his.

EPIPHANIUS, AD 315–403, Bishop of Constantia, author of works directed against heresy in particular.

EUSEBIUS of Caesarea, 3rd–4th century AD, Christian scholar, author of a *Church History* among other works.

GALEN of Pergamon, *c.* AD 129–*c.*199, physician, medical theorist, and author of medical works.

JEROME, Saint, *c.* AD 347–420, Church father, theologian, and historian, author of the Vulgate translation of the Bible.

JULIAN, 'the Apostate', AD 332–62, Roman Emperor who tried to restore the old religion, prolific and eloquent author.

LUCIAN of Samosata, *c.* AD 125–*c.*192, author of humorous and satirical works, largely dialogues, much influenced by the early Cynic author Menippos.

MACROBIUS, 4th–5th century AD, Latin grammarian and Neoplatonist philosopher.

MARCUS AURELIUS, AD 121–80, Roman Emperor with Stoic sympathies, author of the *Meditations*, a philosophical notebook.

MAXIMUS the Confessor, *c.* AD 580–662, monk and theologian; a florilegium containing apophthegms and extracts on religious and moral themes, of unknown authorship, is referred to under his name.

MUSONIUS RUFUS, 1st century AD, Roman Stoic philosopher.

PHILO of Alexandria, 20 BC–AD 54, Greek philosophical writer of Jewish birth.

PHILODEMUS of Gadara, *c.*110–*c.*40 or 35 BC, Epicurean, author of works on a wide variety of subjects partly recovered from papyri found at Herculaneum

PHILOSTRATUS the Younger, *c.* AD 170–*c.*250, author of, among other works, a life of the Neopythagorean sage and wonder-worker Apollonius of Tyana.

PLUTARCH of Chaeronea, AD 46–after 125, author of biographies, moral treatises, and other works; he records many anecdotes of philosophers, usually in elaborated form.

SENECA, *c.*4 BC–AD 65, Roman statesman who served as an adviser to Nero, and author of, among other things, philosophical treatises and moral letters in a Stoic vein.

SEXTUS EMPIRICUS, 2nd–3rd century AD, Greek physician whose philosophical works are our fullest source of information for ancient Sceptical philosophy; he provides an account of the sceptical epistemological views of the Cyrenaics.

SIMPLICIUS of Cilicia, *c.* AD 490–*c.*560, late Neoplatonist philosopher, author of commentaries on Aristotle and Epictetus.

STOBAEUS, i.e. Joannes of Stobi in Macedonia, 5th century AD, compiler of a very large anthology of extracts from ancient Greek authors, thematically arranged.

STRABO, 64 BC–after AD 24, Greek author of geographical and lost historical works.

TELES of Megara, 3rd century BC, author of Cynic diatribes, short unsophisticated moral discourses which contain references to Diogenes, Crates, and Bion.

TERTULLIAN, *c.* AD 160–*c.*220, Latin Christian author.

VALERIUS MAXIMUS, 1st century AD, author of a Latin collection of anecdotes of the Romans and Greeks.

VITRUVIUS, 1st century BC, Roman architect and engineer, author of a book on architecture.

XENOPHON, *c.*428–*c.*354 BC, an Athenian who was a friend of Socrates in his early years, served as a soldier in Asia, and became a versatile author after being exiled from Athens.

SELECT BIBLIOGRAPHY

The fragments, testimonies, and apophthegms for both the early Cynics and the Cyrenaics are collected in G. Giannantoni, *Socratis et Socraticorum Reliquiae*, 4 vols. (Naples, 1990); valuable notes (in Italian) on various matters, often extending over many pages, can be found in the fourth volume. Giannantoni had previously compiled a collection of the fragments of the Cyrenaics, with Italian translations and a full introduction, *I Cirenaici* (Florence, 1958); there is another collection compiled by Erich Mannebach, *Aristippi et Cyrenaicorum Fragmenta* (Leiden and Cologne, 1961). J. F. Kindstrand's collection of the fragments of Bion, *Bion of Borysthenes* (Uppsala, 1976), also contains discussions of many aspects of early Cynicism in the introduction and notes. A. J. Malherbe, *The Cynic Epistles* (Missoula, 1977), provides the Greek texts of the apocryphal Cynic letters with rather rough and ready English translations, but the best edition, with excellent German translations, is that by E. Müseler, *Die Kynikerbriefe*, 2 vols. (Paderborn, 1994). Malherbe also includes the letters of Socrates and the Socratics (containing the apocryphal correspondence of Aristippos), which have been edited and discussed by Liselotte Köhler, *Die Briefe des Sokrates under Sokratiker* (Leipzig, 1928; Philologus Supplementband 20.2), with German translations, and by Jacopo Bolzan, *Socratis et Socraticorum Epistolae* (Padua, diss., 2009),with Italian translations.

Léonce Paquet, *Les Cyniques grecs: fragments et témoignages* (Ottawa, 1975), offers French translations of a wide range of Cynic material over the whole history of the movement, while G. Luck, *Die Weisheit der Hunde* (Stuttgart, 1997), offers a much fuller collection in German. Pierre Gouirand, *Aristippe de Cyrène: le chien royal* (Paris, 2005), provides a French translation of all the Cyrenaic fragments and testimonies, with the sources arranged in chronological order; and there is also another French collection, M. Onfray, *L'Invention du plaisir: fragments Cyrénaiques* (Paris, 2002). There is an edition of Diogenes Laertius, a main source for both the early Cynics and the Cynics, in the Loeb series with a good parallel translation by R. D. Hicks, *Lives of the Eminent Philosophers* (London, 1925).

As a general introduction to the history of the Cynic movement, D. R. Dudley, *A History of Cynicism from Diogenes to the Sixth Century AD* (London, 1937), is still very useful, and there is an excellent survey of more recent date by William Desmond, *Cynics* (Berkeley, 2008). To these may be added a volume of essays edited by R. Bracht Branham and M.-O. Goulet-Cazé, *The Cynics: The Cynic Movement in Antiquity and its Legacy* (Berkeley, 1996), which also covers the later reception of Cynicism, as does

H. Niehues-Pröbsting, *Der Kynismus des Diogenes und der Begriff des Kynismus* (Munich, 1979). M.-O. Goulet-Cazé and R. Goulet, eds., *Le Cynisme ancient et ses prolongements* (Paris, 1993), is a very fine collection of papers about Cynicism (many in French, some in English, German, and Italian), while M. Billerbeck, ed., *Die Kyniker in der modernen Forschung* (Amsterdam, 1991), is a collection of classic articles, mostly in German or English, extending back over a century and a half. F. Sayre, *The Greek Cynics* (Baltimore, 1949), is something of an oddity. Although much of interest can be found in R. Höistad, *Cynic Hero and Cynic King* (Uppsala, 1948), the approach will not appeal to those who would attach more value to evidence from the apophthegmatic tradition. M.-O. Goulet-Cazé, *L'Ascèse cynique: un commentaire de Diogène Laërce VI 70–71* (Paris, 1986), is a more specialized study which throws much light on the early Cynics, as does the same author's later work *Les Kynika du Stoicisme* (Stuttgart, 2003; Hermes Einzelschriften 89). Luis E. Navia has written a number of accessible works about the early Cynics and their forebear Antisthenes in recent years, *Diogenes of Sinope: The Man in the Tub* (Westport, 1998), *Diogenes the Cynic: The War Against the World* (Amherst, 2005), *Classical Cynicism: A Critical Study* (Westport, 1996), *Antisthenes of Athens: Setting the World Aright* (Westport, 2001), and has also compiled a bibliography, *The Philosophy of Cynicism: An Annotated Bibliography* (Westport, 1995).

K. von Fritz, *Quellenuntersuchungen zur Leben und Philosophie des Diogenes von Sinope* (Leipzig, 1926; Philologus Supplementband 18), is a study of the sources for the early traditions about Diogenes. Oliver Overwien, *Die Sprüche des Kynikers Diogenes in der griechischen und arabischen Überlieferung* (Stuttgart, 2005; Hermes Einzelschriften 92), offers a detailed study of the apophthegmatic tradition for Diogenes, taking into account the Arabic as well as the Greek sources. Translations of the apophthegms preserved in Arabic can be found in the collection of papers edited by Goulet-Cazé and Goulet (see above), D. Gutas, 'Sayings by Diogenes Preserved in Arabic', 475–519. A. Packmohr, *De Diogenis Sinopensis apopthegmatis [sic] quaestiones selectae* (Münster, 1913), is still of interest for its discussion of some particular sayings and anecdotes, especially for the comparative material provided. T. S. Brown, *Onesicritus* (Berkeley 1949), is a monograph on this interesting character who associated with Diogenes for a time and later met Cynic-like ascetics in the East.

Some further papers relating to early Cynicism:

H. Bannert, 'Numismatisches zu Bigraphie und Lehre des Hundes Diogenes', *Litterae Numismaticae Vindobonenses* 1 (1979), 49–63.

E. K. Borthwick, 'The Cynic and the Statue', *Classical Quarterly* 51 no. 2 (2001), 494–8.

Philip Bosman, 'Selling Cynicism: The Pragmatics of Diogenes' Comic Performances', *Classical Quarterly* 56 no. 1 (2006), 93–104.

F. Caizzi, 'Antistene', *Studi Urbinati* 38 (1964), 48–99.

V. Emeljanow, 'A Note on the Cynic Short Cut to Happiness', *Mnemosyne* ser. 4, 18 (1965), 182–4.

Percy Gardner, 'Diogenes and Delphi', *Classical Review* 7 no. 10 (1893), 437–9.

M.-O. Goulet-Cazé, 'Une liste de disciples de Cratès le Cynique en Diogène Laërce 6.95', *Hermes* 114 (1986), 247–52.

——, 'Le Cynisme est-il une philosophie?', in M. Dixsaut, ed., *Contre Platon* (Paris, 1993), 273–313.

R. F. Hock, 'Simon the Shoemaker as an Ideal Cynic', *Greek, Roman and Byzantine Studies* 17 (1976), 41–53.

Kristen Kennedy, 'Hipparchia the Cynic: Feminist Rhetoric and the Ethics of Embodiment', *Hypatia* 14 no. 2 (199), 48–71.

J. F. Kindstrand, 'Diogenes Laertius on the "Chreia" Tradition', *Elenchos* 71–2 (1986), 214–43.

——, 'The Cynics and Heraclitus', *Eranos* 83 (1985), 113–24.

J. Moles, 'The Cynic's Attitude to Moral Corruption', *Journal of Hellenic Studies* 103 (1983), 103–23.

——, 'The Woman and the River', *Apeiron* 17 no. 2 (1983), 125–30.

Maria Noussia, 'Parodia e Filosofia in Cratete Tebano', in R. Pretagostini and E. Dettori, eds., *La cultura Ellenistica: l'opera letteraria e l'esegesi antica* (Rome, 2004), 127 35.

Susan Prince, 'Socrates, Antisthenes and the Cynics', in Sara Ahbel-Rappe and Rachana Kamtekar, eds., 'A Companion to Socrates' (Oxford, 2005), 75–92.

Audrey N. M. Rich, 'The Cynic Conception of Autarcheia', *Mnemosyne* 4th series 9.1 (1956), 23–9.

C. T. Seltman, 'Diogenes of Sinope, Son of the Banker Hikesias', *Transactions of the International Numismatic Congress* (London, 1936), 121.

W. Tarn, 'Alexander, Cynics and Stoics', *American Journal of Philology* 60 (1939), 41–70.

M. Winarczyk, 'Theodoros *ho Atheos* und Diogenes von Sinope', *Eos* 69 (1981), 37–42.

The only complete book devoted to the Cyrenaics in English is V. Tsouna, *The Epistemology of the Cyrenaic School* (Cambridge, 2004), which provides a detailed analysis of their sceptical epistemological views. There is a more general survey in German, K. Döring, *Der Sokratesschüler Aristipp und die Kyrenaiker* (Stuttgart, 1988), and mention should also be made of the very full introduction to Giannantoni's collection of the Cyrenaic fragments (see above). Aristippos is briefly discussed in W. K. C. Guthrie, *Socrates* (Cambridge, 1971), 170–9, and there is somewhat longer and perhaps more perceptive discussion in Jean Humbert, *Socrate et les petits Socratiques* (Paris, 1967). See also W.-R. Mann, 'The Life of Aristippos', *Archiv für Geschichte der Philosophie*, 1978 (1996), 97–119. J. Classen, 'Aristippos', *Hermes* 86 no. 2 (1958), argues with some cogency that the elder Aristippos did not formulate the teachings that are recorded for the school. The nature of Cyrenaic hedonism is examined in Tim O'Keefe, 'The Cyrenaics on Pleasure, Happiness and Future-Concern', *Phronesis* 47 (2002), 395–416. Two papers on the later members of the school: P. Laks, 'Anniceris et les plaisirs psychiques', in J. Brunschwig and M. Nussbaum, eds., *Passions and Perceptions* (Cambridge, 1993), 18–49, and Wallace Matson, 'Hegesias the Death-Persuader: Or, the Gloominess of Hedonism', in *Philosophy* 73 no. 286 (Oct. 1998), 553–7.

SAYINGS AND ANECDOTES

PART 1
DIOGENES AND THE EARLY CYNICS

I · A HUMOROUS PORTRAIT OF DIOGENES AND ARISTIPPOS

1 ZEUS: Bring forward the next!

HERMES: What, that grubby creature from the Black Sea?*

ZEUS: Yes, that one.

HERMES: Hey, you there with the knapsack and the bare shoulder, come over and walk in front of the people here. I'm offering a manly way of life for sale, a most excellent and noble life, a free life; who wants to buy?

BUYER: What on earth do you mean, auctioneer? You're offering a free man for sale?

HERMES: Yes, indeed.

BUYER: But aren't you afraid that he'll accuse you of kidnapping and have you hauled up in front of the Areiopagos?*

HERMES: Oh, he's not bothered at all about being sold, since he thinks he's perfectly free whatever happens.

BUYER: But what use could one possibly make of such a filthy creature, in such a wretched state as that? Unless perhaps one could set him to work digging the ground and fetching water.

HERMES: Not only that, but you could also use him as a doorkeeper, you'd find him more reliable than any dog. In point of fact, he's even called a dog.

BUYER: Where's he from, and what way of life does he recommend?

HERMES: Well, ask him, that's the best thing to do.

BUYER: But he's looking so fierce and sullen that I'm afraid he might bark at me if I go too close, or, by heaven, even bite me! Don't you see how he has raised his stick, and is knitting his brows, and is scowling in a threatening and furious manner?

HERMES: Don't be afraid, he's quite tame really.

BUYER: Then first, my good fellow, where do you come from?

DIOGENES: Everywhere.

BUYER: How do you mean?

DIOGENES: You're looking at a citizen of the world.

BUYER: Is there anyone whom you strive to emulate?

DIOGENES: Yes, Heracles.*

BUYER: Then why aren't you wearing a lion-skin? Though I'll admit that your club looks like his.*

DIOGENES: Why, this old cloak is my lion-skin, and like him I'm fighting a campaign against pleasure, not at anyone else's bidding, but of my own free will, since I've made it my purpose to clean up human life.

BUYER: A noble resolve. But tell me, what are your main abilities? Do you practise any craft?

DIOGENES: I'm a liberator of humanity, a healer of human ills. In short I have set out to be a prophet of truth and plain speaking.

BUYER: Very well, Mr Prophet; and if I buy you, what manner of training will you give me?

DIOGENES: I'll start by taking hold of you and stripping you of your luxuries, and will incarcerate you in poverty and make you wear a shabby cloak; and then I'll make you toil away until you come close to dropping, and make you sleep on the ground, drink nothing but water, and be satisfied with any food that you come across. If you have any money, I'll urge you to go off and throw it into the sea;* and you'll not give another thought to your wife and children and homeland, all of that will seem a pile of nonsense to you, and you'll leave your family home to set up residence in a tomb, or lonely tower, or storage-jar. You'll have a knapsack filled with lupin seeds* and scrolls written on both sides. Leading such a life, you will profess to be happier than the King of Persia; and even if you were to be flogged or stretched on the rack, you'd consider that no cause for distress.

BUYER: How do you mean, feel no pain at getting flogged? It's not as if I have armour to protect me like a crab or tortoise!

DIOGENES: You can apply that notorious line from Euripides, with a slight emendation.

BUYER: Which line?

DIOGENES: '*Your mind will feel the pain, but not your tongue.*'* These are the things that will be chiefly required of you: you must be bold and headstrong, and abuse everyone without exception, king and commoner alike, for in that way you'll gain everyone's admiration and be considered manly and brave. You must assume an alien mode of speech and snarling voice, just like the yapping of a dog, and assume a sullen expression, and a manner of walking that is in accord with your face; in short, everything about you must be bestial and savage. Away with all modesty, decency, and moderation, and wipe off any blushes from your face once and for all. Pick out the spots that are most crowded with people, and in those very places set out to be solitary and unsociable, suffering neither friend nor stranger to approach; for to allow that would undermine your power. Do boldly in front of everyone things that no decent person would do even in private, and choose the most absurd ways to satisfy your lusts; and at last, if you care to do so, eat an octopus or cuttlefish raw and die!* Such is the happiness that we can promise you.

BUYER: Off with you! This life that you talk of is revolting and inhuman.

DIOGENES: Ah yes, but it is a very easy one, my friend, and practicable for all to follow. For you will have no need of any education, or doctrines, or any of that drivel, but this provides you with a short cut to fame.* And even if you're a quite ordinary man, a tanner, a fish-seller, carpenter, or money-changer, there's nothing to stop you from becoming an object of wonder, provided only that you have the necessary shamelessness and impudence, and learn how to abuse people in the proper manner.

BUYER: I certainly don't want you for anything like that, but you might perhaps be of some use as a boatman or gardener, if this man here will let you go for a couple of obols at the most.

HERMES: Then he's yours, do take him. We're only too glad to get rid of him, because he's utterly exasperating, always shouting, and always reviling and running down everyone without exception.

ZEUS: Call someone else forward, the Cyrenean,* the man dressed in purple, the one wearing a crown.

HERMES: Attention now, everyone, here's a very expensive article, one that calls for a rich buyer. This is a most pleasant life, an altogether blissful life. Who wants to wallow in luxury? Who wants to buy this most delicate creature?

BUYER: Come forward, my man, and tell me what you can do; I'll buy you if you're useful for anything.

HERMES: Don't bother him, my friend, don't put any question to him, he's far too drunk to answer, he won't be able to get his tongue round the words, as you can see.

BUYER: Would anyone with any sense at all buy such a degenerate and dissolute character* as a slave? What is more, he stinks of perfume, and look how he stumbles and lurches when he tries to walk! All the same, Hermes, you can tell us what he is good for and what he seeks to achieve.

HERMES: Well, in short, he'd make an excellent companion for an amorous and profligate master, just the man to drink with and make merry with at parties with flute-girls. Furthermore, he's quite an expert when it comes to sweet-cakes and knows all the secrets of fine cooking, and, in short, he's a connoisseur of every kind of pleasure. He was educated in Athens and has served also with the tyrants of Sicily, who held him in the highest esteem. His main doctrines can be summarized as follows: despise everything,* profit from everything, and draw pleasure from whatever you can.

BUYER: You'd better look around for someone else, for one of those rich people who are rolling in money; I'm in no position to buy the life of a buffoon.

HERMES: I'm afraid it looks, Zeus, as if he's going to remain unsold and be left on our hands.

(Lucian, *Philosophies for Sale* 7–12)

II · DIOGENES' CONVERSION TO THE ASCETIC LIFE

Exile from Sinope to Athens

2 Diogenes was born in Sinope* as a son of the banker Hicesias. Diocles* reports that he had to go into exile because his father, who was in charge of the state bank, had re-stamped the currency;* Euboulides* states, however, in his book on Diogenes that it was Diogenes who did this, and that he was thus obliged to wander abroad together with his father. Diogenes himself in his *Pordalos* does in fact admit* to having re-stamped the currency. Some claim that when he was acting as superintendent of the mint, his workmen tried to persuade him to do this, and he thus went to Delphi,* or to the Delian oracle in his homeland, to ask whether he should accede to this suggestion; and when the god gave him his permission to alter the political currency, he failed to understand the proper meaning and

adulterated the coinage. His crime was detected and, in some accounts, he was banished, while according to others he left of his own accord out of fear. Others again say that the money was entrusted to him by his father and he debased it; his father was imprisoned as a result and died, while he himself fled into exile and travelled to Delphi, where he asked, not whether he should re-stamp the currency, but what he should do to gain the greatest reputation, and it was in response to this question that he received the above-mentioned oracle.

(Diogenes Laertius 6.20–1; G2)

3a To someone who said to him, 'The Sinopeans have condemned you to exile', he replied, 'Yes, and I've condemned them to stay where they are.'

(Diogenes Laertius 6.49; G11)

3b To someone who said to him, 'The Sinopeans have condemned you to exile from the Black Sea, Diogenes the Dog replied, 'And I've condemned them to remain there, *by the high cliffs of the inhospitable sea.'**

(Plutarch, *On Exile* 7, 602a; G11)

4 To someone who reproached him for his banishment, he replied, 'But it was because of that, you wretch, that I turned to philosophy.'

(Diogenes Laertius 6.49; G13)

5 When he was reproached one day for having falsified the currency, he said, 'That was at a time when I was just as you are now; but what I am now, you will never be.' And to another who made the same reproach, he replied, 'And there was once a day when I would piss in my bed, but no longer.'

(Diogenes Laertius 6.56; G4)

Meeting with Antisthenes and Conversion to Philosophy

6a On arriving in Athens he ran across Antisthenes;* and although Antisthenes rebuffed him because he did not want to accept any pupils, Diogenes won his way through his persistence. When

Antisthenes once raised his stick against him, he offered his head,* saying, 'Go on then, hit me, for you'll not find any wood that's hard enough to keep me away until such time as you have something to say to me.' And from that time forth he became his pupil, and being an exile, strove to live a simple life.

(Diogenes Laertius 6.21; G19)

6b When Antisthenes had exhorted many people to turn to philosophy and they had paid no attention, he finally lost patience and would allow no one to come near him; and so he even drove Diogenes from his company. When Diogenes proved rather persistent and held his ground, he then threatened to lay into him with his stick, and even struck him on the head. All the same, Diogenes did not go away, but pressed himself forward yet more insistently, being most eager to hear Antisthenes, and would say, 'Strike me if you wish, I'll offer you my head, but you'll never find a stick strong enough to drive me away from your discourses'; whereupon Antisthenes welcomed him most kindly.

(Aelian, *Historical Miscellany* 10.16; G19)

6c Now since Antisthenes was unwilling to accept any pupils, and he could not rid himself of the ever-persistent Diogenes, he finally threatened to hit him with his stick if he would not go away; and Diogenes, so the story goes, lowered his head before him and said, 'There is no stick so hard that it could deter me from following you.'

(Jerome, *Against Jovinian* 2.14; G19)

7 It was in this way too that Diogenes used to praise his master Antisthenes, as though he were reviling him; 'This man', he said, 'turned me from a rich man into a beggar, and made me live in a storage-jar rather than a spacious house.' This was better expressed than if he had said, 'I am grateful to him because he turned me into a philosopher and a man of consummate virtue.'

(Macrobius, *Saturnalia* 7.3.21; G21)

8 When Diogenes asked him for a tunic, he [Antisthenes] told him to fold his cloak double.

(Diogenes Laertius 6.6; G23)

9a As Theophrastos* recounts in his *Megaric*, he once saw a mouse running this way and that, not looking for anywhere to lie down, not having any fear of the dark, not yearning for any of the things that are regarded as desirable, and from its example discovered the way out of his difficulties.

(Diogenes Laertius 6.22; G172)

9b Diogenes was bereft of all company and left all alone. He neither received anyone, because he was so poor, nor did other people invite him into their houses, because he put them off by his accusatory manner and the way in which he disapproved of all that they said and did. So Diogenes was thoroughly dejected and was eating barley-bread and leaf-tips, this being all that he had at hand. A mouse came along and fed on the crumbs that dropped from his hand; and as Diogenes watched it busy at work, he smiled and became more cheerful and contented, saying, 'This mouse has no need of any of the luxuries of the Athenians, and yet you, Diogenes, are downcast because you are not dining with the Athenians.' And so he achieved contentment of mind when it was most needed.

(Aelian, *Historical Miscellany* 13.26; G172)

9c They told a similar story about Diogenes of Sinope at the time when he was first embarking on philosophy. The Athenians were celebrating a festival with public feasts and shows, and people were gathering together for merriment and night-long revelries. Diogenes for his part had curled up in a corner of the market-place to go to sleep, and now fell prey to thoughts that disconcerted him to no small degree and threatened his resolve. Without any external compulsion he had embarked on an arduous and unnatural way of life, and was now sitting there all alone, deprived of all good things. But then, so the story goes, a mouse crept forward and busied itself with the crumbs of his barley-cake; the sight of this revived his spirits, and he said to himself by way of rebuke and self-reproach: 'What are you to say of this, Diogenes? That while your leavings provide this little animal with a feast and due nourishment, you, noble creature that you are, are complaining and lamenting because you cannot get drunk over there, and lie back on soft brightly-coloured cushions.'

(Plutarch, *On Progress in Virtue* 5, 77ef; G172)

10 Antisthenes' most famous follower was the great Diogenes, who was mightier than King Alexander as one who vanquished nature. . . . According to Satyros,* who wrote biographies of illustrious men, he folded his cloak double* to guard against the cold, and had a knapsack for a larder; he carried a stick because of the frailty of his poor body, and in his old age would use it to support his limbs. He was commonly known as *hemerobios*,* that is to say, as one who lived from hand to mouth, because he begged for his present needs from anyone whom he encountered, acquiring his food in that way from others. He made his home in gateways and the public arcades. When he wriggled into his jar,* he would joke that he had a rolling house which could be moved to accord with the seasons. For in the cold of winter he would turn the mouth of his jar toward the south, and in summer toward the north, and as the sun changed its position in the sky, Diogenes would move his headquarters accordingly.

(Jerome, *Against Jovinian* 2.14; G175)

11 According to some, he was the first to fold his cloak double because he also had to sleep in it, and he carried a knapsack to carry his food, and would use any place for any purpose, whether for eating, or sleeping, or talking. And he used to say, pointing to the portico of Zeus and the Pompeion,* that the Athenians had provided him with excellent homes. He began to lean on a stick only when his strength declined, but from then on he carried it everywhere, not in the city, to be sure, but when he was on the road, along with his knapsack, as is reported by Olympiodoros, who was a magistrate at Athens, and by Polyeuctos the orator, and Lysanias, son of Aischrion.* He had written to someone asking him to look out for a little house for him, but when the man was slow about it, he set up home in a storage-jar in the Metroon,* as he himself attests in his letters. In the summer he used to roll in the sand, and in the winter embrace snow-covered statues, using every means to train himself to endure hardship. . . . He used to walk barefoot in the snow and do the other things mentioned above.

(Diogenes Laertius 6.22–3 and 6.34; G174 and 176)

12a For a time he used a wooden cup for drinking, but on seeing a boy drinking from the hollow of his hand, he smashed his cup on the ground, saying, 'I hadn't realized that nature had provided me with a cup.'

(Jerome, *Against Jovinian* 2.14; G175)

12b On seeing a youth using his hollowed hand to scoop up a drink from some water that was flowing by, Diogenes immediately threw away the cup that he had used for drinking, saying that nature had provided him with hands that were better and more useful for that purpose.

(*Gnomologium Vaticanum* 185; G158)

12c They say that Diogenes always carried a wooden cup around with him in his knapsack, to enable him to scoop up water to drink, but when, as he was once crossing over a stream, he saw someone scooping up water in his hands and drinking from them, he hurled his cup into the stream, saying that he no longer had need of it because his hands would serve the purpose.

(Simplicius, *Commentary on the 'Encheiridion' of Epictetus* 32; G160)

13a To those who advised him to seek out his runaway slave, he said, 'How absurd if Manes can live without Diogenes, but Diogenes cannot live without Manes!'*

(Diogenes Laertius 6.55; G441)

13b When his slave ran off, Diogenes did not mind in the least, saying that it would be most strange if Diogenes could not live without him when he could live without Diogenes.

(Stobaeus 4.19.47; G441)

13c When Diogenes left the city of his birth, he was accompanied by one of his household slaves, Manes by name; but finding life with Diogenes to be unbearable, this Manes ran away. When people urged Diogenes to go out in search of him, he said, 'Wouldn't it be shameful that when Manes has no need of Diogenes, Diogenes should have need of Manes?' This slave wandered off to Delphi, where he was torn apart by dogs, and so paid the penalty for his misconduct in a way that accorded with the name of his master.

(Aelian, *Historical Miscellany* 13.28; G441)

14 When asked where he was from, he said, 'I'm a citizen of the world.'*

(Diogenes Laertius 6.63; G355)

15a He used to say that all the curses of tragedy had lighted upon his head, for he surely was

> *'Without city or home, bereft of his native land,*
> *A beggar, a wanderer living from day to day'.**

(Diogenes Laertius 6.38; G263)

15b Diogenes said that he had suffered all that is found in tragedy, for he was *a beggar, a wanderer, living from day to day*; 'But all the same, although these are my circumstances, I am fully prepared to compete in happiness with the King of the Persians.'

(*Gnomologium Vaticanum* 201; G263)

15c Diogenes of Sinope used constantly to say to himself that he had suffered the curses of tragedy in full measure and stood firm, for he was

> *'A wanderer without a home, bereft of his native land,*
> *A beggar dressed in rags, living from day to day'.*

And yet he took no less pride in all of this than did Alexander in ruling over the world, on returning to Babylon after having conquered India.*

(Aelian, *Historical Miscellany* 3.29; G263)

III · THE SAGE AS BEGGAR

True Wealth and Relative Values

16 When asked by Aristippos what he had gained from philosophy, he replied, 'To be rich without having an obol.'*

(*Gnomologium Vaticanum* 182; G361)

17 When asked who is rich among men, he replied, 'He who is self-sufficient.'*

(*Gnomologium Vaticanum* 180; G241)

18 He used to reason as follows: 'Everything belongs to the gods; the wise are friends to the gods; friends hold all things in common; *ergo*, everything belongs to the wise.'*

(Diogenes Laertius 6.37; G353)

19 Diogenes said that poverty aids us to philosophy of its own accord,* for what philosophy attempts to persuade us by means of arguments, poverty compels us to in very deed.

(Stobaeus 4.32.11; G223)

20 On seeing someone behaving in a craven manner in the face of poverty, Diogenes encouraged him to be of good heart by quoting these words from Homer:*

> *'Come now, friend, stand at my side and watch me at work.'*

(*Codex Ambrosianus Graecus* 409, no. 116; G225B)

21 When he once arrived at a customs post, he was asked whether he was carrying any valuables, and replied that indeed he was. On failing to find anything in his search, the customs official accused Diogenes of making fun of him, but he bared his chest and declared, 'I'm carrying this vessel filled with any number of good things, but you are unable to see them because you keep the eyes of your soul firmly closed.'

(*Codex Patmos* 263, no. 60; G471C)

22 During the night a thief attempted to pull his money-bag from under his head; and on becoming aware of this, he said, 'Take it, you wretch, and allow me to get some sleep!'

(*Gnomologium Lindenbrogium* no. 1; G243)

23 He would often loudly proclaim that the gods have granted human beings the means to an easy life, but this has been hidden from sight* because they seek for honey-cakes and perfumes and the like.

(Diogenes Laertius 6.44; G322)

24a Things of great value, he said, are sold for a song, and vice versa;

for a statue will sell for three thousand drachmas, and a day's supply of barley-flour for two coppers.

(Diogenes Laertius 6.35; G323)

24b [May I recount] what Diogenes did with the man who declared that Athens was an expensive city. He took him in hand and led him off to a perfume-seller, and asked how much a half-pint of myrrh cost. 'A mina',* replied the seller, and Diogenes cried out, 'The city is indeed expensive!' And then he led the man off to a butcher's shop and asked the price of a choice cut of meat. 'Three drachmas', replied the butcher, and Diogenes said, 'The city is indeed expensive!' Next, to a seller of fine wools, where he asked the price of a full fleece; 'a mina' was the reply, and he cried again, 'The city is indeed expensive!' 'Here now', he said, and took the man to a lupin-seller and asked, 'How much for a quart?' 'A copper',* was the reply, and Diogenes cried, 'How cheap the city is!' And then again to a seller of dried figs: 'Two coppers.' And to a seller of myrtle-berries, 'Two coppers'; 'How cheap the city is!' So the fact of the matter is that the city is not cheap or expensive in itself, but expensive if one lives expensively, and cheap if one lives cheaply.

(Teles pp. 12.5–13.13 Hense; G222)

His Manner of Eating

25 Diogenes said that other people lived to eat, but he ate to live.

(Stobaeus 3.6.41; G182)

26 Diogenes said that people eat for the sake of pleasure, but for that same reason are unwilling to desist from eating.

(Stobaeus 3.6.40; G182)

27 When he was once at a drinking-party and was given a large helping of wine, he poured it away; and when some people reproached him, he said, 'But if I drank it all, it is not only the wine that would be lost, but me too!'

(Maximus 30.14; G192)

28 When some mice crept on to his table, he said, 'Look, even Diogenes has scroungers* to support!'

(Diogenes Laertius 6.40; G173)

29 Asked whether the wise eat cakes, he said, 'Cakes of every kind, just like everyone else.'*

(Diogenes Laertius 6.56; G189)

30 When someone made fun of the sage Diogenes, laughing to see a philosopher like himself eating cakes, he said, 'Philosophers partake of everything, but not in the same way as everyone else.'*

(*Gnomologium Vaticanum* 188; G189)

31 When he was once wolfing down cakes at a dinner, and somebody questioned him about this, he said that he was merely eating a better kind of bread.

(Athenaeus 3, 113f; G190)

32a When he was once dining on olives and found a cake included among them, he threw it away, saying, '*Stranger, stand out of the pathway of kings!*',* and on another occasion, '*He lashed it on its way.*'*

(Diogenes Laertius 6.55; G494)

32b On being given some white bread, he threw the coarse-milled bread out of his knapsack, saying, '*Stranger, stand out of the pathway of kings.*'

(Stobaeus 3.17.15; G494)

33 As he was once eating in a temple, and some loaves of black bread were set on the table, he picked them up and threw them away, saying that nothing unclean should enter a temple.*

(Diogenes Laertius 6.64; G349)

34 When asked what wine he most liked to drink, he replied, 'Somebody else's.'*

(Diogenes Laertius 6.54; G193)

35 When asked at what hour one should dine, he replied, 'If you are rich, when you want, if you are poor, when you can.'*

(Diogenes Laertius 6.40; G183)

Cynic Shamelessness

36 It was his practice to do all things in public, including those connected with Demeter and Aphrodite.* He would thus argue as follows: 'If taking a meal is nothing improper, then neither is that improper in the market-place; now taking a meal is in fact nothing improper, so neither is it improper to take one in the market-place.' He would regularly masturbate in public* and used to say, 'If only one could put an end to hunger by rubbing one's stomach!'

(Diogenes Laertius 6.69; G147)

37a He masturbated in the market-place one day and said, 'If only one could do away with hunger by rubbing one's stomach!'

(Diogenes Laertius 6.46; G147)

37b To those who reproached him for masturbating, he would say, 'If only by rubbing my stomach, I could put an end to hunger and need!'

(Athenaeus 4, 158f; G147)

37c He [Chrysippos in his *Republic*] praises Diogenes for rubbing his genitals in public and saying to those who were present, 'If only I could also rub hunger out of my stomach in such a way!'*

(Plutarch, *On Stoic Self-Contradictions* 21, 1044b; G147)

38 When he was once reproached for eating in the market-place, he said, 'Why, it was in the market-place that the hunger took me.'

(Diogenes Laertius 6.58; G186)

39 For asses likewise, said Diogenes, turn aside for food and drink just as the fancy takes them.

(Simplicius, *Commentary on Aristotle's 'On the Heavens'*, p. 148, 19–20; G185)

40 When asked why he was eating in the public portico, he replied, 'I see that steersmen too and other craftsmen bring their food to their work.'*

(*Gnomologium Vaticanum* 196; G187)

41 When reproached for drinking in a tavern,* he said, 'And when I want a haircut too, I go to a barber's.'

(Diogenes Laertius 6.66; G194)

42a When someone expressed a wish to study philosophy with him, Diogenes gave him a fish to carry and told him to follow in his footsteps; the man threw it away out of shame,* and when Diogenes ran across him again some time later, he burst out laughing and said, 'Our friendship was brought to an end by a fish!'

(Diogenes Laertius 6.36; G367)

42b Diocles* gives another version of this story. Someone said to Diogenes, 'I'm yours to command', and Diogenes led him off and gave him a half-obol's worth of cheese to carry; and when the man refused, Diogenes exclaimed, 'Our friendship has been brought to an end by a half-obol's worth of cheese!'

(Diogenes Laertius 6.36; G367)

43 When someone dropped some bread and was ashamed to pick it up again, Diogenes, wanting to teach him a lesson, tied a piece of string around the neck of a wine-jar and dragged it through the Ceramicos.*

(Diogenes Laertius 6.35; G188)

The Art of Begging

44 When he was in need of money, he would say to his friends that he was asking for what he was owed, and not for charity.*

(Diogenes Laertius 6.46; G234)

45 When some people praised somebody for having given him money, he said, 'But you aren't praising me for having deserved to receive it.'

(Diogenes Laertius 6.62; G248)

46 When he was once invited to a dinner, he refused to go, saying that on the last occasion they hadn't been properly grateful.

(Diogenes Laertius 6.34; G467)

47 When begging for money (as he did at the beginning* because of his poverty), he used to say, 'If you have given to someone else before, give to me as well; and if you've given to no one else, then make a start with me.'

(Diogenes Laertius 6.49; G249)

48 One day he begged for money from a statue,* and when asked why he was doing so, replied, 'I'm getting practice in being refused.'

(Diogenes Laertius 6.49; G247)

49 When asked why people give to beggars but not to philosophers, he replied, 'Because they expect that they may become lame and blind, but never that they will become philosophers.'

(Diogenes Laertius 6.56; G366)

50 He said that it was one and the same fault to give to those to whom one ought not, and to fail to give to those to whom one ought.

(Maximus 8.27; G366)

51 When someone asked for his cloak to be returned to him, he said, 'If you gave it to me, I own it; if you lent it to me I'm still using it.'

(Diogenes Laertius 6.62; G252)

52 He asked a spendthrift for a mina, and when the man enquired as to why he asked just an obol* from everyone else, but a mina from him, Diogenes replied, 'Because I expect to get money from them in the future, but whether I will get any more from you lies in the laps of the gods.'

(Diogenes Laertius 6.67; G253)

53 He was once begging from a skinflint, and the man was slow to respond. 'Come on, man,' said Diogenes, 'I'm asking you for money to feed myself, not to pay for my funeral.'*

(Diogenes Laertius 6.56; G251)

54 He once asked a disagreeable man for some money, and when the man said, 'If you can persuade me', replied, 'If I were capable of doing that, I would have persuaded you to go away and hang yourself.'

(Diogenes Laertius 6.59; G250)

55 On receiving a piece of small change from Diotimos of Carystos, he said:

> *'May the gods grant you your heart's desire,*
> *A husband and a home',**

(for Diotimos was thought to be somewhat effeminate).

(Aelian, *Historical Miscellany* 4.27; G235)

IV · SELF-CHARACTERIZATION

The True Man and the Crowd

56a He lit a lamp in full daylight and walked around with it, saying, 'I'm searching for a man.'*

(Diogenes Laertius 6.41; G272)

56b He once lit a lamp in daylight and walked around; and when some people asked him why he was doing that, he said that he was searching for a man.

(Maximus 70.20; G272)

57 He would call human beings only those who have a knowledge of what is truly human, just as those who have a knowledge of grammar are grammarians, or of music are musicians.

(*Codex Patmos* 263, no. 55; G331B)

58 When he came back from the Olympic Games, someone asked him if there had been much of a crowd. 'A considerable crowd,' he replied, 'but hardly a man to be seen.'

(Diogenes Laertius 6.60; G273)

59 As he was coming out of the baths, someone asked if there were many men bathing there, and he said, 'No'; but when asked if there was much of a crowd, he replied, 'Yes indeed.'

(Diogenes Laertius 6.40; G274)

60 One day he shouted, 'Hey, men!', and when some people came along, he struck them with his stick, saying, 'I called for men, not scum!'

(Diogenes Laertius 6.32; G278)

61 When asked where in Greece he had seen good men, he replied, 'Men nowhere at all, but boys in Sparta.'

(Diogenes Laertius 6.27; G280)

62 When someone asked him, as he was returning from Sparta to Athens, where he had been and where he was going, he replied, 'From the men's quarters to the women's.'*

(Diogenes Laertius 6.59; G282)

63 When an Athenian once reproached Diogenes, saying that he was always praising the Spartans and yet did not care to go and live among them, he replied, 'But a doctor, being a man who is responsible for bringing people to good health, does not carry out his business among those who are healthy.'

(Stobaeus 3.13.43; G281)

As True Victor

64 After the race in armour* at the Olympic Games, Diogenes ran forward and proclaimed himself as the Olympic victor over all mankind in human excellence.

(Demetrius, *On Style* 260; G449)

65 Diogenes used to say that he had seen many men competing in wrestling and in running, but no one competing to surpass in human excellence.

(Stobaeus 3.4.111; G450)

66 He said that many men compete in digging and kicking,* but no one at all in the pursuit of human excellence.

(Diogenes Laertius 6.27; G450)

67 Diogenes used to say that it is absurd that, if athletes and singers gain mastery over their stomach and pleasures for the sake of their voice or body, no one despises these things for the sake of his soul's good order.

(Stobaeus 3.5.39; G451)

68 Diogenes said that no exercise is of any value unless it aims at the good order and fitness of the soul, as opposed to that of the body.

(Stobaeus 3.7.17; G292)

69a When the herald proclaimed at the Olympic Games, 'Dioxippos is victor over men!',* Diogenes said, 'No, he's victor over slaves, it's I who am victor over men.'

(Diogenes Laertius 6.43; G76)

69b When someone said that he had been victor over men at the Pythian Games,* Diogenes replied, 'No, it's I who am victor over men, and you over slaves.'

(Diogenes Laertius 6.33; G76)

70a As the Athenian Olympic victor Dioxippos was being driven into Athens in the way that is customary for victorious athletes,* a crowd gathered together from all directions and gazed at him admiringly; and among others a woman of exceptional beauty arrived to have a look at him. On seeing her, Dioxippos was at once overcome by her beauty, and could never stop gazing at her and turning back to look at her, as his face kept changing colour, so that it did not escape the attention of many who were there that the man was looking at her in no casual fashion. His state of mind was recognized most clearly by Diogenes of Sinope, who remarked to those around him, 'Just look at how that great athlete of yours has been caught in a neck-lock by a slip of a girl!'

(Aelian, *Historical Miscellany* 12.58; G452)

70b Diogenes was watching the Olympic victor Dioxippos as he was being driven past in a chariot, and saw how he could not keep his eyes off a beautiful woman who was watching the procession, but kept gazing at her and turning back to look at her. 'Look at that,' he said, 'the athlete has been caught in a neck-lock by a slip of a girl!'

(Plutarch, *On Curiosity* 12, 521b; G452)

70c Seeing an Olympic victor repeatedly turning to gaze at a woman of easy virtue, Diogenes said, 'Look at this fire-breathing ram of ours, caught in a neck-hold by the first wench he comes across!'

(Diogenes Laertius 6.61; G452)

71 He used to say that he imitated the chorus-masters, for they too set the note somewhat high* so that others may strike the right note.

(Diogenes Laertius 6.35; G266)

Striving Against the Current

72 He walked into a theatre against the flow as everyone was streaming out, and when asked why he was doing so, replied, 'Why, this is what I seek to do my whole life through.'

(Diogenes Laertius 6.64; G267)

73 He walked around backwards in the public arcade, and when people laughed at him, said, 'Aren't you ashamed that while you're walking in the wrong direction along life's path, you scoff at me for walking backwards?'

(Stobaeus 3.4.83; G267)

74 Someone said that Diogenes was out of his mind.* 'It's not that I'm out of my mind,' he replied. 'It's that I don't have the same mind as you.'

(Stobaeus 3.3.51; G427)

75 One day, when he had been talking in a serious fashion and no one had drawn near, he began to whistle; and as people gathered round him, he reproached them for earnestly pressing forward to listen to nonsense, but holding back and reacting with disdain when it came to serious matters.

(Diogenes Laertius 6.27; G314)

76 Diogenes used constantly to say to himself; when most people sing your praises, consider yourself worthy of none, and when no one praises and all condemn, that you are worthy of much.

(*Codex Vaticanus Graecus* 633, fo. 119; G435)

77 He would ridicule good birth and reputation and everything of that kind, calling them gaudy embellishments of vice.

(Diogenes Laertius 6.72; G353)

78 When someone asked him, 'Who are the noblest of men?', he replied, 'Those who despise riches, reputation, pleasure and concern for life, and are thus able to overmaster their opposites, poverty, ill-repute, suffering, and death.'

(Stobaeus 4.29.19, G362)

79a When someone asked him how one can best gain a reputation, he replied, 'By holding reputation in contempt.'

(Lucian, *Defence of the Portrait-Study* 17; G302)

79b When someone asked him how one can gain a reputation with the greatest rapidity and ease, he replied, 'By being able to hold reputation in contempt.'

(Nicephorus Gregoras, *Byzantine History* 21.5.7; G302)

80 To someone who told him, 'Many people laugh at you', he replied, 'Yes, but I'm not laughed down.'

(Diogenes Laertius 6.54; G430)

81 When a good person is insulted, the insult is indeed inflicted, but it has no effect on him because he views it with contempt. So when someone insulted Diogenes, and someone else said to him, 'That man has insulted you, Diogenes', he replied, 'But I for my part suffer no insult or ridicule.'*

(Olympiodoros, *Commentary on Plato's 'Gorgias'*, 476a, 22.2; G270)

82 When someone said to him, 'Most people laugh at you', he replied, 'And doubtless donkeys laugh at them;* but just as they pay no heed to the donkeys, I pay none to them.'

(Diogenes Laertius 6.58; G431)

83 The man from Sinope would go up to women from the brothels and abuse them, so the story goes. With what in mind? To be able to bear insults with equanimity in return for insults.

(Gregory Nazianzen, *Carmina* 1.2, 25.494–6; G271)

84 When someone told him that he was pretending to be a philosopher without really being one, he replied, 'Then I'm better than you at least in the fact that I do actually want to be one.'

(*Gnomologium Vaticanum* 174; G365)

85 To someone who said to him, 'You play the philosopher without knowing anything at all', he replied, 'Even if I merely pretend to wisdom, that is itself the mark of one who aspires to it.'

(Diogenes Laertius 6.64; G364)

As Dog

86 Some schools took their name . . . from nicknames that were applied by way of a gibe, as was the case with the Cynics.

(Diogenes Laertius 1.17)

87 Diogenes used to say, 'Other dogs bite their enemies, but I my friends, so as to save them.'*

(Stobaeus 3.13.44; G149)

88 When Polyxenos the dialectician* grew indignant at the fact that

people were calling Diogenes a dog, he said, 'You too should call me "Dog"; Diogenes is merely my nickname; I am indeed a dog, but one of noble breed who watches over his friends.'

(*Gnomologium Vaticanum* 194; G149)

89 When asked what sort of things he did to be called a dog, he said, 'I fawn on the people who give me something, bark at those who don't, and sink my teeth into scoundrels.'

(Diogenes Laertius 6.60; G143)

90 When asked what kind of dog he was, he said, 'When hungry, a Maltese, and when full, a Molossian,* dogs whom everyone praises but no one dares to go out hunting with,* because of the hardships involved; and you likewise are incapable of sharing my life, because you are afraid of suffering.'

(Diogenes Laertius 6.55; G143)

91 As he was eating his meal in the market-place, the bystanders kept shouting out, 'Dog!' 'It's you who are the dogs', he retorted, 'who keep pressing round me as I eat.'

(Diogenes Laertius 6.61; G147)

92 At a dinner some people were tossing bones to him as though he were a dog; but he rid himself of them by pissing on them as though he were a dog.

(Diogenes Laertius 6.46; G146)

93a To some boys who crowded round him, saying, 'Watch out that he doesn't bite us', he said, 'Don't be afraid, lads, dogs don't feed on beets.'*

(Diogenes Laertius 6.45; G145)

93b When a pair of cowards hid away from him, he said, 'Don't worry, a dog doesn't feed on beets.'

(Diogenes Laertius 6.61; G145)

94 He used to say that he was the kind of dog whom everyone praised, but that none of those who praised him dared accompany him on the hunt.*

(Diogenes Laertius 6.33; G144)

95 The people of Athens called Diogenes 'the Dog' because he made the ground his bed and would spend the night in the streets in front of doors; but Diogenes liked this nickname because he saw that it was appropriate to the way in which he conducted himself. For he knew, as Plato recounts about the nature of dogs,* that it is their way to love those whom they know and to fawn on them, whilst they growl at those whom they do not know, and that they distinguish enemies from friends, not because they have any knowledge of good and evil, but because they either know people or do not know them. The philosopher must be of such a nature that he does not hate someone because that person does not give him anything, but rather that he should regard as a friend anyone whom he sees to be in possession of virtue, and recognize someone as alien to him in so far as he sees badness in him. Whilst a dog recognizes someone as a friend because he is accustomed to seeing him, the philosopher is able to rely on his understanding, in preference to his eyes, to distinguish a friend from an enemy, so that he should approach the one and keep the other at a distance, not so as to satisfy his anger, or indeed to bite him, but to restore him to his proper mind through admonition and cure him, and, as though through bites, to expose and bring to light his hidden failings through admonition. If someone is a dog of such a kind, it is not a house alone that he protects, and not only the person who feeds him, but he keeps watch over human beings in general, not to ensure that they do not lose their property, but rather that they do not get robbed of their integrity and mutual harmony.

(Themistius, *On Virtue* 43 ff. Sachau)

V · A SHORT CUT TO PHILOSOPHY AND VIRTUE

The Cynic Approach to Philosophy

96 Such are the lives of the various Cynics. We will now add an account of the doctrines* that they hold in common, for we consider this too to be a philosophical school, and not, as some maintain, simply a way of life. They choose to dispense with logic and physics,* much like Ariston of Chios,* to concentrate entirely on ethics. Diocles ascribes to Diogenes* what others attribute to Socrates, reporting him as saying that 'We must enquire into *whatever of good and ill comes to pass within our halls*'. They also dispense with the standard subjects of study.* Antisthenes used to say accordingly that those who have not yet acquired proper self-mastery should not study literature, so as not to become distracted by extraneous interests. They reject geometry too, and music, and all such studies. Diogenes thus remarked, when someone showed him a clock,* that it was 'a useful device to save one from being late for dinner'. And to someone who gave a musical recital in front of him, he said,

> "*'Tis wisdom that governs men and cities well,*
> *Not the twanging of lyres and whistling of flutes.'**

They maintain, furthermore, that the end is to live in accordance with virtue, as Antisthenes says in his *Heracles*,* just as with the Stoics; for the two schools have a certain affinity with one another. It has thus been said that Cynicism is a short cut to virtue. The same manner of life was also adopted by Zeno of Citium.*

They also hold that we should live a simple life, feeding only to sustain ourselves, wearing only a single cloak, and scorning wealth, repute, and high birth. Some indeed are vegetarians and drink nothing but cold water, and are contented to live in whatever shelter they can find, even storage-jars, like Diogenes, who used to say that it is the privilege of gods to need nothing, and of those who are like the gods to need little.*

They hold, furthermore, that virtue can be taught, as Antisthenes asserts in his *Heracles*, and can never be lost once acquired; and that the wise man is worthy of love, and can never go astray, and is a friend to all who are like him; and that we should leave nothing to fortune. All that falls between virtue and vice they hold to be indifferent,* in the same way as Ariston of Chios.

(Diogenes Laertius 6.103–5)

Useless Culture

97 He marvelled that the grammarians should enquire into the

misfortunes of Odysseus while remaining ignorant of their own;* that the musicians should tune the strings of their lyre while allowing the disposition of their soul to remain out of harmony; that the mathematicians should gaze up at the sun and moon and yet fail to see what lies beneath their feet;* that the orators should be so earnest in praising justice and yet never practise it.

(Diogenes Laertius 6.27–8; G374)

98 The plays entered for the festival of Dionysos* he called big puppet-shows for fools.

(Diogenes Laertius 6.24; G487)

99 A young man was once delivering a recitation, and Diogenes, who had filled the fold of his cloak with lupin seeds, began to swallow them down directly opposite him; and when he had captured the attention of the crowd,* he professed to be quite astounded that everyone should have turned away from the speaker to look at him.

(Diogenes Laertius 6.48; G393)

100 On hearing that a young man who had been associating with all the sophists was eager to associate with him too, he said,

> '*Come not here, you turncoat, to snivel at my feet.*'*

(*Gnomologium Vaticanum* 193; G498)

101 A geometer accused Diogenes of being uncultivated and ignorant. 'You'll have to forgive me', he replied, 'for not having learned what Cheiron never taught Achilles.'*

(Stobaeus 3.31.118; G373)

102 To someone who was talking about astronomical matters, he said, 'And how many days did it take you to get down from the sky?'*

(Diogenes Laertius 6.39; G371)

103 When someone asked Diogenes about how things proceed in the heavens, he said, 'I've never been up there.'

(Tertullian, *To the Nations* 2.2; G337)

104a An astronomer was pointing in the market-place to a diagram representing the stars, and was saying that 'these here are the wandering stars';* on hearing this, Diogenes said, 'Don't lie, my friend, it's not these that are wandering astray, but those over there'—pointing to the people standing around.

(Stobaeus 2.1.23; G372)

104b An astronomer was drawing a diagram of the stars in the market-place and saying 'these are the wandering ones'. 'Oh no, you wretch,' cried Diogenes. 'It's not those that are roaming astray, but these people here, who are standing around you and gazing at you as if you had just come down from the sky.'

(*Gnomologium Parisinum* 7)

Training to Virtue

105 He used to say that there are two kinds of training,* one mental and the other bodily. Through constant physical exercise, mental impressions are produced which facilitate the realization of virtuous actions. The one kind of training cannot achieve its full effect without the other, since good health and strength belong no less among the qualities that are essentially required, both for the soul and for the body.

He put forward arguments to prove that physical exercise can ease the way to the attainment of virtue. It can be seen how in the handicrafts and other arts, the craftsmen acquire remarkable dexterity through the constant practice of their art, and how flautists and athletes likewise come to excel in their respective fields through assiduous and unceasing effort; and if they had changed the scope of their training so that it was also carried over to their soul, their labours would have proved neither fruitless nor ineffective.

Nothing whatever in life, he would say, can be brought to a successful conclusion without training; it is capable of overcoming anything. It is thus necessary that, instead of engaging in useless exertions, we should choose those that are in accordance with nature if we are to live a happy life; but through their foolishness, people are unhappy. For in fact the very despising of pleasure is itself a very great source of pleasure provided that one has exercised oneself in that beforehand; and just as those who have become habituated to a life of pleasure find it most disagreeable to cross over to a contrary form of life, so those who have undertaken the opposite course of training find greater pleasure in scorning pleasure than in the pleasures themselves.

Such was the way in which he would argue and he certainly seems to have acted accordingly, re-stamping the currency in very truth, by not ascribing the same worth to merely conventional values as to those that accord with nature; and he thus maintained that his way of life was of the same stamp as that of Heracles,* in so far as he set freedom above all else.

(Diogenes Laertius 6.70–1)

True Happiness is Founded in Invulnerability to Fortune

106a Diogenes said that true pleasure lies in having one's soul in a calm and cheerful state, and that without that, the riches of a Midas or Croesus will bring no benefit; and if one suffers any distress at all over matters small or great, one is not happy but wretched.

(*Gnomologium Vaticanum* 181; G300)

106b He said that happiness is this and nothing else, to be of truly good heart and never distressed, wherever one is and whatever the moment may bring.

(Stobaeus 4.39.20; G301)

106c He said that true happiness is this, that one's mind and soul should be perpetually at peace and in good cheer.

(Stobaeus 4.39.21; G306)

107 But we always blame anything other than our own perversity and bad nature, accusing old age, poverty, the circumstances, the day, the hour, the place; and thus Diogenes claimed to have heard the voice of Vice accusing herself and saying, '*No one other than I myself is to blame for all these ills.*'*

Teles, 8.4–9.2 Hense; G468)

108 To someone who said life is bad, he said, 'Not life, but life lived badly.'

(Diogenes Laertius 6.55; G310)

109 To one who said, 'I'm ill-suited to philosophy', he replied, 'Then why live at all, if you have no interest in living well?'

(Diogenes Laertius 6.65; G362)

110 Diogenes said that people procure what they need to live, but not what they need to live well.

(Stobaeus 3.4.85; G311)

111 Diogenes would constantly say that to manage our lives properly, we need either reason or a rope.*

(Diogenes Laertius 6.24; G303)

112 When he was once in Sparta and saw his host preparing with great eagerness for a festival, he said, 'And doesn't a good man consider every day to be a festival?'

(Plutarch, *On Tranquillity of Mind* 20, 477c; G464)

113 When someone asked him what he had gained from philosophy, he said, 'This, if nothing else, that I'm prepared for every fortune.'

(Diogenes Laertius 6.63; G360)

114 Diogenes said that he thought he could see Fortune storming out to attack him and exclaiming, '*But that mad dog alone I cannot hit!*'*

(Stobaeus 2.8.21; G148)

115a When he fell prey again to some mishap, he would say, 'Thank you, Fortune, for having confronted me in such a manly fashion!'; and on such occasions he would walk away whistling.

(Stobaeus 4.44.71; G351)

115b When things came about that were unexpected and contrary to his wish, he would say, 'Thank you, Fortune, for training me to virtue by means of such afflictions.'

(*Codex Patmos* 263, no. 58; G331E)

Empty Dialectic

116 To someone who professed to be a philosopher but engaged in sophistical quibblings, he said, 'You wretch, you defile what is best in a philosopher's life by your means of argument, and yet you claim to be a philosopher.'

(Stobaeus 3.33.14; G363)

117 When someone proved by an impeccable deduction that he had horns,* he touched his forehead and said, 'Well, *I* don't see any.' And likewise, when somebody said there is no such thing as motion,* he got up and walked around.

(Diogenes Laertius 6.38–9; G479)

118 It is pleasant to record how wittily Diogenes responded to a sophism of the kind that I mentioned above, when a dialectician from Plato's school put it forward in the hope of making fun of him. For when the dialectician had asked, 'That which I am, you are not?' and Diogenes had assented, and he had then added, 'Now I am a human being', and Diogenes had assented to that too, he concluded: 'So it follows that you are not a human being.' 'Now that', replied Diogenes, 'is false, but if you want it to become true, start off with me.'

(Aulus Gellius, *Attic Nights* 18, 13.7–8; G480)

Confrontations with Plato

119 He used to refer to the discourse of Plato as a waste of time.*

(Diogenes Laertius 6.24; G487)

120 Plato defined man as a two-footed animal without wings,* and was applauded for it; so Diogenes plucked a cock and brought it into the lecture-hall, saying, 'Here's Plato's man!' As a result the definition was supplemented with the phrase 'having broad nails'.

(Diogenes Laertius 6.40; G63)

121 When Plato was once talking about his Ideas* and used the terms 'tableness' and 'cupness',* Diogenes remarked, 'I can see a table and a cup, but in no way this tableness and cupness.' 'Of course not,' replied Plato, 'because you have the eyes that are needed to see a cup and table, but lack the intellect through which tableness and cupness can alone be beheld.'

(Diogenes Laertius 6.53; G62)

122 On hearing Plato praised, Diogenes said, 'And what's so wonderful about him, a man who has practised philosophy all this time and never caused pain to anyone?'*

(Plutarch, *On Moral Virtue* 12, 452d; G61)

123 Diogenes asked Plato if he was writing a book of laws,* and he said yes. 'That's odd, haven't you written a *Republic?*' 'Yes, I have.' 'Well then, didn't your republic have laws?' 'Of course it did.' 'Then why on earth do you need to be writing laws again?'

(Stobaeus 3.13.45; G64)

124a Diogenes once asked Plato for three figs from his garden; and when Plato sent a whole bushel, he exclaimed, 'The same old story—ask him one thing and he'll reply with a thousand!'

(Stobaeus 3.36.21; G55)

124b Diogenes once asked Plato for some wine, and then for some dried figs also; and Plato sent him a whole jar full. 'Now if someone asked you what two and two add up to,' said Diogenes, 'would you answer: twenty? In just the same way, you neither give what is asked of you, nor answer the questions that are put to you.' Such was the way in which he mocked him for being a man who talked without end.

(Diogenes Laertius 6.26; G55)

125 Some also ascribe the following story to him; on seeing him washing vegetables,* Plato came up to him and quietly remarked, 'If you paid court to Dionysios,* you wouldn't need to be washing vegetables', to which he replied in the same calm tone, 'Yes, and if you washed vegetables, you wouldn't need to be paying court to Dionysios.'

(Diogenes Laertius 6.58; G56)

126 One day, at a sumptuous banquet, he noticed that Plato was merely eating olives.* 'How is it', he asked, 'that our philosopher, after having sailed over to Sicily for the sake of these fine dishes, does not enjoy them when they are set out in front of him?', to which Plato replied, 'No, by all the gods, Diogenes, over in Sicily too I lived on the olives and the like for the most part.' 'Then why', said Diogenes, 'did you need to sail to Syracuse? Can it be that Attica was not producing any olives at the time?' But Favorinos in his *Miscellaneous Tales* ascribes this to Aristippos.*

(Diogenes Laertius 6.25; G55)

127 On another occasion, while he was eating some dried figs, he ran across Plato and said, 'You can have a share of these if you like'; and when Plato took them and ate them, he said, 'I invited you to take a share of them, not to gobble down the lot.'

(Diogenes Laertius 6.25; G55)

128 When Diogenes offered Aristotle some dried figs, Aristotle realized that he had some witticism ready to deliver* if he failed to accept them; so he took them, and said that Diogenes had lost his witticism along with his figs. When offered some figs on another occasion, he accepted them, raised them up high as one does with babies, and then returned them, saying, 'Great is Diogenes.'

(Diogenes Laertius 5.18; G68)

129 When reproached for begging when Plato did not, he replied, 'Oh, he begs too, only,

> He holds his head close so that others may not hear.'*

(Diogenes Laertius 6.67; G58)

130a Plato was discussing various points in the presence of Diogenes, who was paying little attention to him. Growing irritated at this, the son of Ariston* said, 'Listen to what I'm saying, dog!' In no way disconcerted, Diogenes replied, 'Well I at least have never returned to the place where I was sold from, as dogs do', alluding to Plato's return to Sicily.*

(Aelian, *Historical Miscellany* 14.33; G59)

130b When Plato called him a dog, he said, 'Oh yes, because I have returned to those who have sold me.'*

(Diogenes Laertius 6.40; G59)

131a One day, when Plato had invited some friends who had come over from Dionysios, Diogenes trampled over his carpets, saying, 'I'm trampling on Plato's empty pride', to which Plato retorted, 'How much vanity you display, Diogenes, in making a show of not being vain!'

(Diogenes Laertius 6.26; G55)

131b Others claim that Diogenes said, 'I'm trampling on the vanity of Plato', to which Plato replied, 'Yes indeed, Diogenes, with vanity of another kind.' Sotion says in his fourth book that it was the Dog* who addressed this remark to Plato.

(Diogenes Laertius 6.26; G55)

132 When Diogenes once invited Plato to share his meal in the market-place, Plato said, 'How charming your unaffectedness would be, if only it were not so affected!'*

(*Gnomologium Vaticanum* 445; G60)

133 Diogenes was once standing outside and got a soaking, and when the bystanders took pity on him, Plato, who also happened to be present, exclaimed, 'if you really want to have occasion to pity him, simply walk away!'

(Diogenes Laertius 6.41; G57)

134a It is said that Plato used to say of Diogenes that he was Socrates gone mad.*

(Aelian, *Historical Miscellany* 14.33; G59)

134b When someone asked him, 'What sort of a man do you consider Diogenes to be?', he [Plato] replied, 'Socrates gone mad.'

(Diogenes Laertius 6.54; G59)

135 Diogenes used to say that Socrates himself had lived a life of luxury; for he had devoted too much concern to his little house, and his little couch, and his sandals* (which Socrates did in fact wear from time to time).

(Aelian, *Historical Miscellany* 4.11; G256)

136 He said that the school of Eucleides was nothing more than gall.*

(Diogenes Laertius 6.24; G487)

VI · THE WORLD OF ILLUSION

Riches and Avarice

137 Illusion,* like a shepherd, leads most men where it wills.

(Stobaeus 3.22.41; G289)

138 Avarice, he said, is the mother-city of all evils.*

(Diogenes Laertius 6.50; G228)

139 He said that wealth is the vomit of fortune.*

(Arsenius p. 209, 11; G220)

140 Those who heap up large stores of wealth he called arch-beggars.*

(Stobaeus 3.10.62; G240)

141 He used to say that neither in a rich city nor in a rich household can virtue make its dwelling.

(Stobaeus 4.31.88; G221)

142 He condemned those who, while they praise honest people for having risen above a desire for wealth, yet at the same time envy the extremely rich.

(Diogenes Laertius 6.28; G237)

143 When asked whether a certain man was wealthy, Diogenes replied, 'I have no idea, because I don't know how he uses his wealth.'*

(*Codex Patmos* 263, no. 54; G246B)

144 An uneducated and pretentious man showed him his beautiful house; 'Very fine,' he said, 'altogether admirable, like those Egyptian temples which are most beautifully fitted out and have cats or apes set up inside.'*

(*Codex Ambrosianus Graecus* 409, no. 117; G236B)

145a When someone conducted him into a magnificent house and warned him not to spit, and he then wanted to clear his throat, he spat into the man's face, saying that he could not find any worse place. This tale is also recounted about Aristippos.*

(Diogenes Laertius 6.32; G236)

145b While being received in the house of a man who had devoted considerable care to his many possessions, while leaving only himself in utter neglect, Diogenes cleared his throat and looked around him, but instead of choosing any nearby spot, spat directly at the master of the house. And when the man grew angry and asked why he had done that, he said that he could see nothing in the house that had been so neglected as its owner. For every wall was adorned with wonderful paintings, and there were images of the gods on the floor portrayed in magnificent mosaics, and all the furniture was bright and clean, and the coverings and couches were beautifully adorned, leaving their owner as the sole thing there that could be seen to have been neglected; and it is the universal custom in human society to spit in the worst available place.

(Galen, *Protreptic* 8; G236)

146 Diogenes compared the avaricious to people who are suffering from dropsy;* for just as the latter are full of water and yet yearn all the same for drink, so the avaricious too are replete and yet constantly yearn for more, to equally bad effect in both cases, their passions being heightened still further the more they obtain the objects of their desire.

(Stobaeus 3.10.45; G229)

147 To someone who was buying large quantities of land, he said, 'If you weren't held back by your love of money, there wouldn't be a spot left to which you could extend your lust for endless acquisition.'

(*Codex Patmos* 263, no. 67; G246D)

148 On seeing an avaricious man being carried out for burial, he said, 'After living a life that was no life he's left a living to others.'*

(*Codex Palatinus Graecus* 297, no. 71, fo. 118r; G231)

149 When reproached for his poverty by someone of bad character, Diogenes said, 'I've never seen anyone put to torture because of his poverty, but any number because of their wickedness.'

(Stobaeus 4.32.12; G224)

150 When someone reproached Diogenes for his poverty, he said, 'I've never seen anyone, you wretch, playing the tyrant because of poverty, but because of riches one and all.'*

(Stobaeus 4.33.26; G225)

Self-Indulgence and Excess

151 He said that just as house-slaves are at the beck and call of their masters, so bad people are at the beck and call of their desires.

(Diogenes Laertius 6.66; G318)

152 Those who are in thrall to their stomach and sexual organs and sleep he called triple-slaves.*

(*Gnomologium Vaticanum* 195; G180)

153 He thought it most odd that when slaves see their masters eating like gluttons, they do not steal some of the food for themselves.

(Diogenes Laertius 6.28; G444)

154 To a man who was having his shoes put on by his servant, he said, 'You won't be absolutely happy until he wipes your nose as well; and that will come about when you have lost the use of your hands.'*

(Diogenes Laertius 6.44; G322)

155 He said that the stomach is a whirlpool* that sucks down one's livelihood.

(Diogenes Laertius 6.51; G181)

156 He said that the houses that have the most food in them also have many mice and weasels;* and that the bodies that take in much food draw in many diseases likewise.

(Stobaeus 3.6.37; G195)

157 Diogenes laughed at those who lock away their treasures with bolts and locks and seals, but throw open their own body* with all its windows and doors, namely their mouth and genitals and eyes and ears.

(Stobaeus 3.6.17; G317)

158 It is not from barley-eaters that tyrants arise, said Diogenes, but from those who dine on sumptuous fare.

(Julian, *Oration* 9, 199a; G196)

159 He compared the dissolute to those fig-trees that grow on the precipices, whose fruit is never tasted by any human being, but is eaten by crows and vultures.*

(Diogenes Laertius 6.60; G321)

160 Most rich people can be compared with fruit trees and vines that grow in inaccessible and precipitous locations; for just as the fruit of the latter is not gathered by human beings, but only consumed by crows and similar creatures, so likewise the money of the dissolute, instead of being put aside for appropriate use, is squandered on spongers and whores, and on the most shameful indulgences and emptiest fancies.

(Stobaeus 4.31.48; G242)

161 Seeing a 'for sale' sign on the house of a wastrel, he said, 'I knew that after such a binge you'd soon vomit up your owner.'

(Diogenes Laertius 6.47; G233)

162a Seeing a young spendthrift who had squandered his inheritance feeding on bread and olives, and drinking water, he said, 'If you'd breakfasted in that way by force of reason, you wouldn't be dining in that way by force of necessity.'

(*Gnomologium Vaticanum* 169; G191)

162b Seeing a spendthrift feasting on olives in a tavern, he said, 'If you'd breakfasted in that way, you wouldn't be dining in that way.'

(Diogenes Laertius 6.50; G191)

Sex and Love

163 Love, he said, is the occupation of the unoccupied.*

(Diogenes Laertius 6.51; G198)

164 Lovers, he said, attain their pleasure in their misfortune.

(Diogenes Laertius 6.67; G199)

165 Diogenes offered some advice that was rather coarse in its expression but substantially true when he said, 'Go to a brothel, lad, and learn that what is worthless differs not at all from what is highly prized.'*

(Plutarch, *On the Education of Children* 7, 5c; G398)

166 Good-looking courtesans* he compared to a deadly honey-mixture.

(Diogenes Laertius 6.61; G209)

167 Diogenes called the most beautiful courtesans 'queens', since many men will fulfil their every command.

(Stobaeus 4.21.15; G208)

168 To one who was pressing a courtesan to grant him her favours, he said, 'Why so eager, you wretch, to obtain what it is better for you to fail in?'

(Diogenes Laertius 6.66; G210)

169 On the golden statue that Phryne* had dedicated at Delphi

Diogenes inscribed the following words: A gift from the licentiousness of the Greeks.

(Diogenes Laertius 6.60; G212)

170 Diogenes the Cynic is generally acknowledged to have been the
most steadfast of all men in every activity that demands self-control
and endurance, but for all that, even he engaged in sexual activity, because he wanted to free himself from the discomfort that is caused by
the retention of the seminal fluid, rather than for the sake of any good
that he sought in the pleasure that accompanies its emission. One
day, at any rate, so the story goes, when he had arranged for a courtesan to visit him and she was slow to arrive, he grasped his sexual
organ in his hand and contrived an emission through masturbation;
and afterwards, when the woman arrived, he sent her on her way, saying that he had already sung the marriage-song with his hand.*

(Galen, *On Affected Parts* 6.15; G197)

171 As Diogenes was once wrestling with an attractive boy, his penis
began to stir; and when the boy took alarm and drew back, he said,
'Don't be afraid, lad, I'm not of the same mind as that.' *

(Demetrius, *On Style* 261; G410)

172 When asked what is the right time to marry, he replied, 'For
those who are young, not yet, for those who are older, never at all.'*

(Diogenes Laertius 6.54; G200)

173 Diogenes considered that there is nothing cheaper than an
adulterer, who will throw away his life for what can be bought for a
drachma.*

(Stobaeus 3.6.39; G218)

174 How can one mention this saying of Diogenes without shud-
dering? Something that the philosophers of this world have not been
ashamed to cite as something worthy of recall, we can neither repeat
nor hear without a sense of shame. When (so the story goes) someone was due to be punished for the crime of adultery, Diogenes said,
'Don't buy with your life what is sold for a gift.'

(John Cassian, *Conferences* 13.5; G219)

Against Effeminacy in Young Men

175 One day he saw a young man behaving in an effeminate manner. 'Aren't you ashamed', he said, 'that you should have worse intentions for yourself than nature had? For nature made you a man, and yet here you are, forcing yourself to become a woman.'

(Diogenes Laertius 6.65; G403)

176 When he was asked something by an effeminately dressed young man, Diogenes refused to say anything to him unless he first pulled up his clothes to show whether he was a woman or a man.

(Diogenes Laertius 6.46; G403)

177 To a youth who was complaining of the large numbers of men who were pestering him with their attentions, he said, 'Then stop displaying the signs of your unnatural lusts.'*

(Diogenes Laertius 6.47; G409)

178 One day he saw a young man engaging in philosophy. 'It is a fine thing', he said, 'that you should cause the lovers of your body to turn to the beauty of your soul.'

(Diogenes Laertius 6.58; G397)

179 Seeing a young man who was fair of form and attracted admirers on that account, he said, 'You should endeavour, young man, to turn lovers of your bodily beauty to love of your soul.'

(*Gnomologium Vaticanum* 176; G397)

180 To a young man playing *kottabos** in the baths, he said, 'The better you are, the worse you are.'

(Diogenes Laertius 6.46; G401)

181 Seeing a young man going off to dine with some satraps,* he dragged him off to his relations and told them to keep a good eye on him.

(Diogenes Laertius 6.46; G402)

182 To one who prided himself on his good looks, he said, 'Aren't you ashamed to attach such importance to your youthful charms, which are only yours on loan and for a short time at that?'

(*Gnomologium Parisinum* 229)

183 To one who had perfumed himself, he said, 'Watch out that the fine smell on your head doesn't cause a stink in your life.'

(Diogenes Laertius 6.66; G325)

184 On seeing a young man who had anointed himself with perfume, Diogenes the Dog said, 'The fine smell around your head is creating a stink in your life.'

(*Codex Parisinus Graecus* 1168, no. 14; G407B)

185 Seeing a young man beautifying himself, he said, 'If that's for men, you're a wretch; if it's for women, you're a rogue.'*

(Diogenes Laertius 6.54; G405)

186 To wear one's hair over-short and one's garments fine beyond necessity is, according to the saying of Diogenes, the behaviour of a wretch or a rogue.

(Basil, *De Legendis Libris Gentilium* 7; G165)

187 On observing how a young man was priding himself on his expensive cloak, he said, 'Stop priding yourself on sharing in the good qualities of a sheep.'

(*Gnomologium Vaticanum* 177; G407)

Miscellaneous

188 One day, as Metrocles* recounts in his *Anecdotes*, he broke in on a young men's drinking-party with his head half-shaved,* and was greeted with blows. Afterwards he inscribed the names of his assailants on a white tablet, and walked around with it hung around his neck until he had brought disgrace on them, and they were reproached and condemned by everyone.

(Diogenes Laertius 6.33; G412)

189 The Dog called the wine-shops the mess-halls of Attica.*

(Aristotle, *Rhetoric* 3.10, 1411a 24–5; G184)

190 Diogenes delivered a discourse on moderation and self-control, and when the Athenians applauded him for it, cried, 'To hell with the lot of you, since you contradict me in everything that you do!'

(Stobaeus 2.15.43; G283)

191 When Diogenes went to Olympia and saw some young men from Rhodes* at the festival dressed in sumptuous clothing, he laughed and said, 'Sheer vanity!'; and when he then ran across some Spartans in mean and filthy tunics, he said, 'Just another kind of vanity!'

(Aelian, *Historical Miscellany* 9.34; G288)

192 He had his feet anointed with perfume,* saying that from one's head the perfume passes into the air, while from one's feet it passes up into one's nostrils.

(Diogenes Laertius 6.39; G324)

193 When he was once dining with King Antigonos*and some scented water was brought in, he rubbed it into his knees; and when the king asked, 'Why are you doing that?', he replied, 'Because when I am lying in bed, I hold my knees up to my nostrils.'

(*Gnomologium Parisinum* 8)

VII · RELIGION AND SUPERSTITION

On Religious Practices

194 He criticized people for the way in which they prayed, saying that they asked for the things that seemed good to them, and not for those that truly are.*

(Diogenes Laertius 6.42; G350)

195 It made him angry that people should sacrifice to the gods for good health, and yet at those very sacrifices feast* to the detriment of their health.

(Diogenes Laertius 6.28; G345)

196 Diogenes said, 'People pray to the gods for good health, and yet most of them consistently act in such a way as to damage their health.'

(Stobaeus 3.6.35; G345)

197 To a couple who were sacrificing to the gods in the hope of having a son, he said, 'But you don't sacrifice to ensure what kind of a person he'll turn out to be?'

(Diogenes Laertius 6.63; G343)

198 On seeing someone being purified in a lustral rite,* he said, 'Poor wretch, don't you know that, just as sprinklings of water cannot deliver you from errors of grammar, they will be no more effective in delivering you from the errors of your life?'

(Diogenes Laertius 6.42; G326)

199a When the Athenians urged him to have himself initiated, and said that initiates obtain a privileged position in Hades,* he said, 'It would be absurd if Agesilaos and Epaminondas* are to lie in the mud while utterly worthless people, just because they have been initiated, are to dwell in the Isles of the Blest.'

(Diogenes Laertius 6.39; G339)

199b When Diogenes heard these lines by Sophocles about the Mysteries:

> *Thrice-blessed*
> *Are those mortals who have beheld the Mysteries*
> *When they depart to Hades, for they alone will know*
> *Life there, while others meet with nought but evil,**

he said, 'Do you mean to say that Patakion the thief* will meet with a better lot than Epaminondas, just because he has been initiated?'

(Plutarch, *How a Young Man Should Listen to Poets* 4.21 ef; G339)

200 When someone marvelled at all the votive offerings on Samothrace,* he said, 'There would have been a good many more if they were also offered up by those who were *not* saved.'

(Diogenes Laertius 6.59; G342)

201 One day he saw a woman assuming a none too decorous posture* as she was supplicating the gods; and wanting to free her of her superstition (as Zoilos of Perga records) he went up to her and said, 'Aren't you afraid, my good woman, that the god may be standing behind you—for everywhere is full of his presence—and then your posture would be none too decent.'

(Diogenes Laertius 6.37; G344)

202 To Asklepios he dedicated a pugilist* who, whenever people prostrated themselves, would run up to them and give them a beating.

(Diogenes Laertius 6.38; G341)

203 When he was once gathering figs and the custodian said to him, 'A man hanged himself from that tree not long ago', he replies, 'Very well, then, I'll clear it.'*

(Diogenes Laertius 6.61; G348)

204 The philosopher Diogenes once entered a temple of Heracles as evening was falling, and seizing hold of the wooden image of Heracles, mockingly said, 'Well then, Heracles, the time has now come for you to serve me as once you served Eurystheus,* and to perform this thirteenth labour of cooking my lentil soup'; and with these words, he thrust it into the fire.

(Oracles of the Greek Gods, no. 70, ed. K. Buresch, *Klaros* (1889); G131)

205 One day, on seeing the custodians of the temple-treasures leading away a man who had stolen a bowl, he said, 'The big thieves are arresting the little thief.'

(Diogenes Laertius 6.45; G462)

Against Superstition

206 He used to say that when in this life he saw pilots, doctors, and philosophers, man struck him as being the most intelligent of creatures, but when, on the other hand, he saw diviners and dream-readers* and those who consulted them, and those who prided themselves on their reputation and wealth, he then thought there could be no creature more foolish than man.

(Diogenes Laertius 6.24; G375)

207 To those who allowed themselves to be disturbed by their dreams, he used to say that, while they paid little enough attention to what they were doing while they were awake, they devoted all their concern to fancies that they dreamed up while they were asleep.

(Diogenes Laertius 6.43; G327)

208 A man who was highly superstitious once remarked to Diogenes, 'I could break your head in with a single blow', to which he retorted, 'And I for my part could make you tremble with fear simply by sneezing from the left.'*

(Diogenes Laertius 6.48; G346)

209 To someone who marvelled at having found a snake coiled around a bolt,* he said, 'That's nothing to wonder at, it would have been stranger by far if you'd seen the pestle coiled around the outstretched snake!'

(Clement of Alexandria, *Stromata* 7.4.25.1; G463)

210 When Agesilaos of Cos recounted a dream, Diogenes said, 'You look into how you act and talk in your dreams, but fail to see where you are making a false step while you are awake.'

(*Codex Patmos* 263, no. 59; G471B)

Do the Gods Exist?

211 Diogenes the Cynic used to say that Harpalos,* who had enjoyed a successful career as a pirate in those days, offered telling witness against the gods, by having lived so long in such good fortune.

(Cicero, *On the Nature of the Gods* 3.83; G335)

212 The prosperity and good fortune of the wicked, so Diogenes used to say, provides telling evidence against the power of the gods.

(Cicero, *On the Nature of the Gods* 3.88; G335)

213 When asked, 'Do the gods exist?', he replied, 'I don't know, all I know is that it is expedient that they should.'*

(Tertullian, *To the Nations* 2.2; G337)

214a To someone who said to him, 'Are you the Diogenes who doesn't believe in the existence of the gods?', he replied, 'And how could I be, when I consider you to be hateful to the gods?'*

(Epictetus 3.22.90–1; G334)

214b When Lysias the pharmacist asked him whether he believed in the gods, he replied, 'And how could I not, when I regard you as being hateful to the gods?'

(Diogenes Laertius 6.42; G334)

Unholy Paradoxes in Writings ascribed to Diogenes

215 He said that wives should be held in common, recognizing no other union than that between the man who persuades and the woman who yields to persuasion; and for that reason, he thought that sons too should be held in common. He also held there to be nothing improper in stealing from a temple* or eating the meat of any kind of animal; nor even anything ungodly in consuming human flesh, as is plain from the custom of some foreign peoples. According to right reason, so he argued, every substance is to be found in all others* and throughout all things; so in bread, for instance, there are particles of meat, and in vegetables, particles of bread, and also particles of every other substance in every other, in so far as they pass in through certain invisible pores* and enter into combination with it in vaporous form, as he makes clear in his *Thyestes*, if the tragedies were indeed written by him, and not by Philiscos of Aegina,* a pupil of his, or by Pasiphon,* son of Loucianos, as Favorinos claims in his *Miscellaneous Histories*, saying that they were written after the death of Diogenes.

(Diogenes Laertius 6.72–3; G132 and 128)

216 Since you have read so much, what do you think of the things that are to be found in the works of Zeno, Diogenes, and Cleanthes?* They teach cannibalism, fathers are to be cooked and eaten by their own sons, and if anyone should prove unwilling and throw away his share of the abominable meal, he who refuses to eat will himself be eaten. Can any voice be found that is more ungodly than that of Diogenes, who teaches children to bring their own parents to sacrifice* and devour them?

(Theophilus, *To Autolycus* 3.5; G134)

217 Cleanthes in his book *On the Way to Dress* mentions it [the *Republic*]* with praise as a work of Diogenes, and gives a general account of its contents, with further discussion of some particular points; and Chrysippos in his work *On the State and Law* makes mention of it. . . . In his work *On the State*, while talking about the uselessness of weapons,* he says that such a view was also stated by Diogenes, which is something that he could only have written about in his *Republic*. In the treatise *Things which should not be chosen for their own sake*, Chrysippos states that Diogenes laid down in his state that knucklebones should serve as legal currency.* This is to be found in the work of which we are talking and also in the first book of the treatise *Against those who have a different idea of practical reason*. In his work *On the life in accordance with reason* he also makes mention of [Diogenes' *Republic*], together with the many impieties contained in it, to which he gives his approval; and he frequently mentions the work and its contents with praise in the fourth book of his treatise *On the beautiful and pleasure*. And in the third book of his work on justice he speaks of cannibalism as a teaching. . . . Diogenes himself in his *Atreus*, *Oedipus*, and *Philiscos* acknowledges as his own teachings most of the foul and impious ideas that are to be found in the *Republic*. Antipater* in his work *Against the Philosophical Schools* mentions Zeno's *Republic* and the doctrines that Diogenes expounds in his *Republic*, expressing amazement at their impassibility. And some say that the *Republic* is not by the Sinopean but by someone else . . .

We must now go on to summarize the noble thoughts of these people,* expending as little time as possible in describing their opinions. It pleases these holy people, then, to assume the lives of dogs, to speak shamelessly and without restraint to everyone without distinction, to masturbate in public, to wear a doubled cloak, to abuse young men whether they love them or not, and whether or not the young men willingly surrender themselves or have to be forced . . . boys are held in common by all . . . they have sexual relations with their own sisters and mothers and other close relatives, and with their brothers and sons. To achieve sexual gratification, there is nothing that they will abstain from, not even the use of violence.* The women make advances to men, and seek to persuade them in every way to have intercourse with them, and if they fail in their efforts, offer themselves in the market-place to anyone whatever. Everyone misbehaves with everyone else, husbands have intercourse with their maidservants, wives abandon their husbands to go off with those who better please them. The women wear the same clothing as men and take part in the same activities, differing from them in no way at all.

(Philodemus, *On the Stoics* 13 ff.; G126)

218 The following books are attributed to him.*The dialogues *Cephalion, Ichthyas,* *The Jackdaw, Pordalos,* *The People of Athens, The Republic, The Moral Art, On Wealth, On Love, Theodoros, Hypsias, Aristarchos, On Death*; a collection of letters; and seven tragedies,* *Helen, Thyestes, Heracles, Achilles, Medea, Chrysippos, Oedipus.*

Sosicrates, however, in the fourth book of his *Successions*, and Satyros in the fourth book of his *Lives*, claim that none of these are by Diogenes, and Satyros says that the little tragedies are the work of Philiscos of Aegina, a friend of Diogenes; while Sotion in his seventh book says that the only genuine works of Diogenes are *On Virtue, On the Good, On Love, The Beggar, Tolmaios, Pordalos, Cassandros, Cephalion, Philiscos,* *Aristarchos, Sisyphos, Ganymedes*, the *Anecdotes*, and the *Letters.*

(Diogenes Laertius 6.80; G117)

VIII · POLITICIANS AND RULERS

Diogenes and the Orators of Athens

219 He called the orators the lackeys of the crowd,* and crowns of honour efflorescences* of fame.

(Diogenes Laertius 6.41; G501)

220 The orators and all who speak for the sake of fame he called 'thrice-human'.*

(Diogenes Laertius 6.47; G501)

221 Words spoken solely to please are like choking honey.

(Diogenes Laertius 6.51; G505)

222 When asked what is the finest thing of all in life, he said, 'Plain speaking.'*

(Diogenes Laertius 6.69; G473)

223 Diogenes said that reproof is another person's benefit.*

(Stobaeus 3.13.42; G307)

224 He said that the orators are very earnest about justice in their speeches, but not at all in their actions.

(Diogenes Laertius 6.28; G504)

225a When some stranger wanted to see Demosthenes he pointed him out with his middle finger, saying, 'There you are, the demagogue of Athens!'*

(Diogenes Laertius 6.34; G502)

225b Do you not know that Diogenes pointed out one of the sophists in this way, by stretching out his middle finger, and when the man flew into a rage, remarked, 'That's the man you asked me about, I've pointed him out to you!'*

(Epictetus 3.2.11; G276)

226 As Diogenes was taking a meal in a tavern one day, he saw Demosthenes walking by and called out to him; and when Demosthenes paid no heed, he said, 'So you're ashamed, are you, Demosthenes, to come into a tavern? And yet your master comes in every day!'*

(Aelian, *Historical Miscellany* 9.19; G503)

227 He once caught Demosthenes the orator eating a meal in a tavern, and when Demosthenes tried to draw back, called out, 'You'll only be that much further in!'

(Diogenes Laertius 6.34; G502)

228 And he scoffed at him, saying that he was a Scythian in his speeches, but a dainty man of the city in battle.*

(Plutarch, *Lives of the Ten Orators* 847F)

229 When Anaximenes* was once delivering a discourse, Diogenes distracted the audience by holding up some salt fish; and when Anaximenes grew angry, he said, 'An obol's worth of salt fish has broken up Anaximenes' lecture!'

(Diogenes Laertius 6.57; G506)

230 Seeing the servants of Anaximenes moving a large amount of furniture, he asked, 'Who does that belong to?', and when they replied, 'To Anaximenes', he said, 'Isn't he ashamed to possess all that when he doesn't even possess himself?'*

(Maximus 12.43; G507)

231 He once went up to Anaximenes the rhetorician, who was rather stout, and said, 'Give us beggars a share of your belly, it will be both a relief for you and a blessing for us.'

(Diogenes Laertius 6.57; G506)

Confrontations with Philip of Macedon

232a Dionysios the Stoic recounts that after the battle of Chaironeia,* Diogenes was arrested and brought in front of Philip; and when he was asked who he was, he replied, 'A spy who has come to observe your insatiable greed',* a response which so impressed the king that he set him free.

(Diogenes Laertius 6.43; G27)

232b And was not Diogenes plain-speaking, who, when he entered Philip's camp as the king was advancing to fight against the Greeks, and was hauled in front of him as a spy, said, 'Yes, I have indeed come as a spy, to observe the greed and folly of a man who is shortly about to stake his crown and life on a single throw of the dice'?

(Plutarch, *On Exile* 16, 606bc; G27)

233 Diogenes of Sinope went to Philip straight after the battle of Chaironeia and rebuked him for his behaviour toward the Athenians, saying that although he claimed to be a Heraclid, he was destroying by force of arms those who had taken up arms on behalf of the Heraclids.*

(Philostratus, *Life of Apollonius* 7.2.3; G29)

234a When it had been reported that Philip was about to attack Corinth,* and all the citizens were hard at work and absorbed in their tasks, Diogenes began to roll his jar back and forth; and when someone asked, 'Why are you doing that, Diogenes?', he replied, 'Because when everyone is toiling away, it would hardly be proper for me to do nothing; so I'm rolling my jar,* having nothing else to turn my hand to.'

(Diogenes Laertius 6.69; G26)

234b When I saw and heard this, my friend, I was reminded of the following tale of the man of Sinope. On receiving news that Philip was advancing against them, the Corinthians were all thoroughly agitated and set to work, one man attending to his weapons, another fetching stones, another repairing the walls, another shoring up the battlements, and everyone making himself useful in one way or another. At the sight of this activity, Diogenes, since he had nothing to do for his own part (for no one had called on his services in any way), girded up his cloak in a determined manner and rolled the jar in which he had made his home up and down the Craneion;* and when one of his friends asked him, 'Why are you doing that, Diogenes?', he replied, 'Well, for my part I'm rolling my jar so as not to give the impression that I'm the only idler among all these people who are so hard at work.'

(Lucian, *How to Write History* 3; G25)

235 The saying of Diogenes, 'Aristotle breakfasts when Philip pleases,* and Diogenes when Diogenes pleases.'

(Plutarch, *On Exile* 12, 604d; G30)

Confrontations with Alexander the Great

236a As he was sunning himself in the Craneion,* Alexander stood over him and said, 'Ask whatever you wish of me', and he replied, 'Stand out of my light.'

(Diogenes Laertius 6.38; G33)

236b But Diogenes took a greater liberty, in the true Cynic fashion, and when Alexander asked him if he had need of anything, replied, 'For the present, that you should stand a little out of my sun', for Alexander was preventing him from sunning himself.

(Cicero, *Tusculan Disputations* 5.32.92; G33)

236c On seeing him sitting in the sun, Alexander stood over him and asked him if he wanted anything; and when Diogenes demanded nothing other than that he should stand a little out of his light, he was so impressed by his spirit that he remarked to his friends, 'If I were not Alexander, I should be Diogenes.'

(Plutarch, *On Exile* 15, 605de; G32)

236d The Greeks held a general assembly at the Isthmus and voted to embark on an expedition against the Persians with Alexander, who was proclaimed as their leader.* Many statesmen and philosophers came to congratulate him, and he hoped that Diogenes of Sinope, who was living in Corinth, would do likewise; but since he paid not the slightest heed to Alexander, but remained at his leisure in the Craneion, Alexander himself went to see him and found him stretched out in the sun. At the approach of so many people, Diogenes sat up a little and fixed his eyes on Alexander. And when the king greeted him and asked him if there was anything that he wanted, he said, 'Yes, that you should stand a little out of my sun.' It is said that Alexander was so impressed by this, and by the arrogance and grandeur of spirit of a man who could treat him with such disdain, that he said to his courtiers, who were laughing and joking about the philosopher as they were walking away, 'But I'll tell you this, if I were not Alexander, I would be Diogenes!'

(Plutarch, *Life of Alexander* 14, 671de; G32)

237 Alexander once appeared before him and said, 'I'm Alexander, the Great King.'* 'And I', he replied, 'am Diogenes the Dog.'

(Diogenes Laertius 6.60; G34)

238 Alexander came up to him and said, 'Aren't you afraid of me?' 'Well, tell me this,' asked Diogenes, 'are you a good thing or a bad one?'; and when Alexander replied, 'A good one', he said, 'Then who's afraid of what is good?'

(Diogenes Laertius 6.68; G40)

239 Alexander stood over him while he was asleep and said,

> *'To sleep the whole night through ill befits a man of counsel'*

to which he replied while half-asleep,

'Who has people to watch over and a multitude of cares.'
(Epictetus 3.22.92; G39)

240 Seeing Diogenes asleep in a jar, he said, 'A jar-full of wits', at which the sage rose up and said, 'O mighty king,

> *Rather the least drop of fortune than a jar-full of wits*
> *For when it is absent, one's wits feel the misfortune.'*

(*Gnomologium Vaticanum* 97; G38)

241 When Diogenes asked Alexander for a drachma, he replied, 'That's no proper gift for a king to bestow'; and when Diogenes said, 'Then give me a talent', he replied, 'And that's no proper thing for a Cynic to ask!'

(*Gnomologium Vaticanum* 104; G35)

242 Alexander filled a dish with bones* one day and sent it to Diogenes the Cynic; on receiving it, Diogenes said, 'A meal befitting a dog, but not a gift befitting a king.'

(*Gnomologium Vaticanum* 96; G35)

243 Diogenes said that Alexander was not content to be a man, but was too foolish* to be capable of being a god.

(*Codex Vaticanus Graecus* 96, fo. 88v, no. 13; G35b)

244 When the Athenians voted that Alexander should be honoured as Dionysos, he said, 'Then for my part you can make me Serapis!'*

(Diogenes Laertius 6.63; G36)

245 Demetrios says in his book *On the Men of the Same Name* that Alexander died in Babylon on the same day as Diogenes* died in Corinth. He was an old man in the 113th Olympiad.*

(Diogenes Laertius 6.79; G92)

246 To someone who was praising the good fortune of Callisthenes,* saying that he was enjoying great luxury as a member of Alexander's retinue, Diogenes said, 'Oh no, he's fallen into a wretched plight, for he has to breakfast and dine whenever Alexander pleases.'

(Diogenes Laertius 6.45; G30)

247 When Alexander was once sending off a letter to Antipater by a certain Athlias, Diogenes, who happened to be present, said, 'From a wretch born of a wretch through a wretch to a wretch.'*

(Diogenes Laertius 6.44; G37)

248 When reproached for accepting a cloak from Antipater, he replied,

> *'The glorious gifts of the gods are not to be disdained.'*

(Diogenes Laertius 6.66; G52)

249 When Crateros urged that he should visit him, he said, 'I'd prefer to lick salt in Athens than enjoy sumptuous fare at the table of Crateros.'*

(Diogenes Laertius 6.57; G51)

250 When Perdiccas* threatened to have him killed if he failed to come to him, he said, 'That's nothing remarkable, a poisonous beetle or tarantula could do as much.'

(Diogenes Laertius 6.44; G50)

Diogenes and Dionysios of Syracuse

251a Plato never saw Dionysios when he was in Corinth,* being already dead by that time, but Diogenes of Sinope said to him, on first encountering him there, 'How little you deserve this life that you are presently living, Dionysios.' But when Dionysios then came up to him and said, 'It's very good of you, Diogenes, to sympathize with me in my misfortunes', Diogenes retorted, 'What, do you really suppose that I feel sympathy for you, rather than anger that a slavish creature like you, who deserved to grow old and die in his tyrant's halls as your father did, should be living with us here in pleasure and luxury instead?'

(Plutarch, *Life of Timoleon* 15, 243c; G54)

251b For a tyranny is not actually a 'beautiful winding-sheet',* as someone said to Dionysios, no indeed, the fact that he was unable to renounce his monarchy with its many injustices made his misfortune all the more complete, and it was thus very aptly that Diogenes, when he later saw Dionysios's son living as a private citizen in Corinth after having lost his tyranny, addressed him in these terms: 'This life of yours, Dionysios, is not at all what you deserve, for you should not be living among us here in freedom and without a fear, no, you should be dragging out your life over there, like your father before you, walled up in your tyrant's citadel into your old age.'

(Plutarch, *On Whether an Old Man should Engage in Affairs of State* 1, 783cd; G359)

252 When asked how Dionysios treated his friends, he said, 'Just like sacks;* for while they are full, he hangs them up, and when they are empty, he throws them away.'

(Diogenes Laertius 6.50; G53)

253 On being asked by a tyrant which bronze is best for a statue, he replied, 'That from which Harmodios and Aristogeiton were cast.'*

(Diogenes Laertius 6.50; G358)

IX · THE ENSLAVEMENT OF DIOGENES

How Diogenes was Captured by Pirates and Sold as a Slave

254 When he was sold into slavery he bore it with great nobility of spirit. For while sailing to Aegina, he was captured by pirates* under the command of Skirpalos,* and was carried off to Crete to be offered for sale there. When the auctioneer asked him what he was skilled at, he replied, 'Governing men';* and he then pointed to a Corinthian who was wearing a fine purple-bordered robe, the man called Xeniades* mentioned above, and said, 'Sell me to that man, he could do with a master.' So Xeniades bought him, took him to Corinth, and put him in charge of his children and entrusted his entire household to him.* And he administered it so well in every regard that Xeniades used to go around saying, 'A good guardian-spirit* has entered my house.'

(Diogenes Laertius 6.74–5; G70)

255 Diogenes the Cynic philosopher showed such elevation of mind and greatness of spirit that, when he was captured by pirates and they were mean in their treatment of him, barely giving him enough to keep himself alive, he neither allowed himself to be bowed down by his present ill-fortune, nor to be intimidated by the brutality of his captors, but spoke out as follows: 'How extraordinary it is that if one has pigs or sheep which one is intending to sell, one fattens them up with choice food until they are plump, and yet when one has charge of that finest of creatures, a human being, one lets him starve and constantly keeps him short of food until he has been reduced to a skeleton, and then sells him for a song.' He was then given enough to eat, and when the time came for him to be sold with the other captives, he sat down beforehand and took a bite to eat in the most cheerful spirits, sharing some of his meal with his neighbours; and when one of them could not endure the pressure and became thoroughly despondent, he said, 'Do please stop worrying, just take the moment as it comes,

> *For even Niobe with the beautiful hair remembered to eat,*
> *Although her twelve children had perished in her halls,*
> *Six daughters, and six sons, in the bloom of their youth.'*

(Philo, *That Every Good Man is Free* 121–2; G74)

256a Menippos tells in his *Sale of Diogenes** how, when he was captured and offered up for sale, he was asked what he could do, to which he replied, 'Govern men'; and he then told the auctioneer to make an announcement to ask 'if anyone wanted to buy a master for himself'.

(Diogenes Laertius 6.29; G70)

256b When he was sold at Corinth, the auctioneer asked him, 'What do you know how to do?', and he replied, 'How to govern men.' The auctioneer said with a laugh, 'Then I'll do excellent business, if anyone wants to buy a master!'

(Stobaeus 3.3.52; G75)

257a When he was forbidden to sit down, he said, 'It really makes no difference, people will buy fish however they are lying.'

(Diogenes Laertius 6.29; G70)

257b When Diogenes was being offered up for sale, he made fun of the auctioneer by lying down; and when told to stand up, he declined to do so, saying in a playful and mocking tone, 'And what if you were selling a fish?'

(Plutarch, *On Tranquillity of Mind* 4, 466e; G72)

258 He said he found it extraordinary that if we are buying a pot or a plate, we test it to see whether it rings true, but if we are buying a man, we are satisfied merely to look him over.*

(Diogenes Laertius 6.30; G70)

259a It is said that when he observed that one of the purchasers, who was suffering from the female disease,* was not at all masculine in his appearance, he went up to him and said, 'Why don't you buy me, since it seems to me that you could do with a man.'

(Philo, *That Every Good Man is Free* 124; G74)

259b Diogenes, when he was put up for sale, rebuked one of those degraded creatures in true pedagogical fashion, saying to him with great boldness, 'Come on, young fellow, buy a man for yourself', using that ambiguous expression to encourage him to put a curb on his shameless ways.

(Clement of Alexandria, *Pedagogy* 3.3.16.1; G74)

260 Diogenes the Cynic also served as a slave; but he was sold into slavery after having previously been a free man. When Xeniades of Corinth, who wanted to buy him, asked him whether he had any special knowledge, he replied, 'I know how to govern free men [*liberis*].' Impressed by his response, Xeniades bought him, restored his freedom, and entrusted his sons to him, saying, 'Here are my children [*liberos*]* for you to govern.'

(Aulus Gellius, *Attic Nights* 2.18, 9–10; G77)

261 He used to say to his purchaser Xeniades that he should obey him even though he was a slave; for if a doctor or a steersman were a slave, one would still need to obey him.

(Diogenes Laertius 6.30; G70)

262 He said to Xeniades, who had bought him, 'Be sure that you do as you are told'; and when Xeniades quoted the verse, '*backwards flow the streams to their sources*',* he replied, 'And if you had been ill and had bought a doctor, would you have refused to obey him, saying, '*backwards flow the streams to their sources*'?

(Diogenes Laertius 6.36; G70)

263 Tell me, my friend, when Diogenes was exiled to Athens, or when he was sold by the pirates and came to Corinth, was there anyone else in those days who showed greater frankness of speech than Diogenes? Well then? Or was there anyone else among the men of that time who was freer than Diogenes? Than this man who governed Xeniades, who had purchased him, as a master governs his slave?

(Musonius Rufus, 9, p. 49, 3–9; G73)

264 Such is the way in which Diogenes was set free by Antisthenes,* and said that thenceforth he could never be enslaved again by anyone. And in consequence, how did he conduct himself when he was captured by the pirates? He never called any of them master, did he? And here I am not speaking of the name, for it is not the mere word that I fear, but the state of mind from which the word proceeds. How he rebuked them for not giving enough food to their captives! And how he behaved when he was put up for sale! Did he look for a master? Not at all, but for a slave. And once he had been sold, how he behaved toward his master! He at once began to argue with him, saying that he ought not to be dressed as he was, or have his hair cut in the way that he did, and talked to him about his sons and how they should live their lives. And is there anything so strange in that? After all, if he had bought a trainer, would he have treated him as a servant or a master when it came to gymnastic exercises? And similarly, if he had bought a doctor, or an architect. Correspondingly, in whatever field, it is necessary that the person who possesses the requisite skill should exercise authority over one who lacks it.

(Epictetus 4.1.114–18; G73)

265 When he was an old man, he was captured by the pirate Skirtalos and sold at Corinth to a certain Xeniades; and he remained with his purchaser, choosing not to be ransomed by the Athenians or his relations and friends.

(*Suda* s.v. Diogenes; G71)

As a Pedagogue in Corinth

266 Cleomenes* recounts in his book *On Pedagogues* that the friends of Diogenes wanted to ransom him, but he responded by telling them that they were utterly naive; for lions, he explained, are not the slaves of those who feed them, but rather it is those who feed them that are the slaves of the lions;* for fear is what characterizes a slave, and wild beasts make men afraid of them.

(Diogenes Laertius 6.75; G70)

267 Euboulos* reports in his *Sale of Diogenes* that this was the course that he followed in educating the sons of Xeniades. After their other studies, he taught them to ride, to shoot with a bow, to use a sling, and to hurl javelins; and later, at the wrestling-school, he did not allow the instructor to give them a full athletic training, but only as much as was needed to bring some colour to their cheeks and keep them fit and well. The boys learned by heart many passages from the poets and historians, and from the works of Diogenes himself, and he trained them in every short cut to the development of a good memory. In the house he taught them to serve themselves, and to make do with a simple diet, with water as their drink. He made them wear their hair short and unadorned, and go out dressed in nothing but a cloak, with no shoes on their feet; as they walked, they had to keep silent, and not look around them in the street. He would also take them out hunting with him. They for their part had the highest respect for Diogenes, and would seek favours for him from their parents.

(Diogenes Laertius 6.30–1; G70)

268 The same author tells us that Diogenes grew old in the house of Xeniades, and that when he died, he was buried by the sons of Xeniades. He had once been asked by Xeniades how he wanted to be buried, and had replied, 'Face downwards.' 'And why is that?', asked Xeniades. 'Because after no great while, down will be turned into up.'

He said this because the Macedonians now had the upper hand, and had thus risen to great heights from a humble beginning.
(Diogenes Laertius 6.31–2; G102)

X · MORALISTIC AND TRADITIONAL

269 On seeing a young man blushing, he said, 'Take courage, that's the hue of virtue.'*
(Diogenes Laertius 6.54; G399)

270 To a son who spoke scornfully of his father, he said, 'Aren't you ashamed to speak scornfully of the one who made it possible for you to have such a high opinion of yourself?'*
(Diogenes Laertius 6.65; G396)

271 He said that education is a source of self-control for the young, a consolation for the old, a treasure for the poor, and an adornment for the rich.'
(Diogenes Laertius 6.68; G380)

272 When someone brought his son to him and said that he was highly gifted and extremely well-behaved, Diogenes said, 'Then what need does he have of me?'
(Diogenes Laertius 6.64; G392)

273 One of the youths who associated with Diogenes fell silent when he put a question to him. 'Don't you think', said Diogenes, 'that it is the business of one and the same person to know what one should say and when, and when one should keep silent and toward whom?'
(Stobaeus 3.34.16; G475)

274 When someone asked how one can become a teacher to oneself, he replied, 'By reproaching first of all in oneself those faults that one reproaches in others.'
(Stobaeus 3.1.55; G384)

275 When you worry about another, then you neglect yourself.

(Stobaeus 2.31.61: G315)

276 Diogenes said he would rather meet with failure among the cultivated than with success among the uncultivated.

(*Codex Neapolitanus* II D 22, no. 51; G378)

277 On seeing a child behaving in a disorderly manner, Diogenes struck his pedagogue,* saying, 'Why did you teach him to behave like that?'

(Hermogenes, *Progymnasmata* 3.19; G388)

278 Who will be least subject to fear, who could have greater confidence, than one who is conscious of having committed no bad deed?*

(Stobaeus 3.24.14; G305)

279 When asked how someone in office should approach public affairs, he replied, 'Just as with fire: don't get so close that you get burnt, or keep so far away that you freeze.'*

(Maximus 9.26; G357)

280 When someone reproached Diogenes for entering unclean places, he said, 'The sun too makes its way into middens, but is not defiled as a consequence.'

(Diogenes Laertius 6.63; G269)

281 Seeing an idle man, he said, 'If you avoid the discomforts of the industrious, you'll incur the misfortunes of the neglectful.'

(*Codex Patmos* 263, no. 68; G331C)

282 Seeing someone who was living a shameful life reproaching someone else for the very same thing, he said, 'You're like a pile of ashes trying to blow against the wind.'

(John of Sardis, *Commentary to Aphthonius' Progymnasmata* p. 40, 11–13; G388)

283 To someone who was taking pride in wearing a lion-skin, he said, 'Won't you stop dishonouring the trappings of courage.'*

(Diogenes Laertius 6.45; G465)

284a He said that those who say the right things but fail to do them are no different from lyres, for those too can neither hear nor perceive.

(Diogenes Laertius 6.64; G320)

284b Diogenes said that some people say what is right but do not hear themselves, just as lyres make beautiful sounds but cannot perceive them.

(Stobaeus 3.23.10; G320)

285 On seeing that the Megarians were building large town-walls,* he cried, 'You wretches, it's not about the size of your walls that you should be worrying, but about the people who will be standing on them!'

(Stobaeus 3.7.46; G285)

286 Diogenes gave an excellent reply to someone who asked him for a letter of introduction. 'That you are a man', said Diogenes, 'he will know as soon as he sees you; whether you are a good or a bad one, he will know if he has learned to distinguish between the good and the bad; and if he has not learned that, it would make no difference if I were to write him thousands of letters.'

(Epictetus 2.3.1; G470)

287 On seeing one of the so-called freedmen rejoicing and receiving congratulations from many people around, Diogenes marvelled at their irrationality and lack of judgement. 'It is as if', he said, 'one were to proclaim that, from this day forth, some domestic slave should all at once become a grammarian, or geometer, or musician, when not having even the very slightest knowledge of those arts. So if a mere proclamation does not turn people into experts, so neither does it make them free—which truly would be a miracle—but simply brings it about that they should no longer be slaves.'

(Philo, *That Every Good Man is Free* 157; G445)

288 When asked how fathers and sons should behave toward one another, Diogenes said that they should not wait for one another to ask for something, but should grant it before needing to be asked. It is natural for the father, as one who has taken the lead in bestowing favours, to be quick to feel aggrieved if he is not well treated in return, while the son for his part is apt to become complacent, and not think it necessary to ask his father for something.

(Stobaeus 4.26.23; G394)

289 To the foolish the truth is bitter and unpleasant, while falsehood is sweet and agreeable; and likewise, I believe, for those who have diseased eyes, light causes pain, while darkness brings freedom from pain and is welcome, because it prevents them from being able to see.

(*Excerpts from Manuscripts of Florilegia of John Damascene* 2.31, 22; G313)

290 Diogenes said that it is absurd that, while we pour oil into a lamp to be able to see what is on the table, we are unwilling to pay out anything to become wiser in our minds, so as to be able to recognize what is best for us in life.

(Stobaeus 2.31.74; G316)

291 Diogenes said: from books one should take for use only what is of true value, and the rest one should throw away, just as we do with bones; for we make use of their marrow, while we throw the bones themselves to the dogs.

(*Codex Neapolitanus* II D 22, no. 49; G378)

292 Just as doctors use honey to sweeten the bitterness of their chosen remedies, so wise men make use of good humour to sweeten their dealings with disagreeable people.

(Antonius 2.32.61; G330)

293 Diogenes said that the training of children can be compared to the way in which potters mould their pots; for just as potters shape and fashion the still soft clay according to their wish, but can no longer mould it once it is baked, so likewise with children, if they are not rigorously trained with much effort while they are still young, it becomes impossible to reform them once they are fully grown.

(Stobaeus 2.31.87; G382)

294 Diogenes said that Medea was no sorceress* but a woman of great wisdom; for she took hold of men who had gone soft and whose bodies had become corrupted by luxury, and by making them toil in gymnasia and take steam-baths, she restored them to full vigour and health; and it was because of this that the rumour spread that she rejuvenated people by boiling their flesh.

(Stobaeus 3.29.92; G340)

295 Diogenes said that most people rot themselves alive by softening up their bodies in baths and wasting themselves away in sexual intercourse, and yet when they come to die, arrange for their body to be placed in embalming fluid or honey* to prevent it from rotting too quickly.

(Stobaeus 3.6.36; G104)

On Friendship and Enmity

296 For the man who is suffering many a trouble there is no sure salvation except a good friend.

(Boissonade, *Anecdota Graeca* 1, p. 125, 3–4; G417)

297 Diogenes said that, to come off well in life, one needs either good friends or ardent enemies; for friends instruct you, and enemies expose your faults.

(Plutarch, *How to Tell a Flatterer from a Friend* 36, 74c; G420)

298 Diogenes said that one should behave well toward one's friend, so that he should be one's friend all the more, and likewise toward one's enemy, so that he should become a friend, for it is necessary that we should guard against the reproaches of our friends, and against the schemes of our enemies.*

(*Codex Vaticanus Graecus* 633, fo. 121r; G420)

299 When he was asked how one can best exact revenge against* an enemy, he said, 'By becoming a good and honest man oneself.'

(*Gnomologium Vaticanum* 187; G421)

300 On hearing that one of his acquaintances was associating with people of bad character, he said, 'How absurd it is that when we are intending to set off on a voyage, we take care to select the best travelling-companions, and yet, when we have resolved to live well, we choose whomever chance sets in our path as our companions in life.'

(*Gnomologium Vaticanum* 197; G415)

301 He used to say that we should stretch out our hands to our friends with our fingers unclenched.*

(Diogenes Laertius 6.29; G277)

302 Seeing a rich man in the company of a poor one, he asked, 'Who are these people who are associating together?', and when someone replied, 'They're friends', he said, 'And how is it, then, that one is wretchedly poor and the other exceptionally rich?'*

(*Codex Patmos* 263, no. 66; G246C)

303 Someone told him that his friends were scheming against him. 'And where would we be', he replied, 'if we had to treat our friends and our enemies just the same?'

(Diogenes Laertius 6.68; G419)

304 He who accepts foul words spoken against a friend strikes me as being just as bad as the calumniator himself.

(Boissonade, *Anecdota Graeca* 1, p. 125, 5–6; G418)

305 When someone told him about some abusive remarks that a friend had been making about him, he replied, 'That my friend really said that may be doubted, that you have said it to me is a definite fact.'

(*Gnomologium Monacense Latinum* 24.3; G438)

306 When some perfidious person spoke ill of him, he said, 'I'm glad to have become your enemy, since it's not to your enemies that you seek to bring harm, but to your friends.'

(Maximus 10.25; G428)

307 On seeing shepherds eating a sheep in their tent, a wolf went up to it and said, 'Just think what a fuss they would make if *I* were to do that!'*

(Antonius 1.39.55; G471)

308 Diogenes on a Journey

While on a journey, Diogenes the Dog arrived at a river which was running very high, and stopped by the ford, having no idea how to get across. A man who had experience in ferrying people over noticed that he was at a loss, and went up to him and ferried him over to the opposite bank. Wondering at the man's kindness, Diogenes stood there chiding himself for the poverty that made it impossible for him to repay his benefactor. While he was still reflecting on the matter, the man caught sight of another traveller who was unable to get over and hurried across to help him on his way. Diogenes then went up to the man and said, 'Look here, I no longer feel grateful to you for what you did, for I can see that you're doing this not by your own free decision, but because you're sick in the head.'*

Moral: Those who perform good deeds for good and worthless people alike do not gain a reputation for being generous of mind, but for being short of sense.

(Aesop, *Fables* 65; G331)

Proverbial Wisdom and Gnomic Comparisons

309 When asked what is most precious in life, he said: 'Hope.'*

(Stobaeus 4.46.20; G329)

310 When Diogenes was asked, 'What is most difficult?', he replied, 'To know oneself,* since we all credit so much to ourselves through self-love.'

(Maximus 69.18; G308)

311 When asked what is wretched in life, he said: 'An old man without means.'

(Diogenes Laertius 6.51; G84)

312 When someone asked him, 'What do you consider old age to be?', he replied, 'Life's winter-time.'

(Maximus 41.25: G85)

313 When asked, 'What is a friend?', he replied, 'One soul dwelling in two bodies.'*

(Stobaeus 2.33.10; G416)

314 When asked where the Muses have their dwelling, he said: 'In the souls of the cultivated.'*

(Papyrus Michigan inv. 41.1.6–7; G387)

315 When asked what weighs most heavily on the earth,* he said: 'An uncultivated man.'

(Stobaeus 2.31.75; G377)

316 When asked which weighs more heavily, lead or gold, he replied: 'A lack of culture.'

(*Codex Vaticanus Graecus* 633, fo. 121v; G377)

317 When asked what ages most swiftly among men, he replied: 'Gratitude.'

(Stobaeus 2.46.13; G328)

318 When asked why gold is pale,* he replied, 'Because so many people have designs upon it.'

(Diogenes Laertius 6.51; G227)

319 When asked what animal has the worst bite, he replied, 'Of those that are wild, the informer,* of those that are tame, the flatterer.'

(Maximus 11.31; G423)

320 When asked what are the most dangerous beasts, he replied, 'In the mountains, lions and bears, in the cities, tax-collectors* and informers.'

(Maximus 22.20; G424)

321 He said that it is much better to fall victim to crows than to flatterers,* who devour the best men while they are still alive.

(Athenaeus 6, 245c; G425)

322 Those who are fair of form but uncultivated he compared to perfume-jars filled with vinegar.

(Maximus 44.15; G378)

323 On flattery, as on a memorial stone, only the name of friendship stands inscribed.

(Stobaeus 3.14.14; G422)

324 Education is like a golden crown: for it brings high honour and is bought at high cost.

(Stobaeus 2.31.92; G381)

325 Boastfulness he compared to gold-plated armour, since the outer surface does not correspond to what is within.

(Stobaeus 3.22.40; G306)

326 A man who is rich but ignorant he called a sheep with golden fleece.

(Diogenes Laertius 6.47; G232)

327 Seeing a rich but uncultivated man, he said, 'Look at the golden sheep!'

(*Codex Vaticanus Graecus* 633, fo. 115v; G379)

328 Seeing a youth who was rich but uncultivated, he said, 'Silver-plated filth!'

(Theon, *Progymnasmata* 5.97; G388)

329 Seeing a good-looking youth chattering away in an unseemly fashion, he said 'Aren't you ashamed to draw a leaden blade from an ivory scabbard?'

(Diogenes Laertius 6.65; G411)

330 Good men he called images of the gods.

(Diogenes Laertius 6.51; G354)

331 Diogenes was admonishing a man of thoroughly bad character, and when someone asked him what he was doing, he replied, 'Scrubbing an Ethiopian to turn him white.'*

(Antonius 2.32.60; G385)

332 Cure a corpse,* admonish the old, it's all just the same.

(Maximus 16.12; G383)

Misogynistic and Racial Humour

333a Seeing two women conferring together, he said, 'The adder's borrowing poison from the viper.'*

(Maximus 39.15; G204)

333b Seeing one woman advising another, he said, 'The adder's acquiring poison from the viper.'

(Papyrus *Sorbonne* 826, no. 3; G204)

334 On seeing a girl learning her letters, he said, 'I see a sword being sharpened.'*

(*Gnomologium Parisinum* 4)

335 Seeing a woman being carried in a litter, he said, 'Not the right cage for the beast!'*

(Diogenes Laertius 6.51; G203)

336 When he saw some women hanging from an olive-tree, he said, 'If only all trees bore such fruit!'*

(Diogenes Laertius 6.52; G202)

337a Seeing a woman being carried away by a river, he said, 'Let the bad be carried away by the bad!'*

(Inscription at Herculaneum, no. 264 Della Corte; G206)

337b When someone pointed out to him that a woman was being carried away by a river, and said, 'Let's try to save her', he replied, 'Oh let the notorious evil be carried away by another evil.'

(*Gnomologium Parisinum* 3)

338 When asked what is bad in life, he said: 'A good-looking woman.'

(*Gnomologium Vaticanum* 189; G201)

339a Seeing a woman who was beautiful but small, he said, 'That's what they call a half-evil.'

(*Gnomologium Parisinum* 2; G206B)

339b Seeing a woman who had only one eye, he said, 'That's what they call a half-evil.'

(*Codex Vaticanus Graecus* 96, fo. 88v, no. 7; G206B)

339c Seeing a woman who was beautiful but small, he said, 'Small is the beauty, but great the evil!'

(*Codex Vaticanus Graecus* 96, fo. 88v, no. 6; G206B)

340 Seeing an Ethiopian eating white bread, he said, 'Look, the night's engulfing the day!'*

(Papyrus Sorbonne 826, no. 4; G466)

341 Seeing an Ethiopian shitting, he said, 'Just like a leaky cauldron!'*

(Papyrus Sorbonne 826, no. 5; G466)

XI · DIOGENES AS WIT

342 Seeing an incompetent archer, he sat down beside the target, saying, 'Just to make sure I don't get shot.'

(Diogenes Laertius 6.67; G455)

343 There was a certain musician who was always abandoned by his audience, and Diogenes greeted him by saying, 'Hello chanticleer'; and when the musician asked why, he said, 'Because your singing makes everyone get up.'*

(Diogenes Laertius 6.48; G454)

344 There was a big lyre-player who was the butt of everyone's criticism but was praised by Diogenes alone; and when asked the reason, Diogenes replied, 'Because, being as large as he is, he sticks to singing to his lyre and doesn't turn to robbery.'

(Diogenes Laertius 6.47; G453)

345 When someone had given a long reading, and was pointing to the blank space at the end of the scroll, Diogenes cried, 'Courage men, I can see land ahead!'*

(Diogenes Laertius 6.38; G391)

346 On entering a school-room and seeing many statues of the Muses there but few pupils, he said, 'Thanks to the gods,* teacher, you've got plenty of pupils!'

(Diogenes Laertius 6.69; G389)

347 Seeing a second-rate wrestler practising as a doctor, he said, 'What's the meaning of this, then? Is this how you're planning to bring down those who once defeated you?'*

(Diogenes Laertius 6.62; G447)

348 When asked why athletes are so stupid, he said, 'Because they're built up from the flesh of swine and oxen.'*

(Diogenes Laertius 6.49; G446)

349 When abused by someone who was bald, he said, 'I'll not insult you in return, but simply congratulate your hair for having taken flight from such an evil head.'

(Maximus 10.24; G458)

350 When someone came up to him and told him that a certain person was speaking badly of him, he replied, 'That's nothing to wonder at, since he's never learned to speak well.'*

(*Gnomologium Vaticanum* 179; G429)

351 To someone who was abusing him, Diogenes said, 'Just as no one would believe me if I were to speak well of you, so no one will believe you when you speak badly of me.'*

(*Gnomologium Vaticanum* 186; G426)

352 When someone abused him saying, 'You're drunk and talking nonsense', he replied, 'But you think I'm talking nonsense when I'm sober.'

(*Codex Vaticanus Graecus* 1144, fo. 216v; G433)

353 When somebody reported to him that someone was saying dreadful things about him, he replied, 'And he's welcome to strike me too when I'm not there.'*

(*Codex Ottobonianus Graecus* 192, fo. 206v; G432)

354a When someone ran into him with a plank* and then cried, 'Watch out!', he said, 'What, are you going to hit me again?'

(Diogenes Laertius 6.41; G457)

354b When someone ran into him with a plank and then said, 'Watch out!', Diogenes struck him with his stick and cried, 'Watch out!'

(Diogenes Laertius 6.66; G457)

355 When someone struck him a blow with his fist, he said, 'Heracles! How did I come to forget that one needs to walk around in a helmet!'*

(Diogenes Laertius 6.41; G456)

356 Meidias,* after assaulting Diogenes, told him, 'There's three thousand to your account.' The next day, Diogenes wound some thongs around his hand,* gave Meidias a thorough beating, and said, 'And *there*'s three thousand to yours!'

(Diogenes Laertius 6.42; G483)

357 When asked what he would want for receiving a punch* on the head, he said, 'A helmet.'

(Diogenes Laertius 6.54; G456)

358a On seeing the son of a prostitute throwing stones into a crowd, he said, 'Take care that you don't hit your father!'

(Diogenes Laertius 6.62; G211)

358b To the son of a prostitute who was throwing stones into a crowd, he said, 'Watch out, lad, or you'll wound your father, whom of course you have no way of knowing.'

(Eustathius on Homer *Iliad* 24.499; G211)

359 He once saw a lad throwing stones at a gibbet. 'Good for you,' he exclaimed, 'you're sure to hit your mark.'

(Diogenes Laertius 6.45; G413)

360 Seeing a young man behaving in a giddy and deranged fashion, he said, 'Young man, your father must have been drunk when he begot you.'

(Plutarch, *On the Education of Children* 3, 2a; G395)

361 When a worthless youth called out to him, 'Hello there, father!', he said, 'How did it come to escape me all this time that I was father to such a rascal of a son!'

(*Gnomologium Parisinum* 6)

362 On seeing someone making a show of being in love with a rich old woman, Diogenes the Dog remarked, 'He hasn't cast his eye on her but sunk his teeth in her.'

(Stobaeus 3.10.60; G239)

363 Seeing an old woman beautifying herself, he said, 'If that's for the living, you're out of your wits, if it's for the dead, don't be too slow about it.'

(Maximus 41.26; G217)

364 A disreputable eunuch had inscribed above the entrance to his house, 'Let nothing evil enter in.'* 'How, then', enquired Diogenes, 'will the master of the house be able to get inside?'

(Diogenes Laertius 6.39; G347)

365 A man who had just got married inscribed above the door to his house,

> *'The son of Zeus, all-victorious Heracles*
> *Dwells within, let nothing evil enter',*

to which Diogenes added the words, 'After conflict, alliance.'*
(Diogenes Laertius 6.50; G347)

366a After listening to two men pleading their case, he passed judgement against the two of them, declaring that the one was surely guilty of theft, but the other hadn't lost anything.*
(Diogenes Laertius 6.54; G461)

366b He once acted as arbiter between two disreputable characters, one of whom was accusing the other of theft. After listening to both, he declared, 'It seems to me that *you* haven't lost anything, while *he* is clearly a thief.'
(*Gnomologium Vaticanum* 190; G461)

367 He saw a hunchback approaching from a distance, and when the man drew close, exclaimed, 'I thought all along, my good fellow, that you were carrying something!'
(*Gnomologium Vaticanum* 199; G460)

368 When someone chided Diogenes on seeing him coming out of a brothel, he said, 'What's the matter then, should I have been coming out of *your* house?'
(*Codex Bodleianus* 50, fo. 108r, no. 6; G211B)

369 With regard to a filthy bath-house he enquired, 'When people have bathed here, where do they go to wash?'
(Diogenes Laertius 6.47; G268)

370a On seeing that the sheep in Megara were covered with leather coats* while the children ran bare, he exclaimed, 'It's evidently better to be a Megarian's ram than his son!'
(Diogenes Laertius 6.41; G284)

370b One day Diogenes arrived in Megara, and saw that the Megarians' sheep were wrapped up in hides, but that their children went naked while pasturing them; 'It's evidently better', he said, 'to be a Megarian's ram than his son.'

(*Gnomologium Vaticanum* 191; G284)

371 On arriving at Myndos* and seeing that the gates were very big while the city was very small, he cried, 'Shut your gates, men of Myndos, or your city will get out!'

(Diogenes Laertius 6.57; G286)

372 A Spartan praised the line from Hesiod which says, 'Not an ox would be lost if your neighbour were not bad'; and on hearing this, Diogenes said, 'Why, to be sure, the Messenians and their oxen have been lost, and you are their neighbours.'*

(Aelian, *Historical Miscellany* 9.28; G287)

373 On seeing Diogenes the Dog embracing a bronze statue* in extremely cold weather, a Spartan asked him whether he was feeling chilly; and when he replied no, the Spartan said, 'Then what's so wonderful in what you're doing?'

(Plutarch, *Spartan Sayings* 233a; G177)

Homeric Jokes and Verbal Humour

374 On seeing a good-looking youth lying in a careless posture, he said, 'Wake up,

Lest while you are lying there someone fix a spear in your back!'

(Diogenes Laertius 6.53; G499)

375 On seeing a man who had been caught stealing purple, he said,

'Purple death and mighty fate laid hold of him.'

(Diogenes Laertius 6.57; G495)

376 On seeing a clothes-thief, he said,

> *'What doest thou here, my good friend?*
> *Or hast thou perhaps come to plunder some corpses?'**

(Diogenes Laertius 6.52; G492)

377 On seeing someone buying food at great expense, he said,

> *'Doomed to a swift death will you be, my child, by what you buy!'**

(Diogenes Laertius 6.53; G493)

378 Seeing a son of a flute-player who had a very high opinion of himself, he said, 'Young man, you're even more puffed up than your mother was.'*

(*Gnomologium Vaticanum* 173; G207)

379 On seeing a runaway slave sitting beside a well, he said, 'Take care, lad, or you'll end up inside!'*

(Diogenes Laertius 6.52; G443)

380 On seeing a clothes-thief at the baths, he said, 'Have you come here for a rubbing or the robing?'*

(Diogenes Laertius 6.52; G484)

381 On seeing an Olympic victor pasturing (*nemonta*) sheep, he said, 'How quickly you have passed, my friend, from Olympia to Nemea!'*

(Diogenes Laertius 6.49; G448)

382 When asked where a youth who had been selling his favours had come from, he said, 'Evidently from Tegea.'*

(Diogenes Laertius 6.61; G400)

383 On seeing a wretchedly bad painting of two Centaurs, he asked, 'And which of these is Cheiron?'*

(Diogenes Laertius 5.51; G485)

XII · OLD AGE AND DEATH

The Proper Response to Age

384a To those who said to him, 'You're an old man and ought to take things easy from now on', he replied, 'What, if I were running in a long-distance race, would I ease up when approaching the finishing-line, rather than strain all the harder?'

(Diogenes Laertius 6.34; G83)

384b One of his friends advised him that, now that he was growing old, he should relax a little on account of his age; he replied that this was the same as though, when someone was running in a foot-race and approaching the finishing-line, he were to advise him to slacken his pace, when he ought to be advising quite the opposite, that he should strain to the utmost.

(*Gnomologium Vaticanum* 202; G83)

385 And you should act as befits your circumstances. You have grown old? Do not seek for what is proper to the young. You are weak? Do not seek for what is proper to the strong, but rather, act as Diogenes did when someone took advantage of his weakness to force him back and seize him in a neck-hold, for he did not allow himself to be disconcerted, but pointed to a column and said, 'There, my good man, throw *that* over!'*

(Teles 10.6–11.1; G469)

The Question of Suicide

386 Diogenes was suffering from pain in his shoulder, because he had been wounded, I think, or perhaps for some other reason. Since the pain seemed to be very severe, someone who was on bad terms with him scoffed at him, saying, 'Why don't you die, Diogenes, and free yourself from your sufferings?', to which Diogenes retorted, 'Those who know what they should do in life, and what they should say, those are people for whom it would be better to stay alive', indicating that he placed himself in that category; 'As for you,' he continued, 'since you have no knowledge of what you should say or do, it would be an excellent thing if you were to die; but it would be proper for me, as one who has knowledge of these things, to stay alive.'

(Aelian, *Historical Miscellany* 10.11; G81)

387a When Antisthenes was lying mortally ill, Diogenes showed him a dagger, saying, 'If you have need of a friend.'

387b He [Antisthenes] died of an illness. Diogenes came to visit him, and asked, 'Do you have need of a friend?' And one day he came to him with a dagger, and when Antisthenes cried, 'Who will deliver me from my sufferings?', he showed him the dagger and said, 'This will', to which Antisthenes retorted, 'I said from my sufferings, not from my life!' It seems that he showed a certain weakness of character in putting up with the illness because he was over-attached to life.

(Diogenes Laertius 6.18; G24)

388 When his body had become crippled by paralysis, Speusippos sent a message to Xenocrates* inviting him to take over his school. It is reported that as he was being conveyed to the Academy in a little carriage, he came across Diogenes and called out to greet him; 'No,' replied Diogenes, 'I can't return your greeting if you can endure to live in such a state as that.'

(Diogenes Laertius 4.3; G66)

389 When Speusippos was suffering from paralysis in his limbs, Diogenes urged him to bring his life to an end; but he replied, 'It's not in our limbs that we live, but our soul.'

(Stobaeus 4.52.17)

Death and Burial

390 When asked whether death is an evil, he said, 'How can it be an evil, if we are not even aware of it when it arrives?'

(Diogenes Laertius 6.68; G87)

391 Very wise too was the remark of the Cynic Diogenes, who when he had sunk into sleep and was close to death, and his doctor roused him to ask if he was suffering any distress, replied, 'None at all, for the one brother is forestalling the other', that is to say, sleep and death.*

(Plutarch, *Consolation to Apollonius* 12, 107e; G88)

392 To someone who was lamenting over the fact that he was going to die in a foreign land, Diogenes said, 'Why all this fuss, poor fool? Wherever you start, from the road to Hades is just the same.'*

(Maximus 36.19; G86)

393 One day he fell ill in a tavern and was in danger of his life; and when someone asked who would carry him out for burial if he died, he said, 'The owner of the inn.'*

(*Gnomologium Vaticanum* 200; G442)

394 When someone asked him whether he had a slave-girl or slave-boy, he said no. 'But when you die, who will carry you out for burial?' 'Whoever wants the house.'

(Diogenes Laertius 6.52; G442)

395 Some say that when he was dying, he instructed that they should throw him out unburied, to allow every wild beast to have a share of him, or shove him into a pit and sprinkle a little earth over him;* or according to others, that they should throw him into the Ilissos, so that he might be of use to his brothers.*

(Diogenes Laertius 6.79; G101)

396 Diogenes said that if he were ripped apart by dogs, he would have a Hyrcanian burial,* or if he were [devoured] by vultures, [he would have a Bactrian burial],* but if no animal should venture near him, time would grant him an even finer burial with the aid of those two most excellent things, the sun and the rain.

(Stobaeus 4.55.11; G103)

397a Antigonos* once said to him, 'If you scorn any expense while still alive, Diogenes, how will you avoid falling prey to dogs when you die?' 'Do you suppose', he replied, 'that I carry my staff around with me to no purpose? It will be lying at hand when I die, and I will strike any dogs that come near me'; and when the king said, 'But how will you be aware of them?', he replied, 'Well, if I'm not aware, what will it matter to me?'

(*Gnomologium Parisinum* 9)

397b Diogenes was a rougher character [than Socrates], and although he held the same views on this matter, he expressed it more brutally in the Cynic fashion, ordering that he should be thrown out unburied. When his friends exclaimed, 'What, to fall prey to birds and beasts?', he replied, 'Not at all, you must lay my stick down beside me to enable me to drive them away.' 'But how will you be able to do that', they said, 'since you will no longer be conscious?' 'Well, if I'm not aware of anything, how can it harm me to be ripped apart by wild beasts?'

(Cicero, *Tusculan Disputations* 1.43.104; G105)

The Death of a Sage

398a He is said to have been almost ninety years old when he died. As to the manner of his death, several different tales are recounted. Some say that he was afflicted by colic after eating an octopus raw* and died because of that, while others claim that he deliberately held his breath. This is stated, for instance, by Cercidas of Megalopolis,* who writes as follows in his meliambics:

> He is now no more, the Sinopean,
> The staff-bearer with the doubled cloak who fed on the air,
> But has gone off because he pressed his lips and teeth together
> And held his breath; for he was Diogenes in very truth,*
> A son of Zeus and hound of heaven.

Others again say that he tried to divide an octopus among some dogs, and was so badly bitten on the tendon of his foot that he perished. His friends, however, according to Antisthenes* in his work *The Philosophical Schools*, thought it likely that he died by holding his breath. For he happened to be living at that time in the Craneion, the gymnasium just outside Corinth, and when his friends came to visit him in their usual way, they found him wrapped up in his cloak and assumed that he must be asleep, even though he was not usually a long or deep sleeper. When they pulled his cloak aside, however, they found that he was no longer breathing, and presumed that he had deliberately held his breath* to make his departure from this life.

A quarrel then arose, so it is said, between his friends as to who was to bury him, indeed they even came to blows. But when the city-fathers and leading men arrived, they had him buried beside the gate that leads to the Isthmus; and above his grave they set a pillar with a dog in Parian marble on the top. Subsequently the citizens also honoured him with bronze statues, on which these verses were inscribed:

> *Even bronze yields to time, but your glory,*
> *O Diogenes, will remain intact through all eternity,*
> *Since you taught mortals the doctrine of self-sufficiency*
> *And showed them the easiest path through life.*

(Diogenes Laertius 6.76–8)

398b As one approaches Corinth, one sees among other memorials* alongside the road that of Diogenes of Sinope, who is buried near the gate, and is known among the Greeks as the Dog.

(Pausanias 2.2.4; G107)

399 When Diogenes of Sinope was ill and close to death, he dragged himself off with some difficulty, and threw himself down on a bridge which lay close to the gymnasium; and he instructed the superintendent that, as soon as he could see that he was dead, he should throw his corpse down into the Ilissos.* So little concern did Diogenes have for either death or burial.

(Aelian, *Historical Miscellany* 8.14; G100)

400a His courage and self-control are revealed too in the story of his death. For while he was travelling in his old age to the Olympic Games, which were celebrated in Greece in the presence of large crowds of people, he is said to have been overcome by a violent fever on the way, and to have lain down by the side of the road. His friends wanted to put him on an ass or in a cart, but he refused, and said as he was being moved under the shade of a tree, 'Leave me, I beg you, and travel on to watch the games. This night will prove me either the victor or the vanquished. If I defeat the fever, I will come to the games; but if the fever defeats me, I will make my way down to the

Underworld.' And during the night he choked himself,* saying, 'I'm not dying but shutting out the fever through my death.'

(Jerome, *Against Jovinian* 5.17; G99)

400b Listen to what he said to the people who walked by while he was lying sick with a fever: 'You wretches,' he cried, 'aren't you going to stop? You'll travel all the way to Olympia to see worthless athletes do battle with one another, and yet you have no wish to see a man fighting it out with a fever?'

(Epictetus 3.25.58; G99)

401 He expired after being bitten in the leg by a dog* and refusing to have any treatment.

(*Suda* s.v. Diogenes; G96)

402a Diogenes undertook to eat an octopus raw so as to remove the need for the use of fire* in the preparation of meat; and with many people standing around him, he veiled his face in his cloak and brought the meat up to his mouth. 'It is on your behalf', he said, 'that I am taking this action and running this risk.' A noble risk, by Zeus! For is it not the case that, just like Pelopidas for the liberty of the Thebans, or like Harmodios and Aristogeiton* for that of the Athenians, our philosopher hazarded his life in a battle with a raw octopus, to reduce our life to the level of that of a beast!

(Plutarch, *On the Eating of Meat* 1.6, 995cd; G93)

402b Diogenes the Cynic used fire as little as possible, and even went so far as to swallow down an octopus raw, saying, 'It's on your behalf that I'm undertaking this.'

(Plutarch, *On Whether Fire or Water is More Useful* 2, 956b; G93)

XIII · IMMEDIATE FOLLOWERS OF DIOGENES

Monimos of Syracuse

403 Monimos of Syracuse was a pupil of Diogenes, and, as Sosicrates* reports, was in the service of a Corinthian banker. This banker

used to receive regular visits from Xeniades, the man who had purchased Diogenes,* and he gave such a favourable account of the qualities of Diogenes in both word and deed as to inspire Monimos with
feelings of love for the man. Monimos then pretended to go mad,
and threw around all the money and small change that was on the
counter, until his master dismissed him; whereupon he immediately
attached himself to Diogenes. He often associated with Crates the
Cynic too, and adopted a similar way of life, at the sight of which his
master became all the more convinced that he was mad.*

He acquired such a reputation that even Menander, the writer of
comedies,* makes mention of him. For in one of his plays, the *Groom*,
he refers to him in these terms:

> There was a man named Monimos, Philo, a wise one,
> But none too famous—Who carried a knapsack?—
> Not one but three.*Never did he use a saying
> Like 'Know thyself', by heaven, or other of the quoted
> Proverbs, no, he went much further, the dirty beggar,
> And declared all human suppositions to be illusion.

He was a man of such gravity that he despised empty opinion and
sought only for truth. He wrote light poems leavened with a hidden
seriousness* and two books, *On Impulse* and an *Exhortation to
Philosophy*.

(Diogenes Laertius 6.82–3; G VG 1)

404a Xeniades of Corinth* . . . says that nothing is true, and perhaps
also Monimos of Syracuse when he says that everything is illusion,*
which is thinking of non-existent things as if they had existence.

(Sextus Empiricus, *Against the Mathematicians* 8.5; G VG 2)

404b There have been not a few, as I have previously mentioned,
who have said that Metrodoros and Anaxarchos* and Monimos too
did away with the criterion* . . . Anaxarchos and Monimos because
they likened existing things to stage-painting and supposed them to be
similar to the impressions that we experience in sleep or madness.*

(Sextus Empiricus, *Against the Mathematicians* 8.87–8; G VG 2)

404c 'Everything is what you suppose it to be.' For the words that
were addressed to the Cynic Monimos* are clear enough, and clear

too the value of that saying, if one accepts its inner meaning, so far
as it is true.

(Marcus Aurelius, *Meditations* 2.15; G VG 3)

405 Monimos said that money is the vomit of fortune.*

(Stobaeus 4.31.89; G VG 4)

406 Monimos the Cynic philosopher said that it is better to be blind
than to be uneducated; for the one takes us into the ditch and the
other into the pit.*

(Stobaeus 4.31.88; G VG 5)

Onesicritos, Androsthenes, and Philiscos

407 Onesicritos* was born in Aegina according to some accounts,
but Demetrios of Magnesia says that he was from Astypalaia. He too
was one of the notable followers of Diogenes. He seems to have followed a rather similar course to that of Xenophon; for just as Xenophon participated in the expedition of Cyrus, he participated in that
of Alexander,* and just as Xenophon wrote the *Education of Cyrus*,*
he wrote an account of the education of Alexander; and as Xenophon
wrote in praise of Cyrus,* he wrote in praise of Alexander. And their
manner of writing is also quite similar, except that Onesicritos, as an
imitator, falls short of his model.

(Diogenes Laertius 6.84; G VC 1)

408 The man [Diogenes] possessed extraordinary persuasive powers,
so that he could overcome anyone whatever with his arguments. It is
thus recounted that a certain Onesicritos of Aegina* sent one of his
two sons, Androsthenes, to Athens, and that after hearing Diogenes
speaking, he chose to remain there. So Onesicritos then sent his elder
son Philiscos (whom we have already mentioned*) to search for his
missing son; but Philiscos too was detained there in just the same
way. When, thirdly, the father himself arrived there, he was drawn no
less than his sons* to join in the pursuit of philosophy, such was the
spell that Diogenes exercised on the people through his discourses.
Among those who listened to him were Phocion,* known as the

Honest, and Stilpo* of Megara, and many others who engaged in public life.

(Diogenes Laertius 6.75–6; G VC 2)

Hegesias and Drymos

409 Among the other pupils of Diogenes were Menandros, known as Drymos ('Oakwood'), who was an admirer of Homer, and Hegesias of Sinope, known as Cloios ('Dog-collar'), and Philiscos of Aegina, as already mentioned.

(Diogenes Laertius 6.84)

410 When Hegesias once asked to be lent some of his writings, he [Diogenes] replied, 'You're an idiot, Hegesias; you'd choose real figs rather than painted ones, and yet you'd pass over real training for virtue to apply yourself to written precepts.'*

(Diogenes Laertius 6.48)

Crates of Thebes

411 Crates, son of Ascondas, was born at Thebes. He was one of the illustrious pupils of the Dog. According to Hippobotos, however, he was a pupil not of Diogenes but of Bryson the Achaean.* . . . He was known as the 'Door-opener'* because he would enter every house to admonish and advise. . . . He was at his prime in the 113th Olympiad.*

Antisthenes recounts in his *Successions* that it was the sight of Telephos, in a tragedy,* carrying a basket and looking altogether miserable, that first caused him to become attracted to Cynic philosophy. So he sold all his property—for he came from a prominent family—and collecting together two hundred talents by that means, he distributed the money among his fellow-citizens. And he devoted himself with such perseverance to philosophy that Philemon,* the author of comedies, refers to him, saying,

> And in summer he would wear a thick cloak,
> So as to be like Crates, and in winter rags.

Diocles reports that Diogenes persuaded him to abandon his land to sheep-pasture, and to throw any money that he possessed into the sea. And Alexander, so he says, once stayed in the house of Crates, just as Philip once stayed in that of Hipparchia.* Relations would often visit and try to turn him aside from his course, but he would chase them off with his stick, and remained steadfast. Demetrios of Magnesia recounts that he deposited his money with a banker on the condition that, if his sons turned out to be ordinary men,* he should hand it over to them, but if they became philosophers, he was to distribute it among the people; for they would have no need of anything if they lived as philosophers.

Eratosthenes* reports that he had a son named Pasicles by Hipparchia (whom we will talk about presently), and that when this son came of age, he took him to a brothel* and said that this was the nature of his father's marriage. The marriages of adulterers, he said, are a matter for tragedy, having exile or murder as their reward, while the marriages of those who associate with women of easy virtue are a matter for comedy, for as a result of dissolute behaviour and drunkenness they turn men crazy. He also had a brother named Pasicles, who was a pupil of Eucleides.*

(Diogenes Laertius 6.85 and 6.87–9)

XIV · SAYINGS, ANECDOTES, AND VERSES OF CRATES

How Crates Disposed of his Property

412a When he died, he left 30 talents to the Thebans,* saying that if his son proved worthy of him, he would have no need of money, while if he proved unworthy, even that much would not be enough.

(*Gnomologium Vaticanum* 387; G4)

412b He sold off his property and deposited the money with a banker, saying that if his children became philosophers, he should hand over the money to the people, but if not, should give it to his children.

(*Suda* s.v. Crates; G4)

413 And poverty, according to Epictetus,* is nothing terrible; for otherwise it would have seemed so to Crates of Thebes too, who handed over all of his possessions to his city, saying, 'Crates robs Crates of all that he owns.'* He thought that he had set himself free by doing this, and set a crown on his head as though to celebrate his emancipation, now that he had exchanged his prosperity for poverty.

(Simplicius, *Commentary on Epictetus' 'Encheiridion'* 5; G6)

414a Abandoning his land to sheep-pasture, he climbed on to an altar and cried, 'Crates frees Crates of Thebes from slavery!'

(*Suda* s.v. Crates; G4)

414b They say that he presented all his property to the people of Thebes, saying, 'Crates on this day sets Crates free!'

(Origen, *Commentary on Matthew* 15.15; G9)

414c This Crates, who was a wealthy man, threw all his money into the sea to pursue philosophy, saying as he threw it, 'Crates of Thebes sets Crates free!'

(*Codex Ottobonianus Graecus* 388, fo. 6r; G7)

415 Crates of Thebes in Boeotia, who was a Cynic too, used to say that destitution is the beginning of freedom.

(Epiphanius, *Against Heresies* 3.2.9; G16)

As Adviser to Families

416a The philosopher Crates, who would enter every house and always be received with honour and affection, used to be called 'the Door-opener'.

(Plutarch, *Convivial Questions* 2.1.6, 632e; G18)

416b Crates of Thebes is said to have visited households in which there was discord, and to have settled the quarrels with words of peace.

(Antonius 1.26.70; G18)

416c He was called the Door-opener because he would fearlessly enter whatever house he wished.

(*Suda* s.v. Crates; G18)

416d Crates, the famous pupil of Diogenes, was honoured by his contemporaries in Athens as though he were a household god.* No house was ever closed to him, and no father of a family ever had such a dark secret that Crates was excluded from becoming involved, fittingly and seasonably, in his capacity as arbiter and mediator in all family disputes and quarrels. The poets recount how Heracles of old, through his indomitable courage, vanquished dreadful monsters, human and animal alike, and cleared the whole world of them; and this philosophical Heracles achieved just the same in his combat against anger, envy, greed, and lust, and all other monstrous and shameful urges of the human soul. All these plagues he drove out of people's minds, purifying households and taming vice, he too going half-naked and being recognizable by his club, a man who had been born, moreover, at that same Thebes in which Heracles is supposed to have entered the world. Now before he became the true Crates, he belonged to the most eminent circles in Thebes, he was of noble birth, had a host of servants, and a luxurious house with a large entrance-hall,* and he himself was finely dressed and endowed with large estates. But when he came to recognize that his inheritance provided him with no security, with no sure stay in life, and that all the riches in the world cannot assure a good and happy life . . .*

(Apuleius, *Florida* 22; G18)

The Blessings of Poverty

417a When Demetrios of Phaleron* sent him some bread and wine, he reproached him, saying, 'If only the springs brought forth loaves of bread too!' So it is plain that he drank water alone.

(Diogenes Laertius 6.90; G33)

417b The Cynic Crates, according to Sosicrates in his *Successions*, rebuked Demetrios of Phaleron for sending him, in addition to a knapsack full of bread, a flagon of wine also. 'If only the springs', he said, 'brought forth loaves of bread too!'

(Athenaeus 10, 422cd; G33)

418 He said that one should not accept gifts from anyone whatever; for it is not right that virtue should call on the support of vice.

(Antonius 1.29.39; G55)

419 Zeno of Citium recounts in his *Anecdotes* he once sewed a sheep-skin on to his cloak without thinking twice about the matter.

(Diogenes Laertius 6.91; G40)

420 He had as his home-country Ignominy and Poverty, which are secure against the assault of Fortune, and he was a fellow-citizen of Diogenes, who was immune to all schemings of envy.*

(Diogenes Laertius 6.93; G31)

421 On visiting the market-place and seeing some people selling and other people buying, Crates said, 'These people account one another happy because one does the opposite of the other; but I account my-self happy because I no longer play either part, being neither a seller nor a buyer.'

(Stobaeus 3.5.52; G51)

422 Crates said that it was not to his wealth that he owed his reputation, but to his poverty.

(Stobaeus 4.33.27; G53)

423 Although he had only a knapsack and a rough cloak, Crates spent his whole life laughing and joking as though he were at a festival.*

(Plutarch, *On Tranquillity of Mind* 4, 466e; G46)

Miscellaneous Sayings and Anecdotes

424 When Alexander asked him if he would like his native city to be rebuilt,* he said, 'What's the point? Perhaps another Alexander will merely destroy it again.'

(Diogenes Laertius 6.39; G31)

425 He used to say that it is impossible to find anyone who is wholly free of fault, but just as in a pomegranate there is always some rotten seed.

(Diogenes Laertius 6.89; G36)

426 When Crates saw a monument of the courtesan Phryne*

standing at Delphi, he cried out that it was standing there as a monument to the licentiousness of the Greeks.

(Plutarch, *On the Fortune of Alexander* 2.3, 336cd; G28)

427 To a rich young man who was being followed by a crowd of flatterers, Crates said, 'Young man, I pity you for being so utterly alone!'

(Stobaeus 3.14.20; G52)

428 He said that those who surround themselves with flatterers are as helpless as calves which have fallen among wolves; for neither the one nor the other are with fit company, but only with such as are scheming against them.

(Diogenes Laertius 6.92; G54)

429 On seeing a young man beautifying himself, Crates the Cynic said that he was like a smooth and level road along which many a traveller would make an easy passage.

(*Gnomologium Vaticanum* 381; G58)

430 On seeing a young man walking around on his own, Crates asked him what he was doing there all alone; and when the youth replied, 'I'm talking to myself', Crates said, 'Beware now, and take good heed of this: that's a bad man that you're talking to!'

(Seneca, *Letters to Lucilius* 1.10; G56)

431a Crates was in the habit of running a certain distance each day, and would say, 'I'm running for the sake of my spleen, for the sake of my liver, for the sake of my stomach.'

(Themistius, *On Virtue* p. 59; G63)

431b He was ugly to behold, and when he carried out his exercises, people would laugh at him. As he raised his arms, he used to say to himself, 'Courage now, Crates, this is for the good of your eyes and of your whole body; and there will come a day when you will see these people, who are now laughing at you, become shrivelled up by illness, and then they will account you happy and reproach themselves for their idleness!'

(Diogenes Laertius 6.91–2; G40)

432 He said that we should pursue philosophy until generals come to seem no different from donkey-drivers.*

(Diogenes Laertius 6.92; G47)

433 He made a deliberate habit of railing at prostitutes to train himself to endure foul abuse.

(Diogenes Laertius 6.90; G27)

434 He once so annoyed the harpist Nicodromos that the man struck him in the face; to which he responded by sticking a little sign to his forehead with the inscription 'Nicodromos did this'.*

(Diogenes Laertius 6.89; G36)

435 Having a request to make of the master of the gymnasium, he laid hold of him by his hips; and when the man bristled at that, he said, 'What, don't these form part of you just as much as your knees?'*

(Diogenes Laertius 6.89; G36)

436 He was once flogged at Thebes by the master of the gymnasium (or else at Corinth by Euthycrates), and when he was then dragged out by his feet, he called out, as if without a care in the world:

'Caught by the foot and hurled from heaven's threshold.'

According to Diocles, however, it was Menedemos of Eretria who dragged him out in this way. For since he was a good-looking man who was reputed to be on intimate terms with Asclepiades* of Phlious, Crates grasped him by the thighs and said, 'Is Asclepiades at home?',* which so angered Menedemos that he dragged him out, giving him occasion to cite this verse.

(Diogenes Laertius 6.90–1; G35)

437 It is said that when Demetrios of Phaleron had been banished from his homeland* and was living in dishonour and in very mean circumstances in Thebes, he was none too pleased to see Crates approaching him, expecting a Cynic tongue-lashing and harsh words. But Crates treated him with consideration and spoke to him about the nature of exile, saying that it brings nothing bad in its train, and that it is wrong to get upset about being delivered from public life, with all its perils and uncertainties. At the same time, he did his best to put new heart in him and console him. Now becoming more cheerful and regaining his courage, he said to his friends, 'How unfortunate that under the pressure of affairs and through lack of time, I never came to know such a man as that.'*

(Plutarch, *How to Tell a Flatterer from a Friend* 27, 69cd; G34)

438 Zeno recounts that Crates was once sitting in a cobbler's workshop reading Aristotle's *Exhortation to Philosophy*,* which the author had dedicated to Themison, King of Cyprus, saying that no one was better fitted to become a philosopher than he; for he was immensely rich, and so would be able to apply his wealth to that purpose, and he was held moreover in high respect. While Crates was reading out aloud from the book, the cobbler listened attentively as he was stitching his shoes, and Crates remarked, 'It seems to me, Philiscos,* that I should write an exhortation to philosophy for you; for I see that you are better fitted for philosophy than that man whom Aristotle was writing for.'

(Teles p. 46, 6–14 Hense; G42)

Fragments from the Verses of Crates

439 The following playful verses are ascribed to him:

> There is a city, Pera* in the wine-dark sea of folly,
> Fair and fat, though filthy, with nothing much inside.
> Never does there sail to it any foolish stranger,
> Or lewd fellow who takes delight in the rumps of whores,
> But it merely carries thyme* and garlic, figs and loaves,
> Things over which people do not fight or go to war,*
> Nor stand they to arms for small change or glory.

And then there was his 'Account-book'* which was in everyone's mouth, running like this:

> Mark down ten minas for the cook, a drachma
> For the doctor, five talents for a toady,
> Less than nothing for good counsel, a talent
> For a tart, and for a philosopher, three obols.

. . . Here are some further verses by him:

> *This I own, what I have learned and thought, and the Muses'*
> *Solemn precepts; but all my riches are gone like empty smoke.* *

This too is ascribed to him:

> *Hunger brings a halt to love, or if not hunger,*
> *Time, or if those are of no avail, a noose.* *

(Diogenes Laertius 6.85–6)

440 *Glorious children of Mnemosyne and Olympian Zeus,*
Pierian Muses, hearken to my prayer! *
Grant me food without fail for my belly,
Which has ever made my life simple and unenslaved . . .
Make me useful rather than sweet to my friends. *
Glorious goods I do not wish to gather, as one
Who yearns for the wealth * of a beetle or riches of an ant;*
No, I wish to possess righteousness and collect riches
Which are easily borne, easily gained, and conducive to virtue.
If these I win, I will propitiate Hermes and the holy Muses
Not with costly offering but with pious virtues.

(Julian *Oration* 6, 199c; G84)

441 And Crates moreover composed a *Hymn to Frugality*:

> *Hail, Goddess and Queen, beloved of the wise,*
> *Frugality, worthy offspring of glorious Temperance,*
> *Your virtues are honoured by all who practise righteousness.*

(Greek Anthology 10.104; G77)

442 So Crates, who believed that civil strife and despotism were brought about in the main by luxury and extravagance, offered the following humorous recommendation:

> *Do not throw us into strife*
> *By preferring fine dishes to lentil soup.* *

(Plutarch, *Rules for the Preservation of Health* 7, 125f; G72)

443 *If you but gather some lentil soup* * and beans in a pot,*

You will easily raise a trophy, friend, for the rout of penury.*

(Teles fr. 7, in Stobaeus 3.1.98; G73)

444   *You have no idea what power a knapsack holds,*
             And a quart of lupins,* and freedom from care.

(Teles p. 44, 3–5, Hense; G83)

445   *Hard it is that there should be hunger at harvest-time.*

(Julian, *Misopogon* 369b)

446 On seeing Crates shivering with cold in the winter, he [Stilpo] said to him, 'It seems to me, Crates, that you could do both with a new coat and a change of mind';* irritated by this, Crates replied to him with the following parody:

> *And Stilpo too I beheld, suffering bitter woes,**
> *In Megara,* where, they say, the bed of Typhoeus lies;**
> *There he argued* without end, with many a comrade around him,**
> *As they wore away their time pursuing virtue in word alone.**

(Diogenes Laertius 2.118; G67)

447   *And Asclepiades of Phlious, and the Eretrian Bull.**

(Diogenes Laertius 2.126; G68)

448   *And Micylos* too I beheld,*
             Carding wool and his wife too carding it with him,
             Striving in the dread fray to escape Starvation's assault.

(Plutarch, *That We Ought Not To Borrow* 7, 830c; G69)

449 There is a work of Crates in circulation entitled *Letters*, which contains some excellent philosophy in a style that sometimes approaches that of Plato. He also wrote tragedies marked with philosophy of a most elevated character, as can be seen, for instance, in this:

> *Not one tower does my country have, not one roof,*
> *But for home and city, the entire earth lies*
> *At my disposition for a dwelling.*

(Diogenes Laertius 6.98; G80)

450 *You reproach me for my age as though it were a great evil,*
Yet he who fails to reach old age falls prey to death,
And all of us desire it; but when it comes along,
We are aggrieved, so ungrateful we are by nature.

(Stobaeus 4.50.8; G85)

451 *For Time has bent me down, the wise craftsman,*
Who brings all that he makes to weakness.

(Stobaeus 4.50.56; G82)

452 When he realized that his end was drawing near, he chanted these verses to himself,

'Hunchback, it's time for you to go down to the halls of Hades.'

For he had become bowed down by the years.

(Diogenes Laertius 6.92)

Crates in the Cynic Diatribes of Teles

453 Hence the reply offered by Crates to someone who asked, 'What will I gain by turning to philosophy?' 'You will be able', he said, 'to open up your purse with an easy heart, and draw out your money to give it away open-handedly, rather than as people do nowadays, turning away, and hesitating and trembling, as if their fingers were paralysed. You, by contrast, on having a full purse, will view it in such a way as to feel no distress at seeing it emptied, and will easily be able to decide to put your wealth to proper use; and when you no longer have it, you will no longer yearn for it, but will live fully contented with what is presently available to you, feeling no desire for what you do not have, and no dissatisfaction with your present circumstances.' If anyone wants to deliver himself or another person from want and need, he should not set out in search of riches. That would be as if, says Bion,* when trying to relieve a hydroptic of his thirst, one were to provide him with springs and rivers rather than attempting to cure him of his dropsy.* By drinking in quantity he would surely burst rather than be relieved of his thirst, and likewise one can never be satisfied when one is insatiably greedy, and avid for good repute, and superstitious. So if you want to deliver your son from want and need, do not send him to Ptolemy to amass riches, or otherwise he will come back full of false pretensions and you will have accomplished nothing. No, it is to Crates that you should send him, for he was capable of transforming the greedy and extravagant into free-spirited people who were contented to live a simple life. And Metrocles* recounts accordingly, so it would seem, that as long as he was studying with Theophrastus and Xenocrates, he was afraid, even though much was being sent to him from home, that he might perish from hunger, and was constantly short of money and in want; but afterwards, when he went on to study with Crates, he was able to support one of his comrades in addition, even though nothing was now being sent to him. For previously he had felt obliged to wear shoes, and brand new ones moreover, and a fine cloak too, and to have slave-boys to accompany him, and live in a large house, where he could receive visitors regularly to dinner, offering them good white bread, meats of no mean quality, and sweet wine, such that all was luxurious. For among these people, this was adjudged to be the way of life that befitted a gentleman. But when he came over to Crates, there was none of all that. Having adopted simpler ways, he was contented with a rough cloak, and barley-bread, and vegetables, without ever yearning for his former way of life or being unhappy with his present one. To protect ourselves against the cold, we seek out a thicker tunic, but he folds his cloak double and so walks around as if he had two layers of clothing. If he needs to rub himself down with oil, he goes into the public baths and makes do with oil that has already been used. And sometimes he makes his way to the ovens in the smithies, where he fries his sprats, pours a little oil on them, and sits down to dine. During the summer he sleeps in the temples, during the winter in the baths; and so he suffers no need or want, as had formerly been the case, but is satisfied with what his present circumstances provide, and has no wish for servants.

(Teles p. 38, 4–31, 14 Hense; G44)

454 If the happiness of human life had to be judged by the predominance of pleasure, says Crates, then no one would ever be happy; for if one tries to make a reckoning for every stage of our life, one will find that suffering predominates by far. In the first place, the half of all this time in which one lies asleep is of no value for good or bad; and then one's first years, in which one is being reared as a child, are full of travails. The little child is hungry, but the nurse lays it down to sleep; it is thirsty, but she washes it; it wants to sleep, but she shakes a rattle. Once he has escaped from his nurse, he is taken in hand by the pedagogue,* and the trainer, and those who set out to teach him his letters, and music, and drawing. He advances in age: there are added the teachers of arithmetic, geometry, riding; he is woken up at an early hour, and has no time to himself. He has become a cadet,* and now has others again to be afraid of, the commander, the drill sergeant, the superintendent of the gymnasium; he is beaten by all of these, kept under close watch, and seized by the throat. He has left the cadets, now having reached the age of twenty, and still has to fear the gymnasiarch and general, and pay good heed to them. If it is necessary to keep watch, they will be watching; or to stay awake and keep guard, they will be on guard; or embark on a ship, they will be embarking. He has become a man, and reaches his prime; he serves in the army, undertakes a mission on behalf of his city, he governs, commands, directs a choir, presides at the games; at which point he deems happy that life that he led as a child. He has passed his prime and reaches old age; once again he has to be looked after like a child, and yearns for his youth, *'Oh youth, how dear it was to me, while old age weighs more heavily than Etna!'* And so I am unable to see how anyone has ever lived a happy life, if happiness is to be measured by the predominance of pleasure.

(Teles p. 49, 3–51, 4 Hense; G45)

XV · THE FOLLOWERS OF CRATES AND LATER CYNICS

Hipparchia of Maroneia, the Wife of Crates

455 Hipparchia, the sister of Metrocles, was also greatly attracted by the doctrines of this school; both of them came from Maroneia.* She fell in love with the teachings and way of life of Crates, and showed no interest at all in any of her suitors, whatever their wealth, or high birth, or beauty; no, Crates meant everything to her. She even threatened her parents with suicide if she were not allowed to marry him. They therefore appealed to Crates to talk the girl around, and he made every effort, until finally, on finding himself unable to persuade her, he stood up, removed all his clothing right in front of her, and said, 'Here is your bridegroom, here are his possessions, make your choice accordingly; for you will be no fit companion for me if you do not share the same way of life.' The girl made her choice, adopted the same form of dress, and went around with her husband, living with him in public and accompanying him to dinners.*

Once she went to a banquet held by Lysimachos,* where she refuted Theodoros,* known as 'the Atheist', by means of the following sophism: 'Whatever action Theodoros carries out without it being regarded as wrong, Hipparchia too could carry out without it being regarded as wrong; now Theodoros commits no wrong if he strikes himself; so neither does Hipparchia commit any wrong if she strikes Theodoros.' Having no reply to offer to this argument, he tried to pull up her cloak; but Hipparchia was neither alarmed nor perturbed by that, as one might expect a woman to be. And when he then said to her, '*Who is this who has abandoned her shuttle and loom?*',* she replied, Why, it is I, Theodoros; but do you suppose I have made a bad decision in my regard when, instead of spending further time at the loom, I have devoted it to my education?' These tales and a great many others* are recorded about this female philosopher.

(Diogenes Laertius 6.96–8; G VI 1)

456 He [Crates] married Hipparchia of Maroneia and called this marriage a 'dog-marriage'. By her he had a son named Pasicles.

(*Suda* s.v. Crates; G VH 19)

457 When someone else said that marriage and life with a woman seemed to him to be an obstacle if one wants to become a philosopher, Musonius* replied, 'It was no obstacle for Pythagoras, or for Socrates, or for Crates, all of whom lived with a wife; and one could hardly claim that anyone else pursued philosophy better than they did. Crates, indeed, had no home, no household goods, no possessions, but was married nonetheless; and having no roof of his own, he spent his days and nights in the public arcades of Athens along with his wife.

(Musonius 15, p. 70, 11–17 Hense; G VH 20)

458a What is so surprising, then, in the fact that the adherents of the Cynic philosophy, and the followers of Zeno of Citium, and Cleanthes and Chrysippos,* declare this [sodomy] to be morally indifferent? And to have intercourse with a woman in public, however shameful that might strike us as being, is not regarded as such among some people in India; they have intercourse in public without the least concern, as we have also heard with regard to the philosopher Crates.*

(Sextus Empiricus, *Outlines of Pyrrhonism* 3.24, 200; G VH 21)

458b Whereas most men withdraw into private to have intercourse with their wives, Crates had intercourse with Hipparchia in public.

(Sextus Empiricus, *Outlines of Pyrrhonism* 1.14, 153; G VH 21)

Metrocles of Maroneia and Others

459 Metrocles of Maroneia was the brother of Hipparchia. He had previously been a pupil of Theophrastos the Peripatetic,* and had fallen into such a bad state of mind that, when he had once let off a fart while delivering a discourse, he had been thrown into such despondency that he had shut himself up in his house, intending to starve himself to death. When Crates heard of this, he came to visit him, having been invited to do so, and deliberately ate a quantity of lupins* before setting off. He tried to persuade Metrocles by argument that he had done nothing so very bad, since it would have been quite a wonder if he had not released the trapped air as nature demanded; but in the final resort Crates farted in his turn, and so managed to put new heart in him, reassuring him by acting in just the same way as he had done. From that time onward Metrocles became his pupil and attained some standing as a philosopher.

According to Hecaton* in the first book of his *Anecdotes*, he burnt all his writings, saying, '*These are all but phantoms of infernal dreams.*'* Others say, however, that he set fire to his notes of Theophrastus' lectures, saying, '*Draw hither, Hephaistos, Thetis now has need of you.*'*

He used to say that certain things can be bought with money, while others are acquired through time and effort, such as education. Wealth, he said, causes nothing but harm, unless one makes proper use of it. He died at a great age, having choked himself.*

(Diogenes Laertius 6.94–5; G VL 1)

460 His [Crates'] pupils* were Theombrotos and Cleomenes.

Theombrotos had Demetrios of Alexandria as his pupil, while Cleomenes had Timarchos of Alexandria and Echecles of Ephesos as pupils. Echecles also attended the lectures of Theombrotos, however, which were attended by Menedemos too, of whom we will speak presently. Menippos of Sinope also became a prominent member of this school.

(Diogenes Laertius 6.95)

461 Menedemos was a pupil of Colotes of Lampsacos.* According to Hippobotos, he advanced to such a degree of imposture that he went around in the guise of a Fury,* saying that he had come from Hades to take note of sins that were committed, so as to be able to report them, on his return, to the deities below. This was the manner of his dress: he wore a dark tunic reaching down to his feet, with a red belt tied around it, and an Arcadian hat on his head with the twelve signs of the zodiac embroidered on to it, and tragic buskins,* and he had an enormously long beard, and carried an ash-wood staff in his hand.

(Diogenes Laertius 6.102)

462 Menippos too was a Cynic. He was a Phoenician by descent, and was born as a slave, as Achaicos reports in his *Ethics*. Diocles states in addition that his master was from Pontus* and was a man named Baton; but that later, as a result of very importunate begging and avarice, he managed to become a citizen of Thebes.

There is not a trace of seriousness to be found in him, his books are full of mockery,* and in some regards similar to those of Meleager,* who was a contemporary of his. Hermippos says that he lent out money by the day and was called usurer-by-the-day* in consequence; for he used to make loans on shipping and demanded securities, which enabled him to amass a considerable fortune. In the end, however, he fell victim to a plot, and was deprived of all that he had. In his despair he hanged himself, and so took leave of this life. We have composed this little poem about him:

> *A Phoenician by birth, but a Cretan dog,*
> *Usurer-by-the-day, so he came to be called,*
> *You are doubtless acquainted with Menippos.*
> *People broke into his house at Thebes one day,*

> *And he lost everything; not knowing what it really means*
> *To be a dog,* he hanged himself.*

According to some, the books ascribed to him are not really his work,*
but were written as a joke by Dionysios and Zopyros of Colophon,
who passed them on to Menippos as one who was well able to dispose
of them. . . .

The books left by this Cynic are thirteen in number:

A visit to the world below*

Wills

Letters presented as having been written by the gods*

Against the natural philosophers, mathematicians, and
    grammarians

On the birth of Epicurus and

The honouring of the twentieth day* by members of his school
(and some others).*

(Diogenes Laertius 6.99–101)

Zeno of Citium, Founder of the Stoic School

463 Zeno, son of Mnaseas or Demeas, was born at Citium in Cyprus,
a Greek city which had also become home to Phoenician settlers. . . .
He was a pupil of Crates, as has already been mentioned. . . . This
is the way in which he came to meet Crates. While on a voyage from
Phoenicia to Peiraeus* with a cargo of purple,* he suffered a shipwreck, and after making his way to Athens, sat down by a bookseller's
store (he was then a man of about thirty). He began to read the second book of Xenophon's *Memorabilia*,* which so pleased him that he
asked where men such as Socrates might be found. Just at that moment, Crates happened to pass by, and the bookseller pointed to him
and said, 'Follow that man.' From that time onward Zeno became a
pupil of Crates, but although he was very zealous in other respects in
his attachment to philosophy, he was too modest to be able to adopt
the shamelessness of the Cynics. So Crates, wanting to cure him of
his bashfulness,* gave him a jar of lentil soup to carry through the
potter's district; and on seeing that he was ashamed and was trying
to hide it from sight, Crates struck the jar with his stick and broke it;
and as Zeno took to flight with the lentil soup running down his legs,
Crates cried out, 'Why are you running away, my little Phoenician?
Nothing dreadful his happened to you!'

He was, then, a pupil of Crates for some time, and when he wrote his *Republic*, some people joked that he had written it on the dog's tail.* . . . Eventually he left Crates and studied with the philosophers mentioned above for twenty years.

He is thus reported to have said, 'I made a profitable voyage when I was shipwrecked.' Or in some accounts, he made that remark while he was still with Crates. Some authors record another version of the story in which he was already in Athens when he heard that his ship had been wrecked, and he then said, 'Thank you, Fortune, for having driven me in this way to philosophy!' Others again say that it was only after he had sold his cargo in Athens that he turned to philosophy.

(Diogenes Laertius 7.1–5, with omissions)

464 He [Crates] once gave his pupil Zeno of Citium a pot of lentil soup to carry, and when Zeno, being worried about what people would think of him, tried to hide the pot amidst the crowd, Crates smashed it with his stick; and when the soup dripped down Zeno's legs and he blushed for shame, Crates said, 'Courage my little Phoenician, it's nothing terrible, only soup!'

(*Gnomologium Vaticanum* 384; G VH 41)

465 He [Zeno] once made a hollow lid for his oil-flask, and used to carry money around in it, so as to have some change at hand to pay for anything that his master Crates might need.

(Diogenes Laertius 7.12; G VH 38b)

466 Apollonius of Tyre recounts that when Crates seized Zeno by the cloak to drag him away from Stilpo, Zeno said, 'My dear Crates, the right way to take hold of a philosopher is by the ears; so persuade me and drag me off by those; but if you resort to force, my body will be with you but my mind will remain with Stilpo.'*

(Diogenes Laertius 7.24; G VH 38)

XVI · POSTSCRIPT: BION OF BORYSTHENES

The Life of Bion

467 Bion was a citizen of Borysthenes* by birth; as to who his parents were and through what circumstances he came to turn to philosophy, he himself reveals clearly enough in what he said to Antigonos.* For when the king asked him,

> *Who are you, and whence do you come?*
> *From what city and from what parentage?',**

he replied, knowing that malicious reports had already been spread about him, 'My father was a freedman, who wiped his nose on his sleeve'—meaning by this that he was a seller of salt-fish—'a Borysthenite by birth, but with no face to show,* but only the branding* on his face, a token of his master's venom. My mother was such a woman as a man of that condition might marry, she came from a brothel. And then my father, because he defrauded the customs* in some way, was sold into slavery along with his family. Being a not unattractive young man, I was bought by a rhetorician,* who left me his entire property at his death. And I burnt his books, scraped together all my resources, and came to Athens, where I turned to philosophy. *This is the lineage, this the blood, of which I boast of having sprung.** That is my story, then. So Persaios and Philonides* really ought to leave off recounting it: you may judge me by who I am.'

In truth Bion was a man of versatile mind, an artful sophist, and one who provided detractors of philosophy with plenty of material;* on occasion he was sociable,* and he knew how to poke fun at vanity.

Bion initially preferred the Academic doctrines, at the time in which he was listening to the discourses of Crates.* Then he adopted the Cynic way of life,* putting on a rough cloak and knapsack; for what else could have enabled him to change over to complete insensibility? After that he went over to the Theodorean teaching and followed the lectures of Theodoros the Atheist,* who employed every kind of sophistical argument; and after that he attended the lectures of Theophrastos the Peripatetic.*

He adopted a showy style, and liked to turn everything to ridicule, making use of vulgar expressions. Because he mixed together every style of speech, Eratosthenes is said to have remarked of him that he was the first to deck out philosophy in a flowery dress.* He was clever too at parody; here is an example of that:

> *Oh my friend Archytas,* born to the harp, happy in his conceit,*
> *Most skilled in rousing men to the utmost strife.*

And he poked fun at music and geometry in general.

He was a man of expensive tastes, and would thus move from one city to another, sometimes contriving to put on quite a show. At Rhodes, for example, he persuaded the sailors to dress up in philosopher's dress* and follow him around; so when he walked into the gymnasium with them in tow, he immediately became the centre of attention. He was in the habit also of adopting young men to make use of them for his pleasures, and to gain protection as a result of their affection. On the other hand, he was extremely self-centred, and placed much insistence on the maxim that 'friends hold all things in common'.* And so he enlisted not a single disciple, even though a great many people attended his lectures. There were, however, some who allowed themselves to be led by him into shamelessness. One of his intimate friends, Betion, is thus said to have once remarked to Menedemos,* 'Well, I for my part, Menedemos, spend the night with Bion, and don't think that I have come to any harm by it.'

In conversation he would talk in a thoroughly impious manner, having benefited in this regard from the teachings of Theodoros. Subsequently, however, when he fell ill, so the people of Chalcis claim—for it was there that he died—he was persuaded to wear an amulet* and to repent of his insults against the gods. He was in a very bad way for lack of nurses, until Antigonos sent him a couple of his servants. And according to Favorinos in his *Miscellaneous History*, the king himself followed after them in a litter.

Bion in Teles' Discourse on Self-Sufficiency

468 Just as a good actor must play to the best of his ability whatever role is assigned to him by the dramatist, so also must the man of worth play whatever role he is assigned by Fortune. For like a poetess, says Bion, she assigns now a leading role, now a secondary one, and sometimes the role of a king, and sometimes that of a beggar. So if you have a secondary role, do not aspire to a leading one; for otherwise you will be acting discordantly. You fulfil your role well as a ruler, and I as someone who is ruled, he says; you have many people to command, and I just one, having become a pedagogue; and you, being wealthy, can dispense liberally, while I for my part accept it from you with confidence, without grovelling, or abasing myself, or complaining of my lot. You make good use of a multitude of things, and I of just a few; for it would be wrong to suppose, he says, that what is expensive nourishes and can be used with benefit, whereas, on the other hand, one cannot make use of slight and inexpensive resources, if one is temperate and free of pretension. So if things could speak with a human voice like us, says Bion, and could plead their cause, would not Poverty, he says, be the first to say, 'Why do you attack me, man?', like a slave who pleads his cause with his master after having taken refuge at an altar, 'Why are you attacking me? Have I stolen anything from you? Don't I fulfil your every order? Don't I regularly bring you my earnings?' Could not Poverty say to her accuser, 'Why are you attacking me? Have you ever been deprived of anything of value because of me? Such as moral wisdom? Justice? Courage? Surely you do not lack anything that you really need? Aren't the roadsides full of wild vegetables, and the springs full of water? And don't I offer you as many beds as there are places on earth? And leaves for your bedclothes? Is it impossible for you to live happily in my company? Don't you see old women chattering merrily away as they eat a barley-cake? Don't I provide you with hunger as a cheap and excellent seasoning for your food? Isn't it the case that those who are hungry eat with the most pleasure and have the least need of appetizers? And those who are thirsty drink with most pleasure and yearn the least for drink that does not lie at hand? Who is it, then, who hungers for cakes or thirsts for fine Chian wine? Isn't it true that people seek for such things through sheer self-indulgence? Don't I provide you with housing at no expense, the baths in winter, the temples in summer? And what finer house could you have in summer, says Diogenes, than the Parthenon that I have, so well-aired and so magnificent? 'If Poverty were to speak like this, what could you say in response? I think for my part that I would be left speechless. But we always blame anything other than our own perversity and bad nature, accusing old age, poverty, circumstances, the day, the hour, the place; and Diogenes thus claimed to have heard the voice of Vice accusing herself and saying, '*No one other than I myself are to blame for* *all these ills.'** Most people, however, are lacking in sense and ascribe the blame not to themselves but to things outside. It is like the bite that one can get when one takes hold of a wild beast, says Bion; if you grasp a snake by its middle, you will get bitten, but if you seize it by the head, nothing bad will happen to you. And likewise, he says, the pain that you may suffer as a result of things outside yourself depends on how you apprehend them, and if you apprehend them in the same way as Socrates, you will feel no pain, but if you take them in any other way, you will suffer, not on account of the things themselves, but of your own character and false opinions.

(Teles fr. II 5.2–9.8 Hense; K16A, 17, 21)

Moral Wisdom and Useless Knowledge

469 Slaves who are of good character are free men, while free men who are of bad character are slaves to many a desire.

(Stobaeus 3.2.38; K11A)

470 And Bion of Borysthenes did well to say that one should not derive one's pleasures from the table, but from the wisdom of one's mind.

(Athenaeus, *Deipnosophists* 10, 421e–f; K14)

471 He used to say that moral wisdom* surpasses the other virtues to the same degree as sight surpasses the other senses.

(Diogenes Laertius 4.51; K12A)

472 When asked, 'What is foolishness?', he said, 'An impediment to moral progress.'

(Stobaeus 3.4.87; K19)

473 False opinion, he said, is a hindrance to progress.

(Diogenes Laertius 4.50; K20)

474 He said that vain opinion is the mother of all grief.*

(Diogenes Laertius 4.48; K22)

475 And the philosopher Bion used to say that just as the suitors, when they found themselves unable to approach Penelope,* coupled with her maidservants instead, so likewise those who are unable to attain to philosophy wear themselves out with other studies which are of no worth.

(Plutarch, *On the Education of Children* 10, 7c–d; K3)

476 Bion used to say that the scholars, as they enquire into the wanderings of Odysseus, fail to examine where they themselves have gone astray,* and are going astray in that very activity by toiling over matters that are of no use.

(Stobaeus 3.4.52; K5A)

477 Bion used to say that the astronomers are most absurd who, when they fail to see the fish on the sea-shore, claim to know those in the heavens.*

(Stobaeus 2.1.20; K6)

Wealth and Avarice

478 Bion the sophist said that avarice is the mother-city of all evils.*

(Stobaeus 3.10.37; K35A)

479 If anyone wants to deliver himself or another person from want and need, he should not set out in search of riches. That would be as if, says Bion, when trying to relieve a hydroptic* of his thirst, one were to provide him with springs and rivers rather than attempting to cure him of his dropsy. By drinking in quantity he would surely burst rather than be relieved of his thirst, and likewise one can never be satisfied when one is insatiably greedy, and avid for good repute and superstitious.*

(Teles in Stobaeus 4.33.1; K34)

480 Bion said that it is absurd for people to strive for riches, which fortune bestows, avarice guards, and benevolence disperses.

(Stobaeus 4.31c.87; K38A)

481 Bion said, 'Riches are not given to the wealthy by fortune, but loaned to them.'

(Stobaeus 4.41.56; K39B)

482 As long as a person is insatiable, niggardly, slavish, and full of false pretences, he is bound to remain in want and need.—But how can people be in want of what they already have?—And how, says Bion, can money-changers be in want of riches which they already have beneath their hands? Plainly because what they have does not really belong to them; and likewise with those other people [the insatiable and miserly].

(Teles fr. IVA, p. 36.6–9 Hense; K41)

483 Bion used to say that just as shabby purses, even if they are of no value in themselves, are held to be of value in so far as they have money in them, so likewise, wealthy men who are of no worth are held to be of worth for what they possess.

(Stobaeus 4.31a.33; K42a)

484 He said of a miserly rich man, 'That man doesn't own his wealth, his wealth owns him.'

(Diogenes Laertius 4.50; K36)

485 He said that misers look after their property as if it belongs to them, but gain no more benefit from it than if it belonged to somebody else.

(Diogenes Laertius 4.50; K37)

486 Bion neatly remarks that it hurts the bald no less to have their hair pulled out than it hurts those who have a full head of hair. You may be sure that the same applies to the poor and the rich, that they suffer the same distress: for in both cases their money clings to them, and cannot be torn away without them feeling it.

(Seneca, *On Tranquillity of Mind* 8.3; K44)

487 To someone who had devoured his entire inheritance, he said, 'The land swallowed up Amphiaraos,* but you have swallowed up your land.'

(Diogenes Laertius 4.48; K45)

488 Bion said that a good magistrate will lay down his office having increased, not his wealth, but his reputation.

(Stobaeus 4.5.23; K43A)

489 Wealth is the sinews of business.*

(Diogenes Laertius 4.48; K46)

Religion and Superstition

490 When Crates asked him [Stilpo]* whether the gods take pleasure in adoration and prayers, he is said to have replied, 'Don't ask me about such matters in the street, you fool, but when we are alone'; and it is said similarly that when Bion was asked whether the gods exist, he replied:

> *'Will you not scatter the crowd from me, wretched old man?'**

(Diogenes Laertius 2.117; K25)

491 So it was a neat remark that Bion made, I think, when he asked how people could reasonably pray to Zeus for good children when Zeus could not even procure that for himself.*

(Clement of Alexandria, *Protreptic* 4.56.1; K29)

492 'And is it such a marvel', says Bion, 'if a mouse has gnawed through a sack,* not having anything to eat? The real marvel would be, as Arcesilaos* jokingly remarked, if the sack had devoured the mouse.'

(Clement of Alexandria, *Stromata* 7.4.24.5; K31A)

493 When Bion persistently ran down the diviners, he [Menedemos] said that he was simply slaying the dead.*

(Diogenes Laertius 2.135; K32)

494 He [the superstitious man] sits outside his house in sackcloth or wrapped up in filthy rags, and often rolls naked in the mud* as he confesses his sins or errors, such as having eaten or drunk the wrong thing, or having walked along a path contrary to some divine indication.* But if he is very fortunate and only moderately in thrall to superstition, he sits at home and has himself purified by fumigations and magical procedures, as old women, so Bion says, bring along whatever they please* and attach and fasten it to him as though to a peg.

(Plutarch, *On Superstition* 7, 168d; K30)

495 He said that people in Hades would suffer a much worse punishment if they were made to fetch water in vessels that were intact, rather than in ones that have holes bored through them.*

(Diogenes Laertius 4.50; K28)

496 Bion says that if God punishes the children of the wicked,* that is even more ridiculous than a doctor administering medicines to a son or grandson to cure the illness of his father or grandfather.

(Plutarch, *On the Delays of Divine Justice* 19, 561c; K27)

497 Bion put forward arguments to prove at one time that everyone is sacrilegious, and at another time that no one is. When he feels inclined to throw everyone down from the Tarpeian Rock,* he says, 'Whoever takes anything and consumes or puts to his own use what belongs to the gods, commits sacrilege; but everything belongs to the gods, so whatever anyone takes, he takes from the gods, to whom all things belong; so anyone who takes away anything whatever commits sacrilege.' And then, by contrast, when he bids people to break into the temples and pillage the Capitol without fear of divine punishment, he says that no one can commit sacrilege, because whatever anyone takes away, he removes from one place that belongs to the gods to another place that belongs to the gods.

(Seneca, *On Benefits* 7.7.1; K33)

Sex and Love

498 Beauty is another's good.*

(Diogenes Laertius 4.48; K54)

499 To those who say that beauty exercises a tyrannical power, he would say, 'Oh yes, a tyranny that can be brought down by a hair.'*

(Stobaeus 4.21b.23; K55)

500 In an even more vulgar vein, the sophist Bion used to refer to the hairs of beautiful youths as Harmodioi and Aristogeitones,* because when they make their appearance, lovers are liberated by them from a beautiful tyranny.

(Plutarch, *Amatorius* 24, 770b; K56)

501 He even abused Socrates, saying that if he felt desire for Alcibiades and held back, he was a fool, or if he did not, there was nothing remarkable in his behaviour.*

(Diogenes Laertius 4.49; K59)

502 He cast reproach on Alcibiades, saying that, as a boy, he led husbands away from their wives, and when he grew up to become a young man, drew wives away from their husbands.

(Diogenes Laertius 4.49; K60)

503 When asked if one should marry, he said, 'If she's ugly, you'll find her hard to bear, if she's beautiful, you'll find you have to share.'*

(Diogenes Laertius 4.48; K61A)

Miscellaneous

504 When reproached for not trying to win over a youth,* he said, 'One can't catch a soft cheese on a hook.'

(Diogenes Laertius 4.47; K58)

505 It is impossible to please the mass of people, so Bion thought, unless one becomes a honey-cake or good Thasian wine.

(Dio Chrysostom 66.26; K18)

506 To be unable to endure ills is itself a great ill.

(Diogenes Laertius 4.48; K23)

507 When asked who is subject to the greatest anxiety, he said, 'He who aspires after the greatest prosperity and happiness.'

(Diogenes Laertius 4.48; K24)

508 On seeing an envious man with a very glum expression on his face, Bion the sophist said, 'Either something very bad has happened to him, or something very good to somebody else.'*

(Stobaeus 3.38.50; K47A)

509 To an envious man who was looking very glum, he said, 'I don't know whether something bad has happened to you, or something good to somebody else.'

(*Gnomologium Vaticanum* 158; K47B)

510 Bion compared people like this [i.e. those who readily offer their ear to flatterers] as jugs who can easily be carried away by their ears.*

(Plutarch, *On Not Letting Ourselves Be Bullied* 18, 536a; K51)

511 It was thus foolish and simple-minded of Bion to say, 'If a field could be made more fertile and fruitful by being praised, it would not seem amiss to do that rather than to dig and work away at it; so there would be nothing improper in praising a man also, if it is beneficial and productive to those who are praised'; for a field cannot be made worse by being praised, but a man can become puffed up and cor-rupted if he is falsely and undeservedly praised.

(Plutarch, *How to Tell a Flatterer from a Friend* 16, 59a; K50)

512 We should keep a close eye on our friends to see what kind of people they are, so that one should not be thought to associate with rogues, or to turn away people of worth.

(Diogenes Laertius 4.51; K49)

513 Bion used to say that, as with Hesiod, pupils come in three races,* the gold, the silver, and the bronze; the gold are those who pay and learn, the silver those who pay and do not learn, and the bronze those who learn but do not pay.

(Stobaeus 2.31.97; K78A)

514 When the Athenians concentrated their attention on rhetoric, he taught philosophy at Rhodes;* and to those who criticized him for that, he said, 'When I have brought wheat to market, how can I sell barley?'

(Diogenes Laertius 4.49; K4)

515 And it was a witty response too that Bion made to the lines of Theognis,

> *Any man bowed down by poverty can neither do*
> *Nor say anything, since his tongue is tied.**

—'How can it be, then, that being poor as you are, you talk all this nonsense and tire us with your empty chatter?'

(Plutarch, *On How a Young Man should Listen to Poets* 4, 22a; K53)

516 When, during a discussion over the wine, he noticed that a young man was keeping silent, he said, 'If you're well educated and keeping silent, you're badly educated,* but if you're ill-educated, you've plainly had a good education.'

(*Gnomologium Vaticanum* 159; K77)

517 To a relentless chatterer who sought his help, he said, 'I'll do what I can, provided only that you don't come along yourself, but send others to plead on your behalf.'*

(Diogenes Laertius 4.50; K74)

518 When someone asked him why he failed to benefit from his own advice, he replied, 'Neither do medicine-boxes which contain excellent medicine draw any benefit from it themselves.'

(*Gnomologium Vaticanum* 157; K75)

519 When someone snatched away the upper part of the fish, Bion turned to seize it back, and he then gobbled it down and recited the verse, *'But Ino finished the work on the other side.'**

(Athenaeus 8, 344a; K81)

520 While making a sea-voyage in very bad company, he ran across some pirates; when his companions said, 'We're done for if we're discovered', he replied, 'And I'm done for if we're not.'

(Diogenes Laertius 4.50; K79)

521 Bion said that boys throw stones at frogs in fun, but the frogs do not die in fun but in real earnest.

(Plutarch, *On the Cleverness of Animals* 7, 965ab; K76)

Old Age and Death

522 Old age, he said, is the harbour of all ills; for at any rate, all of them take refuge there.

(Diogenes Laertius 4.48; K62A)

523 He said it is not right to heap reproaches on old age, to which, he said, all of us aspire to attain.

(Diogenes Laertius 4.51; K63)

524 He said that old age is the dregs of life.

(*Gnomologium Vaticanum* 163; K64)

525 When people are young, he said, they have courage, but they only reach the height of their wisdom in old age.

(Diogenes Laertius 4.50; K65)

526 He used to say that the path to Hades is an easy one; people set off along it at any rate with their eyes shut.

(Diogenes Laertius 4.49; K66)

527 Bion said that there are two things that foretell the nature of death, the time preceding our birth and sleep.

(*Gnomologium Vaticanum* 160; K67)

528 Just as we leave a house, says Bion, when the landlord, having failed to receive the rent, takes out the door, removes the tiles from the roof, and shuts up the well, so likewise, he says, I leave my poor body when nature, which has lent it to me, deprives me of the use of my eyes and ears, and of my hands and feet; I do not resist, but as when leaving a banquet, I depart without any ill-feeling, so also do I depart from life itself: when the hour comes, '*Climb into the shelter of the boat.*'*

(Teles 15.11–16.4; K68)

529 It is this opinion [i.e. that death is a great evil] that gives rise to all those horrible forms of mourning, such as begriming one's body, tearing at one's cheeks like a woman, and striking oneself on the chest, thighs, and head; it is this that makes Agamemnon, in Homer and Accius* alike, '*oft tear in grief his unshorn locks*'. Hence that witty remark by Bion, that it was exceedingly silly of the king to tear out his hair in his grief, as though his sorrow would be alleviated by baldness.

(Cicero, *Tusculan Disputations* 3.26.62; K69)

530 Disputes over burial, says Bion, have provided the basis for many a tragedy.*

(Teles in Stobaeus 3.40.8; K70)

531 He would condemn those who burn the dead* as if they are devoid of sense, and yet invoke them* as though they were still in possession of their senses.

(Diogenes Laertius 4.48; K71)

532 Let anyone run over in his mind the various things that cause us to be happy or sad, and he will recognize the truth of what Bion said: 'All the affairs of human beings resemble their beginnings, and their life is no more sacred and serious than their conception, they return to nothing after having been born out of nothing.'

(Seneca, *On Tranquillity of Mind* 15.4; K72)

XVII · ANTISTHENES AS FORERUNNER OF CYNICISM

From the Life of Antisthenes by Diogenes Laertius

533 Antisthenes, son of Antisthenes, was an Athenian, but it was said that he was not of pure Athenian birth; and accordingly, when someone sneered at him for this, he retorted, 'The mother of the gods too is a Phrygian';* for his mother was thought to have been a Thracian. So when he fought with great valour at the battle of Tanagra,* he gave Socrates occasion to remark that a man born to Athenian parents could hardly have turned out so brave.* He for his own part cast scorn on the way in which Athenians prided themselves on having

sprung from the earth,* saying that this did not mean that they were of any higher birth than snails and locusts.

He was initially a pupil of Gorgias the rhetorician,* hence the rhetorical style of the language that he employs in his dialogues, and especially in his *Truth* and *Exhortations*. Hermippos* recounts that at the gathering for the Isthmian Games, he had intended to deliver an address in which he would censure and praise the Athenians, Thebans, and Lacedaimonians; but he abandoned this plan when he saw a great many people arriving from those states. After a time, however, he attached himself to Socrates, and profited so greatly from him that he urged his own pupils to join with him in becoming fellow-pupils of Socrates. Since he was living in the Peiraeus, he used to walk forty stades* to the city each day to listen to Socrates, from whom he learned the art of endurance, and by emulating his impassivity of mind, became the original founder of the Cynic philosophy. And he argued that hardship* is a good thing, pointing to the great Heracles and to Cyrus,* drawing one example from the Greeks and the other from the barbarians. . . .

These were some of his teachings. He set out to show that virtue can be taught, and that true nobility belongs only to the virtuous; that virtue suffices to ensure happiness, requiring nothing further apart from the strength of a Socrates;* that virtue is founded in actions, and does not require a great many words or much learning; that the wise man is self-sufficient, for all that belongs to others belongs to him too; that ill-repute is a good thing, of equivalent value to hardship; that the wise man will conduct his duties as a citizen not in accordance with the established laws, but according to the law of virtue; that he will marry in order to have children, through union with the best-endowed women; and that he will feel love, since only the wise know who are worthy to be loved.

Diocles ascribes the following sayings to him. To the wise man nothing is alien or impracticable. The good man is worthy to be loved. One should ally oneself with those who are at once courageous and just. Virtue is a weapon of which one cannot be deprived. It is better to fight with a few good men against all who are bad than to fight with a multitude of bad men against a few who are good. One should pay good heed to one's enemies since they are the first to recognize one's errors. One should value an honest man above a relation. Virtue is the same for a woman as for a man. What is good is honourable and what is bad is shameful. Regard all that is wicked as alien. Wisdom is the most secure fortification, since it can neither collapse nor be betrayed. One must construct a fortress for oneself through one's own impregnable reasonings.

He used to converse in the gymnasium of the Cynosarges* ('the White Dog'), not far outside the city gates, and it is from that, so some people claim, that the Cynic school acquired its name. Antisthenes himself was nicknamed Haplokuon* ('Plain Dog'), and he was the first to fold his cloak double, according to Diocles, and to make do with that single garment and to carry a staff and knapsack. Neanthes states likewise that he was the first to double his cloak.* Sosicrates says, however, in the third book of his *Successions*, that Diodoros of Aspendos* was the first to do this, and that he also let his beard grow and used to carry a stick and knapsack.

Of all the Socratics, Antisthenes is the only one to be praised by Theopompos,* who says that he was most accomplished and could win over whomever he pleased by the charm of his discourse, as is plain too from his own writings and from Xenophon's *Symposium*. It would seem that the most manly part of the Stoic school can trace its origin to him.

(Diogenes Laertius 6.1–2 and 6.10–14)

534 *Antisthenes argues in Xenophon's* Symposium *that true wealth lies in being satisfied with little:*

'And now for your part', said Socrates, 'what is it that you most pride yourself on, Antisthenes?' 'On my wealth,' he replied. Whereupon Hermogenes asked him if he had plenty of money; but he swore that he owned not a penny. 'Well, a large amount of land, then?' 'Perhaps sufficient to enable Autolycos here to dust himself with it.'* . . .

'Well now,' said Socrates, 'the time has come for you to explain to us, Antisthenes, how it is that, with such scanty means, you pride yourself on your wealth.' 'Because it is my conviction, gentlemen, that people's wealth and poverty are located, not in their property, but in their soul. For in everyday life, I see many people who, although they already have a considerable fortune, regard themselves as being so poor that they will take on any amount of effort or risk if only it will enable them to add more to their possessions; and I also know of brothers with whom one finds that, although both have an equal inheritance, one of them has enough—and indeed more than enough—to cover his expenses, while the other is in the utmost want. I know, furthermore, of certain despots who have such a greed for wealth that they will commit worse crimes than those who are in dire want. For it is of course out of want that people turn to theft, or burglary, or the slave-trade; but there are some despots who destroy entire families, commit mass-murder, and often even enslave entire cities for the sake of money. For such people I feel great pity, though, since they are in the grip of a very cruel disease; for in my view they are in the same plight as one who has large possessions and eats a great deal without ever being able to satisfy his hunger.* But as for me, my wealth is so great that I can barely discover any part of it; and yet all the same I am sufficiently well provided to be able to eat until I no longer feel any hunger, to drink until I no longer feel any thirst, and have clothes enough to ensure that, when I go outside, I feel no chillier than Callias here with all his abundant riches; and when I get back home again, the walls serve me, so I think, as the warmest of tunics, and the roofs as the thickest of cloaks, and I have sufficient bedclothes to ensure that it is quite a business to wake me in the morning. If I feel any need for sexual gratification, I am so well satisfied with what the moment provides, so that the women whom I approach welcome me with the utmost joy,* having no one else at all who wants to court their favours. Well then, all of this furnishes me with so much pleasure that, in every case, I am inclined to pray for less rather than more, fancying that some of this is more pleasurable than is good for me.

But of all my wealth of possessions, I consider this to be the most precious, that even if I were to be robbed of what I presently have, I know of no form of work that would be so mean as to fail to provide me with adequate support. For whenever I feel a desire to indulge myself, I do not buy delicacies in the market-place (those are too expensive for me) but draw from the store-house of my soul. And when it comes to pleasure, besides, I think it much better to await the promptings of need before partaking of anything, rather than to share in any of your costly fare, as now when I am drinking this fine Thasian wine which chance has set before me without my having any real thirst for it. Yes, and it is surely also the case that those who live a simple life are more honest than those who make it their aim to amass worldly goods. For those who are most satisfied with what they have are least likely to covet the possessions of others.

It is worth noting, furthermore, that wealth of the kind that we are envisaging also makes people more generous. Just look at Socrates here, from whom I acquired these riches of mine; he did not dole them out to me by weight or measure, but simply delivered over to me as much of it as I could carry. And now for my own part, I am not mean or grudging with anyone, but pass on this wealth that I have in my soul to anyone who wants it. Yes, and my choicest possession of all is, as you can observe, that I am always at my leisure, so that I can go off and see what is worth seeing, or hear what is worth hearing, and, what I value first and foremost, I can spend the whole day at leisure with Socrates here. And he likewise does not reserve his admiration for those who can come up with the most money, but spends his time in the company of those whom he finds pleasing.'

(Xenophon, *Symposium* 3.8 and 4.34–44)

PART 2

ARISTIPPOS AND THE CYRENAICS

XVIII · ARISTIPPOS OF CYRENE

Pleasure, Adaptability, and Living for the Moment

535 Aristippos was born at Cyrene, but came to Athens, being drawn there, so Aeschines* reports, by the fame of Socrates. He taught as a sophist according to Phanias of Eresos,* the Peripatetic, and so became the first follower of Socrates to charge fees, and sent money to his master. One day, after he had sent him eighty minae, Socrates returned the money to him, saying that his divine sign* would not allow him to accept it; for he was in fact displeased by this course of action. Xenophon was ill-disposed toward him, and in consequence wrote the discourse on pleasure, placed in Socrates' mouth, which is directed against him.* Theodoros* too speaks badly of him in his work *On the Philosophical Schools*, as does Plato too in his work *On the Soul*,* as I have mentioned elsewhere.

He was a man who was skilled in adapting himself to place, and to time, and to person, and played his role in the manner that befitted each circumstance; he thus enjoyed the favour of Dionysios* above all others, because he always made the best of any situation. He drew pleasure from what was presently available to him, and made no effort to procure the enjoyment of what was not present; and in consequence Diogenes used to call him the royal dog.* Timon sneered at him too on account of his luxurious ways, saying, '*Such is the luxurious nature of Aristippos who fondled error.*'* . . .

The following works are ascribed to the Cyrenaic philosopher,* a history of Libya in three books, dedicated to Dionysios, and a single work containing twenty-five dialogues, some written in the Attic dialect and others in the Doric, namely: *Artabazos*; *To the Shipwrecked*; *To the Exiles*; *To a Beggar*; *To Lais*; *To Poros*; *To Lais about her Mirror*; *Hermeias*; *A Dream*; *To the Master of the Cups*; *Philomelos*; *To his Friends*; *To those who Reproach him for having a Taste for Old Wine and Courtesans*; *To those who Reproach him for the Extravagance of his Table*; *Letter to his Daughter Arete*; *To One in Training for Olympia*;

Questionings; another book of *Questionings*; *Treatise for Dionysos*; another, *On the Statue*; another, *On the Daughter of Dionysios*; *To One who Considered himself Dishonoured*; *To One who Undertook to Offer Advice*.

Some say that he also wrote six books of diatribes, while others, including Sosicrates of Rhodes, say that he wrote nothing at all. According to Sotion in his second book, and Panaitios, he composed the following works:* *On Education*; *On Virtue*; *Exhortation to Philosophy*; *Artabazos*; *The Shipwrecked*; *The Exiles*; six books of Diatribes; three Treatises;* *To Lais*; *To Poros*; *To Socrates*; *On Fortune*.

He laid down that the final end is smooth movement resulting in sensation.*

(Diogenes Laertius 2.65–6 and 83–5)

536 Aristippos was a companion of Socrates who founded the so-called Cyrenaic doctrine from which Epicurus drew material* when expounding his own account of the ultimate end. Aristippos was very voluptuous in his way of life and a lover of pleasure, but he never lectured in public about the nature of the end.* He did say, however, that the foundation of happiness lies potentially in the enjoyment of pleasures. For by constantly speaking about pleasure, he led his followers to suppose that he was suggesting that living pleasurably is the ultimate end.

(Aristocles, cited in Eusebius, *Preparation for the Gospel* 14.18.31, 763d–764a; G173)

537 Aristippos was thought to have made a very sound point when he urged people not to worry afterwards about things that have gone by, or worry in advance about those that are yet to come. For such an attitude is a sign of confidence and gives proof of a cheerful frame of mind. He recommended that one should concentrate on the present day, and indeed on the very part of it in which one is acting and thinking. For only the present, he said, truly belongs to us, and not what has passed by or what we are anticipating: for the one is gone and done with, and it is uncertain whether the other will come to be.

(Aelian, *Historical Miscellany* 14.6; G174)

538 All the philosophical schools have contended about the choice of enjoyment; and that which is known as the Cyrenaic school took its origin from Aristippos the Socratic, who taught that the enjoyment of pleasure is the end of life, and that happiness resides in that. And he taught also that pleasure is confined to the moment, thus assuming the same attitude as the debauched, who attach no value to the memory of past pleasures or hope of future ones, but judge that the good is to be found in the present alone, and that past or future enjoyment means nothing to us, the former because it no longer exists, and the latter because it does not yet exist and is moreover uncertain; just as those who live for luxury and pleasure are concerned only to fare well in the present moment. And his life was in full accord with his teachings, for he lived in the utmost luxury and extravagance, amidst perfume, fine clothing, and women. He consorted openly with the courtesan Lais,* and rejoiced in all the extravagances of Dionysios, even though he was often insulted by him.

(Athenaeus 12, 544ab; G174 and 53)

Profiting from Socrates

539 On meeting Isomachos* at the Olympic Games, Aristippos asked him what Socrates was saying in his discourses to draw young people to him as he did, and on picking up a few scraps and samples of his conversation, was so strongly affected that he virtually collapsed and became altogether pale and lean, until he finally sailed off to Athens and quenched his burning thirst at the spring, and came to know the man, and his discourses and his philosophy, the aim of which was to recognize one's own faults and to free oneself from them.

(Plutarch, *On Curiosity* 2, 516c; G2)

540 To a lawyer who successfully pleaded a case on his behalf and then asked him, 'What benefit did Socrates bring you?',* he replied, 'This at least, that what you said about me in your speech was true.'

(Diogenes Laertius 2.71; G10)

541 When he was once reproached for having paid an orator to plead a case for him, he replied, 'Yes, and when I want to give a dinner, I hire a cook.'

(Diogenes Laertius 2.72; G12)

542 When asked how Socrates had died, he said, 'As I would wish to die.'

(Diogenes Laertius 2.76; G13)

543a When asked what he had gained from philosophy, he said, 'To be able to associate with everyone with absolute confidence.'

(Diogenes Laertius 2.68; G104)

543b When asked what he had gained from philosophy, he said, 'To be able to associate without fear with all whom I encounter.'

(*Gnomologium Vaticanum* 36; G104)

544a When he was due to meet Pharnabazos,* satrap of the King, and someone said to him, 'Have courage, Aristippos', he replied, 'If you have anything else to say, say it; for after having associated with Socrates, I'm not afraid of any man's company.'

(*Gnomologium Vaticanum* 43; G108)

544b When he was once staying in Asia and was captured by the satrap Artaphernes,* and someone said to him, 'You are cheerful even in the face of this?', he replied, 'Yes, you fool, how can I have greater reason to be cheerful than when I am about to converse with Artaphernes?'

(Diogenes Laertius 2.79; G107)

545 When asked what he had gained from philosophy, he said, 'To be able to do without constraint what others only do through fear of the law.'*

(*Excerpts from Manuscripts of Florilegia of John Damascene* 2.13.146; G105)

546 When asked in what respect philosophers surpass other people, he replied, 'If all the laws were repealed, we would continue to live in just the same way.'

(Diogenes Laertius 2.68; G105)

547 When Plato once expressed himself in a manner that was rather too dogmatic, to his way of thinking, Aristippos said, 'Our friend would never have spoken like that',* meaning Socrates.

(Aristotle, *Rhetoric* 2.23, 1398b 29–31; G16)

548 Plato came to visit him one day while he was unwell, and when Plato asked how he was faring, Aristippos replied that a man of good character will fare well even when he has a fever, while one of bad character will fare badly even when he does not.

(*Gnomologium Vaticanum* 30; G18)

549 Since he had gained money from his teaching, Socrates asked him, 'Where did you get so much money?', to which he replied, 'Where you got so little.'

(Diogenes Laertius 2.80; G4)

550 To one who accused him of accepting money even though he was a pupil of Socrates, he replied, 'To be sure, I do, for Socrates too, when someone sent him food and wine, would take a little and send the rest back. But he has the foremost men of Athens as his provisioners, while I have only Eutychides, a purchased slave.'

(Diogenes Laertius 2.74; G3)

551 Someone brought him his son as a pupil, and he demanded five hundred drachmas as a fee; and when the man said, 'Why, I could buy a slave for that', Aristippos replied, 'So go off and buy one, and then you'll have two.'

(Diogenes Laertius 2.72; G5)

552 He said that teachers deserve to receive handsome fees from their pupils, from the gifted ones because they learn so much, and from the incompetent ones because they cause so much bother.*

(*Excerpts from Manuscripts of Florilegia of John Damascene*, 2.13, 145; G6)

553a He said that he took money from his friends not for his own personal use, but so that they might come to know what money ought to be used for.

(Diogenes Laertius 2.72; G7)

553b He said that he demanded fees from his pupils, not so as to improve his own life, but to teach them to spend their money on the right things.

(*Gnomologium Vaticanum* 24; G7)

Luxury and Expensive Living

554a When Plato once reproached him for having bought a large amount of fish, he said that he had paid only two obols* for them; and when Plato then remarked that he too would have bought them at that price, Aristippos replied, 'Then it looks, Plato, as if it is not I who am greedy, but you who are too fond of your money.'

(Athenaeus 8, 343cd; G17)

554b When someone reproached him for being extravagant in his food, he replied, 'Wouldn't you have bought this if you could have acquired it for three obols?', and when the man agreed, he said, 'It would seem, then, that it is not I who am over-fond of pleasure, but you who are over-fond of money.'

(Diogenes Laertius 2.75; G69)

555a When Plato once reproached him for having bought a costly fish for twelve drachmas, he asked Plato whether he would have bought the same fish for a drachma; and when Plato agreed that he would, he said that this was a matter of no account, 'for what is worth one drachma to Plato is worth a dozen to Aristippos'.

(*Gnomologium Vaticanum* 40; G17)

555b It is said that he once ordered a partridge to be bought for him at a cost of fifty drachmas; and when someone reproached him, he said, 'Wouldn't you have bought it for an obol?', and when the man said yes, replied, 'Well, fifty drachmas mean no more to me.'

(Diogenes Laertius 2.66; G17)

556 Polyxenos the sophist* once paid him a visit, and on seeing that women were present and expensive food was laid out, he reproached him for this. Shortly afterwards, Aristippos asked him, 'Can you join us today?', and when Polyxenos accepted the invitation, he said, 'Then why the reproaches? For it seems that it is not the food to which you object, but the expense.'

(Diogenes Laertius 2.76–7; G17)

557 When he was once reproached for his extravagant way of life, he said, 'If there were anything wrong with that, it wouldn't be so much in evidence at the festivals of the gods.'*

(Diogenes Laertius 2.68; G68)

558a Taking delight one day in the scent of a perfume, Aristippos exclaimed, 'A curse on those effeminates for having brought such a fine thing into disrepute!'

(Seneca, *On Benefits* 7.25; G65)

558b When Charondas, or, according to others, Phaedo,* asked, 'Who is it that stinks of perfume?', Aristippos said, 'Why me, poor wretch that I am, and the still more wretched King of the Persians; but consider that, just as no other creature is any the worse for smelling good, the same is true of me too. So a curse on those catamites who have cast discredit on our lovely perfume!'

(Diogenes Laertius 2.76; G63)

559 Aristippos lived a soft and luxurious life. Through a series of questions, he once developed this sophistic argument: if a horse is anointed with perfume, that does not cause it to lose any of its distinctive excellence as a horse, or if a dog is perfumed, any of its distinctive excellence as a dog, so no more does it do so for a man, he concluded.

(Clement of Alexandria, *Pedagogy* 2.8.64.1; G66)

560 If a shoe is too big, it is unusable, but that is not at all the case with an excess of riches; for while the excessive size of the shoe impedes one's movements when one tries to make use of it, it is possible to make use of any amount of riches either in whole or in part according to the circumstances.

(Stobaeus 4.31.128; G75)

Money and Non-Attachment

561 When his servant was carrying some of his money on the road and was struggling under the load, he said, 'Pour most of it away and carry only as much as you can manage.'*

(Diogenes Laertius 2.77; G79)

562a When he was once making a sea-voyage, he came to realize that he was on a pirate-vessel. So he took out his money and began to count it, and then, as if by accident, let it drop into the sea, making a show of sorrow at the loss. According to some accounts he added that it was 'better for the money to be lost through Aristippos than Aristippos through the money'.

(Diogenes Laertius 2.77; G79)

562b He was given handsome sums of money by Dionysios, and took it with him when he sailed away. On realizing that the sailors were plotting against him because of it, he moved away from the middle of the ship to the side, and ordered that his money-jar should be emptied on to the deck, as though he were intending to count the money. As the ship tossed in the sea, however, he cast it over the side into the depths. When the sailors grew angry at this, he said, 'Better that the money should be lost through me than that I should be lost through the money.'

(*Gnomologium Vaticanum* 39; G82)

563a While sailing to Athens, Aristippos the Cyrenaic philosopher suffered a shipwreck, and was taken in by the Athenians; when asked what he would say to his friends when he got back to Cyrene, he replied, 'To take only such supplies with them as they could swim off with if they were shipwrecked.'*

(*Gnomologium Vaticanum* 23; G50)

563b After his ship went down while he was making a sea-voyage, Aristippos was washed up on the shores of Syracuse, but he was immediately reassured when he saw a geometrical diagram in the sand, concluding from this that he had arrived among Greeks and civilized people, rather than among barbarians. Subsequently, after arriving at the gymnasium of the Syracusans, he recited these verses, '*Who will welcome the wandering Oedipus this day with even the meanest gifts?*',* and some people came up to him and, recognizing who he was, at once provided him with all that he needed. Some people who were about to sail off to Cyrene, his home-city, asked if he had any message to send to his fellow-citizens, and he said to tell them to equip themselves with such things as they could swim off with if they too should suffer a shipwreck.

(Galen, *Protreptic* 5; G50)

563c Aristippos the Socratic philosopher, after being cast up on the beach at Rhodes by a shipwreck, noticed that some geometrical figures had been inscribed there. 'Be of good hope,' he exclaimed to his companions, 'I see signs of human presence!'; and he headed at once for the city of Rhodes, and arrived directly at the gymnasium, where he discussed philosophical matters and was offered gifts, sufficient not only to provide for himself, but also to furnish his companions with clothing and all the necessities of life. Subsequently, when his companions wanted to return to their homeland, they asked him what message he wanted to be carried home, and he instructed them to say: that their children ought to be provided with such objects and travel-supplies as it would be possible for them to swim away with in the case of a shipwreck.

(Vitruvius, *On Architecture* 6.1.1; G50)

563d Aristippos advised the young only to take such travel-supplies with them as they could swim off with if they were shipwrecked.

(*Excerpts from Manuscripts of Florilegia of John Damascene* 12.13.138; G50)

564 On meeting him after a shipwreck,* enveloped in a double cloak (that is to say, folded in two) and wretchedly dressed, Plato praised him, saying, 'Every form of outward appearance and every circumstance suits Aristippos, full of wisdom as he is, who thus knows how to make use of small things as of great.'

(Pomponius Porphyrion on Horace, *Letter* 1.17.23; G45)

565a And yet people marvel at Aristippos the Socratic for the fact that, whether he was wearing a simple cloak or fine Milesian robes, he retained a dignified bearing.

(Plutarch, *On the Fortune of Alexander* 1.8, 330c; G56)

565b Straton,* or, according to some accounts, Plato, once said to him, 'To you alone is it granted to be equally happy to appear in fine robes or in rags.'

(Diogenes Laertius 2.67; G57)

566 When he was once asked how a wise man differs from one who is not, he replied, 'Send the two out naked among strangers, and then you will know.'

(Diogenes Laertius 2.73; G120)

567 He said that one should accustom oneself to living on little so as to do nothing shameful for the purpose of gaining wealth.

(*Gnomologium Vaticanum* 29; G76)

568 Most people pass over what is best and most agreeable in their circumstances to hasten to the things that are tiresome and unpleasant. Aristippos was not a man of that kind, however, but was capable, when balancing up what was good and bad in his present situation, of rising up toward the better side and so lightening his spirits. When he had once lost a fine piece of land, he thus asked one of those people who made a great show of sympathizing and condoling with him, 'Isn't it true that you have only one small piece of land while I have three farms left over?', and when the man agreed, then said, 'So isn't it I who should be condoling with you?'

(Plutarch, *On Tranquillity of Mind* 8, 469c; G74)

Sexual Pleasure and Non-Attachment

569 He consorted with the courtesan Lais,* as Sotion relates in the second book of his *Successions of the Philosophers*. To those who reproached him for this, he replied, 'I possess Lais but am not possessed by her.'* For the best thing is to master pleasures without becoming subjected by them, not to abstain from them.'

(Diogenes Laertius 2.74–5; G96)

570 On seeing Aristippos dressed in sumptuous robes, Socrates smeared some dirt on the seat on which he was about to sit; and when Aristippos sat down on it without the least concern, he remarked,

'I thought all along that you possess these clothes and are not possessed by them.'

(*Gnomologium Vaticanum* 493; G97)

571 The man who masters pleasure is not the one who abstains from it, but the one who enjoys it without allowing himself to be carried away by it; in just the same way as the master of a horse or ship is not the one who has nothing to do with it, but the one who guides it where he wants.

(Stobaeus 3.17.17; G98)

572 When he was once entering the house of a courtesan, and one of the lads who was with him blushed, he said, 'It's not going in that is bad, but being unable to get out again.'

(Diogenes Laertius 2.69; G87)

573 When Dionysios once told him to choose out one courtesan from a group of three, he carried off all three of them, saying, 'It did Paris no good* at all to choose out one from three!' But when he had taken them as far as the doorway, he let them go.

(Diogenes Laertius 2.67; G86)

574 To someone who reproached him for living with a courtesan, he said, 'Well then, if one is taking a house, does it make any difference whether many people have lived there before, or no one at all?' 'No difference.' 'Or if one is sailing in a ship, whether thousands have sailed in it before, or no one has?' 'Not the least difference.' 'Then it makes no difference at all', Aristippos concluded, 'whether the woman with whom one lives has lived with many men before or with none.'

(Diogenes Laertius 2.74; G90)

575 When Diogenes said to him, 'Aristippos, you're living with a public whore; so either turn Cynic like me or leave off', Aristippos replied by asking, 'Does it by any chance seem improper to you, Diogenes, to live in a house where others have lived previously?' 'By no means.' 'Or to sail in a ship in which many others have sailed?' 'No again.' 'So neither is there anything improper in living with a woman with whom many others have previously slept.'

(Athenaeus 13, 588f; G92)

576 Each year Aristippos used to spend two months with her [Lais] in Aegina during the festival of Poseidon; and when his servant reproached him for this, saying, 'You gave all this money to this woman, and she takes a tumble with Diogenes* for free', he replied, 'I reward Lais richly so that I may enjoy her, not to prevent anyone else from doing so.'

(Athenaeus 13, 588e; G92)

577 When someone spoke badly of Lais to him, saying that she did not love him, he replied that he did not suppose that wine or fish loved him either, but he happily took his pleasure in both of them.

(Plutarch, *Amatorius* 4, 750e; G93)

Interchanges with Dionysios

578 When Dionysios* once asked Aristippos why he had come to him, he said it was to hand over a share of what he had in return for a share of what he did not have. Or in some accounts, he offered this reply: 'When I had need of wisdom, I went to Socrates, but now that I have need of money, I've come to you.'

(Diogenes Laertius 2.77–8; G38)

579 To someone who criticized him for having left Socrates to go to Dionysios, he replied, 'But I went to Socrates for education, and to Dionysios for diversion.'*

(Diogenes Laertius 2.80; G38)

580 Hegesandros* recounts further that the servants of Dionysios once spattered Aristippos with water, and when Antiphon* mocked him for putting up with this, he replied, 'And if I had been out fishing, would I have gone away and abandoned my work?'

(Athenaeus 12, 544d; G36)

581 He bore it patiently when Dionysios spat at him, and when someone reproached him for this, he said, 'If the fishermen put up with being spattered with seawater to catch a gudgeon, shouldn't I put up with being sprinkled with wine to take a blenny?'*

(Diogenes Laertius 2.67; G36)

582a When he was once constrained by Dionysios to talk about some philosophical point, he said, 'It would be absurd that you should learn from me how to speak, and yet venture to teach me when to speak.' Dionysios was so annoyed by this that he made him take a place at the end of the table, to which Aristippos responded by saying, 'You evidently wanted to make this a place of honour!'

(Diogenes Laertius 2.73; G36)

582b Hegesandros recounts that when he was once assigned a rather dishonourable place at table, he showed no sign of being disconcert-ed, and when Dionysios asked him what he thought of this place com-pared to the one that he had occupied the day before, he replied that it was much the same: 'For the place up there', he said, 'has no value today without me, but yesterday was the most splendid of all because of me; while today this one has become a seat of honour because of my presence, and yesterday's has lost its lustre because I am no longer there.'

(Athenaeus 12, 544c; G36)

583a One day, during a drinking-party, Dionysios ordered everyone to dress in purple and dance. Plato declined, saying,

> *'Never could I put on women's raiment'*,

But Aristippos for his part put on the robes, and as he was about to dance responded wittily,

> *'For even amidst the Bacchic revels*
> *She who enters chaste will not be corrupted.'*

(Diogenes Laertius 2.78; G31)

583b Dionysios pressed Aristippos to take off his old cloak and dress in purple robes, and Aristippos complied; he then asked Plato to do the same, but Plato said,

'Never could I put on women's raiment',

to which Aristippos responded, 'But the same poet says,

> *Even amid the Bacchic revels*
> *She who enters chaste will not be corrupted.'*

(Stobaeus 3.5.38; G34)

584 He [Dionysios] regularly offered him [Plato] large gifts of money, but Plato would not accept them, and Aristippos, who was present to see this, said that Dionysios had adopted a safe form of magnanimity; for he offered little to people like him who needed more, but a great deal to Plato who would not take anything.

(Plutarch, *Life of Dion* 19.7; G28)

585 When Dionysios once said to him,

> *'Whoever comes to a tyrant's court*
> *Becomes his slave though free he comes'*,

he retorted,

> *'No slave is he, if free he come.'**

So Diocles states in his work *On the Lives of the Philosophers*, though others attribute this story to Plato.

(Diogenes Laertius 2.82; G30)

586 When Dionysios asked him why philosophers come to rich men's doors,* while the rich do not come to those of philosophers, he replied, 'Because philosophers know what they have need of, while the rich do not.'

(Diogenes Laertius 2.69; G106)

587 When someone said that he constantly saw philosophers at the doors of the rich, he replied, 'Yes, just as doctors are always visiting the sick; but no one would prefer for that reason to be ill rather than to be a doctor.'

(Diogenes Laertius 2.70; G106)

588 When someone asked him why he associated with people of bad character, he replied, 'Just as doctors are always with the sick.'*

(*Gnomologium Vaticanum* 37; G106)

589 He asked Dionysios for some money, only to be told, 'But didn't you say that the wise man would never be at a loss?' Aristippos replied, 'Well, give me the money and then we'll look into the question', and once he had been given it, said, 'So you see now that I was not at a loss?'*

(Diogenes Laertius 2.82; G40)

590 He once received some money from Dionysios while Plato took a book; and when someone criticized him for this, he said, 'Well, it's money that I have need of, while Plato has need of books.'*

(Diogenes Laertius 2.81; G39)

591 When he was asked by the tyrant Dionysios when he would stop asking him for money, he replied, 'When you stop giving it; and that will come about when we no longer find pleasure in one another's company.'

(*Gnomologium Vaticanum* 35; G40)

592 When he was once seeking a favour from Dionysios on behalf of a friend and met with no success, he fell down at the tyrant's feet; and when someone mocked him for that, he retorted, 'It's not I who am to blame but Dionysios, for having his ears in his feet.'

(Diogenes Laertius 2.79; G37)

593 When Dionysios once said to Aristippos, 'I've gained no benefit from you', he replied, 'All too true, for if you had, you would have rid yourself of your tyranny as though of a sacred disease.'*

(Stobaeus 4.8.23; G41)

594 One day Simos, Dionysios' steward, who was a Phrygian and a dreadful rogue, showed him some luxurious houses paved with mosaics; and as he was doing so, Aristippos coughed up some phlegm and spat it into his face, and when he grew angry at that, said, 'I couldn't see any more suitable place.'*

(Diogenes Laertius 2.75; G42)

595 When he was once reproached by Plato for his extravagant way of life, he replied, 'Doesn't Dionysios strike you as being a good man?', and when Plato agreed, said, 'Yet Dionysios lives more extravagantly than I do, so it seems that there is nothing to prevent a man from living both extravagantly and well.'

(Diogenes Laertius 2.76; G70)

Confrontations with Diogenes

596a One day Aristippos saw Diogenes washing raw vegetables* at a spring and said, 'If you attended the courts of princes, Diogenes, you wouldn't be feeding on those', to which he retorted, 'And if you for your part fed on such food, Aristippos, you wouldn't be haunting the courts of princes.'

(*Gnomologium Vaticanum* 192; G48)

596b As Diogenes was once washing vegetables, he saw him [Aristippos] walking by and said, 'If you'd learned to make do with these, you wouldn't be haunting the courts of princes', to which Aristippos retorted, 'And if you for your part knew how to associate with human beings, you wouldn't be washing vegetables.'

(Diogenes Laertius 2.68; G44)

597 It is said that Aristippos, after having invited Diogenes to the baths, made sure that everyone left before them, and then put on the shabby cloak of Diogenes, leaving him his own purple robes. When Diogenes then came out, being unwilling to put on the robes, and asked for his own cloak to be returned to him, Aristippos reproached the Cynic for being a slave to his own reputation, because he preferred to freeze rather than be seen in purple robes.*

(Acron, Scholium to Horace, *Letter* 1.17, 30; G45)

Miscellaneous Sayings and Anecdotes

598a As he was once sailing to Corinth, he was caught by a storm and was thrown into great alarm; and when someone remarked to him, 'We ordinary folk are not scared, and yet you philosophers are behaving like cowards', he replied, 'Yes, to be sure, since the lives that we are worrying about are not of equivalent value.'

(Diogenes Laertius 2.71; G49)

598b When Aristippos was once on a sea-voyage, a storm blew up and he became greatly alarmed. One of his fellow-travellers remarked to him, 'So you're afraid too, Aristippos, just like anyone else?', to which he replied, 'Yes, of course; for in your case, during this present danger, you have only your wretched life to worry about, while for me it is a life of true happiness that is in peril.'

(Aelian, *Historical Miscellany* 9.20; G49)

599a Aristippos had once grown angry with Aeschines,* and when someone asked him, 'What's become of your friendship, Aristippos?', he replied, 'It's gone to sleep, but now I'll wake it up again'; and he went to Aeschines and said to him, 'Do I strike you as being in such a thoroughly bad way, and so beyond cure, as to be inaccessible to your reproaches?', to which Aeschines replied, 'There's nothing to wonder at in the fact that you, who surpass me by nature in every respect, should have been the first to recognize the right course of action.'

(Plutarch, *On the Control of Anger* 14, 462d; G24)

599b After once growing angry with Aeschines, he said to him shortly afterwards, 'Shouldn't we make up our quarrel and stop talking nonsense? Or are you waiting for someone to reconcile us over a bowl of wine?', to which Aeschines replied, 'I'm only too glad.' 'Remember then,' said Aristippos, 'that although I am the older, it was I who made the first approach', and Aeschines replied, 'Yes indeed, by Hera, you're absolutely right, for you're a much better man than I am—it was my part to start the quarrel, and yours to open the way back to friendship.'

(Diogenes Laertius 2.82–3; G24)

600 On seeing someone who was in a temper and was growing the more angry the more he spoke, Aristippos the Cyrenaic philosopher said, 'We should not allow our words to be guided by anger, but use our words to put a check on our anger.'

(Stobaeus 3.20.63; G109)

601 Aristippos was once outwitted in argument by a man who was very self-assured, but was otherwise devoid of sense and reason. On seeing him rejoicing and swelling with pride, Aristippos remarked, 'And yet I, who have been defeated, am going off to enjoy a sweeter sleep than you who have defeated me.'

(Plutarch, *On Progress in Virtue* 9, 80c; G111)

602a When subjected to abuse one day, he moved away; and when the man chased after him and said, 'Why are you fleeing?', he replied, 'Just as you have the freedom to insult me, I have the freedom not to listen.'

(Diogenes Laertius 2.70; G112)

602b Moving away from a man who was abusing him, Aristippos said, 'Just as you are master of your tongue, I am master of my ears.'

(*Gnomologium Monacense Latinum* 35.1; G112)

603 One day Aristippos ran across a man who had wronged him, and who now turned aside to avoid meeting him. 'It is not you who should be fleeing from me', cried Aristippos, 'but I from you, since it is you who are the villain!'

(*Gnomologium Vaticanum* 27; G113)

604 Aristippos said that it is generally ridiculous to pray to the gods for benefits and ask them for any particular thing,* for it is not when patients ask their doctors for some food or drink that they give it to them, but when they judge that it will be of benefit to them.

(*Gnomologium Vaticanum* 32; G132)

605 When asked what is admirable in life, Aristippos said, 'A man of sound and moderate character, because even when he falls in with many bad people, he will not be corrupted.'

(Stobaeus 3.37.24; G35)

606 It is better to be a beggar, he said, than to be uneducated; for beggars merely lack money while the uneducated are lacking in humanity.*

(Diogenes Laertius 2.70; G125)

607 To someone who asked him in what respect his son would be better for having an education, he said, 'In this, if nothing else, that when he's at the theatre he won't just be one stone sitting on another.'*

(Diogenes Laertius 2.72; G128)

608 When he was reproached by his fellow-citizens for spending so much time with the young, talking to them about wisdom, he replied, 'And yet I see that you, my dear fellow-citizens, never set out to break in old horses, but only the foals.'

(*Gnomologium Vaticanum* 45; G130)

609 To someone who boasted that he could drink large amounts without getting drunk, he said, 'Yes, and so can a mule.'

(Diogenes Laertius 2.73; G118)

610 When a courtesan said to him, 'I'm expecting a child by you', he replied, 'You can no more be sure of that than, after passing through a clump of thistles,* you could say that you had been pricked by one particular thistle.'

(Diogenes Laertius 2.81; G88)

611 When someone reproached him for not having returned some money that he had borrowed, he said, 'But shouldn't you be reproaching yourself for not having rightly judged the man to whom you were giving the money?'

(*Gnomologium Vaticanum* 31; G85)

612 When someone presented him with a knotty riddle and said, 'Untie that one!', he replied, 'Why do you want it untied, you silly man, when it provides us with quite enough of a problem even while it is still tied up!'

(Diogenes Laertius 2.70; G116)

A Dialogue with Socrates in Xenophon's Memorabilia

613 [Socrates:] 'If, then, we classify those who exercise self-control in all these respects as being fit to rule, should we not classify those who are incapable of doing so as being people who can have no claim to rule?' He [Aristippos] agreed to this too.

'Well now, since you know the category to which each of these two kinds of people deserves to be assigned, have you ever given any thought as to which of these categories you should properly assign yourself?'

'I have indeed,' said Aristippos, 'and I would not dream of classing myself among those who aspire to rule. For when one considers what a business it is to provide for one's own needs, it seems to me that one would have to be a complete idiot not to confine oneself to that, but also to saddle oneself with the further responsibility of having to provide for the needs of all one's fellow-citizens as well. That one should deprive oneself of so many things that one desires in order to put oneself at the head of a state, and so expose oneself to the vagaries of the law if one should fail to fulfil every last wish of the community is surely the very height of folly. For states claim the right to treat their rulers just as I treat my domestic slaves. I expect my servants to provide me in full measure with all that I may need, but that they should not take any of it for themselves, whereas states regard it as the duty of their rulers to provide them with as many good things as possible, while they themselves touch none of it. So if anyone should want to incur no end of bother both for himself and others, I would educate him in the manner suggested, and allow him to take his place among those who are fit to rule; but for my own part I would class myself among those who want to live as easy and pleasant a life as possible.'

Socrates then asked, 'So would you like us to examine whether those who rule or those who are ruled live a more pleasant life?' 'Yes indeed,' said Aristippos. 'Let us start, then, by considering the nations that we are familiar with. In Persia it is the Persians who rule, while the Syrians, Lydians, and Phrygians are ruled. In Europe the Scythians rule, while the Maeonians are ruled, and in Africa, it is the Carthaginians who rule while the Africans are ruled. Which of these two classes, do you suppose, lives the more pleasant life? Or among the Greeks, to whom you yourself belong, who seems to you to live a more pleasant life, those who rule or those who are ruled?'

'But for my part,' said Aristippos, 'I wouldn't class myself among the slaves either, but it seems to me that there is a middle path which I try to follow, which leads neither through rule nor through slavery, but through freedom; and this is the road that leads most surely to happiness.'

'Now if this path of yours,' replied Socrates, 'which leads neither through rule nor through slavery, could also avoid passing through human society, there might perhaps be some sense in what you are saying. If, however, living among men as you do, you have it in mind neither to rule nor to be willing to cater to the wishes of the rulers, you can presumably see how the stronger know how to make the weaker lament their predicament both in public and in private, and treat them like slaves? Or has it escaped you that they gather in the harvest that others have sown, and cut the trees that others have planted, and that they lay siege to the weaker in every way if they are unwilling to serve them, until they are induced to accept slavery to avoid a hopeless struggle with those who are stronger? So too in private life, do you not see that those who are brave and powerful enslave and plunder those who are cowardly and weak?'

'Yes,' he replied, 'but to escape those very evils, I do not shut myself up in a single community, but am a stranger everywhere', to which Socrates replied, 'That is certainly a clever move, since ever since the death of Sinis, Sceiron, and Procrustes,* no one ever causes harm to strangers.'

(Xenophon, *Memorabilia* 2.1.7–14)

XIX · THE CYRENAIC SCHOOL UNDER THE YOUNGER ARISTIPPOS

The Cyrenaic Succession

614 Now that we have given an account of his [Aristippos'] life, let us pass on now to review the Cyrenaics who followed after him, some of whom were called Hegesians, others Annicerians, and others again, Theodoreans.

This is how things stand.* Aristippos had as pupils his daughter Arete,* Aithiops of Ptolemais, and Antipatros of Cyrene. Arete had as her pupil [her son] Aristippos, who was known as the Mother-taught;

and he had as his pupil Theodoros, who was known as the Atheist, and subsequently as 'God'. Antipatros* had as his pupil Epitimides of Cyrene, who had as his pupil Paraibates, who in turn had Hegesias the Death-persuader and Anniceris as his pupils.

(Diogenes Laertius 2.85–6)

The Family of Aristippos

615 After he [the elder Aristippos] had been summoned home repeatedly by his father, but had never obeyed him, his father wrote to say that he would sell him into slavery in accordance with the laws of the land; to which Aristippos responded by writing to ask his father to wait a little while longer, since he would then become more valuable, and could be sold for a higher price.

(*Gnomologium Vaticanum* 42; G134)

616a Someone accused him of casting off his son* as though he were not his own offspring. 'Phlegm too and spit', he replied, 'are things that we know to be born from us, but since they are useless, we cast them as far away from us as possible.'

(Diogenes Laertius 2.81; G135)

616b When his son grew dissolute,* he shut him out of the house; and when his wife reproached him for not seeking a reconciliation, and constantly repeated that he was after all his own offspring, Aristippos spat and said, 'This too comes from me, but I cast it out because it riles me.'

(*Gnomologium Vaticanum* 25; G136)

617 Aristippos [the Younger] was happy to be called the Mother-taught because he had been educated in philosophy by his mother [Arete] alone; you need to be clear, however, about which Aristippos I am talking, not the great one who was a disciple of Socrates, but that one's grandson through his daughter. Now the mother loved her son Aristippos, as is natural, and instilled him with learning, striving to show him what was of value in her view and that of his grandfather.

(Themistius, *Oration* 21, 244b; G IVB 3)

618 He [the elder Aristippos] had as a follower, among others, his daughter Arete, who after giving birth to a son, named him Aristippos; and since she herself educated him to philosophy, this Aristippos was called the Mother-taught. He [the younger Aristippos] clearly defined the end* as living pleasurably, introducing the idea that pleasure is connected with motion. For he said that our constitution has three possible states, one in which we suffer pain, which may be compared to a storm at sea, another which may be compared to a gentle rocking of the waves, and finally a third state which is intermediate in nature, in which we neither suffer pain nor enjoy pleasure, this being comparable to a calm sea. It is of these affections alone, he said, that we have any consciousness.

(Aristocles, cited in Eusebius, *Preparation for the Gospel* 14.18, p. 764ab; G IVB 5)

The Teachings of the Cyrenaic School under the Younger Aristippos

619 Those who remained faithful to the teaching of Aristippos and were known as Cyrenaics professed the following doctrines. They maintained that there are two basic states, pleasure and pain, the former being a smooth motion and the latter a rough motion. No pleasure is different from any other pleasure, nor is one more pleasant than another. All living creatures find pleasure agreeable and are repelled by pain. By pleasure, it should be noted, they mean physical pleasure, which is also the ultimate end, as Panaitios* states in his book *On the Philosophical Schools*, and not the settled pleasure that follows from the removal of pains and is a kind of freedom from disturbance, which Epicurus accepts* and proclaims as the end. They think, furthermore, that the end is different from happiness; for our end is particular pleasure, while happiness is the sum of the various particular pleasures, among which are included those that have passed by and those that are yet to come.

Particular pleasure is desirable for its own sake, whereas happiness is desirable not for its own sake, but for the sake of the particular pleasures. The proof that pleasure is the end can be found in the fact that, from our earliest childhood, we are instinctively drawn to it and, after having attained it, seek for nothing more, whilst there is nothing that we so strive to avoid as its opposite, pain. Pleasure is good, moreover, even if it is derived from the most shameful actions, as Hippobotos relates in his book *On the Philosophical Schools*. For even if the action is improper, it is no less the case that the pleasure that arises from it is desirable and good.

The removal of pain, on the other hand, as envisaged by Epicurus, is not regarded by them as being pleasure, any more than the absence of pleasure is pain. For they hold that both pleasure and pain are founded in motion, whereas neither the absence of pain nor the absence of pleasure is motion, the absence of pain being, as it were, the condition of one who is asleep. They say that it is possible that some people, through a kind of perversity, may not pursue pleasure; and not all pleasures and pains of the mind arise from bodily pleasures and pains. For in fact the mere prosperity of our homeland may be a source of joy to us, as in the case of our own prosperity. They deny, however, that pleasure is attained through the recollection or anticipation of good things, as was thought by Epicurus; for with time, the movement of the soul becomes exhausted.

They hold, furthermore, that pleasure is not derived from the mere sensation of sight or hearing. We listen, for instance, with pleasure to those who imitate the sounds of mourning, whereas we find genuine mourning hard to bear. The absence of pain and pleasure they call intermediate states. They asserted that bodily pleasures are far superior to mental ones, and bodily pains much worse than mental ones; that is why wrongdoers are punished with physical pains. Suffering they considered to be harder to bear, while pleasure is more in conformity with our nature, and hence they concerned themselves above all with the fostering of the latter. Although pleasure is desirable in itself, the things that give rise to certain pleasures are often irksome and quite the opposite of pleasurable, so that to accumulate the pleasures that are productive of happiness seems to them a most disagreeable business.

They do not accept the idea that every wise person lives an entirely pleasant life, or every fool an unpleasant one, but only that this is broadly the case. It is sufficient even that we enjoy each particular pleasure as it presents itself. They say that practical wisdom is a good thing, though it is not desirable for its own sake, but only for what it brings; that a friend is good for the advantages that he brings us, just as we cherish a part of our body as long as we have it. Some virtues may be found even in the foolish. Bodily training can contribute to the acquisition of virtue. The sage will yield neither to envy, nor to love, nor to superstition, since all such feelings are founded in empty opinion; he will feel distress and fear, however, these being natural sentiments. And wealth is productive of pleasure, but not desirable in itself.

They hold that affections are intelligible, but not the causes from which they arise. They renounced the study of nature because of its manifest unintelligibility, but cultivated logic because of its usefulness. Meleagros, however, in the second book of his work *On Philosophical Opinions*, and Cleitomachos in the first book of his work *On the Philosophical Schools*, say that they considered both natural philosophy and dialectic to be useless, since anyone who has properly mastered the theory of good and evil will also be capable of speaking well, and will be free from superstition, and will have escaped the fear of death.

They also maintained that nothing is intrinsically just, honourable, or base, but things are merely held to be so by convention and custom. A good person will nevertheless do nothing improper because of the penalties and ill-repute that follow from such actions. The sage really does exist. They allow that progress can be achieved both in philosophy and in other matters. They say that the pain suffered by one person can exceed that suffered by another, and that the senses are not always reliable guides to the truth.

(Diogenes Laertius 2.86–93)

620 [Epicurus 10, for the distinction between Cyrenaic and Epicurean hedonism] When we [the Epicureans] say, then, that pleasure is the ultimate end, we do not mean by that the pleasures of the dissolute, or those founded in sensual indulgence, as some suppose us to do as a result of ignorance, disagreement, or misrepresentation; no, by pleasure we mean the absence of bodily pain and mental disturbance. It is not an uninterrupted succession of drinking-parties and carousals, or sexual indulgence with boys or women, or the enjoyment of fish and other delights of a luxurious table, which produce a pleasant life, but the sober exercise of reason, as we carefully examine the grounds for choosing or avoiding each particular thing, and banish the vain opinions through which the greatest disturbance seizes hold of the soul.

(Diogenes Laertius 10.131–2; from Epicurus, Letter 10, to Menoiceus)

Cyrenaic Scepticism

621 So Socrates thought in this way, and after him, the school of

Aristippos of Cyrene, and later that of Ariston of Chios,* sought to assert that in pursuing philosophy, we should concentrate on the moral questions alone; for such questions are within our capacity and are useful, while those relating to nature, by contrast, are beyond our grasp, and would be of no use even if they were open to investigation.

(Eusebius, *Preparation for the Gospel* 15.62.7, 854c; G166)

622 Next there are those who claim that affections* alone are apprehensible; this is asserted by some philosophers from Cyrene. These thinkers maintained, just as if weighed down by a deep sleep, that they knew nothing whatever, unless somebody at their side should strike or prick them; for they said that when they were being burned or cut, they recognized that they were undergoing something: as to whether what was burning them was fire, or what was cutting them was iron, that they could not say.

(Aristocles, cited in Eusebius, *Preparation for the Gospel* 14.19.1, 764b–d; G218)

623 The Cyrenaics say, then, that the affections are the criteria of truth, and that they alone are apprehensible and undeceptive, but that none of the things that produce the affections are apprehensible or undeceptive. That we feel the affection of whiteness, or of sweetness, can be stated, so they say, infallibly, truly, and firmly, without risk of refutation; but that the thing that produces the affection in us is white or sweet is impossible to affirm. For it is possible that we could feel the affection of whiteness under the effect of something that is not white, or the affection of sweetness under the effect of something that is not sweet. For just as one who is suffering from vertigo or jaundice receives a yellowish affection* from everything, or one suffering from ophthalmia* a reddish affection, or one who presses on his eye comes to see two images, or someone in a state of madness sees Thebes twice over* and imagines the sun to be double, so it is true that in all these cases, the people suffer some affection, such as of yellowness, redness, or redoublement, but it must be considered false that what produces these affections is yellow, red, or double, and we are thus obliged to conclude that we can grasp nothing beyond our own affections.

Thus we must posit either that affections are appearances or that the things that produce them are. Now if we say that our affections

are appearances, all appearances must be said to be true and apprehensible; while if we apply that name to the things that produce the
affections, then all appearances are false and inapprehensible. For the
affection that occurs in us reveals nothing more than itself. It thus
follows, if we are to speak the truth, that the affection alone is an
appearance for us, whilst that which is outside us and produces the
affection may perhaps exist, but does not appear to us.

And so with regard to our own affections, we are all free from error,
but with regard to what lies outside us, we are all subject to error, the
former being apprehensible, but the latter inapprehensible because
our mind is too weak to distinguish it in view of the positions, dis-
tances, motions, changes, and all the multitude of other causes. And
so they say that there is no criterion that is common to all human
beings, but that common names are assigned to objects. All people in
common call something white or sweet, but they do not share something in common that is white or sweet; for each person is aware of
his own particular affection, but is incapable of telling whether the
affection comes to him or to his neighbour from a white object, since
he does not experience the affection of his neighbour, any more than
his neighbour experiences his. Since we share no affection in common, it would be rash to declare that what appears to me to be of a
certain nature appears likewise to my neighbour too. For perhaps I
am so constituted to experience an affection of whiteness under the
effect of what strikes me from outside, while another person has his
senses so organized as to be affected differently. So what appears to
us is by no means common to us all. And that in fact, owing to the
different constitutions of our senses, we are not all moved in the same
way, is evident from the case of those who are suffering from jaundice, or ophthalmia, or are in a normal state. For just as the first group
are affected in a yellowish manner, the second in a reddish manner,
and the third in a whitish manner by the same object, so it is probable
that those who are in a normal state, in accordance with the different
constitution of their senses, will not be moved in the same manner by
the same object, but differently according to whether a person has
grey eyes, or blue eyes, or dark eyes. So we apply common names to
objects, but have our own particular sense-affections.

(Sextus Empiricus, *Against the Mathematicians* 7.191–8; G213)

624 To act is one thing, to suffer is another. If opposite affections are suffered in relation to the same thing, they agree that the specific nature of the agent is not defined, because the same thing could not produce different affections at the same time. Hence the Cyrenaics claim that the affections alone are apprehensible, while the objects themselves are inapprehensible. For I apprehend, they say, that I am being burned, but that fire is of such a nature as to burn is uncertain; for if it were of such a nature, all things would be burned by it.

(*Anonymous Commentary to Plato's 'Theaetetus', Berlin Papyrus* 9782, col. 65, 18–39; G214)

XX · THE OTHER CYRENAICS

The Teachings of Hegesias' Branch of the School

625 Those who were known as the Hegesians* adopted the same ends, pleasure and pain. Neither gratitude, nor friendship, nor beneficence, have any real existence in their view, because we do not choose any of these for their own sake, but for the advantages that we can draw from them, and when those are no longer to be found, the things themselves cease to exist also. Happiness is altogether impossible, since the body is afflicted with many sufferings, and the mind shares in the sufferings of the body and is troubled accordingly, and fortune, furthermore, prevents many of our hopes from being realized; so for these reasons happiness cannot exist.* Life and death can both be desirable.* They supposed that nothing is pleasant or unpleasant by nature, and as a result of deficiency, or novelty, or surfeit, some can find pleasure and others displeasure in the same things. Poverty and wealth count for nothing with regard to pleasure, since the rich do not experience pleasure in a different way from the poor. Slavery and freedom make no difference when it comes to the calculation of pleasure, and neither do nobility and low birth, or good and bad repute. If to the foolish life is advantageous, to the wise it is a matter of indifference. The wise man does everything for the sake of his own personal interest, because he thinks that no one else is of equal value to himself; for even if he could reap the greatest benefits from another person, these would not measure up to those that he could provide for himself. They placed no value on the senses, furthermore, because they do not provide accurate knowledge, but said that we should do whatever appears to be in accordance with reason. They said that we should forgive people for their faults, since no one commits a fault of his own free will, but only under the constraint of some passion. And we should not hate people, but try to show them a better way. The sage will not surpass others so much in the choice of goods as in the avoiding of evils, since he makes it his end to live without pain or distress,* a result which will be achieved best by those who make no distinction between the causes of pleasure.

(Diogenes Laertius 2.93–6; G IV F 1)

Hegesias as 'Death-Persuader'

626 Hegesias of Cyrene: he maintained that neither friendship nor gratitude exist; according to him, these do not exist in themselves, but a person who has need of things offers gratitude, while one who possesses somewhat more confers benefits. He also said that for the foolish, life is a good thing, while for the sage, death is,* for which reason some have called him the Death-persuader.*

(Epiphanius, *Against Heresies* 3.2.9; G IV F 2)

627a To tell the truth, death separates us from bad things and not from good; and it was this thought that Hegesias of Cyrene developed with such eloquence that King Ptolemy* had to forbid him from speaking about the matter in his lectures, because many of his pupils resolved to commit suicide after having heard him.

(Cicero, *Tusculan Disputations* 1.34.83; G IV F 3)

627b What value should we attach to the eloquence of Hegesias the Cyrenaic? He portrayed the evils of life in such a vivid manner that, once he had introduced such a miserable idea of the human lot into the hearts of his listeners, he inspired many of them with the desire to seek a voluntary death, to such a point that King Ptolemy forbade him to discuss the matter any further.

(Valerius Maximus, 8.9, ext. 3; G IV F 5)

628 The book of Hegesias that I referred to is called *The Man who Starved himself to Death*; it tells how a man set out to starve himself to death, and when his friends tried to restrain him, responded by enumerating all the miseries of human life.

(Cicero, *Tusculan Disputations* 1.34.84; G IV F 4)

629 Through his arguments Hegesias persuaded many of his listeners to starve themselves to death.

(Plutarch, *On Affection for Offspring* 5, 497d; G IV F 6)

The Teachings of Anniceris' Branch of the School

630 While agreeing with them [the Hegesians] in other regards, the Annicerians* admitted that friendship, gratitude, and respect for one's parents do have a place in life, and that one may sometimes act out of love of one's country. As a consequence the sage, even if he has his troubles, will nonetheless be happy,* even if few pleasures accrue to him. The happiness of a friend is not desirable for its own sake, since it is not perceptible even to one who is close to him. Reason is not sufficient on its own to enable a person to have confidence in himself and to rise above the opinions of the crowd, but it is necessary that we should educate our character to overcome the bad dispositions that have developed in us over a long period of time. A friend should be welcomed not merely because of his usefulness (for otherwise, if that were to fail, we would have nothing to do with him), but also out of a natural feeling of goodwill,* on the account of which we are even willing to put up with hardships. For although pleasure is accepted as the end, and we are distressed at being deprived of it, we willingly endure the privation nonetheless because of the affection that we feel for our friend.

(Diogenes Laertius 2.96–7; G IV G 3)

631 Those known as the Annicerians, from the Cyrenaic school, laid down no general definition of the end of life, but ascribed a specific end to each action, the pleasure that arises from the action itself. These Cyrenaics reject Epicurus' definition of pleasure, namely the removal of pain, calling that the condition of a corpse; for we rejoice on account not only of pleasure, but also of the company of others and their esteem.

(Clement of Alexandria, *Stromata* 2.21.130.7–8; G IV G 4)

632 And if it is the case that the night does not take away our happiness, why should it be taken away by a day that resembles the night? On this subject Antipatros* the Cyrenaic made a remark which is far from inept even if it is a little coarse: when some lasses were once condoling with him over his blindness, he said, 'Why trouble yourselves? Do you suppose the night does not bring pleasures of its own?'

(Cicero, *Tusculan Disputations* 4.38.112; G IV C 1)

Theodoros the Atheist

633 Those who were called the Theodoreans derived their name from the Theodoros mentioned above, and followed his doctrines. Theodoros was a man who entirely rejected the customary beliefs about the gods. I have chanced upon a book of his entitled *About the Gods*, which is by no means contemptible; it was from this book, so they say, that Epicurus drew most of the things that he said about this matter.

Theodoros was a pupil of Anniceris and of Dionysios the dialectician,* as Antisthenes reports in his *Successions of the Philosophers*. He regarded joy and grief as being the supreme good and evil,* the one deriving from wisdom and the other from foolishness. Wisdom and justice he viewed as goods, and their opposites as evils, while he held pleasure and pain to be of intermediate value. He rejected friendship because it exists neither between the foolish nor between the wise; for in the case of the foolish, when the advantage to be gained from it is removed, the friendship too disappears, whilst the wise are self-sufficient and have no need of friends. He said, furthermore, that it is reasonable for the wise man not to risk his life for his country, since he should not throw away his own wisdom to bring benefit to fools.

He said that the world is our country. Theft, adultery, and sacrilege are justifiable on occasion, since none of these acts is foul by nature, if one puts aside the common opinion* that is held about them, which is merely designed to keep fools in check. The wise man will indulge his passions with those whom he loves quite openly and without any embarrassment. He would thus develop arguments such as this: 'Is a woman who is expert in grammar useful in so far as she is expert in grammar?' 'Yes.' 'And a boy or youth who is expert in grammar useful in so far as he is expert in grammar?' 'Yes.' 'And again, is a woman who is beautiful useful in so far as she is beautiful, and a boy or youth who is beautiful useful in so far as he is beautiful?'

'Yes.' 'And a beautiful boy, then, or youth will be useful for that for which he is beautiful?' 'Yes.' 'Then he is useful for having sexual intercourse with.' And when this was conceded, he concluded, 'So if someone engages in intercourse in so far as that is useful, he commits no wrong, nor does he commit any wrong by making use of beauty for that which it is useful for.' It was through such arguments based on question and answer* that he would uphold his view.

It seems that he was called 'god'.* Stilpo once questioned him as follows: 'Is it the case, Theodoros, that you are who you declare yourself to be?' 'Yes.' 'And you say that you are god?' 'Indeed.' 'Then you are god.' And when Theodoros showed himself satisfied with this, Stilpo said with a laugh, 'But on those grounds, you wretch, you could admit to being a jackdaw too and a host of other things.'

One day Theodoros was sitting beside the hierophant Eurycleides.* 'Tell me, Eurycleides,' he said, 'who are those who violate the Mysteries?' And when the hierophant replied, 'Those who reveal them to the uninitiated', Theodoros said, 'Then you yourself are violating them when you expound them to the uninitiated.' And in truth, he would hardly have escaped from being hauled in front of the court of the Areiopagos* if Demetrios of Phaleron had not come to his rescue. Amphicrates, however, in his book *About Famous Men*, claims that he was condemned to drink hemlock.* ...

It is said that when he was once walking around in Corinth with a large train of pupils, Metrocles the Cynic,* who was washing chervils, cried out to him, 'Hey, you sophist, you wouldn't need so many pupils if you'd been contented to wash vegetables!', to which Theodoros retorted, 'And if you'd learned to associate with human beings, you'd have no use for these vegetables.' As has already been mentioned, a similar story is also told of Diogenes and Aristippos.*

Such, then, was Theodoros and his teachings. He finally departed for Cyrene and lived there with Megas,* continuing to be held in high honour. When he was initially expelled from Cyrene,* he is said to have made this witty remark, 'This is an excellent thing that you're doing, men of Cyrene, to drive me out of Libya into Greece!'

(Diogenes Laertius 2.97–101; G IV H 13)

Theodoros at the Court of Lysimachos

634 While he was staying at the court of Ptolemy, son of Lagos,* the king once sent him to Lysimachos* as an ambassador. He expressed himself with such boldness on this occasion that Lysimachos asked him, 'Tell me, Theodoros, wasn't it you who was expelled from Athens?', to which he replied, 'Yes, because the city of Athens was no more able to bear me than Semele was able to bear Dionysos,* and cast me out.' And when Lysimachos then said, 'Take care that you never come back to us again', he replied, 'I shan't, unless Ptolemy sends me.' Mithras, the treasurer of Lysimachos, who was present at the meeting, remarked, 'So it seems that it is not only gods whom you refuse to recognize, but kings also.' 'And how could it be the case', replied Theodoros, 'that I do not recognize the gods, when I consider you to be hateful to the gods?'*

(Diogenes Laertius 2.102–3; G IV H 13)

635 When Theodoros, known as the Atheist, had been banished from Athens, so the story goes, and had taken refuge at the court of Lysimachos, one of the officials there reproached him for his banishment, mentioning at the same time why this had come about, because he had been condemned for atheism and the corrupting of the young, to which he replied, 'I have not been banished, but have suffered the same fate as was also suffered by Heracles, son of Zeus. For when he was put off the ship by the Argonauts,* it was not because he had done anything wrong, but because he was weighing down the ship, being as heavy on his own as an entire crew and cargo, and so caused his fellow-travellers to fear that the ship might founder. And so I too have had to change my home, because the citizens of Athens were unable to measure up to the loftiness and greatness of my mind, and I thus fell prey to their envy.' When Lysimachos then went on to ask, 'Weren't you banished from your native land through envy?', he replied, 'Not through envy, but because the superiority of my nature was such that my country could not contain it; for as when Semele was pregnant with Dionysos and was unable to bear him for the complete term, Zeus, overcome by anxiety, drew the unborn child from her belly before the full term, and appointed the child to be of equal rank with the heavenly deities; and so it was with me too, since my country was too small to bear the huge burden of my philosophical genius, some divine spirit or god decided to remove me and set me down in Athens.'

(Philo, *That Every Good Man is Free* 127–30; G9)

636a When Lysimachos threatened to have him crucified, he replied,
'If you are to make such horrible threats, do please address them to
your courtiers; for it makes no difference to Theodoros whether he
rots in the ground or in the air above.'*

(Cicero, *Tusculan Disputations* 1.43.102; G IV H 8)

636b When a tyrant threatened to have him killed and then left unburied, the philosopher Theodoros replied, 'Do as you please, you
have a half-pint of blood in your power; as for the burial, how foolish
you are if you suppose that it matters a whit to me whether I rot above
the ground or beneath it.'

(Seneca, *On Tranquillity of Mind* 14.3; G IV He 8)

637 It would be absurd to contend that Theodoros lost his freedom
of speech [because of his exile], that man who, when King Lysimachos said to him, 'So your country has cast out a man such as you',
replied to him, 'Yes, because I was too much for it to bear, just as
Dionysos was too much for Semele.' And when the king showed him
Telesphoros* shut up in a cage with his eyes gouged out, and said
to him, 'That's how I treat those who injure me', he replied, 'And
what does it matter to Theodoros whether he rots above the ground
or beneath it?'

(Plutarch, *On Exile* 16, 606b; G IV H 9)

638a When threatened with death by Lysimachos, Theodoros replied, 'What a truly amazing feat, to have acquired the power of a
poisonous fly!'*

(Cicero, *Tusculan Disputations* 5.40.117; G IV H 7)

638b When Theodoros of Cyrene had once spoken with excessive
boldness to Lysimachos, and the king threatened him with death, he
replied, 'Aren't you ashamed, Lysimachos, great king that you are, to
threaten those who are just, when unable to vanquish them, with what
a poisonous fly can achieve?'

(*Gnomologium Vaticanum* 352; G IV H 7)

638c When King Lysimachos threatened to have him killed,

Theodoros said, 'I'd failed to realize that it isn't the power of a king that you have, but that of a draught of hemlock.'

(Stobaeus 3.2.32; G IV H 7)

639 Theodoros of Cyrene said that there can never be any sufficient pretext to justify the wise man in taking his own life; and accordingly he posed this question: to disdain human misfortunes, and to feel oneself driven by them to take one's own life, how can that not conflict with the position of one who has said that only the noble is good, and only the shameful is bad?

(Stobaeus 4.52.16; G IV H 26)

640 This son of Phocion,* [Phocos] so they say, turned out to be a thoroughly worthless man, and conceived a passion for a girl who lived in a brothel. He happened to be present while Theodoros was putting forward this argument in the Lyceum: 'If there is nothing wrong in ransoming a male friend, the same is true with regard to a female friend; and if there is nothing wrong with ransoming a male companion, the same is true of a companion woman';* and so assuming that this argument held good in relation to his own situation, he paid for the deliverance of his prostitute companion.

(Plutarch, *Life of Phocion* 38.3; G IV H 6)

PART 3
APOCRYPHAL LETTERS

XXI · SELECTIONS FROM THE CYNIC LETTERS

Antisthenes Shows Diogenes the Short Cut to Virtue and Happiness

641 *Diogenes 30, to Hiketes**

I have come to Athens, father, and when I heard that a pupil of Socrates* was teaching about how to achieve happiness, I went to visit him. He happened to be delivering a discourse at the time about the two paths that lead to happiness,* and said that there are only two such paths, not many, and that one is short and the other long. So everyone can choose which he would prefer to travel along. On hearing these words, I remained silent for the present, but when we returned to him on the following day and he spoke again about the two paths, I asked him to show them to us. And he stood up quite willingly from his seat and led us into town,* and then straight through it until we were by the Acropolis. Once we were close by, he pointed to two paths leading up it, one of them short, but steep and difficult, the other long, but gentle and easy. 'Those are the two paths', he said, 'that lead up to the Acropolis, and the paths that lead to happiness are of the same character. So each of you must choose which you prefer to follow, and I will guide you on your way.' Being frightened of the short path because it was so difficult and steep, the others shrank from taking it and asked him to guide them up by the long and easy route; but I did not allow myself to be intimidated by the difficulties and chose the steep and difficult path; for when it comes to striving for happiness, one must be ready to pass even through fire and swords.

Once I had chosen this path, he stripped me of my tunic and robes, and dressed me in a rough cloak folded double; and he hung a knapsack around my shoulders, placing some bread and oat-brew* inside along with a cup and bowl, and attaching an oil-flask and scraper to the outside; and he also gave me a staff. When I had been provided with this equipment,* I asked him why he had dressed me in the double cloak. He replied, 'So that you may be able to protect yourself against the heat of summer and cold of winter.' I then asked, 'But wouldn't a single cloak suffice for that?', to which he replied, 'By no means, for although it would be a relief for you in the summer, it would ensure more misery for you in the winter than a man can endure.' 'And why have you hung the knapsack around me?' 'So that you may be able to carry your home around with you wherever you go.' 'And why did you place the cup and bowl inside?' 'Because you will need to drink and eat; and other food moreover when you have no cress.' 'And why did you attach the oil-flask and scraper?' 'The one to help you in your exertions, the other to clear away the oil and dirt.'* 'And why the staff?' I asked. To ensure your safety,' he replied. 'How do you mean?' 'Why, you must use it as the gods have used it, to belabour scoundrels.'*

On the Cynic Name and Way of Life

642 *Diogenes 7, to Hiketes*

Do not be distressed, father, that I am called a dog, and that I wear a doubled cloak, and carry a knapsack over my shoulders and a staff in my hand. For there is no point in getting upset over such things, when you should instead be pleased that your son is satisfied with little, and is free from the false opinions to which all people, Greeks and foreigners alike, are enslaved. The name of dog, moreover, quite apart from the fact that it is not meant literally but should be interpreted symbolically, is a quite honourable one; for I am called a dog of heaven,* because I liken myself to that, by living in accordance not with mere opinion but with nature, free under Zeus, measuring what is right by him rather than by my fellow-men. Homer writes, furthermore, that Odysseus, the wisest of the Greeks, wore such clothing on Athene's orders while returning home from Troy; so this is accordingly an honourable form of dress, since it is generally acknowledged to have been an invention not of human beings but of the gods.

> *First she gave him a cloak, tunic, and other clothing,*
> *Pitiful and dirty, begrimed with filthy smoke,*
> *Then she slung around him a large hide of a swift deer,*
> *Shorn of hair, and gave him a staff and miserable knapsack.**

So you should be reassured, father, about the name by which they call us, and about our clothing, since the one is pleasing to the gods, and the other is the invention of a goddess.

643 *Diogenes 12, to Crates*

On hearing that there is a short cut that leads to happiness, most people hurry forth, just like ourselves, to pursue philosophy; but when they set foot on the path and see how rough and difficult it is, they draw back as though overcome by weakness, and then put the blame not on their own feebleness, but on our insensitivity to hardship. So let them sink down into their pleasures in accordance with their intention; but if they live in such a way, they will fall victim not only to the same hardships which they criticize us for, but worse still, for they will become shamefully enslaved to every circumstance. But as for you, you should persist in your training as you have begun it, and make every effort to contend against pleasure and hardship in equal measure; for it is proper for us to make war against both of these equally, the one because it leads to shameful actions, the other because it diverts us from noble actions through fear.

644 *Diogenes 26, to Crates*

Remember that I have given you poverty as the principle that should govern your entire life, and therefore endeavour neither to lay that principle aside of your own accord, nor to allow it to be taken away from you by anyone else. For it is not improbable that the Thebans will surround you again* and accuse you of being unhappy. But you for your part should regard your rough cloak as a lion's skin, and your stick as a club, and your knapsack as being the land and sea from which you gain your sustenance; for in that way the spirit of Heracles should rise up within you, giving you the power to rise above every adversity. Now if you have any lupin seeds or dried figs left over, be sure to send some to me.

645 *Diogenes 10, to Metrocles*

You should feel confident, Metrocles, not only about your clothing, name, and way of life, but also about begging from people for what you need to support yourself, for there is nothing shameful in that. Kings and potentates ask their subjects too for money, soldiers, ships, and food; and those who are unwell ask their doctors for remedies, not only against fever but also against cold and hunger; and lovers ask their favourites for kisses and caresses, and they say that Heracles even took on strength from the unfeeling. Now it is not for mere charity that you are begging, or to be given something in exchange for something of lesser value; no, for the salvation of all, you are asking for what nature requires, to enable you to do the same things as Heracles,* son of Zeus, and so give back in exchange something much more valuable than what you receive. And what may that be? That in doing this, you are battling not against truth but against false opinion, which you should fight against everywhere, even when nothing is pressing you to do so; for to make war against such things is the sign of a noble disposition. Socrates used to say that the wise do not beg but ask for what is theirs;* for everything belongs to them as it does to the gods. And this he would attempt to establish on these grounds,* that the gods are masters of all, that friends hold all things in common, and the sage is a friend of god. So you will simply be asking for what already belongs to you.

646 *Diogenes 44, to Metrocles*

It is not only bread and water, and a bed of straw, and a rough cloak, that teach temperance and hardiness, but also, if I may use the expression, the shepherd's hand.* If only I had been able to make that known to Paris, who was once a cattle-herd.* So you should adopt that practice too, wherever you are hurrying to, since it accords with our way of life. As for intemperate intercourse with women, which takes up so much free time, you may bid that farewell. For one who is hastening along the short cut to happiness, dalliance with women brings no benefit; and for many ordinary men too, such activity brings its penalty likewise. But you for your part will take your place among those who have learned from Pan* to make use of your hand; and do not draw back even if some call you a dog, or something still worse, for having adopted this way of life.

Diogenes Visits Olympia and Confronts an Athlete

647 *Diogenes 38, to an unrecorded recipient*

After the games were concluded, you left Olympia and travelled away; but since I am exceptionally fond of sightseeing, I stayed behind to watch the rest of the festival. I hung around in the central precinct, along with the rest of the crowd, and as I wandered back and forth, I looked now at the people who were offering things for sale, and now at those who were giving poetic recitals, or at the philosophers, or at the diviners. At one point, as someone was holding forth about the nature and power of the sun, and was winning everyone over, I stepped forward among the crowd and asked, 'How many days is it then, Mr Philosopher, since you came down from the sky?'; but he was unable to offer me any response. All the bystanders deserted him and went their various ways, so now finding himself left all alone, he gathered up his charts of the heavens and put them into his box.

After that I went up to a diviner. He was sitting in the middle of a crowd, and was more splendidly wreathed than Apollo himself, the inventor of the diviner's art. So I stepped forward and put a question to him: 'Now are you a very good prophet or a bad one?' And when he replied, very good, I held up my stick and asked, 'Well then, what am I going to do? Will I hit you or not?' He pondered the matter for a moment and said, 'You won't.' Whereupon I struck him, laughing as I did so, while the bystanders cried out in shock. 'Why did you cry out like that?' I said. 'Since he was all too clearly a bad prophet, he was beaten.'*

As the bystanders deserted this man too and went away, other people in the market-place, on hearing of this episode, also dispersed from where they had been gathered and followed me from that time forth. While accompanying me, they often heard me talking about hardiness and endurance, and were often in a position to observe me exercising such endurance and living in such a manner. As a result, some brought me money, and others items that could be sold for money, while many also invited me to meals. From people of worth I accepted as much as was necessary to satisfy my natural needs, but from worthless people I accepted nothing at all; and if people were duly grateful* to me for accepting on the first occasion, I accepted from them again, but from those who showed no gratitude I accepted nothing more. I applied the same test to those who wanted to give me foodstuffs, accepting it from those who would gain some benefit but taking nothing from the rest, since I thought it improper to take anything from anyone who would receive nothing in return.

Nor did I eat with everyone who invited me, but only with those who were in need of my care, namely those who imitated the King of the Persians in their way of life. And when I once went to visit the house of a young man* who was the son of very wealthy parents, I was invited to recline in a room which was adorned throughout with paintings and gilding, so that there was no place at all where one could spit. When I wanted to clear my throat, I thus looked all around, and being unable to find anywhere to spit, I spat on the young man himself. When he reproached me for this, I replied, 'Well Sir'— addressing him by his name—'do you blame me for what happened rather than yourself, when you have so adorned the walls and floors of the room, leaving yourself alone unadorned as the only suitable place for me to spit on?' He replied, 'It seems that you are alluding to my lack of education, but you won't be able to say that ever again, since I'll not allow you to leave me behind by even a single step.' And so from the next day, after distributing his property among his relations, he took up a knapsack, doubled his cloak, and followed me. Such were my deeds in Olympia after you left.

648 *Diogenes 31, to Phainylas*

I was travelling to Olympia after the end of the games, and on the day after, the pancratiast Cicermos* met me on the way. He was wearing an Olympic crown on his head, and was being accompanied home by a large crowd of his friends. I took him by the hand and said, 'My poor friend, you really ought to spare yourself all this misery, and free yourself from the delusion that brings you back from Olympia in such a state that you are no longer recognizable to your own parents. Tell me now,' I continued, 'what reason do you have to be so proud, so that you are wearing this crown, carrying this palm branch,* and are dragging such a crowd of people behind you?' 'It is because I have been victorious over everyone else in the pancration at Olympia.' 'Oh how amazing,' I exclaimed, 'over Zeus too and his brother?' 'Not over them.' 'But you challenged all the other competitors one after another?' He again said no. 'So presumably you have fought against the various opponents who were assigned to you by lot?'* 'To be sure.' 'Then how can you be so bold as to say that you would have defeated those who were eliminated by other competitors? Well then? And was it only men who were competing in the pancration at Olympia?' 'There were boys too,' he said. 'And you defeated those, true man that you are?' 'No, because they weren't in my class.' 'Then you defeated everyone who was drawn against you in your own class?' 'Indeed.' 'Tell me now,' I said, 'wasn't your class that of the adults?' 'To be sure.' 'And what class was Cicermos competing in?' 'You mean me? Among the adults.' 'So did you defeat Cicermos?'* 'Of course I didn't,' he replied. 'So you have neither defeated the boys, nor all of the adults, and yet you are so bold as to claim that you were victor over all? And who', I asked, 'did you have for your opponents?' 'The foremost men of Greece and Asia.' 'And were they stronger than you, or much the same, or weaker?' 'Stronger.' 'You say that they were stronger, and yet they were defeated by you?' 'They were of the same strength.' 'And how could you defeat people of equivalent strength unless they were weaker than you? Or are you the only person who is capable of doing that? Well? In point of fact, there is no one who doesn't prevail over people of inferior strength. You should say farewell, then, to all of this, Cicermos, and no longer compete in the pancration, or against men to whom you will be inferior before long, when you arrive at old age. You should turn instead to things of true value, and learn to practise endurance, not under the blows of puny men, but under those of fate, and not under the blows that come from leather thongs and fists,* but under those of poverty, of disrepute, of low birth, of exile. For when you have trained yourself to think light of these things, you will live a happy life and meet a tolerable death; but if you pursue them, you will live in misery.' As I explained these things to him, he threw his palm branch to the ground, pulled the crown from his head, and had the strength to call off his journey.*

Diogenes Meets a King and an Ex-Tyrant

649 *Diogenes 33, to Phanomachos*

I was sitting in the courtyard* sticking pieces of papyrus together, when Alexander, son of Philip, came up and stood directly in front of me, cutting off my sunlight. Being no longer able to see the joins of the sheets, I looked up, and then recognized who it was. On recognizing me in my turn as I glanced up, he greeted me and offered me his right hand. So I returned his greeting and addressed him as follows: 'You truly are invincible, young man, seeing that you are able to achieve the same things as gods; for look, just as the moon is said to eclipse the sun when it gets in front of it, you too have achieved that here when you came in and stood beside me.' Alexander exclaimed, 'You'll have your joke, Diogenes', to which I replied, 'How do you mean? Can't you see that I'm unable to get on with my work because I can't see, as though it were night? And although I have no interest in talking with you now, I am actually talking with you.' 'So King Alexander holds no interest for you?' 'None at all,' I replied, 'since his wars do not affect anything of mine, nor am I being plundered, as are the Macedonians and Spartans, and others too who serve a king.' 'But I could be of interest to you because of your poverty.' 'What poverty?' I asked. 'That poverty of yours', he said, 'which makes you have to beg for all your needs.' 'Poverty does not rest', I replied, 'in having no money, nor is begging a bad thing, but real poverty lies in desiring everything, as is the case with you, and violently too. Thus the springs and the earth help me out in my poverty, as do even caves and goat-hides too, and no one makes war against me on account of it, either on the land or sea; but as I was born, mark it well, so also do I live. But for your position neither the earth nor sea is found to be an ally. . . . You try to climb up to heaven, paying no heed to Homer when he warns us not to strive for that, and describes the sufferings of the Aloadai* to teach us to live within our proper limits.'

As I was making all these points in a most inspired tone, Alexander was overcome with great awe, and leaning toward one of his companions, he said, 'If I had not been born as Alexander, I would have been Diogenes.' He then asked me to get up and tried to take me away with him, urging me to accompany him on his campaigns; and it was only with reluctance that he let me go.

650 *Diogenes 8, to Eugnesios*

I arrived in Corinth from Megara, and as I was walking through the market-place, I found myself by a children's school. Since the children were reciting their verses in a pitiful manner, it occurred to me to ask who their teacher was, and they replied: Dionysios, the tyrant of Syracuse.* Thinking that they were teasing me and had not given an honest reply, I came forward, sat down on a bench, and quietly awaited his return; for I was told that he had gone out shopping. Before long, Dionysios duly returned, and I greeted him, adding, 'A pity that you're teaching,* Dionysios.' Supposing that I was sympathizing with him for having fallen from his tyrant's throne and being obliged to live in these circumstances, he said, 'It's good of you to commiserate with me in my misfortunes, Diogenes', to which I retorted, 'I meant what I said, but what upsets me is not that you should have been deprived of your tyrannical power, Dionysios, but that you are now living as a free man here in Greece, and have escaped with your life from the troubles in Sicily, in which you deserve to have died after having brought such dreadful things to pass on land and sea.'

Two Letters of Misanthropic Tone

651 *Diogenes to Zeno*

One should neither marry nor rear children, since our race is weak, and marriage and children burden human weakness with many a trouble. Those who embark upon marriage and child-rearing with a view to ensuring their support in the future do in fact repent of their decision later, when they come to realize that they are only incurring additional hardships, ones that they could have avoided from the beginning. One who has risen above human passions, however, considers that what he possesses in himself is sufficient to enable him to win through, and so avoids all thought of marriage and the rearing of children. 'But all human life on the earth would then die out! So how', you will ask, 'will we have anyone to succeed us?' If only stupidity would vanish from the earth and everyone were to become wise! But for now, it would seem, only such as are persuaded by us will leave no succession, while people in general will remain unconvinced and contrive to have children. But even if the human race were to disappear, would that be any greater cause for lament than if the procreation of flies and wasps were to come to a stop? For this is the manner of speech of people who have not observed the true nature of things.

(*Cynic Letters*, 47)

652 *28, Diogenes the Dog to the so-called Greeks, a plague on you*

This is how it stands with you, even if I should not say it: you may have the appearance of human beings, but in your souls you are apes.

There is no limit to your pretences, but you understand nothing. Nature punishes you accordingly, for in devising laws for yourselves, you have incurred the greatest and most severe delusion through them, and take them as witnesses to the evil that dwells within you. Never are you at peace, but pass the whole of your lives at war until old age, since you are bad and friends to the bad, and envy one another as soon as you see that someone has a slightly softer cloak, or a little more money in his purse, or a sharper turn of expression, or a superior education. Never do you judge anything according to sound reason, but fall back into relying on what is plausible, superficially convincing, and commonly accepted, and find fault with everything; but in fact you know nothing, just as was the case with your ancestors before you, but are duped by ignorance and foolishness, and suffer torment, and rightly so. It is not only the Dog who hates you, but also nature herself, for rarely do you have any occasion for joy, but much for distress, both before and after your wedding-day, for you are already corrupted and disaffected by the time that you marry.

How many men, and ones of note too, have you killed, some in wartime out of greed, and others in what passes for peacetime, through charges that you have brought against them in the courts? And have not many been hung on crosses, and many been slaughtered by public executioners, and others made to drink poison at the orders of the state, and others again tied to the wheel, plainly because you held them to be criminals? Would it not be better, you poor fools, to attempt to educate such people rather than to execute them? For corpses are of no use whatever to us, unless we are to eat them like the meat from sacrificial beasts, but we have every need of good men, you fools! You educate the illiterate and uncultivated by teaching them their letters and the so-called arts, so as to have them at your disposal whenever you may have need of them; so why do you not also educate the unjust so as to make use of them when you have need of just men? Presumably because you also have need of unjust men when you want to gain control of a city or army through surreptitious means. And this is not yet the worst of it. Whenever you set out to achieve good things through force, one can see that what is better too suffers in the process, and whomsoever you lay your hands upon, you fools, you ill-treat and chastise, even though it is you yourselves who deserve the greater punishment. And at the gymnasia, when the so-called festival of Hermes* is celebrated, you eat and drink, become intoxicated, and have intercourse with men and women alike, doing all of this both in secret and openly. The Dog cares nothing for any of these things, but you are eager for them all.

And when you hinder the Cynics from following a natural and true way of life, how should you not be offending against them? While I for my part, as a Cynic, chastise you with my words, nature punishes all of you likewise in very deed; for death, which you so fear, hangs over you one and all. Now I have often seen beggars who enjoy good health because of their privations, and rich people who are ill because of the incontinence of their accursed stomach and sexual organs. For in so far as you indulge these passions, you enjoy the titillations of pleasure for a short while, but these then occasion great and grievous pains. And then you will gain no benefit from your house or its columns with their fine capitals, but will be stretched out on your gold and silver couches suffering torture, and rightly so. Nor will you be able to summon up enough strength to swallow down the remains of your delicacies with their seasonings, you who are bad and friends to the bad. But if you have any sense, hearken one and all to the wise Socrates and to me, from the time of your youth onwards, and either learn self-control or hang yourselves. For there is no other way in which you can live, unless you want to pass through your life as though in a drinking-party until, after drinking too much and becoming wildly intoxicated, you are overcome by vertigo and colic, and have to be carried away by others, no longer being capable of coming to your own aid. While you are living a riotous life, and are revelling in the thought of the great things that you supposedly have at your beck and call, there arrive the public executioners whom you call doctors; and whatever enters their mind, that they will say and do. Setting to work in the proper manner, they cut and cauterize and bind, and apply their remedies both inside and outside the body. And should you regain your health, you offer no thanks to the so-called doctors, but say that one should offer up thanks to the gods; and if you fail to recover, you blame the doctors.

For my part, however, more joy than sorrow falls to my share, and more knowledge than ignorance. For I engaged in regular discussion with the wise Antisthenes, who would talk only to those whom he knew about nature, reason, and truth, but avoided other people, having no time for beasts and children, who, as was remarked in a letter,* cannot understand the words of a Cynic. Barbarians that you are,

I call a plague upon you, until, instead of merely speaking the Greek language, you also become true Greeks. For at present the so-called barbarians have much better taste with regard to both the place and the manner in which they live, and those who call themselves Greeks are waging war against the barbarians,* while the barbarians simply think it necessary to protect their own home, being contented with what they have. But nothing is ever enough for you, since you are greedy for glory, and devoid of reason, and good for nothing at all.

On Death and Burial

653 *Diogenes 25, to Hippon*

You have asked me to write to you about what I have come to think about death and burial, as though you could not become a fully accomplished philosopher unless you had first learned from me even about what lies beyond this life. For my part, though, I regard it as sufficient to live virtuously in accordance with nature, and that is something that lies within our power. Just as events before our birth have been left in the hands of nature, so likewise that which follows after our life should be entrusted to her, for what she has once brought into being so also will she dissolve. And do not be worried that I am unaware of what happens next. I have arranged in any case that a stick should be laid down beside me after I have breathed my last, so that I may be able to drive off any beasts that might cause me any harm.*

Three Letters from Crates

654 *Crates 34, to Metrocles*

You can be assured that I was most distressed to hear that Diogenes had fallen into the hands of pirates, and if it were not for the fact that one of the captives was ransomed and came to Athens, my feelings would still have been the same at the present moment. But as it is, this man arrived and cured me of my distress, by telling me that Diogenes bore the calamity with such an easy mind that, when the pirates were neglecting our people, he once went so far as to say to them, 'Look here, what are you up to? If you were taking pigs to market, you would take proper care of them, so they would bring you more profit when sold; but when it comes to us, whom you intend to sell like pigs, you fail to take proper care of us. Or do you not suppose that we too will fetch a higher price for you if we look plump, and less if we are skinny? Or do you think that because human beings are not eaten, there is no need to look after them in the same way? No, you should be well aware that everyone who is buying a slave looks to this one point alone, whether their body is well filled out and of good size. And I can tell you the reason moreover, it is because they buy a human being too to make use of his body and not of his mind.' And from then onwards, the pirates no longer neglected us, and we were duly grateful to Diogenes.

When we arrived at a city where the pirates would be able to make some small profit from us, they conducted us to the market-place, where we stood and wept. Diogenes for his part took out some bread to eat, and offered some to us. When we declined to accept it, he said, '*Even Niobe with the beautiful hair remembered to eat*';* and after citing this verse jokingly and with a laugh, he continued, 'Do please stop putting on such a display and weeping because you are about to become slaves, as if it were the case that, before you fell into the hands of the pirates, you really were free and not in fact slaves, and to bad masters moreover.* Now, perhaps, you will fall into the hands of good masters, who will rid you of the luxury that has so corrupted you and install endurance and self-control instead, those most precious goods.' As he was saying this, the buyers who were standing around listened to his words and marvelled at his composure. When some asked whether he had any special knowledge, he replied that he knew how to govern men, 'so if there is anyone among you who needs a master, let him step forward and reach an agreement with the sellers'; and when they laughed at him and said, 'Who is there, who as a free man himself, stands in need of a master?', he replied, 'All who are of bad character, who value pleasure and hold all effort in scorn, the attitudes that most incite us to vice.' As a result of what he said, people contended to buy Diogenes; he was not sold, however, but the pirates drew him down from the block, took him home with them, and promised him his freedom* if he would show them some of the things that he claimed to know when he was put up for sale.

As a consequence [of what this man told me], I did not return home to procure the ransom-money, nor am I writing to ask you to provide it. Rather, you too should rejoice that Diogenes is still alive even though he was captured by pirates, and that things have come to pass that would seem incredible to most people.

655 *Crates 20, to Metrocles*

After you left us to go home, I went down to the young men's wrestling-school, and after having oiled myself, began to run. On catching sight of me, the young men burst out laughing, but not wanting to break off my exercises too early, I urged myself on with the words, 'Come on, you are toiling for the good of your eyes, of your head, of your ears, of your feet'; and when the young men overheard what I was saying, they stopped laughing and followed my example, beginning to run in their turn. From that time onward, they did not merely rub themselves with oil, but actually started to take some exercise, and thus did not live lives that rendered them liable to illness as before. So they felt grateful to me, as being responsible for their improved health, and would not leave me, but followed me around wherever I went, listening to what I had to say, and imitating my words and actions. I have written this letter to you so that you too should not go running on your own, but rather in places that are frequented by young people, since we ought to devote some care to them, in view of the fact that hardiness can be taught more quickly through deeds than words, this being a feature peculiar to the philosophy of Diogenes.

656 *Crates 6, to his friends*

You should practise philosophy more often than you breathe, since to live well, which is what philosophy brings about, is to be valued above the mere life that is supported by your breathing; and you should practise philosophy not as everyone else does, but according to the pattern introduced by Antisthenes and perfected by Diogenes. If this form of philosophy may be a difficult one, it also provides a shorter route. To reach happiness, as Diogenes used to say, one should be ready even to pass through fire.

Letters from Crates and Diogenes to Hipparchia

657 *Diogenes 3, to Hipparchia*

I admire you for the eagerness with which, woman though you are, you have aspired to philosophy, and for having become, moreover, a member of our particular school, which even men have shied away from because of the harsh demands that it makes. But having embarked upon this course, make sure that you also carry it through to a proper conclusion. And you will achieve this, I am confident, if you do not fall behind your husband Crates, and if you write regularly to me, your benefactor in philosophy.

658 *Diogenes 43, to the citizens of Maroneia*

You have done well to change the name of your city, so as to call it Hipparchia, as at present, instead of Maroneia; for it is better for you to be named after Hipparchia, a woman to be sure but a philosopher, than after Maron, a man who was a wine-seller.*

659 *Crates 1, to Hipparchia*

Return with all speed, you will still be able to catch Diogenes alive (for he is coming near the end of his life, yesterday indeed he almost died), so that you may be able to offer him your final greeting, and learn how much philosophy can achieve, even in the most frightening circumstances.

660 *Crates 28, to Hipparchia*

Women are not inferior by nature to men. The Amazons, for instance, who accomplished such great deeds, fell in no way short of men; so if you bear this in mind, you should not fail to be their equal. For you could hardly persuade me that you are becoming enfeebled at home.* How shameful it would be if, having shared the Cynic way of life up until now, and having gained renown for your choice of husband and scorn of wealth, you were now to change your mind and turn back when you are half-way along the path.

661 *Crates 29, to Hipparchia*

It is not because we are indifferent about everything that our philosophy is called Cynic, but because we perseveringly endure what others, because of their weakness or false opinions, find it beyond their power to bear; and it is for that reason rather than the former that we have come to be called dogs. So stand firm and continue to share the Cynic life with us (for you are by no way inferior to us by nature, any more than female dogs are inferior to male ones), so that you may succeed in freeing yourself from nature too as from custom, to which all are enslaved because of their baseness.

662 *Crates 31, to Hipparchia*

Reason is the guide of the soul, a noble thing and the greatest good for human beings. So seek to acquire it by whatever means possible. For then you will assure yourself of a happy life and gain a precious possession. Seek out wise men, even if you have to travel to the ends of the earth.

663 *Crates 30, to Hipparchia*

The tunic that you wove for me I have sent back to you, because it is not permissible for those who live a life of hardship to wear such clothes, and so that I may induce you to put aside such work, which you have embarked on with great zeal so as to gain a reputation with the public of being a woman who cherishes her husband. Now if I had married you for such reasons, you would be doing very well to give me such proofs of your affection; but if I did so for the sake of philosophy, to which you aspire likewise, you should bid farewell to such occupations, and try to be of benefit to humanity by helping people to improve their lives; for that is what you have learned both from me and from Diogenes.

664 *Crates 32, to Hipparchia*

Some people have arrived from you bringing me a new tunic,* which you have made for me, so they tell me, so that I may have it to protect me against the cold of winter. While I must commend you for the care that you have shown for me, I must reproach you, however, for still behaving like an ordinary woman, rather than following the philosophic life to which I have exhorted you. So come back at last, if you really care for me, and do not pride yourself on things such as this; rather, you should endeavour to achieve those things for whose sake you wanted to marry me, leaving the spinning of wool, which is of minor benefit, to those women who have not aspired to the same things as you have.

665 *Crates 33, to Hipparchia*

I have just learned that you have given birth* and had an easy delivery; for you told me nothing about this. Thanks be to god and to you. You are convinced, I presume, that taking pain saves one from suffering pain, for you would surely not have given birth with such ease unless, during your pregnancy, you had toiled like an athlete. Now most women, when they are pregnant, sink back into a life of ease, with the result that, when they give birth, their children, if they survive, remain sickly. If what had to happen has duly come to pass, make sure that you take good care of this little pup of ours. Let his bathwater be cold, his swaddling-clothes a rough cloak, and his food be milk, but not too much of it. You should rock him to sleep in a tortoise shell, for that, so they say, serves to protect against the diseases of childhood. When the child is able to speak and walk, you should fit him out, not with a sword, such as Aithra gave to Theseus,* but with a stick and rough cloak and knapsack, which provide a surer defence for men than swords, and then send him off to Athens. As for the rest, I will make it my business to rear him as a stork* for my old age rather than a dog.

XXII · CORRESPONDENCE OF ARISTIPPOS

666 *Diogenes 32, to Aristippos**

I have heard that you have been disparaging me, and that when you are with the tyrant,* have never lost an opportunity to abuse me for my poverty, saying that you once caught me at the well washing chicory to eat with my bread.* But I wonder, my good friend, how you can venture to criticize the poverty of those who value things of true worth, especially when you have been a disciple of Socrates, who wore the same rough cloak in winter and summer and at all times whatever, and who shared it with the women, and did not acquire the seasoning for his food from the gardens and cook-shops, but from the gymnasia. But it would seem that this has escaped your mind because you spend your time at those richly laden Sicilian tables. I will not remind you of the high value that is placed on poverty, especially at Athens, nor will I try to defend myself on this point (for I do not need to refer to you in judging what is good for me, in the way that you refer to others, for it is enough for me to be sure about such matters in my own mind), but rather I will remind you about Dionysios and his happy retinue, in which you take such delight; when you are eating and drinking at sumptuous banquets—may I never have anything to do with such things!—and must constantly see some men being whipped, others being fixed to a stake, and others again taken away to the stone-quarries,* while the wives of some, the children of others, and the slaves of more, are taken away to suffer the outrages not only of one person or of the tyrant himself, but of many infamous men, and when you see yourself drinking there under constraint and having to remain, and going off and trying to get away, but finding yourself unable to escape because you are held back by your golden fetters—I remind you of all of this in return for your insults.

How much better do we live, I say, we who know how to wash chicory, but do not know how to pay court to Dionysios, than do you, who stand at the tyrant's side with your advice and hold sway over the whole of Sicily. But may it be granted to you, however much you arrogantly rail against us, to recover your good sense, so that your passions are no longer in conflict with your reason.*

667 *Aristippos 27, to his daughter Arete**

I have received the letters that you have sent to me on repeated occasions, in which you have asked me to return to Cyrene as soon as possible, saying that you have not met with good treatment from the state officials, and that your husband is not capable of administering your property, because he is so reserved and is accustomed to living far away from the turmoil of the city. I did in fact try to gain leave from Dionysios to sail away to you, but fate stood in my way, and I fell ill at Lipari.* I have found that Sonicos and his friends behaved in an exemplary manner toward me, taking excellent care of me. . . . With regard to what you wrote, wondering about what respect you could count on from the slaves who have been set free by me, who said in fact that they would never abandon Aristippos as long as they would be able to satisfy me and you, you should place entire confidence in them; for enough will be left over to them from my way of life for them not to turn to the bad. I advise you to arrange your affairs with the officials in such a way as to enable you to profit from my advice, namely that you should not foster excessive desires. For in that way you will be able to pass the days of your life with the greatest equanimity, having nothing but disdain for all that is superfluous. And in point of fact these people will not carry their wrongdoing against you so far as to leave you in real want. You still have those two gardens left to you, which will suffice even to enable you to live in some luxury; and the estate in Berenice,* even taken on its own, will not fail to provide you with what is needed for a very satisfactory way of life. I am not recommending that you should hold small things in scorn, but that you should not allow yourself to be disturbed by small matters, given that anger is out of place even with regard to major ones.

If, when I have reached my natural end, you would seek to fulfil my wishes, give young Aristippos as good an education as possible, and go to Athens and pay respect to Xanthippe and Myrto,* who have often implored me to have you initiated into the Mysteries.* So pass a pleasant life in their company, and allow the officials to do you whatever wrong they wish (for they would not carry that so far as actually to take your life). Try to live in good accord with Xanthippe and Myrto as I did with Socrates, improving yourself through their friendship; for there no show of pride has any place. If Lamprocles, son of Socrates,* who associated with me in Megara, should come to Cyrene, do your best to show him hospitality and honour him equally with your own son. If you no longer wish to rear your daughter,* because of the many troubles associated with that. . . .

Above all else, I enjoin you to take good care of little Aristippos, so that he may be worthy of us and of philosophy; for that is the true inheritance that I bequeath to you. If the state officials in Cyrene have hostile designs against all the rest, when it comes to philosophy, you have not written anything to me to suggest that anyone has taken that away from you. So you should rejoice, good lady, to be rich in this wealth that lies within your possession, and ensure that your son comes to share in it, he whom I would have wished to have as my own son. Since I will die filled with such riches, I trust in you to conduct him along that path that befits good men. Keep well and do not worry about me.

668 *Antisthenes 8, to Aristippos**

It is unworthy of a philosopher to stay at the courts of tyrants and attend Sicilian banquets, no, he should rather remain in his own country and be satisfied with simple fare. You consider, however, that the advantage of being a man of substance lies in this, in being able to amass riches and to count the most powerful men among one's friends. For all that, riches are not necessary to us, and even if they were necessary, it would not be honourable to acquire them in such a way, or to make friends with a mob of ignorant people and even tyrants. I advise you, then, to leave Syracuse and Sicily. But if, as you say, you have a great love of pleasure and attach yourself to things which are not suitable for a man of reason, you should go off to Anticyra, for you would benefit from a draught of hellebore,* which is indeed much better than the wine of Dionysios. For the wine induces grave madness, while the hellebore puts a stop to madness; and then you would be greatly improved from your present state, to the degree that health and wisdom differ from disease and madness. Keep well.

669 *Aristippos 9, to Antisthenes*

Our lot is indeed a miserable one, Antisthenes, miserable to no slight degree. And after all, how could it not be when we are living with a tyrant, and are eating and drinking extravagantly day after day, and are anointed with some of the most fragrant perfumes, and are dressed in soft robes from Tarentum? And no one will deliver me from the cruelty of Dionysios, who is holding me here as a hostage who is not lacking in renown, and as a witness, furthermore, to the discourses of Socrates, and is feeding and anointing and clothing me in the manner that I have described. It is evident that he has neither fear of divine justice nor respect for humanity to subject me to such treatment! And now matters are going from bad to worse, since he presented me with three Sicilian women* of quite exceptional beauty and a large sum of money in addition.

So you do well to be concerned about the misfortunes of others, and I for my part rejoice in the happiness that you are enjoying, so repaying you for your kindness. Put aside some dried figs to make sure you have some for the winter, and also some Cretan barley-meal; for those do indeed seem to be of greater value than riches. Wash and drink at the fountain of the Nine Springs,* and wear the same rough and filthy cloak in summer and winter alike, as befits a free man who lives in Athens as a democrat.

As for me, from the moment that I arrived in a city and island under tyrannical rule, I knew that I was fated to suffer a miserable lot there, just as you have written; and now the Syracusans cast pitying glances at me, as do the Agrigentans, Gelans, and other Sicilians who are staying in the city. As punishment for having been crazy enough to throw myself into such misfortune, I call down curses on myself, which I richly deserve. May these evils not take leave of me, given that having reached such an age and passing for wise, I have not wished to suffer from hunger and cold, and incur ill-repute, or grow a long beard. I am sending you some large white lupin seeds, so that you may have something to chew on after delivering your discourse on Heracles* to the young men; for they say that you talk and write in no mean manner about such things.

670 *Aeschines the Socratic 10, to Aristippos*

I have written to Plato too to ask him to do what he can to ensure that the Locrian youths* are saved, and I am confident that it is not out of place to ask you to do the same. You are aware of the ties of friendship that bind me to them, and know that Dionysios was mistaken to suppose that they had committed any wrong. So try to do this as soon as possible. Keep well.

671 *Aristippos 11, to Aeschines*

Those young men whom you wrote to me about, the Locrians, have been released from their imprisonment and will not die. Nor will they suffer any loss of money, even though they have come close to death. Do not say anything to Antisthenes, though, about the fact that I have saved your friends. For he does not approve of anyone including tyrants among their friends, but prefers that one should seek out barley-merchants and tavern-keepers, to see if any are selling barley-groats and wine at an honest price in Athens, or offering good thick tunics for sale when the Scironian winds* are blowing; and he prefers, moreover, to dance attendance on Simon.*

672 *Simon the cobbler 12, to Aristippos*

I hear that you have been casting scorn on our wisdom at the court of Dionysios. I admit to being a cobbler and working at that trade, and I am prepared accordingly to cut whips, if it should be necessary, to punish foolish people who think fit to wallow in luxury, contrary to all that Socrates taught. But it will be Antisthenes who brings you to order, foolish children that you are, for you have written to him making fun of our discussions. Call to mind hunger and thirst, however,

for these can achieve great things for those who are striving to be of
sound mind.

673 *Aristippos 13, to Simon*

It is not I who am making fun of you, but Phaedo, by claiming that
you have become better and wiser than Prodicos of Ceos, saying that
you have refuted him with regard to the encomium of Heracles*
that he composed. For my part I admire and praise you for the fact
that you abound with wisdom, although only a cobbler, and have
long been able to induce Socrates and the most handsome and noble
youths to sit with you in your workshop. Such men as Alcibiades, son
of Cleinias, and Phaidros, son of Myrrhinous, and Euthydemos,* son
of Glaucos, and from among men prominent in public affairs,
Epicrates the Shield-bearer* and Eurysthenes, and many another; so
no doubt even Pericles,* son of Xanthippos, if he had not been so
busy as a general fighting his wars, would have sought out your company. And now we well know what kind of a man you are since
Antisthenes is constantly at your side.

You could do well to come to Syracuse too to practise your philosophy; for whips and leatherwork are in high demand here. And are
you not aware that I, as a regular wearer of shoes, contrive to arouse
admiration everywhere for your craft, whereas Antisthenes, since he
walks barefoot, does nothing other than deprive you of work and
profit, by persuading the young men and the Athenians in general to
wear no shoes? So consider, then, how much of a friend I am to you,
I who approve of comfort and pleasure. If you profess to call Prodicos
sagaciously to account, you have failed to recognize what implica-
tions that has for you; for otherwise you would admire me, and you
would laugh at the imposture of those who wear their beards long
and carry heavy sticks, and are filthy and louse-ridden and have long
nails like wild beasts, and propound teachings that are damaging to
your trade.

EXPLANATORY NOTES

No abbreviations have been used for sources except in the case of Diogenes Laertius, who is referred to as DL; further information can be found on the ancient sources in the Note on the Ancient Sources, p. xxxi.

PART 1: DIOGENES AND THE EARLY CYNICS

1 *creature from the Black Sea*: i.e. Diogenes, who came from Sinope on the coast of the Black Sea.

Areiopagos: an ancient high court at Athens at which people were tried for serious crimes, especially homicide.

Heracles: through a selective interpretation of his mythology, Heracles was adopted as an exemplar by the Cynics, as a hero who had lived an arduous life and performed labours that had benefited the human race.

club looks like his: Diogenes and other Cynics often carried a heavy staff which could be compared to Heracles' club, and their doubled cloak was sometimes compared to his lion-skin.

throw it into the sea: this refers in particular to a story that was told about Diogenes' follower Crates, who came from a wealthy family (see 411 and 414c).

lupin seeds: the seeds or beans of the yellow lupin (*Lupinus luteus*) were eaten as a cheap food and naturally appealed to the Cynics, figuring in their anecdotes, e.g. 99.

but not your tongue: adapted from Euripides, *Hippolytus* 612; in the original, 'My tongue swore the oath, but my mind remained unsworn.'

octopus . . . raw and die: this was one account of Diogenes' death (see 398 and 402).

short cut to fame: since the Cynic path was a purely practical one, demanding that those who embarked on it should adopt an arduous way of life, it was often described as a short cut to virtue (see 96 and 641); it is suggested here that Diogenes is primarily interested in using it as a short cut to notoriety.

the Cyrenean: i.e. Aristippos.

degenerate and dissolute character: this is more of a caricature than the preceding portrayal of Diogenes, since Aristippos, although a hedonist, was neither dissolute—if that implies a loss of self-control and a moral decline—nor an inveterate drunkard. He was said, indeed, to have disowned his own son because of his dissolute behaviour (see 616b).

despise everything: i.e. take nothing so seriously that you would be pained if you came to be deprived of it.

2 *Sinope*: a Greek city on the south coast of the Black Sea; for the tale of
   Diogenes' exile and other biographical traditions; see further pp. xiv ff.

   Diocles: of Magnesia, probably 1st century BC, author of two books about
   philosophers; Diogenes Laertius refers to him quite frequently, although
   he was evidently not one of his main sources.

   re-stamped the currency: Diogenes used this phrase in a figurative sense to
   describe his project of rejecting conventionally accepted values in favour
   of those that are truly in accordance with nature; the idea that he had
   been exiled from his native city for adulterating the currency was probably a legend inspired by this use of language, although it is not inconceivable that there is some historical truth in the story.

   Euboulides: perhaps to be identified with the Eubolos who wrote about
   Diogenes' enslavement (see 267 and note); there was a Euboulides of
   Miletos who was a member of the Megarian school (DL 2.108 ff.), but it
   seems unlikely that he would have written a life of Diogenes.

   in his Pordalos does in fact admit: nothing else is recorded about this work,
   which has a suitably Cynic title, suggesting a connection with farting (*porde*
   meaning 'a fart', and *pordaleos* meaning 'flatulent'). The present report may
   be misleading, since that work may actually have spoken about re-stamping
   the currency in a figurative sense; one cannot assume that Diogenes
   Laertius was speaking from direct knowledge of the book. The works
   ascribed to Diogenes were of questionable authenticity: see 218 and note.

   went to Delphi: according to this story, Diogenes was acting in obedience
   to the oracle of Apollo in carrying out his project of overturning accepted
   values; he initially supposed that he was being given permission to re-
   stamp the currency in a literal sense, but only later discovered the
   'proper' (i.e. figurative) meaning of the expression. This tale was doubtless inspired by a famous story that was told about Socrates. It was said
   that Chaerephon, a close friend of his, put a leading question to the
   oracle by asking whether there was anyone wiser than Socrates, and was
   duly told that there was no one, a response which supposedly played an
   important part in prompting Socrates to embark on his philosophical
   mission (according to an account put into the mouth of Socrates himself
   in Plato's *Apology*, 21a ff.). It would thus have been tempting to imagine
   that Diogenes might have received similar divine sanction for his own
   philosophical mission. This resulting tale is no more likely to have been
   historical than the comparable one that was told about Zeno, the founder
   of Stoicism (DL 7.2); when Zeno asked the oracle what he should do to
   live the best life possible, he was told to 'take on the complexion of the
   dead', which he interpreted as meaning that he should study the writings
   of the ancients, so gaining his first impulse to philosophy.

3b *the inhospitable sea*: Euripides, *Iphigeneia in Tauris* 253. The Greeks
   referred to the Black Sea, which could be dangerous to mariners because
   of sudden storms, by the euphemistic name of the Euxine or 'Hospitable'
   Sea. It was a standing joke that it is a blessing to be exiled from some

remote and provincial places; after recounting this anecdote about Diogenes, Plutarch tells a comparable tale about the musician and wit Stratonicos; on being told by his host on the island of Seriphos that fraud was punishable there by exile, he asks, 'Then why not commit fraud to get away from this confinement?' (602ab). When detained by King Berisades in his realm by the Black Sea, Stratonicos exclaimed, 'Goodness me, you don't mean to stay here yourself?' (Athenaeus 8, 349d). Compare also the anecdote about Theodoros' exile at the end of 633.

6a *ran across Antisthenes*: an immediate follower of Socrates who favoured a moderately ascetic life (see 534); he was traditionally regarded as the master of Diogenes, whether or not that was in fact the case (see pp. xv f.).

offered his head: the tradition suggested that Antisthenes had few pupils and was harsh with them (DL 6.4), and that he would discuss his ideas at the gymnasium of Cynosarges, just outside Athens (DL 6.13; see 533 and note). He had followers nonetheless, who were known as *Antistheneioi* (Aristotle, *Metaphysics* 1043b24). This present story may have been inspired by a well-known tale about the Athenian statesman Themistocles. When Eurybiades, a Spartan naval commander, raised his stick against him during an argument, he said, 'You may hit me if you like, but you must listen to me', and Eurybiades was so impressed by his spirit that he let him have his say (Plutarch, *Life of Themistocles* 11).

9a *Theophrastos*: the successor of Aristotle as head of the Peripatetic school, c.370–c.287, a younger contemporary of Diogenes; this story of the mouse was thus in circulation at an early period and may well have been derived from something that Diogenes actually said. Theophrastos is recorded as having written a 'Compendium of Diogenes' (DL 5.43), which is more likely to have been a collection of sayings and anecdotes than of Diogenes' writings; if so, it would have been an important early source for this anecdotal material.

10 *Satyros*: Peripatetic author of biographies, 3rd to 2nd century BC.

folded his cloak double: a *tribōn* or rough cloak, which was sufficiently capacious to be cool in summer, but could be folded double for warmth in the winter; it became emblematic of the Cynic way of life.

hēmerobios: the word is quoted in Greek in this Latin text; literally living a day, and thence living on a bare sufficiency gained from day to day, in the manner described here.

his jar: in this case a very large clay jar, of the kind that was used as a water cistern.

11 *portico of Zeus . . . Pompeion*: the Stoa of Zeus Eleutherios was a large two-aisled portico in the west corner of the Agora at Athens, while the Pompeion was a handsome public building where the sacred objects for the Panathenaic procession (*pompē*) were kept.

Lysanias, son of Aischrion: presumably the grammarian Lysanias of Cyrene, one of the masters of Eratosthenes; Polyeuctos of Sphettos was an anti-Macedonian orator who was a contemporary of Demosthenes, and Olympiodoros an Athenian citizen of the same period who played a minor role in public affairs.

11 *Metroon*: the temple of the mother of the gods in the Agora at Athens.

13a *without Manes*: since Manes was a standard name for slaves in comedy, etc., this is merely a manner of speaking, and should not be taken as implying that Diogenes' slave was actually called Manes (even if Aelian makes that assumption in 13c); the story is most probably fictional in any case.

14 *citizen of the world*: *kosmopolitēs*; in addition to indicating that Diogenes regarded himself as belonging to no particular state, this response carries the deeper suggestion that he sought to live in accordance with nature rather than with the laws and customs of any state.

15a *'Without city or home ... day to day'*: a fragment from tragedy of unknown origin, fr. adesp. 284 Nauck; it has been suggested that it came from the lost *Oedipus* of Euripides, or indeed the 'tragedy' of that name ascribed to Diogenes himself. We are plainly intended to think of Oedipus first and foremost in any case, wandering abroad in a state of dispossession after his terrible secret has been revealed. This quotation is repeated in a different form in 15c.

15c *after having conquered India*: Alexander conquered nothing more than a small corner of India, of course; it heightens the symbolic contrast with Diogenes to present him as ruler of the world.

16 *obol*: a silver coin of low value; there were 6 obols to a drachma, which was roughly what a skilled workman could expect to earn in a day.

17 *'He who is self-sufficient'*: this may be compared with two sayings attributed to Socrates. 'To someone who asked who is richest, Socrates replied, "He who is satisfied with the least." For self-sufficiency is wealth by nature' (Stobaeus 3.5.31); 'When Socrates was asked how one can become wealthy, he said, "By being poor in one's desires"' (Stobaeus 3.17.30).

18 *everything belongs to the wise*: a little argument put together through the combining of two syllogisms; it can be interpreted in two senses, as implying that the wise possess all that is truly valuable (consisting in internal qualities that render them invulnerable to fortune, rather than in the possession of external goods), or in a more humorous sense, as implying the sage, as god-like, can rightfully demand material support from others.

19 *poverty aids us to philosophy of its own accord*: literally, poverty is a self-taught (*autodidaktos*) aid to philosophy, i.e. something that aids us to philosophy of its own accord without our needing external instruction. Stobaeus also records Diogenes as saying that 'poverty is self-taught virtue' (4.32.12), which comes to much the same, since the life of philosophic virtue is envisaged in the present saying. In particular, poverty helps people to achieve the crucial Cynic virtue of self-control by forcing them to be moderate in their desires. A very similar saying is ascribed to Xenophon (e.g. *Gnomologium Vaticanum* 414).

20 *words from Homer*: *Iliad* 17.179; Hector, the leading Trojan warrior, is inviting Glaucos to observe his prowess in battle.

23 *hidden from sight*: this reverses Hesiod's mythical account in which the gods hid the means to an easy life from human beings as a result of a sequence of events set in course by Prometheus, who contrived that the gods should get the worst portion at sacrifices and then stole fire for mortals (see Hesiod, *Works and Days* 42 ff.). Diogenes suggests, on the contrary, that we have in fact been granted the means to an easy life, but we have hidden it away from ourselves because we crave unnecessary luxuries. One may compare the little parable that was supposedly told to Onesicritos (see **407** and notes) by the Indian ascetic Calamos, Strabo 1.15.64.

24b *'A mina'*: a hundred drachmas; thus an extremely expensive item in relation to workmen's wages.

quart . . . copper: a *choinix* was a dry measure equivalent to something less than a quart; a *chalkos*, 'copper piece', was an eighth of an obol or forty-eighth of a drachma; a day's supply of this favourite Cynic food of lupin seeds could thus be bought at negligible expense.

28 *scroungers*: parasites; a *parasitos* is literally one who dines with another, a guest, but the term came to be applied above all to those who cadged free meals from the rich.

29 *just like everyone else*: two conflicting patterns can be observed in this series of anecdotes, **29–33**; if Diogenes is offered cakes as against bread (or white bread as against black bread), he happily accepts what comes along in some anecdotes, whereas in others he rejects the more luxurious food in favour of the simpler. This could reflect conflicting views about this matter within the Cynic tradition; or alternatively, anecdotes which portray Diogenes acting like a parasite could have been invented to poke fun at him—although he may have been quite happy to present himself humorously in that guise, just as he presents himself elsewhere as a dog who fawns on the people to wheedle gifts out of them. It looks, then, as if we are fated to remain ignorant as to whether Diogenes had any scruples about eating honey-cakes.

30 *not in the same way as everyone else*: the point seems to be that the philosopher will maintain his detachment; he will be happy to accept small luxuries like this if they come his way, but not be in thrall to any desire for them. It has been suggested, with some plausibility, that Diogenes' reply in **29** originally carried the same meaning, until a couple of words dropped out of the text. When Demonax, a Cynic from the time of the Roman Empire, was asked whether he ate honey-cakes, he replied, 'Do you suppose that bees make their honey only for fools?' (Lucian, *Life of Demonax*, 52).

32a *stand out of the pathway of kings*: Euripides, *Phoenician Women* 50; words addressed to Oedipus by the charioteer of Laios, king of Thebes, shortly before Oedipus kills Laios in the resulting fracas, not realizing that he is his father. The humour lies not only in the bathos, but also in the fact that Diogenes is rejecting a nobler food in favour of a humbler one. In the alternative version in 32b, Diogenes cites the verse when throwing out black bread in favour of white. Such incongruous application of familiar verses, especially from Homer, was a favourite form of humour among the Greeks (see the examples in 374 to 377).

32a *'He lashed it on its way'*: a Homeric phrase describing how Zeus whipped his divine chariot-horses to start them on their way, *Iliad* 8.45 (cf. 5.366).

33 *nothing unclean should enter a temple*: *rhuparos*, the adjective which was used to describe black bread made with unhusked grain, literally meant 'dirty' or 'unclean', and white bread of higher quality was described correspondingly as *katharos*, 'clean' or 'pure'; so the joke turns on the suggestion that the coarse bread should be excluded from the temple as being impure (in a religious sense).

34 *'Somebody else's'*: this is typical parasite humour: someone is asked what he considers to be the best wine, and replies, that which he can drink at someone else's expense. One may doubt that this joke was originally connected with Diogenes. As a regular and inexpensive part of people's diet in Athens, wine presented no difficulty for a Cynic if its consumption was kept within proper bounds (cf. 27), although Crates was said to have confined his drinking to water (see 417).

35 *'If you are rich . . . when you can'*: also ascribed to Bion, *Gnomologium Vaticanum* 156.

36 *Demeter and Aphrodite*: i.e. eating and sex, these being the goddesses of corn and of love respectively. Eating in the street was regarded as being very vulgar behaviour, and this was thus a more notable aspect of Cynic shamelessness than one might be inclined to suppose. Dio Chrysostom (8.36; cf. Julian, *Oration* 6, 202bc) also presents Diogenes as defecating in public, but this is not a theme that can be found in the anecdotal tradition.

regularly masturbate in public: there are two points here, that physical desires should be satisfied in the simplest and most direct manner possible, and that sex should be demystified and detached from all connection with love or refined sensuality (both of which are regarded as being a rich source of illusion). Although it could also be suggested that a man would do best to pay for the services of a cheap prostitute, 173, or that the true nature of sex and love is best revealed in a brothel (see 165 and 411), the point could be made even more effectively, and more shockingly, through the public practice of masturbation, which became one of the most notorious features of the legend of Diogenes.

37c *rub hunger out of my stomach in such a way*: the verb used here, *apotripsasthai*, literally means 'rubbing off from oneself' but could also be used in a more general sense 'to get rid of'. This report shows that this practice was an early feature of the legend of Diogenes, since it was accepted as a fact by the early Stoic philosopher Chrysippos (*c*.280–*c*.206). It is difficult to know, all the same, how seriously one should take such reports; it is possible that Diogenes merely talked about the virtues of masturbation, and it was only as a result of subsequent exaggeration that it came to be imagined that he had been in the habit of giving public demonstrations. Cf. **457–8** and note for similar developments with regard to Crates' 'dog-marriage'.

40 *bring their food to their work*: the work of Diogenes is carried out in the streets because that is where he preaches his message and seeks to set an example by his way of life; steersmen or pilots were regularly cited as a parallel for the philosopher in the Socratic tradition, since they used their knowledge to secure people's physical salvation, as a subordinate good, as against the saving of their soul, as the ultimate good.

41 *a tavern*: or wine-shop, not regarded as respectable among more refined citizens; cf. **226–7**.

42a *out of shame*: because he would be acting like a slave; all but the poorest citizens would send a slave to do the shopping, or, if they went along too, leave it to a slave to carry the purchases (and often the money too).

42b *Diocles*: see note to **2**.

43 *through the Ceramicos*: the potter's quarter, a district of Athens; Diogenes' action here seems to have no symbolic import, but simply to be a crazy action undertaken to show that we should not care what people think about us.

44 *what he was owed . . . not for charity*: in the Greek a distinction is drawn between *aitein*, begging for something, and *apaitein*, demanding something back, i.e. asking for what properly belongs to one or is owed to one.

47 *at the beginning*: implying that after he became well-known, people would supply his needs without him needing to beg, which seems plausible enough.

48 *from a statue*: statues were proverbially insensitive: cf. *Gnomologium Vaticanum* 145, 'When asked what is harder than a statue, he [Aristotle] replied, "A man without feeling" '; a symbolic action of a kind that is characteristic of Diogenes, designed to make a point or provoke a question.

52 *mina . . . obol*: there were 600 obols to a mina, which would be an absurd sum for a beggar to request.

53 *feed myself . . . funeral*: in the original there is a play on words between *trophē*, food, and *taphē*, burial.

55 *A husband and a home*: *Odyssey* 6.180–1, words addressed by Odysseus to the Phaeacian princess Nausicaa. This Diotimos is otherwise unknown.

56a *searching for a man*: lighting a lamp in daylight was a proverbially futile action; the search is fated to be a futile one because, although the streets of Athens are crowded, no one knows what it properly means to be a human being; see further p. ix. Only one who has such knowledge, and lives accordingly, can be regarded as a man and a true individual; everyone else is an anonymous member of the crowd. The word translated here as 'man' is not the one that was used to refer to men as opposed to women (the essential point is to have a knowledge of one's true nature as a *human being*, 57), but in developing the idea Diogenes does also make a specific appeal to notions of manliness, because to achieve full humanity according to the Cynic conception it is necessary to embark on an arduous, 'manly' way of life.

62 *men's quarters to the women's*: among wealthier citizens at least, there was a measure of sexual segregation in the Greek home, with the women having special quarters, the *gunaikeion*. A true 'man', in Diogenes' sense, will be more like a hard-living Spartan than an effeminate and self-indulgent Athenian. It hardly needs saying that someone like Diogenes would have received a poor reception in Sparta, where the individual was so strongly subordinated to the state, and it seems unlikely that he ever went there.

64 *race in armour*: a race over two lengths of the stadium in which the athletes would wear a helmet and greaves, and carry a shield; Diogenes would have chosen this as the time to make his proclamation because it was the final contest of the games.

66 *digging and kicking*: this is intended as a dismissive reference to athletics in general. Digging is mentioned as an exercise in the medical literature, and for athletes at the games it would have been a preparatory exercise rather than a competition as such; Epictetus refers to it in that context, 'Then, when it comes to the contest, you have to compete in digging, and sometimes dislocate your wrist, twist your ankle, swallow an abundance of dust.' As for the kicking, that is a scornful allusion to the pancration, a form of all-in wrestling in which kicking was acceptable, almost anything being permitted apart from biting and gouging. Digging could be seen as a vain activity, while kicking could be seen as animal behaviour better fitted to a donkey. The latter point is explicitly brought out in one of the speeches of Dio Chryostom (9.22), in which Dio recounts how Diogenes, while attending the Isthmian Games, once witnessed a fight between two horses that were hitched together, and after one horse had put the other to flight, went up to it and crowned it with a victor's wreath, proclaiming it to be an Isthmian victor because it had won 'in kicking'. The story was doubtless invented by Dio himself.

69a *'Dioxippos is victor over men'*: Dioxippos was a famous Athenian athlete who won an Olympic victory in the pancration in 326. Since there were men's and boys' classes, a victor in the men's class would be formally proclaimed as 'victor over men' in his specific event, giving Diogenes an opportunity to draw his own special distinction between true men and members of the slavish crowd. Although athletes provided a worthy exemplar for the Cynic in so far they submitted themselves to a life of training and hardship, they belonged to the crowd nonetheless because they did so for the sake of glory rather than the good of their soul (cf. 67 and 68).

69b *Pythian Games*: held every four years at Delphi, two years after the Olympic Games; one of the four games of the old athletic circuit, and the most venerable after the Olympic Games.

70a *customary for victorious athletes*: Olympic victors would be welcomed like victorious generals, being driven into the city in a chariot with the emblems of their victory to receive the acclamations of the crowd.

71 *set the note somewhat high*: the reason for this practice is unclear since nothing more is recorded about it, but the point of the analogy is clear enough.

74 *out of his mind*: when Diogenes is accused of being senseless or out of his mind (*anoētos*) he replies that he doesn't have the same mind (*nous*), i.e. the same way of looking at things, as his accuser. The apparently crazy behaviour that led him to be described as Socrates gone mad (134) has its own peculiar logic.

81 *suffer no insult or ridicule*: the point is that one should not be affected by insults and abuse if one does not accept the judgements on which they are founded; Diogenes regards his 'shamelessness', for instance, as a mark of honour rather than a reason for shame.

82 *donkeys laugh at them*: the mindless laughter of fools is compared to the braying of donkeys; a variation on the more frequent comparison in which assault or insult is likened to the kicking of a donkey, as by Socrates in DL 2.12 (cf. Xenophon, *Memorabilia* 2.2.7) and Diogenes himself in the Arabic tradition, to make the point that irrational behaviour deserves simply to be ignored.

87 *to save them*: he uses his biting tongue to shock them into changing over to a better way of life.

88 *Polyxenos the dialectician*: a member of the Megarian school of philosophy who is mentioned in Plato's 13th Letter, 360a, as a friend of the mathematician and sophist Bryson. The school was founded by Eucleides, a disciple of Socrates, and its members were greatly interested in logic and the art of disputation. Polyxenos is shown as being a sympathetic outsider who is upset that Diogenes is called a dog. Diogenes suggests that this is in fact his proper name, i.e. the one that best corresponds with his nature, so that the name that he received from his parents is a mere nickname by comparison; for he is a dog who watches over his friends, by concerning himself for their good (cf. his description of himself as a Molossian, a form of guard-dog, in 90). It is no accident that the language used here, in referring to the noble (*gennaios*) breed of dog, is reminiscent of that used by Plato in his examination of the characteristics of a good watch-dog in the *Republic* (e.g. 375a; see also 95 and note). Polyxenos visited the Syracusan court and figures in one of the anecdotes of Aristippos (see 556).

90 *Maltese . . . Molossian*: a Maltese (Melitaian) was a lady's lap-dog, while a Molossian was a large, hot-tempered guard-dog (cf. Aelian, *History of Animals*, 3.2); the same difference as we might draw between a poodle and a Doberman, making much the same point as in the previous saying. The Molossian could be viewed at the same time as a dog who watches over his friends, as in 88. Part of the humour of this lies in the fact that Diogenes actually begged in anything but a humble manner (see 44–6).

90 *go out hunting with*: the Molossian does not seem to have been used as a hunting-dog and the Maltese was assuredly not; two originally separate sayings (cf. **94**), have been clumsily combined here.

93a *dogs don't feed on beets*: a proverbial phrase. One should think here of the soft and succulent leaves of the beets (rather than their roots, although those were also eaten); by comparing the youths to these, Diogenes is deriding them as being soft and effeminate.

94 *none . . . dared accompany him on the hunt*: i.e. he had very few followers who dared to adopt the arduous Cynic way of life; the 'hunt' was the pursuit of happiness and virtue by the short route.

95 *as Plato recounts about the nature of dogs*: see *Republic* 375a–376c, where the qualities of good watch-dogs are examined to draw a comparison with the qualities that would be required by the guardians in Plato's ideal state. This work by Themistius has survived only in a Syriac version, and the present passage has been translated from Sachau's German translation of that; it expands on some ideas which are implicit in **87–90**.

96 *now add an account of the doctrines*: after recounting the lives of the early Cynics, Diogenes Laertius sets out to offer an account of their teachings (a doxography); Antisthenes is counted among the Cynics here.

dispense with logic and physics: the Cynics are here contrasted with the Stoics in particular, who tried to build up a coherent system in which their ethical theories were founded on a theory of knowledge and a general understanding of the nature of the world; their doctrine was thus divided into three parts, 'logic' (understood in a much broader sense than the modern term), 'physics' (the study of nature and the universe), and ethics. The Cynics thought that it was sufficient to adopt the proper arduous way of life, and that wider theoretical studies were a pointless distraction.

Ariston of Chios: a Stoic philosopher of the 3rd century BC who attached relatively little importance to the non-ethical components of Stoic doctrine. There would continue to be a Cynic strain within the Stoic movement.

Diocles ascribes to Diogenes: Diocles of Magnesia, 2nd–1st century BC; the phrasing suggests that the following saying, which refers to a line from Homer, *Odyssey* 4.392, was more generally ascribed to Socrates, and it is in fact more appropriate to him, pointing as it does to an investigation of moral matters in relation to the shared life of the community. But Socrates and Diogenes did both confine themselves to enquiring into moral matters alone.

standard subjects of study: the encyclical studies, typically grammar, rhetoric, dialectic, geometry, arithmetic, astronomy, and music, but sometimes embracing other subjects too; these could be regarded from two points of view, as providing the sort of knowledge a cultivated gentleman might be expected to possess, or as preparatory studies for philosophy. Diogenes and the Cynics took a radically negative view of them.

a clock: the Greeks would use a *gnomon* or pointer to tell the time, from the length of the shadow cast by it, but something more sophisticated is envisaged here, presumably a water-clock. Plato was supposed to have invented an alarm-clock (Athenaeus 4, 174c). Diogenes' response is a standard joke: parasites were mocked as constantly looking at the shadow on the dial to see whether dinner-time had arrived (Aristophanes, *Assembly-Women* 652, Euboulos in Athenaeus 1, 83).

whistling of flutes: the first line is from Euripides, *Antiope* fr. 205 Dindorf, while the second line was apparently improvised to make the required point.

Antisthenes says in his Heracles: i.e. his work *Heracles, or On Strength*; he used Heracles as an exemplar in a number of works to commend a strenuous way of life.

Zeno of Citium: the founder of Stoicism (see 463–6).

like the gods to need little: a thought from the early Socratic tradition which probably goes back to Socrates himself: cf. Socrates speaking to Antiphon in Xenophon, *Memorabilia*, 1.6.10, 'You seem to suppose, Antiphon, that happiness lies in luxury and extravagance, but I hold that to have want of nothing is divine, and to have want of as little as possible comes closest to the divine . . .'; the same thought is ascribed to Socrates as a saying in Stobaeus 3.5.33.

hold to be indifferent: it could be argued that certain external advantages, such as health, prosperity, and good repute, might be better to have than not to have, even if they are not unequivocally good, and should thus be classed as being naturally preferable, but the Cynics were more radical than the Stoics in this respect, holding that we should be wholly indifferent to everything apart from virtue and the moral good. Ariston was closer to the Cynics on this matter than to the orthodox Stoics.

97 *misfortunes of Odysseus . . . ignorant of their own*: i.e. failing to recognize where they have brought misfortune on themselves through ignorance of what is right and good. The interests of ancient grammarians extended far beyond grammar in the narrow sense, to embrace the study of literature and many aspects of the use of language. Since the travels of Odysseus provided a rich field of study for literary scholars, this was an obvious comparison, which is more neatly expressed in the version ascribed to Bion, 476.

what lies beneath their feet: a frequently expressed thought, most closely associated with an anecdote that was told about Thales, one of the Seven Sages (see 477 and note). The Cynics were in accord with Socrates on this matter, who thought that we should not turn aside from human concerns to study celestial phenomena, which lie beyond the range of our knowledge in any case (see e.g. Xenophon, *Memorabilia* 1.1.11–13, and Plato, *Theaetetus* 173e–174b, which refers to the Thales anecdote).

98 *festival of Dionysos*: the Great Dionysia, the spring festival of Dionsyos at

Athens, at which dramas would be performed in honour of the god. Three poets would enter four plays—three tragedies and a comical satyr-play—for a contest at each festival. Since that is how the plays of Aeschylus, Sophocles, and Euripides first came to be performed, Diogenes is deriding one of the highest manifestations of Greek culture.

99   *captured the attention of the crowd*: to eat lupins during a rhetorical display would be rather like munching potato crisps during a piano recital; part of the joke also lay in the fact that lupins, rather like baked beans, were notorious for causing flatulence (cf. **459**).

100 *snivel at my feet*: Zeus addresses these words to the war-god Ares in *Iliad* 5.498, and then goes on to criticize Ares for loving nothing other than strife, war, and battles; the sophists were particularly associated with forms of 'eristic' argument which aimed at nothing other than victory.

101 *Cheiron never taught Achilles*: the wise centaur Cheiron was supposed to have educated the young Achilles in his cave on Mount Pelion in Thessaly, especially in hunting, the use of weapons, and healing, e.g. *Iliad* 11.831–2, Pindar, *Third Nemean Ode*, 43–52. As one who lived a simple natural life and taught strenuous practical pursuits above all, Cheiron could be regarded as an exemplary educator in the Cynic tradition; the theme can be traced back to Antisthenes, who described how Heracles, an exemplar for the rigoristic Socratics, had benefited from Cheiron's instruction (Eratothenes, *Catasterisms* 40).

102 *to get down from the sky*: this would have been a hoary joke by Diogenes' time; in Old Comedy people were shown as literally making journeys into the sky.

104a *wandering stars*: the Greeks referred to the planets as the 'wandering' stars (*planētes asteres*), and the corresponding verb could be used of people who 'wandered'—i.e. went astray or were led astray—in their thoughts and ideas. This word-play cannot be expressed quite as directly in English.

105 *training*: *askēsis*, hence our term ascetic and asceticism; the Cynic life is a form of training through which one can become inured to any hardship. This is what Diogenes Laertius offers as his specific doxography for Diogenes (as against the general Cynic doxography in **96**).

     Heracles: adopted as a Cynic hero because of his strenuous life and labours on behalf of humanity.

107 *blame for all these ills*: a pseudo-Homeric verse based on *Iliad* 1.335. Diogenes is of course accusing himself in so far he is in the grip of vice.

111 *reason or a rope*: *logon . . . brochon*; one should either learn to live rightly or hang oneself. A similar saying was ascribed to Antisthenes (Plutarch, *Contradictions of the Stoics* 14, 1039e–1040a), and compare Crates' verses about love in **439**. This was plainly a commonplace.

114 *mad dog alone I cannot hit*: at *Iliad* 8.299, Teucros tells Agamemnon that the great Hector alone seems to be immune to his arrow-shots; Hector is

described as being mad in the sense of being seized with battle-frenzy. The mad dog of Athens is impervious likewise to the arrows of fortune.

117 *by an impeccable deduction that he had horns*: this refers to a well-known sophistic argument. If you have never lost something, then you still have it; now you have never lost horns; so it follows that you have horns (DL 7.187; as ascribed to the Stoic Chrysippos, or else to Euboulides).

there is no such thing as motion: some of the paradoxical arguments that were put forward in favour of this proposition were much more subtle than that of the 'horned man'. The argument of Achilles and the tortoise, ascribed to Zeno of Elea, is still widely familiar. If the tortoise is given a lead, Achilles can never overtake it, since the tortoise will have moved further on by the time that Achilles reaches its starting-point, and further on again by the time that he reaches that next point, and so forth indefinitely.

119 *the discourse of Plato as a waste of time*: there is an untranslatable play on words here, between *diatribē* and *katatribē*. *Diatribē* literally meant wearing or rubbing away, and thence the spending of time; and with regard to philosophers especially (as people with whom one spends time in serious discussion), the word also came to be applied to their discourse or lectures. *Katatribē*, as used in the second sense, was more unequivocally negative in tone, referring to the wasting of time. Now *diatribē* could also be used in that last sense, and Diogenes is thus bringing out that negative meaning in relation to Plato's discourse. For another attack against rivals based on such wordplay, see 136.

120 *two-footed animal without wings*: see Plato, *Statesman* 266e and preceding discussion; there is a strong element of humour and self-parody in that section of the dialogue, and this was plainly not intended as a rigorous definition. The specification 'with flat nails' is added in the pseudo-Platonic *Definitions*, 415a, and it was evidently the divergence between the two supposedly Platonic definitions that inspired the invention of this anecdote. It is however a memorable one, being thoroughly Diogenean in tone.

121 *his Ideas*: in relation to Plato's famous theory of 'ideas' or 'forms'; in the present context, one may think of these as being suprasensual archetypes for material objects in any particular class.

Plato . . . used the terms 'tableness' and 'cupness': Plato's use of language is caricatured here; in the *Theaeteus*, 182a, he does add the corresponding *-otēs* ending to adjectives, with due apology, to describe a general quality (thus *leukos* means white, so *leukotēs* could be used as a term for the general quality of whiteness), but there is never any reference in his writings to anything like the 'cupness' (*trapezotēs*) in this anecdote, in which the *-otēs* ending is attached to a noun describing a physical object. It seems likely that it was in fact Antisthenes who invented this usage, with satirical intent; for he is said to have remarked, 'I can see a horse (*hippos*), but horseness (*hippotēs*) I cannot see', and likewise that he could see a man but not 'manness', *anthropotēs* (G VA 149). The present story, in which such language is put in the mouth of Plato himself and Diogenes merely denies that he can see this 'tableness' and 'cupness', may be regarded as a secondary invention. Plato talks about the idea of a table in *Republic* 10, 596b.

122 *never caused pain to anyone*: i.e. he has never shocked anyone into adopting a better way of life, preferring instead to devote himself to theoretical speculations. When treating maladies of the soul, harsh remedies may be required: cf. DL 6.4, of Antisthenes, 'When asked why he reproved his pupils with such a bitter tongue, he replied, "I'm acting just as doctors do with their patients." '

123 *a book of laws*: his late dialogue, the *Laws*, in which he inevitably discussed some of the same subjects as in his earlier *Republic*, though from a different perspective. This is a little parody of the kind of Socratic questioning that can be found in Plato's dialogues.

125 *washing vegetables*: an action symbolizing the simple diet and way of life of a Cynic, a recurring motif in anecdotes that confront Cynics with philosophers who enjoyed a more luxurious way of life by associating with potentates. Compare the similar tales told about Aristippos and Diogenes, 596, and Theodoros and the Cynic Metrocles, 633.

Dionysios: Plato visited Syracuse twice, first when it was under the rule of Dionysios I, and later in 361–360, in the hope of converting Dionysios II into a philosophical ruler. In both cases the experience was an unhappy one.

126 *merely eating olives*: Plato seems to have lived quite austerely and was mocked in comedy as an olive-eater, DL 3.26. He hated the luxurious and dissolute life at the Syracusan court (see *Letter* 7, 326bc), and certainly did not visit it for the sake of its luxuries or for material advantage.

Favorinos . . . Aristippos: in this large encyclopaedic work, Favorinos of Arelata (*c*. AD 80–160) evidently recounted a version of this story in which Aristippos was presented as making fun of Plato in this way, presumably on seeing him eating olives at a banquet in Sicily itself. In the anecdotal tradition, Plato is commonly shown as criticizing Aristippos for buying expensive luxuries for the table (see 554).

128 *some witticism ready to deliver*: not a mere joke, but a *chreia* (see p. xx) designed to make some point of his own at Aristotle's expense; but Aristotle understands his mode of action and short-circuits the process by deliberately failing to respond in the expected way.

129 *so that others may not hear*: *Odyssey* 1.157, 4.70, alluding above all to his supposedly profitable relationship with Dionysios II of Syracuse; some claimed that he had received over 80 talents from him (DL 3.8). Plato was wealthy in his own right.

130a *son of Ariston*: i.e. Plato.

Plato's return to Sicily: Plato was supposed to have been sold into slavery by Dionysios I during his first visit to Sicily, DL 3.18–19, but he returned later during the rule of the younger Dionysios.

130b *because I have returned to those who have sold me*: at first sight this seems rather enigmatic, but if this is taken to be a shorter and less satisfactory version of Aelian's story, Diogenes' response can be interpreted as a sarcastic reference to Plato's own behaviour.

131b *Sotion . . . that it was the Dog*: Sotion of Alexandria, 2nd century BC, author of a book on the successions of the philosophers; he is plainly cited here as the source for the entire story, rather than for an alternative version in which Diogenes addressed the latter remark to Plato.

132 *unaffectedness . . . affected: to aplaston . . . plaston*; his behaviour is not really natural and unaffected, Plato is suggesting, but is contrived for effect. That is in fact true enough of the behaviour of Diogenes in the anecdotes in Sections II and III, where he is usually trying to communicate some message by acting as he does. Whether he could be properly criticized for that would depend on one's interpretation of his motives, i.e. as to whether he was trying to make a useful point or was merely aiming to achieve notoriety.

134a *Socrates gone mad*: whether or not Plato really said this, it seems appropriate, since he did carry some Socratic ideas to a more than eccentric extreme. The idea may have been suggested by the way in which Plato in his writings refers to some naively enthusiastic disciples of Socrates as acting like madmen, as with Chaerephon in *Charmides* 153b and Apollodoros in *Symposium* 173e.

135 *his sandals*: this saying is evidently a later invention designed to stress the originality of the Cynic way of life, by reference to aspects of Socrates' way of life that are mentioned in Plato's dialogues, his sandals in *Symposium* 174a (although it is stressed there that it was most unusual for him to dress up in that way, since he usually went barefoot) and his bed in *Protagoras* 310c.

136 *school of Eucleides . . . gall*: 'he said that the *scholē* of Eucleides was *cholē* (bile, gall, venom)'. Eucleides (Euclid) of Megara was a pupil of Socrates who founded the Megarian school of philosophy. He and his followers devoted much attention to dialectic, and had a reputation for using tricky 'eristic' arguments; this saying of Diogenes suggests accordingly that the school was interested in nothing other than using argument to malicious effect, to make fools of other people. In one of his satirical poems, Timon criticized Eucleides similarly for inspiring the Megarians with a frenzy for disputation (DL 2.107), and Socrates himself was said to have disapproved of this enthusiasm of his: 'On seeing Eucleides devoting himself to eristic arguments, he said, "You'll be able to associate with sophists, Eucleides, but not at all with human beings."' But Stilpo, the third head of the school, seems to have had some sympathy for Cynic moral ideas: see 407 and note.

137 *Illusion: tuphos*, literally smoke or mist, and thence metaphorically vanity

and conceit, and also illusion, vain opinion. It summarized everything that Diogenes and the Cynics fancied that they were battling against.

138   *mother-city of all evils*: a mother-city, *metropolis*, was a city from which colonies were founded, which would usually adopt the same constitution and share many of the characteristics of the mother-city. This is a commonplace which is also ascribed to Democritus (*Gnomologium Vaticanum* 265) and Bion (Stobaeus 3.10.37); avarice was also described as the root of all evil.

139   *vomit of fortune*: primarily ascribed to Monimos, **405**; in *Gnomologium Vaticanum* 216, Demosthenes uses the same expression to describe a rich but uncultivated man.

140   *arch-beggars*: *megaloptōchous*, people who are exceedingly poor; a word not otherwise reported.

143   *how he uses his wealth*: a paradoxical expression of a standard Socratic thought: wealth is an external advantage of no inherent value, and it only comes to be of value by being put to good use.

144   *cats or apes set up inside*: images of the gods Pasht and Thoth; the Greeks liked to make fun of the theriomorphic gods of the Egyptians.

145a *This tale is also recounted about Aristippos*: see **594**, although such a drastic action seems more appropriate to the Cynic. The expanded account that follows explains the point that he was trying to make.

146   *dropsy*: hydropsy or oedema, in which fluid accumulates in soft tissues or cavities of the body; now classed as a symptom rather than a specific disease. Since dropsy is often accompanied by abnormal thirst, it provided an appropriate comparison for the state of mind of people who are suffering from insatiable avarice. Bion also made use of this imagery (see **479**); in Xenophon's *Symposium*, 4.37, Antisthenes describes avarice as a disease but without further specification. The comparison may well have originated with Diogenes (or in some book attributed to him); in the apophthegmatic tradition it is also ascribed to Plato (*Gnomologium Vaticanum* 434), 'Plato said that the rich and insatiable resemble people suffering from dropsy, "for just as those thirst for water when already replete with it, so the others thirst for wealth".'

148   *a living to others*: the oxymoron *abiotos bios* was a proverbial phrase for an unendurable life, a life not worth living; after living such a life, the miser leaves his *bios*—means of life, livelihood, resting in the money that he has accumulated—to those who will inherit it. This play on words, which is also ascribed to Demosthenes (e.g. *Gnomologium Vaticanum* 213), is used to express a paradox that is stated more directly by Bion in **485**, that a miser is exceedingly protective of what he owns, and yet gains no more benefit from it than if it belonged to somebody else.

150   *because of riches one and all*: i.e. for the sake of riches. Diogenes uses the relevant preposition in a slightly different sense in each part of the sentence; he is referring not merely to tyrants in the literal sense, but to anyone who seeks gain by unjust means.

152 *triple-slaves*: *tridoulous*, a current expression which could be used in a variety of contexts, here to mean 'slaves three times over'; the basic thought was a commonplace of popular philosophy: compare, for example, Xenophon, *Memorabilia* 1.5.1 and 1.6.8.

154 *lost the use of your hands*: Plutarch records a comparable tale about Gorgo, daughter of Cleomenes, king of Sparta; when she saw Aristagoras (tyrant of Miletos, late 6th to early 5th century) having his shoes put on by one of his servants, she exclaimed, 'Father, the foreigner hasn't any hands!' (*Sayings of Spartan Women* 240e).

155 *a whirlpool*: in the original Charybdis, the mythical maelstrom that Odysseus had to sail past, *Odyssey* 12.235 ff.; this was a metaphor which was regularly used in comedy in connection with the greedy (e.g. *gastro-charubdis*, Cratinos fr. 428).

156 *mice and weasels*: the Greeks kept weasels to prey on mice, in the same way as cats, but the beasts also seem to have been accused of engaging in undesirable private enterprise; Babrius records a fable (27) in which a weasel complains of ingratitude when about to be drowned, to which the man replies that he may have kept down some pests, but also throttled all the chickens and stripped the house bare, bringing more harm than aid.

157 *throw open their own body*: Stobaeus classifies this saying among those that are concerned with intemperance; people fail to achieve self-mastery and inner fulfilment because they expose themselves to the lure of pleasure through their various senses.

159 *crows and vultures*: *korax*, the Greek word for a crow, sounded much like *kolax*, the word for a flatterer or toady (cf. 321 and note); the dissolute gather people around them who simply want to profit from their weaknesses.

163 *the occupation of the unoccupied*: or the business of the idle, *scholazontōn ascholia*; cf. an apophthegm of Theophrastos in *Gnomologium Vaticanum* 332, 'When asked, what is love, he said, "The passion of an idle mind (*psuchēs scholazousēs*)."' For those who have nothing more serious to attend to, love serves to fill the time.

165 *what is highly prized*: presumably taken from an anecdote that would have provided a more definite context. This could be interpreted in a milder sense, as a lesson for adulterers or those who frequented courtesans, or in a more radical Cynic sense, as indicating the utter worthlessness of love and sex in general.

166 *courtesans*: *hetairai* or 'companion women' were distinguished from *pornai* or prostitutes as being independent women who could be expected to have achieved a certain level of style and accomplishment (e.g. in dance and music, or indeed intelligent conversation). The Cynics were hostile to them not because they had any moral objection to mercenary sex, but because *hetairai* were associated with luxury, expense, and refined sensuality.

169 *Phryne*: a famous *hetaira* or courtesan of the 4th century BC, who was

born at Thespiai in Boeotia and lived in Athens for at least part of her life. She was prosecuted there for profaning the Eleusinian Mysteries, but was acquitted. Her statue at Delphi was made by Praxiteles (Athenaeus 13, 591b), who was also said to have used her as model for his celebrated Cnidian Aphrodite. See also **426**.

170 *sung the marriage-song with his hand*: for the theme of masturbation see 36–7 and notes. The present account is of interest from two points of view. It comes from a work by the highly influential medical writer and theoretician Galen (2nd century AD), and points to the idea that the retention of semen can cause discomfort and indeed harm; and Diogenes is presented as resorting to masturbation, as a happy short cut, when a prostitute— Galen calls her a *hetaira* but that is merely a polite use of language—is slow to arrive. Now a similar story is told in one of the apocryphal letters of Diogenes (42, addressed to the prostitute Melesippe): 'My hand forestalled you in singing the marriage-song before your arrival, being aware that the satisfaction of sexual needs can be contrived with greater ease than for those of the stomach. For Cynic teaching, as you know, is founded in an investigation of nature; and if many would cast reproach on this choice, I am deserving of the greater trust in praising it.' In view of the similarity of language, it may be assumed that Galen was drawing on this letter or one like it. It will be noted that the letter alludes in the first sentence to Diogenes' standard saying about this matter in **37**.

171 *not of the same mind as that*: interpreting the Greek phrase as meaning literally 'I am not the same as that', i.e. as his *kerkis*, penis; he does not identify himself with his involuntary reaction. One of Diogenes' apocryphal letters, 34, touches on this theme in a corresponding manner. If the phrase is interpreted in another way, Diogenes could be suggesting that he is no equal for the boy in that respect, i.e. when it comes to sex, but that seems less appropriate.

172 *not yet . . . never at all*: an old chestnut which originated as folk wisdom—marriage brings all kinds of bothers! It is also ascribed to Thales, one of the Seven Sages of the Archaic period (DL 1.26); when his mother tried to make him marry, he said that it was too soon, and when she tried again during his later life, he said that the proper time had passed. But the saying is appropriate to Diogenes, who rejected marriage along with any kind of settled social life.

173 *can be bought for a drachma*: i.e. he could simply have paid for the services of a cheap prostitute, since it all comes to the same (cf. **165**). A man caught in adultery faced real danger: violent humiliation could be inflicted on him, and a husband could kill him without exposing himself to a charge of murder if he was caught *in flagrante*. It could thus be argued that it was a simple matter of prudence for men to satisfy their sexual desires in some other way that did not expose them to such risk (e.g. Xenophon, *Memorabilia* 2.1.5), and this particular remedy is suggested in a saying ascribed to Antisthenes (DL 6.4): 'On seeing an adulterer in flight one day, he said, "What danger you could have escaped, poor wretch, at the cost of an obol." ' The theme, then, was not of specifically Cynic origin, the Cynic turn lay in using the thought to devalue sex and love in general.

177 *signs of your unnatural lusts*: i.e. the effeminate dress, use of perfume, etc., referred to in the related sayings.

180 *kottabos*: this was a game played at symposia in which wine was flicked from the bottom of a cup at a target. Skill at such a game would be a bad sign because it was associated with drinking-parties and also had erotic connotations, sometimes being used as a love-oracle. The better the youth is at the game, the worse he will be in himself; cf. Antisthenes in Plutarch, *Life of Pericles* 1.5, 'On being told that Ismenias was an excellent flautist, he said, "Yes, but a bad man; for otherwise he wouldn't have been such a good flautist." '

181 *satraps*: these were literally Persian provincial governors, but the term is used here to refer to wealthy and doubtless raffish men—millionaires, nabobs. The use of the word suggests a corrupting atmosphere of Eastern luxury.

185 *a wretch . . . a rogue*: by submitting to a passive homosexual role, he would be committing a misdeed against himself, so rendering himself wretched, while by engaging in adultery, he would be committing a misdeed against another.

188 *Metrocles*: a pupil of Crates (see **459**), so his *Anecdotes* would be a good early source if it was indeed written by him; one may compare a story that was told about Crates, **434**.

with his head half-shaved: as a mark of asceticism; cf. Lucian, *On the Death of Peregrinus* 17, the first thing that Peregrinus does when he embarks on his 'wondrous asceticism' is to half-shave his head and daub his face with mud. Diogenes is making a deliberately provocative demonstration.

189 *mess-halls of Attica*: Spartan men ate together in public messes rather than in their homes like other Greeks; by suggesting that the wine-shops, those centres of rowdy conviviality, were their equivalent in Athens, Diogenes is mocking the Athenians as being vulgar and self-indulgent. He seems to have been in the habit of contrasting them with the Spartans to their disadvantage: cf. **62–3**. Since this saying is recorded by Aristotle, an almost exact contemporary of Diogenes, in his *Rhetoric*, this is the one saying of Diogenes that can be dated with absolute confidence to his own lifetime (if the Dog is indeed him, as we can surely assume).

191 *young men from Rhodes*: rich young Rhodians, as citizens of a wealthy trading-state that was a byword for luxury, form a sharp contrast with typical Spartans, who took a pride in their rough simplicity. Diogenes' own pride in his shabby cloak and simple way of life comes under mockery elsewhere as being a show of vanity (see **597**).

192 *feet anointed with perfume*: although it could be regarded as the very height of luxury to have one's feet anointed with perfume (cf. Athenaeus

553a, citing passages from comedy), Diogenes is clearly poking fun at the use of perfume in this anecdote, by putting the precious ointment to ignoble use.

193 *King Antigonos*: 'the One-Eyed' (382–301), a general and provincial governor under Alexander, and ruler of an Asian kingdom from 306 onward; the notion that Diogenes was ever at his court is plainly absurd.

194 *not for those that truly are*: i.e. they pray for external goods such as wealth or power, which are of equivocal value at best, rather than to become better people. This was a theme that went back to Socrates, e.g. Xenophon, *Memorabilia* 1.3.2.

195 *at those very sacrifices feast*: when animals were sacrificed at festivals in the city, the meat and offal from them would be eaten by the participants, while the bones would be wrapped in fat and burned for the gods on the altar. Since animal meat was very expensive, this was the main or only occasion on which most citizens would eat it.

198 *lustral rite*: such rites, involving ritual sprinkling with water, were employed to purify people from various forms of pollution, notably that incurred by the shedding of human blood.

199a *privileged position in Hades*: people who were initiated into the Mysteries at Eleusis, a short distance from Athens, received a secret revelation which was supposed to assure them of a better lot in the afterlife. The differing fates that initiates and the uninitiated could expect were expressed in figurative terms, through the notion that the initiated would be transferred to the Isles of the Blest, an imaginary place at the ends of the earth where the privileged dead were supposed to enjoy a life of bliss (*Odyssey* 4.561–9, Hesiod, *Works and Days* 167–73), whereas the uninitiated would lie in mud, in accordance with their ritual impurity. The notion that bad people could ensure a better posthumous life for themselves than better ones through purely ritual means is dismissed here as unjust and absurd.

Agesilaos and Epaminondas: Agesilaos (444–360) was a Spartan king of not wholly admirable character who was built up into something of an ideal figure by Xenophon and in the apophthegmatic tradition; Epaminondas (*c*.418–362) was a Theban general and statesman who transformed his state into a leading power in Greece, and was also a man of austere and philosophical character who lived a very simple life. They were thus the kind of people who could be appropriately chosen by Diogenes as examples of admirable foreigners who had not been initiated into the Mysteries (although initiation was also open to non-Athenians).

199b *with nought but evil*: Sophocles fr. 753 Nauck.

Patakion the thief: he seems to have been an Athenian sycophant (i.e. informer) who came to be regarded as a notorious rogue, rather than a thief in the literal sense (Aeschines, *Against Ctesiphon*, Apostolius 14.13, *Suidas* s.v.).

200 *votive offerings on Samothrace*: an island in the northern Aegean; since

the deities known as the gods of Samothrace (who were left unnamed but were often identified with the Kabeiroi) were thought to protect seafarers, those who fell under danger at sea would vow to dedicate an offering to them if they escaped safely. Cicero (*On the Nature of the Gods* 3.89) ascribes a very similar saying to the notorious atheist Diagoras of Melos, 5th century BC.

201 *none too decorous posture*: she was evidently kneeling, which was unusual except in connection with chthonic cults, and could be taken as a sign of superstition. The Zoilos whom Diogenes Laertius cites as his source is otherwise unknown.

202 *he dedicated a pugilist*: slaves could be dedicated to the service of a temple, and here we have the comical idea of one being dedicated to forcibly suppress a servile form of worship, prostration, *proskynesis*, in which the gods were honoured in the same way as an Eastern potentate. People would most often resort to this practice when seeking the help of a god of healing or deliverance like Asclepios; there is also something particularly amusing in the idea of the bruiser inflicting physical harm on those who are approaching a god of healing.

203 *I'll clear it*: the tree has been polluted by being associated with a death, and requires ritual purification before people can eat from it; by playing between different senses of the verb *kathairo*, Diogenes says that he will purify it by clearing it of its fruit.

204 *served Eurystheus*: Heracles, who was honoured both as a hero and a god, was supposed to have performed twelve labours for Eurystheus, king of Mycenae, to expiate for having killed his wife and children in a fit of madness. This story is also ascribed to Diagoras the Atheist, 5th century BC (Athenagoras, *Plea for the Christians*, ch. 4), and since it tells of a positive act of impiety directed against a figure who was held in high honour by the Cynics, it seems more appropriate for Diagoras than for Diogenes. The transfer is easily explicable in view of the similarity of their names.

206 *diviners and dream-readers*: proper arts (*technai*) such as those of navigation and medicine are contrasted with pseudo-arts founded on superstition. The Greeks developed an elaborate pseudo-science of dream-interpretation, as can be appreciated from the surviving treatise by Artemidoros of Ephesos (2nd century AD; actually quite rationalistic in tone); dreams could also be interpreted to divine the future (oneiromancy).

208 *sneezing from the left*: as an involuntary act which occurs suddenly and inexplicably, a sneeze naturally came to be regarded as ominous, and it was a particularly worrying sign if it came from the left, the side of ill omen; cf. Menander fr. 534, in which sneezes are mentioned along with dreams and the hooting of owls as a source of alarm.

209 *a snake coiled around a bolt*: in a similar tale told about Leotychidas II, King of Sparta (Plutarch, *Sayings of Spartans* 224e) the snake is found coiled around the key of a gate, presumably a city-gate, which

could naturally be interpreted as a portent indicating that the security of the place was at risk; here around a *huperon*, a pestle or something shaped like that, here presumably a bolt, giving the portent a similar meaning to that in the other version. In Cicero, *On the Divination*, an unnamed diviner rejects this as being a portent because such a thing is in accord with nature; and cf. **492**.

211 *Harpalos*: not the treasurer of Alexander the Great who sailed off with his treasure and was killed in the following year, but some pirate who plied his trade with lasting success at that time in the seas off Greece; presumably the same as the Skirpalos or Skirtalos who was supposed to have captured Diogenes (see **254** and note).

213 *expedient that they should*: so that wrongdoers should be in fear of divine vengeance.

214a *hateful to the gods*: a similar story is ascribed to Theodoros the Atheist, **634**, but this seems to have been an old joke in any case; cf. Aristophanes, *Knights* 34 ff., where Nicias is asked whether he believes in the gods, and replies that he certainly does because they have formed such a grudge against him.

215 *stealing from a temple*: this was regarded as a particularly heinous crime and was punishable by death; both public and private valuables were often deposited in temples. For the kind of paradoxical argument that could be put forward in defence of temple-robbery, see **497**. Such arguments would have been developed to make points about religion and the nature of the gods rather than to recommend sacrilegious actions in any serious sense.

every substance is to be found in all others: the basic argument here is a naturalistic one, that human flesh is the same as any other kind of meat, and to support that argument, speculations from pre-Socratic philosophy are introduced, presumably in a none too serious spirit, to show that everything is mixed up with everything else within organic substances. Anaxagoras of Clazomenae, 5th century, who argued that 'everything must be in everything', and that 'everything has a portion in everything' (fr. 6 Diels-Kranz), seems to have been the primary source here; Anaxagoras showed a notable interest in the composition of organic substances like meat and bone (see e.g. Aristotle, *On the Heavens* 302a, 28 ff.).

certain invisible pores: an idea proposed by Empedocles (*c*.490–430) and others; see e.g. Aristotle, *On Generation and Corruption* 324b, 25 ff.

Philiscos of Aegina: an immediate follower of Diogenes (see **408** and note); DL mentions elsewhere that Satyros ascribed the tragedies to him (see **218**).

Pasiphon: quite possibly the Pasiphon who was a member of the Eretrian school and was accused of having composed spurious Socratic dialogues, DL 2.61; also mentioned by Plutarch, *Life of Nicias* 4.

216 *Cleanthes*: an early Stoic (331–232), a pupil of Zeno.

bring their own parents to sacrifice: a tragedy entitled *Thyestes* was ascribed to Diogenes (see **215** and **218**); according to Greek legend, Atreus killed the children of his brother Thyestes and served them up as a meal to their unknowing father, because he was so angry with Thyestes for having tricked him out of gaining the Mycenean throne and for seducing his wife. Although it is not known exactly how this theme was treated by Diogenes (if he was indeed the true author) in his 'tragedy', it is recorded that paradoxical arguments were developed in the play to show that there is nothing unnatural in eating human flesh (see **215** and notes). That Diogenes positively recommended there or anywhere else that sons should kill their fathers to eat them is altogether improbable.

217 *the Republic*: in this passage Philodemos (*c.*110 to 40/35), an Epicurean, is discussing the origin of Diogenes' *Republic*. As in the case of the tragedies, the authorship of the work was disputed, but Philodemos argues here that Diogenes was indeed its author, since it was cited as a work of his by Cleanthes and another early Stoic, Chrysippos (3rd century), and the scandalous themes that were developed in both the *Republic* and the tragedies were already taken up by the earliest Stoics. This argument does have real weight, and even if Diogenes himself was not the author of the *Republic*, it must have originated in very early Cynic circles.

uselessness of weapons: in a healthy city in which there is no excess and no accumulation of riches, there would be no need for weapons since no one would have any motive for attacking it; similar thoughts are expressed in Crates' little poem about the city of Pera ('Knapsack'): see **439**.

knucklebones . . . as . . . currency: this is in effect a complete rejection of money in favour of direct exchange; the impracticality of the proposal is the very point of it. Zeno stated accordingly in his own *Republic* that money should have no place either for use in trade or for travelling abroad, DL 7.33.

Antipater: of Tarsus, a leading Stoic philosopher of the 2nd century BC.

these people: i.e. Diogenes, if it was indeed him, and the early Stoics who wrote in a similar vein. Diogenes, as portrayed in the anecdotes, rejected marriage and love and argued that sexual desires should be satisfied as simply and directly as possible; in the Cynic and Stoic utopias, this theme was developed in the most provocative manner that one could imagine, with sexual life being portrayed as an anarchic free-for-all. One should keep in mind, however, that this is a hostile and humourless summary which gives no proper indication of the points that these authors were trying to put over.

not even the use of violence: this aspect of Philodemos' account should be viewed with caution because it conflicts with all that is stated about the basis for sexual relations or love in Cynic and early Stoic sources: cf. **215**, Diogenes recognized no other union than that based on persuasion, and, for the early Stoics, DL 7.130.

218 *The following books are attributed to him*: here we have a catalogue, of unstated origin, which attributes twenty-one works to Diogenes, but DL then goes on to explain that certain authors denied that he had written anything at all, while others denied that he had written some of these works. He cites Sotion (a Peripatetic, 2nd century BC) as giving a list which excludes the works of scandalous content, i.e. the tragedies and *Republic*; this can be seen as reflecting Stoic efforts to disown a disquieting strain in Cynic and the early Stoic literature. Some of the works that Sotion does accept as being genuine, on the other hand, are not to be found in the initial list. Sosicrates (historical writer, early 2nd century), who is reported as rejecting all of Diogenes' writings, rejected all the writings of Aristippos likewise, DL 2.84, and ascribed the writings of Ariston of Chios to another author of the same name, DL 7.163; as to the reasons for his scepticism in the case of Diogenes, nothing specific is recorded, but his judgement on the matter seems to accord with a wider pattern and is unlikely to have been prompted by a desire to dissociate Diogenes from works that might be regarded as shocking. And finally, Satyros (late 3rd century) is mentioned as ascribing the tragedies to Philiscos. These and the *Republic* were assuredly of very early Cynic origin in any case; it is likely enough that quite a few of the works that circulated under Diogenes' name were completely inauthentic, like the apocryphal letters that are translated in the final section of this book.

218 *Ichthyas*: the second head of the Megarian school; in view of his successor Stilpo's connections with the Cynics (see 407 and note), it is interesting that his name should appear as the title of a dialogue ascribed to Diogenes.

Pordalos: see the reference to this work in 2 and the relevant note.

tragedies: these were of course not tragedies in the conventional sense but something very close to parodies, in which the traditional stories were reinterpreted in an often provocative way to make moral points. This seriocomic approach would remain characteristic of Cynic literature.

Philiscos: although this work is not included in the preceding list, Philodemos refers to it in 217 as having a similar content to the *Atreus* and *Oedipus*, which dealt with cannibalism and incest. It is certainly odd to find a work bearing the same name as the disciple of Diogenes who was sometimes credited with having written the tragedies. Perhaps it was a dialogue in which Philiscos appeared. It is possible, of course, that the idea that he wrote the tragedies may have been inferred in some way from this work.

219 *lackeys of the crowd*: a standard theme in Socratic and Platonic philosophy, that orators seek to gratify the people of the city to gain power and reputation, and thus become enslaved to them, whereas the philosopher should engage in a disinterested search for the truth and express that truth regardless of the consequences.

efflorescences: *exanthemata*; as with the corresponding verb, which literally meant to 'put out flowers', this noun could also be used in a figurative sense to refer to an unsightly disorder of the skin, the reddish eruptions that accompany certain diseases. The equivalent English noun can also be used in the latter sense, although the idiom has now become unfamiliar.

220 *'thrice-human'*: in the original an improvised noun (*trisanthropous*), 'men thrice over', coined to parody high-flown expressions like 'thrice-blessed' or 'thrice-wretched' as found in tragedy, etc.; at first hearing this might sound like praise, but is intended in quite the opposite sense, as indicating that the orators are all too human in their lust for reputation and power. DL goes on to explain the point by saying that Diogenes is using the expression in place of 'thrice-wretched' (*trisathlious*).

222 *'Plain speaking'*: *parrhesia*, frankness of speech that may verge on the brutal, the kind of talk that one expects from people who pride themselves on being blunt and always saying what they think irrespective of the feelings of others. Diogenes developed a distinctive kind of Cynic *parrhesia*, cutting and provocative, though often leavened with humour, which was one of the defining features of his activity.

223 *another person's benefit*: *allotrion agathon*, see further in the note to 498; Cynic *parrhesia* is disagreeable but beneficial, by contrast to the flattering speech of the orators, which is sweet to the taste but harmful.

225a *the demagogue of Athens*: Demosthenes (384–322) was the leading Athenian statesman and orator of Diogenes' time; he took the lead in trying to oppose the expansion of Macedonian power into the heartland of Greece, though ultimately without success. He is attacked in these anecdotes as being a typical demagogue who wins his way by flattering the prejudices of the mob, which is naturally far from just. To point to someone with one's middle finger (rather than index finger) was a highly insulting gesture.

225b *I've pointed him out to you*: in the original, 'that's so-and-so', indicating that Diogenes stated the man's name. One may suspect that he was Demosthenes, and that this indicates how the preceding story (which is rather banal in Diogenes Laertius' version) would originally have run. Someone asks after the famous orator, and Diogenes points him out with a scornful remark, using the rude gesture in the knowledge that it will evoke a furious response, so showing up the vanity and irrationality of Demosthenes.

226 *your master comes in every day*: taverns (or more accurately, wine-shops) were regarded as rowdy resorts of the common people; in his prosaic fashion, Aelian feels it necessary to explain the joke, saying that Diogenes was referring to the common people and indicating that politicians and orators were slaves of the mob.

228 *man of the city in battle*: Demosthenes made fierce speeches against Philip of Macedon, but fled (along with many others) when the Athenian line broke at the battle of Chaironeia in 338, at which Philip gained the victory which enabled him to establish himself as the overlord of Greece. It was said that Demosthenes threw away his shield, which was

considered to be a most shameful action (Plutarch, *Life of Demosthenes*
20, 855a). The Scythians were wild inhabitants of the steppes; to 'talk
like a Scythian' was a proverbial phrase for employing a fierce and brutal
manner of speech (Demetrius, *On Style* 216, 297). In battle Demosthenes
proved to be *astikos*, 'urbane', all too refined.

229 *Anaximenes*: of Lampsacos, 390/80–320, an eminent rhetorician who
taught at Athens, but also spent some time at the court of Philip of
Macedon; the probable author of a surviving rhetorical manual, the
Rhetoric to Alexander, and compiler of a universal history. He evidently
made a good living from teaching rhetoric at Athens and from his connections with Macedon, and is presented here as in the following anecdotes as being self-indulgent. Strangely enough, Anaximenes is described
in the *Suda* (s.v. Anaximenes) as being a pupil of Diogenes!

230 *doesn't even possess himself*: i.e. doesn't have charge or control of himself— the Greek verb can carry that meaning.

232a *battle of Chaironeia*: in Boeotia, where Philip II of Macedon defeated the
Thebans and Athenians in 338, and so became able to establish
Macedonian hegemony in Greece. He went on to impose a settlement in
which all the Greek states, except Sparta, became allies of Macedonia as
members of the Corinthian League. Philip was assassinated two years
later in 336, to be succeeded by his son Alexander.

'A spy who has come to observe your insatiable greed': a *kataskopos* was an
observer or inspector and thence a scout or spy. Diogenes has come not
as a spy to gather military intelligence for the opposing army, but as an
observer (and connoisseur) of human stupidity, to gather moral intelligence for the benefit of humanity. Epictetus (1st–2nd century AD) develops this idea at great length, suggesting that it is a prime function of a
Cynic to act as a sort of scout or spy, finding out what is friendly or hostile, good or bad, for human beings, and reporting back the truth without fear or favour (*Discourses* 3, 22.23 ff., cf. 1, 24.3 ff.). Since Epictetus
starts by alluding to this tale of his encounter with Philip (3.22.24), it is
clear that the idea was primarily associated with that anecdote; but the
metaphor may already have been employed more widely in early Cynic
circles, since two works are recorded for Antisthenes with *kataskopos* in
the title (DL 6.17–18).

233 *on behalf of the Heraclids*: Heraclids was a general term for the descendants of Heracles; according to legend, the Athenians had protected the
first Heraclids, the sons of Heracles, from Eurystheus, king of Mycenae,
after the hero's death. Three generations later, some descendants of these
first Heraclids were supposed to have led the Dorians into the Peloponnese,
and to have established the subsequent ruling lines in Argos, Sparta, and
Messenia. The Macedonian kings claimed to be descended from
Archelaos, a son of Temenos, the first Heraclid king of Argos.

234a *about to attack Corinth*: this story can be placed after the battle of
Chaironeia. Philip did in fact march south across the Isthmus of Corinth

into the Peloponnese, but he met with no resistance and there were no further hostilities. He arranged a congress in Corinth in that same year to establish the Corinthian League.

rolling my jar: rolling one's jar became a proverbial phrase for carrying out a futile action by imitation of others, Apostolius 9.24.

234b *the Craneion*: see note to 236a, below.

235 *Aristotle breakfasts when Philip pleases*: in 343 Philip invited Aristotle to become tutor to his son Alexander.

236a *in the Craneion*: a cypress grove just outside Corinth containing a gymnasium, where Diogenes was supposed to have set up home when he was in Corinth. Shortly after coming to the throne in 336, Alexander entered Greece to consolidate his power there, and naturally went to Corinth to be acknowledged as head of the Corinthian League in succession to his father. Since he never visited Athens, any encounter with Diogenes had to take place at Corinth, another city that was associated with the Cynic (whether or not on the basis of any sound tradition).

236d *proclaimed as their leader*: Alexander was chosen to be supreme general for the invasion of Asia at Corinth in 336, but he did not cross over the Hellespont into Asia until 334.

237 *the Great King*: the name that the Greeks applied to the king of the Persians. It was a commonplace in the Socratic tradition that one who is satisfied with little can be as happy as the king of the Persians, and the same thought lies behind the anecdotes that confront Diogenes with Alexander, although Alexander did not achieve his Asian conquests until well after his supposed meeting with Diogenes.

239 *multitude of cares*: see *Iliad* 2.24–5, in which these words are addressed to Agamemnon by a dream sent by Zeus. Diogenes shows his sharpness of mind by adding the second line while half-asleep, indicating at the same time that he is free from servitude to the cares of rule; as one who knows the futility of power and glory, he can sleep without a worry.

240 *feel the misfortune*: the first line at least is a piece of proverbial wisdom, as in Menander, *Monostichs* 240. Although the idea of a jarful of wits or brains might naturally bring Diogenes to mind as a sage who lived in a jar, this anecdote is hardly a happy invention, since the idea expressed in the verses conflicts with the most basic tenets of Cynic thought.

242 *filled a dish with bones*: cf. 92, in which people mock the Dog by tossing bones to him; Diogenes gets the last word here because Alexander's action conflicts with the ideal of kingly liberality, which is a central theme in the apophthegms of kings.

243 *too foolish*: by allowing himself to be governed by insatiable ambition; it is the privilege of the gods to need nothing, and of god-like men to need little, 96.

244 *make me Serapis*: in 424/3 Alexander let it be known in Greece that he wanted to be granted divine honours, and when the matter was debated

in the Athenian assembly, the orator Demades is said to have remarked
that if they begrudged heaven to Alexander, he might deprive them of
their land (Valerius Maximus 7.2 ext. 3, cf. *Gnomologium Vaticanum* 236,
where the same saying is ascribed to Demothenes); the motion was duly
carried, very much under force of necessity, and after Alexander's death
a huge fine of ten talents was imposed on the unfortunate Demades for
having introduced it (Athenaeus 6, 251b, Aelian, *Historical Miscellany*
5.12). The matter invited a humorous response; the orator Lycourgos
asked what kind of a god Alexander would be if worshippers would have
to purify themselves *after* visiting his temple (rather than before in the
usual manner; Plutarch, *Lives of the Ten Orators* 842d). The idea behind
the present saying seems to be that if Alexander could identify himself
with Dionysos, Diogenes could ask to be identified with Serapis as an
exotic equivalent to Dionysos; for Osiris was identified with Dionysos
from an early period (e.g. Herodotus 2.123), and thence with Serapis as
the osirified Apis bull (see Plutarch, *On Isis* 362b). But the anecdote is
anachronistic since the Greco-Egyptian cult of Serapis was first developed by the successor kings in Egypt after the death of Alexander.

245 *on the same day as Diogenes*: a synchronism suggested by the body of
legend that associated the two, and thus not to be taken as having any
sound historical basis, although Diogenes does seem to have died at around
the same period as Alexander (who met his death on 11/10 June in 323).

in the 113th Olympiad: 324–321 BC.

246 *Callisthenes*: of Olynthos, *c*.360–328, a great-nephew of Aristotle, who
accompanied Alexander to the East as a historian.

247 *a wretch*: the messenger's name, Athlias (or possibly Athlios), is suggestive of *athlios* meaning 'wretched'; *athlios par'athliou di'athliou pros ath-
lion*. Athlias seems to be otherwise unrecorded as a personal name.

248 *not to be disdained*: *Iliad* 3.65; Antipater was a Macedonian general who
was appointed to be regent in Macedonia during Alexander's absence,
and was also responsible for maintaining order in Greece.

249 *Crateros*: *c*.370–321, a Macedonian general.

250 *Perdiccas*: one of Alexander's generals, who was briefly regent of his
empire after his death. He would hardly have been likely to have summoned Diogenes to Asia, and this anecdote was evidently transferred
from Theodoros the Atheist (see 638 and note).

251a *Dionysios . . . in Corinth*: Dionysios II, tyrant of Syracuse, took refuge in
Corinth after he was deposed in 334; Plato, who made an unhappy visit
to his court, died three or four years before that. Dionysios lived in very
reduced circumstances in Corinth, and is reputed to have become a
school–teacher (see 650). His fate came to be regarded as symbolic of the
mutability of worldly fortune.

251b *'beautiful winding-sheet'*: when Dionysios I was in grave danger as a result
of a revolt in Syracuse (or, in some accounts, an attack from the

Carthaginians) and was contemplating flight, his friend Heloris was said to have put new heart into him by making this remark, e.g. Diodorus Siculus 14.8.4–6; it was a very famous saying, and the story of Diogenes' meeting with the ex-tyrant was doubtless invented to enable a fitting retort to be put into the mouth of the Cynic.

252 *Just like sacks*: meal-sacks and the like, which would be hung up for use and then thrown away when empty; Dionysios was only interested in people for the use that he could make of them.

253 *Harmodios and Aristogeiton*: two Athenians who tried to assassinate Hippias, tyrant of Athens, and his brother Hipparchos in 514 as a result of personal grievances; although Hipparchos alone was killed and Hippias remained in power for some time afterwards, they came to be admired as liberators and tyrannicides, and Cleisthenes arranged for a bronze statue group of them to be erected in a prominent position in Athens at public expense. This saying seems to have been originally associated with Antiphon, a tragic poet who lived at the Syracusan court in the time of Dionsysios I; the story went that when the question was raised at table as to which was the best form of bronze, he made this reply, provoking the tyrant to have him put to death for his implied support of tyrannicide (Plutarch, *Lives of the Ten Orators* 833bc; this poet Antiphon is wrongly identified there with the rhetorician Antiphon of Rhamnous).

254 *captured by pirates*: although the earliest accounts of this story date back to the 3rd century, quite soon after Diogenes' lifetime, it is plainly fictional in its details and probably enough in its entirety. It is not inconceivable, of course, that Diogenes may have been captured by pirates at some point, if he did indeed wander around Greece as the tradition suggests; and since there are also traditions that suggest that he may have moved to Corinth in the latter part of his life (as the place of his supposed meeting with Alexander and of his death and burial), some have argued that he may have changed his place of residence as the result of some such episode as this. One would not be obliged to assume in that case that he must necessarily have served there as a slave—he could have been ransomed and taken there, for instance, by the rich Corinthian who figures in the story. But it seems more probable on the whole that the whole story was invented as a symbolic fiction, and that it would have been recognized as such by its original audience. The main narrative was composed by Menippos of Gadara in his work entitled *The Sale of Diogenes* (see 256), although the story was subsequently developed in certain respects by other authors (see 266–8). The writings of Menippos of Gadara (who lived in the 3rd century: see 462 and notes) were generally fanciful and humorous in nature, which did not always prevent people from taking them more literally than he intended (see for instance 461 and notes).

Skirpalos: evidently a pirate who was notorious at the time; his name also appears as Skirtalos in a late source, 267, but this is probably just an error. The Harpalos in 211 is presumably the same man.

254 *'Governing men'*: one who knows what is right and has proper control over himself is also qualified to control others, i.e. direct them to the good; this is a standard Socratic theme in the writings of Plato and Xenophon, in which Socrates regularly discussed the kingly or ruling art (e.g. in 613, from Xenophon's *Memorabilia*, where Socrates discusses it with Aristippos). This was the central conceit which provided the basis for the entire narrative, that Diogenes, as a man who had achieved perfect self-mastery through possession of that art, would not only maintain his freedom as a slave, but would come to exercise authority over the man who was supposedly his master.

Xeniades: a wealthy Corinthian aristocrat; probably a purely fictional character invented by Menippos (and certainly not to be identified with the minor philosopher of that name: see 404a and note).

entrusted his entire household to him: this summary by Diogenes Laertius gives an outline of the story, which can be seen as a play in three acts, recounting first how Diogenes behaved toward the pirates, and secondly how he behaved when he was offered up for auction, and finally how he behaved toward his master after he was sold. Menippos would certainly have set the pattern for the first two acts, but the story of his life in Corinth and his pedagogical activities (see 267) seems to have been greatly elaborated by subsequent writers (if that was indeed already a feature of Menippos' account). The main episodes of the story of his capture and sale have been preserved, mainly in the form of a string of brief separate anecdotes, and the tale is filled out accordingly in the following fragments, 255–68.

guardian-spirit: *daimon*, minor or unidentified deity, here in the sense of guardian-spirit, tutelary god; perhaps suggested by language used of Crates, as a good spirit who would advise people in their homes (see 416d and note).

255 *in the bloom of their youth*: *Iliad* 24.602–4. Niobe, the wife of Amphion, a legendary king of Thebes, boasted that she was superior to the goddess Leto because she had so many children while the goddess had only two, provoking Leto to send her son Apollo to shoot Niobe's children with his arrows. Achilles recounts the story in the *Iliad* to urge Priam, king of Troy, to eat something even though he is grieving for the loss of his son Hector.

256a *Menippos . . . Sale of Diogenes*: strangely enough DL does not mention the *Sale of Diogenes* in his list of Menippos' works (462, but the list is explicitly indicated to be incomplete). It seems likely that the auctioneer would have begun by asking Diogenes where he was from (as in Lucian's account of his sale in 1, which would have been inspired by Menippos' work), to receive the familiar reply that he was a citizen of the world (see 14 and note).

258 *merely to look him over*: the point being that buyers are satisfied with an external examination and do not test him to see if he rings true inside.

259a *the female disease*: a form of impotence or eunuchism associated especially with the Scythians. Herodotus, 1.105, refers to some Scythians
who robbed the temple of Aphrodite and were thus punished by the goddess with the affliction known as the female disease. It is discussed in the
Hippocratic treatise *Airs, Waters, Places*, chapter 22, where it is stated
that among the Scythians there are many eunuchs who behave like
women, and it is suggested that excessive horse-riding may be to blame.
In the present context this is doubtless just a way of saying that the man
looked extremely effeminate.

260 *liberis . . . liberos*: this story presumably originated in a Latin source,
since it is hard to think of any Greek equivalent for this play on words.

262 *streams to their sources*: a verse from Euripides (*Medea* 410) which could
be quoted to suggest that the natural order of things had been inverted;
ano potamōn, the streams are running backwards, was a proverbial phrase
which Diogenes, as a contrarian (cf. 72 ff.) and re-stamper of the currency, might well have adopted as his own.

264 *set free by Antisthenes*: i.e. his master had set him on the proper course in
life by delivering him from enslavement to false opinions and superfluous desires.

266 *Cleomenes*: an early Cynic who was a pupil of Crates (see 460); nothing is
recorded about him except that he wrote this work and had two pupils of
his own.

slaves of the lions: not an original analogy. One may compare the notion
of Alcibiades as a lion-cub at Athens, Aristophanes, *Frogs* 1425 ff.,
Plutarch, *Life of Alcibiades* 16; it is not a good idea to keep a lion, but if
you do, you will have to humour his every mood.

267 *Euboulos*: otherwise unknown, perhaps to be identified with the
Euboulides mentioned in 2. He plainly developed this tale of the enslavement of Diogenes into an educational romance, and may well have lived
in the 3rd century BC like Menippos and Cleomenes. It is just possible
that he is the Euboulos who is mentioned in an epigram by Leonidas of
Tarentum, 3rd century, as having 'lived and died sober', as would befit
someone who had Cynic sympathies (*Greek Anthology* 7.452). 288 and
293 may perhaps be fragments from this work.

269 *the hue of virtue*: a commonplace which is variously ascribed in the
apophthegmatic tradition, e.g. to Theophrastos (Antonius 2.71) or
Philoxenos (*Gnomologium Vaticanum* 548); cf. Stobaeus 3.31.8, 'When
Pythias, the daughter of the philosopher Aristotle, was asked which is the
most beautiful colour, she replied, "That which rises up through modesty in the well-born."' Modesty was of course a traditional virtue in
women and the young. 'Plato recommended that the young should possess these three qualities: moderation in their mind, silence on their
tongue, and modesty on their face' (*Gnomologium Vaticanum* 433). This
apophthegm and others of a similar nature in this section show how sayings expressive of traditional morality came to be attached to Diogenes'

name. Some seem more suitable to him than others; this one takes us far from Cynic shamelessness.

270 *to have such a high opinion of yourself*: we owe an absolute moral obligation to our parents for having brought us into being, and reared us and educated us (e.g. Aristotle, *Nicomachean Ethics* 8.12, 1162b, 4 ff.); open criticism of them in front of others is thus an impious act. This apophthegm is also ascribed to Plato, e.g. Stobaeus 4.25.43.

277 *struck his pedagogue*: not a teacher in our sense, but the trusted household slave who had regular charge of male children and was responsible for seeing that they behaved properly; Quintilian (*Institutes of Oratory* 1, 9.5) ascribes this story to Crates.

278 *having committed no bad deed*: one of a series of apophthegms in Stobaeus' anthology suggesting that a good conscience is the source of inner freedom and tranquillity; cf. 3.24.12, 'When asked, "What is freedom?"', Periander replied, "A good conscience"', and 3.24.13, 'When asked who lives an undisturbed life, Socrates replied, "Those who have nothing untoward on their conscience."'

279 *you freeze*: this saying is also ascribed to Antisthenes (Stobaeus 4.4.28, *Gnomologium Vaticanum* 8) and that is doubtless the original attribution; Diogenes had nothing but contempt for any sort of political engagement.

283 *the trappings of courage*: especially in so far as this was the form of dress adopted by the Cynic hero Heracles; in Lucian's sketch (see 1), Diogenes refers to his rough cloak as his lion-skin. Although people would be said to 'don a lion-skin' in a figurative sense when embarking on some brave or noble deed—cf. Plato, *Cratylus* 411a—it seems hard to imagine anyone walking around Athens in such garb.

285 *Megarians . . . town-walls*: Megara was the neighbouring state to Athens on the Isthmus of Corinth, and the Athenians liked to mock its citizens as being uncultivated philistines who were interested only in commerce (see also 370); it may be assumed that neither of these sayings originated with Diogenes himself. The notion that cities should rely on the virtues of their citizens rather than on city-walls was a commonplace that was expressed in a variety of forms; e.g. that the young men of Sparta were its city-walls (Plutarch, *Sayings of Spartans* 210e, 217e; Sparta had no defensive walls).

294 *Medea was no sorceress*: in myth the daughter of Aietes, ruler of a kingdom on the eastern shore of the Black Sea; she helped Jason to seize the golden fleece and returned with him to Greece to become his wife. She was supposed to have used her magical skills to rejuvenate Jason's father Aison (Ovid, *Metamorphoses* 7, 176–293; the story goes back to early epic, *Returns* fr. 6, Davies), or else Jason himself; but Diogenes characteristically reinterprets the story to make a point of his own. Presumably from the lost 'tragedy' *Medea* that was ascribed to him, 218.

295 *embalming fluid or honey*: honey is a good preservative; when, for instance,

Agesipolis I, king of Sparta, died on campaign in northern Greece in 380, his body was immersed in honey to be taken home for burial (Xenophon, *Hellenica* 5.3.19).

298 *schemes of our enemies*: this saying is generally ascribed to Cleoboulos (e.g. *Gnomologium Vaticanum* 370, Maximus 54.42); thus a piece of traditional wisdom that was attributed to one of the Seven Sages, Cleoboulos of Lindos, and transferred secondarily to Diogenes.

299 *exact revenge against*: or 'defend oneself against', the Greek is ambiguous. Cf. *Gnomologium Vaticanum* 432, 'When Plato was asked how one can distress one's enemy, he said, "By setting out to act as well as possible."' Such sayings can be interpreted in two senses. At a prudential level, those who act well provide their enemies with less hold for attack, and at a deeper level, they will gain the advantage over their enemies by surpassing them in what essentially matters, their moral worth.

301 *with our fingers unclenched*: we should hold nothing back, be completely open-handed.

302 *one . . . poor . . . the other exceptionally rich*: there is an implicit reference here to the proverbial thought that friends hold all things in common.

307 *if I were to do that*: in ancient collections this little fable is classed as an attack on gluttony, although one could think of other applications.

308 *you're sick in the head*: although this may strike one as being no more than perverse humour, it was seriously argued in antiquity that the indiscriminate bestowal of benefits is not a virtue, but that any benefits that a person bestows should be proportionate to the merits of the recipient. In Seneca's treatise *On the Benefits* (6.18), this story is recounted to make that very point, suggesting that although the ferryman has performed a good turn for the traveller—in this case Plato rather than Diogenes—he has conferred no benefit on him since he has been acting indiscriminately, and he has accordingly placed him under no obligation. Elsewhere a similar tale is told of the orator Demosthenes (*Gnomologium Vaticanum* 223): when someone readily grants him a loan and he then sees the man doing the same for many others, he remarks, 'I'm no longer grateful to you, since it's not your judgement that's leading you to do this, but some kind of disease.' This was a theme that invited humorous treatment. In Aelian, *Historical Miscellany* 14.14, the musician and wit Stratonicos is initially grateful to be offered hospitality in someone's home during his travels, but when one guest after another is then invited in, he tells his servant that they will be leaving since this is evidently more a hostelry than a home.

309 *'Hope'*: because we still have hope even when we have nothing else at all, a typical piece of folk wisdom of the kind that was ascribed to the Seven Sages of the Archaic period. In Plutarch, *Dinner of the Seven Wise Men* 9, 153d, one of the Seven, Thales, gives this response, along with the explanation, when he is asked what is most common, i.e. most widely shared; and elsewhere another of the Seven, Bias of Priene, replies 'Hope' when asked what is sweet to men (DL 1.87, *Gnomologium Vaticanum* 155).

310 *To know oneself*: the famous Delphic injunction, which acquired a special
     significance in the context of Socratic thought. That it is hard to know
     oneself is a thought that was associated with Thales especially (though
     also with Bias) both in the form of a maxim and as a response to the
     question posed here. Thus in DL 1.36, for instance, Thales is first asked
     'What is hard?', to which he gives this response, and then, 'What is
     easy?', to which he replies, 'To give advice to another', so suggesting that
     we all too easily see where others are going wrong, but find it difficult to
     know ourselves because our conceit and self-regard blind us to our own
     faults—the point that is directly stated in the present apophthegm, here
     ascribed to Diogenes, but elsewhere to Cheilon, another of the Seven
     Sages (Stobaeus 3.21.13).

313 *'One soul dwelling in two bodies'*: cf. Aristotle, *Nicomachean Ethics*
     1168b1 ff., where this saying is considered along with other proverbial
     wisdom about friendship.

314 *'In the souls of the cultivated'*: *mousikos* was a term for a cultivated or
     scholarly person accordingly, while an uncultivated or boorish one was
     amousos.

315 *weighs most heavily on the earth*: the notion that a useless person is no more
     than a burden on the earth was a proverbial one, which can be traced back
     as far as Homer, *Odyssey* 20.379, and the correct answer to this question
     is thus provided by specifying who is the most useless kind of person,
     namely an ill-educated person who is lacking in cultivation. That lack of
     cultivation, *apaideusia*, is a burden is one of the maxims ascribed to Thales
     in the sayings of the Seven Sages (Thales no. 13 in Stobaeus 3.1.172).

318 *why gold is pale*: *chlōros*, primarily meaning pale, but also used of pale
     colours such as yellow and grass-green; often applied to people who are
     pale with fear, as is implied in the present response. One could gain a com-
     parable meaning in English by playing between different senses of the word
     'yellow'. The joke was a traditional one and is recorded in quite similar
     words in a couplet from comedy (scholion to Aristophanes, *Wealth* 204).

319 *informer*: *sukophantēs*, at Athens a man who would bring charges against
     people in the courts for political or personal reasons, or for his own
     financial advantage; at the worst such people would bring false charges,
     or else blackmail the rich by threatening to bring charges against them.

320 *tax-collectors*: i.e. collectors of customs charges, market dues, and the
     like; at Athens direct taxation was imposed only on the resident aliens,
     while wealthy citizens would contribute by undertaking expensive civic
     duties, receiving public honour in return.

321 *to crows than to flatterers*: there is a play on words here, since *korakes*, the
     Greek word for 'crows', differs by only a letter from *kolakes*, the word for
     'flatterers'; and going 'to the crows', furthermore, was an expression for
     going 'to perdition (cf. 'going to the dogs'). According to a more elaborate
     version of this saying, ascribed to Antisthenes, 'it is better to fall in with
     crows than with flatterers, since the former despoil your body while you

are dead, but the latter your soul while you are still alive' (Stobaeus
3.14.17; cf. DL 6.4). Or in a version ascribed to Demosthenes (*Gnomologium
Vaticanum* 206), 'He said that a flatterer differs in this alone from a crow,
that the one eats you alive and the other when you are dead.'

331 *to turn him white*: scrubbing an Ethiopian or black man was a proverbial
phrase for a futile activity, as was the expression 'an Ethiopian cannot be
turned white' with regard to incorrigible people (Apostolius 1.95);
Diogenes is wasting his time on an incorrigible rogue. The corresponding reply in English would be, 'I'm trying to make a leopard change his
spots'. As it happens, in its original source in the Bible, this expression is
cited along with the one used in the Greek saying, 'Can the Ethiopian
change his skin, or the leopard his spots?' (Jeremiah 13: 23).

332 *Cure a corpse*: 'whipping a corpse' (cf. 'flogging a dead horse') was the
standard version of this very common expression for a futile activity, but
it could be adapted to suit the context.

333a *'The adder's borrowing poison from the viper'*: in the Greek, *aspis* and
echidna, referring to the asp or Egyptian cobra, as a highly venomous
African snake, and the viper, as its European counterpart. Here we have
a misogynistic commonplace, by no means peculiar to Greek culture, in
which women are compared to snakes because they are supposed to have
poisonous tongues, especially when it comes to the spreading of malicious gossip; and if two women are seen to be conferring, they can be
said to be passing on their poison. The saying that is put into the mouth
of Diogenes here plainly originated as verse rather than prose, perhaps
coming from comedy. This theme also appears in the Menandrian tradition, in relation to women being taught to read and write; that is not a
good thing to do, because it only provides the viper with additional poison (*Monostich* 261, *Comparison* 1.209–10; also in apophthegmatic form
as a gnomic comparison, Elster appendix, 34). This was evidently an old
motif of popular origin which could be employed in different genres.

334 *a sword being sharpened*: it is her tongue that is being sharpened, writing
will assist her in the spreading of malice; for the implicit analogy, one
may compare the story of Thearidas the Spartan, who when asked, while
whetting his sword, whether it was sharp, replied 'Sharper than slander'
(Plutarch, *Sayings of Spartans* 221c).

335 *'Not the right cage for the beast'*: a litter may resemble a cage, but it is
really quite the opposite of one, since it enables its occupant to travel
around and get up to no good; the suggestion is, of course, that she
should be kept confined at home.

336 *'If only all trees bore such fruit'*: a traditional piece of rough humour also
ascribed to Aesop (*Aesopi Sententia* no. 20 Perry). Aesop sees only one
woman, but this version over-eggs the pudding, with rather absurd
effect, by suggesting that Diogenes saw a number of women hanging
there, like the fruit of a tree. Hanging was a favourite form of suicide in
the ancient world, especially among women.

337a '*Let the bad be carried away by the bad*': that one should not try to cure
one evil with another was a favourite proverbial thought, e.g. Herodotus
3.53, Thucydides 5.65, but Diogenes reverses this by suggesting that it
is fitting to allow one evil to rid the world of another. In an apophthegm
preserved in the Arabic tradition, Socrates makes a similar remark about
a woman who is ill, and it seems reasonable to assume that that was the
original version of the story, since it so neatly inverts the proverbial
phrase. The present version is more outrageous, as is fitting for Diogenes,
even if this is almost certainly a story that has been foisted on him. It is
recorded in graffiti from Herculaneum.

340 *the night's engulfing the day*: cf. *Philogelos* 151a, in which someone
enquires of a procurer with regard to a black prostitute, 'How much for
the night?' There is no hostility or cruelty in the jokes that are recorded
about black people, in contrast to some of the jokes about women.

341 *cauldron*: it would of course have been sooted by being heated over an
open fire.

343 *makes everyone get up*: doubtless a standing joke, it is put in the mouth of
an anonymous speaker in the Greek joke-book *Philogelos* (no. 147).

345 *can see land ahead*: in *Gnomologium Vaticanum* 348 the sophist, orator,
and wit Theocritos of Chios is said to have made this joke at the end of a
long recitation by Anaximenes (who was also a butt of Diogenes' mockery: see **229–32** and notes). The white margin at the end of a scroll would
stand out more sharply against the writing above because there were no
gaps between the words; we should imagine that the reader has been
using his finger to mark his place.

346 *Thanks to the gods*: the corresponding Greek expression literally means
'with the gods'; a similar anecdote was told about the musician Stratonicos
(Athenaeus 8, 348d): 'When he was once teaching the harp (*kithara*), he
had nine statues of the Muses in his classroom, and one of Apollo, but
only two pupils; and when someone asked him how many pupils he had,
he replied, 'With (thanks to) the gods, twelve.' The humour is thus
directed against himself in connection with his own schoolroom. The
attribution to Diogenes is doubtless secondary. The story in **342** was
similarly ascribed to Stratonicos (Maximus 64.14), who was more properly associated with this kind of humour than Diogenes.

347 *bring down those who once defeated you*: there is a play here between two
different meanings of the verb *kataballein*, in the sense of throwing down
in wrestling, and of striking down or killing. Cf. *Gnomologium Vaticanum*
266, 'When he [Demosthenes] once saw a bad wrestler practising as a
doctor, he said, "You've now found a way to bring down many a man!" '

348 *from the flesh of swine and oxen*: athletes in training, especially wrestlers,
boxers, and pancratiasts, adopted a heavy meat diet to build up their
strength and weight; this was in marked contrast to the usual Greek diet,
which rarely included much animal meat. The supposed stupidity of
athletes was a standing joke. A comparable anecdote is recorded in which

Pythagoras tells an athlete to stop building a prison for himself, i.e. for his soul (*Gnomologium Vaticanum* 464); cf. Maximus 27.30, in which the same response is ascribed, doubtless secondarily, to the Cynic Crates: 'Seeing a young athlete taking on a large amount of flesh through wine-drinking, meat-eating, and exercise, he said, "My good fellow, stop creating a mighty prison for yourself." '

350 *never learned to speak well*: i.e. to speak well or rightly in general, a standard response also ascribed to Socrates (DL 2.36), Plato (*Gnomologium Vaticanum* 441, as a direct response to someone who abuses him), and, in slightly different form, to the Spartan Leotychidas (Plutarch, *Sayings of Spartans* 224de).

351 *speak badly of me*: Stobaeus records another version of this anecdote (3.2.40): 'The Socratic who was a Cynic [i.e. Antisthenes] heard someone of bad character speaking ill of Plato; "Leave off," he said, "because you are no more credible when you speak ill of him than he would be in praising you." ' Antisthenes, although not on the best of terms with Plato, does not care to hear someone running him down when he is unworthy to do so.

353 *strike me too when I'm not there*: in *Gnomologium Vaticanum* 222, Demosthenes is said to have made the same remark on being told that he was being abused by Philip of Macedon, whom he had attacked so fiercely in his speeches; the saying is also ascribed to Aristotle in a slightly different form (DL 5.18), 'he may whip me too when I'm not there'. Evidently a standing joke which came to be ascribed to a variety of people in the apophthegmatic tradition.

354a *ran into him with a plank*: this was evidently an old chestnut since Aristotle alludes to the story simply as that of 'the man carrying the plank' without needing to offer any further explanation (*Rhetoric* 1413b29; the phrase is sometimes mistranslated through misunderstanding of the reference). The second version is more distinctively Diogenean, being more drastic and making reference to his staff.

355 *that one needs to walk around in a helmet*: cf. Seneca, *On Anger* 3, 11.2, 'They say that when Socrates once received a blow on the ear, he merely remarked, "How tiresome it is that a man can't tell when he ought to put on a helmet when he goes out for a walk." '

356 *Meidias*: a rich citizen of Athens who slapped Demosthenes in the face while the orator was acting as choir-master at the Dionysian festival; Demosthenes entered a complaint against him for assault, and wrote a surviving speech for delivery in court, but apparently withdrew the case without ever delivering it. Aeschines claimed that he had been bribed to withdraw through a payment of 3,000 drachmas (*Against Ctesiphon* 52). Demosthenes seems to have made rather a fool of himself over this issue, and the present story, in which Diogenes shows the proper way to deal with a bully like that, is a joke at his expense. There is a play between two different senses of the word *trapeza*, table, in the original, which could be used both as a term for a banker's counter and a colloquial term

for someone's face (cf. 'clock' in English). Instead of allowing himself to be bought off with 3,000 drachmas on the counter, Diogenes gives him 3,000, i.e. a great many, blows on the face.

356 *thongs around his hand*: it was the custom for Greek boxers to wind leather thongs around their hands, which provided some protection to the hand, but also rendered their blows more damaging.

357 *want for receiving a punch*: Diogenes is asked what compensation he would want after being assaulted, but replies by saying what protection he would want for himself before being assaulted. Compensation was regularly sought in the courts for outrage against the person or battery.

364 *'Let nothing evil enter in'*: such signs, which were supposed to exercise an apotropaic power in keeping evil influences at bay, were regularly attached to the front of houses. Eunuchs were often regarded as being of bad character.

365 *'After conflict, alliance'*: there is another version of the preceding story in which it is asked how the owner's new wife will be able to get in (*Gnomologium Vaticanum* 564), and this seems to be a variation on that. The new wife has already got in, and Diogenes makes an addition to the inscription to indicate the new state of affairs. The Greek city-states regularly passed from conflict to alliance and back again. Heracles was often invoked as a protective deity and was also portrayed for that reason on amulets.

366a *hadn't lost anything*: this is also recorded as a fable (Phaedrus 1.10), in which a wolf tries to prove a charge of theft against a fox in front of an ape. After listening to each side, the ape concludes, '*You* do not seem to have lost the property for which you are suing, and I am confident that *you* stole that which you so eloquently deny having stolen.' The moral being that one who gains a reputation for deceit will not be believed even when he tells the truth.

370a *with leather coats*: to protect their high-quality wool; Megara was noted for its wool-trade.

371 *Myndos*: near Halicarnassos in Caria, on the west coast of Asia Minor.

372 *you are their neighbours*: Messenia, the land to the west of Sparta, had been reduced to subjection by the Spartans; the quotation comes from Hesiod's *Works and Days* 348.

373 *embracing a bronze statue*: as one of the ascetic practices that he adopted to harden himself, as noted at the end of 11. It seems fair to allow a Spartan a return shot after the preceding anecdote.

374 *in your back*: it was a favourite form of humour in ancient Greece to cite a well-known line from Homer in an incongruous context, sometimes with a slight alteration that affected its meaning. In *Iliad* 8.95 Diomedes tries to rally Odysseus, telling him not to run off lest while he is *fleeing* (*pheugonti*) someone may fix a spear in his back; here Diogenes tells the youth not to lie in an unguarded position, lest while he is *lying* there

(*heudonti*; here evidently lying at his ease rather than actually asleep) someone may fix his 'spear' into him.

375 *laid hold of him*: *Iliad* 5.83. A man has been caught stealing valuable purple robes and faces death for his crime. In the original context, the poet is describing how dark death (*porphureos thanatos*) comes down over a hero's eyes when he is brought down in battle. The adjective *porphureos*, which can vary in its precise meaning, provides the link.

376 *plunder some corpses*: for the latter line, *Iliad* 10.343 and 387. We are to imagine someone stealing clothes at the baths while their owners are lying around naked; this conjures up quite an amusing picture.

377 *what you buy*: in the original, *Iliad* 18.95, the goddess Thetis tells her son Achilles that he will be fated to a swift death 'by what you say (*agoreueis*)', namely that he will kill Hector to avenge the death of his friend Patroclos; for Achilles is fated to meet his own death soon after that of Hector. Diogenes changes *agoreueis* to *agorazeis*, 'what you buy'. The humour lies in the bathos.

378 *even more puffed up than your mother was*: quite a few of the jokes ascribed to Diogenes depend on puns and word-play which are not easily translatable. A handful of such jokes have been picked out by way of example. Here there is a play between 'having the puff' to play a musical instrument and being 'puffed up' or full of oneself. The joke turns on the fact that the women who played the flute at men's parties tended to be regarded as little more than prostitutes, and the young man's airs and graces are therefore in ill accord with his birth. In another version of this story, it is said that the Athenian orator Demades fathered his son Demeas by a flute-playing courtesan, and when this Demeas once assumed grand airs while speaking in the Assembly, the orator Hypereides put him to shame by making this joke (Athenaeus 13, 591f).

379 *end up inside*: in the Greek a play between two different senses of the verb *empiptein*, the runaway slave might 'fall into' the well or 'be thrown into' prison.

380 *a rubbing or the robing*: *ep'aleimmation e ep'all'himation*, i.e. has he come for the oils (which were rubbed into the body to clean it) or for the clothes, a *himation* being a kind of garment. Yet another example of humour about clothes-thieves at the baths, which seems to have been a favourite topic. The word-play is more clever and unexpected than in the average Greek joke of this kind.

381 *Olympia to Nemea*: the Olympic Games and the Nemean Games were two of the four games in the old athletic circuit, and champion athletes would try to amass victories at all four of them; but instead of travelling from one to the other in a literal sense, this one has passed rapidly downhill, so it is suggested, to end up pasturing (*nemein*) sheep. Although the prizes at the games in the old circuit were of purely symbolic value, an Olympic victor would normally receive a monetary reward from his city

and also be able to profit indirectly from his victory. It would thus be unusual for a victor to sink into obscurity and poverty.

382 *from Tegea*: Tegea was a city in Arcadia, but its name is suggestive of the word *tegos*, literally meaning a roof, but here carrying the implied meaning of brothel.

383 *which of these is Cheiron*: Cheiron was the name of the wisest of the Centaurs (cf. 101 and note), but the name was pronounced the same as *cheiron* meaning 'worse'.

385 *throw that over*: just as his opponent would be no match for one of the columns that supported the building, and would feel no shame at that fact, Diogenes submits with equanimity when he finds himself caught at a disadvantage by a younger and stronger opponent.

388 *Speusippos . . . Xenocrates*: Speusippos was Plato's nephew and his successor as head of his school, the Academy, but he invited Xenocrates of Chalcedon, another eminent pupil of Plato, to take over from him in 340 after he suffered a stroke. Xenocrates was confirmed as head of the school in a contested vote after Speusippos died in 339/8.

391 *sleep and death*: brothers both figuratively and in myth, in which they are both sons of Night (Hesiod, *Theogony* 211; cf. *Iliad* 16.672 as brothers). A similar story was recounted about the sophist Gorgias, who was said to have reached the age of 100 (*c*.480–380); when friends asked him how he was faring as he sank into his final sleep, he replied that sleep was now beginning to hand him over to his brother (Aelian, *Historical Miscellany* 2.35).

392 *road to Hades is just the same*: a commonplace, mostly ascribed in the apophthegmatic tradition either to Diogenes or to the pre-Socratic philosopher Anaxagoras (e.g. DL 2.11); the saying is better in Greek because 'hodos', the word for a road, sounds quite similar to 'Hades'.

393 *'The owner of the inn'*: the smell will bury him (cf. Lucian, *Demonax* 66), as is implied more directly in a version in the Arabic tradition.

395 *sprinkle a little earth over him*: i.e. grant him the barest formalities of burial, as did Antigone for her brother Polyneices (Sophocles, *Antigone* 255–6); after expressing the basic thought in drastic Cynic fashion, he concedes that some slight show of respect might be permissible.

might be of use to his brothers: i.e. the fish of this stream in Attica; one may suspect, however, that the original thought was that Diogenes should be of use to his brother *dogs* when thrown out unburied, and that the phrase has become detached from its proper context, as could easily happen when summaries were being compiled. Diogenes was no St Francis.

396 *Hyrcanian burial*: Hyrcania, familiar to readers of Latin poetry for the fierceness of its tigers, lay to the south and south-east of the Caspian Sea. Onesicritos (see 407 and notes) reported that the Hyrcanians threw their aged and infirm to dogs which were kept specifically for that purpose and were known as 'entombers' (Strabo 11.11.3).

vultures . . . Bactrian burial: referring to Zoroastrian burial practice in which corpses would be exposed in high places to be devoured by birds of prey, particularly associated in Greek literature with Bactria (hence the name inserted in this corrupt text), e.g. Plutarch, *Whether Vice is Sufficient to Cause Unhappiness* 3, 499d.

397a *Antigonos*: see **193** and note, an inappropriate interlocutor.

398a *eating an octopus raw*: the tradition that Diogenes died from eating an octopus raw surely originated as a humorous tale. As it happens, someone else from the same general period was supposed to have died from eating an octopus, namely the poet Philoxenos of Cythera (5th–4th century BC), who had a reputation for gluttony. The story goes that he bought an octopus at Syracuse which was two cubits (three feet) long and, in a heroic act of gluttony, consumed all of it in a single sitting apart from the head. He suffered severe indigestion as a consequence, and was warned by a doctor that he would soon die and should settle his affairs; he then set to work to devour what was left of the octopus before taking his leave (Athenaeus 8, 341 ff., quoting an extract from the comic poet Machon, 3rd century BC). One may suspect that it was this tale that inspired the present story about Diogenes, in which the Cynic eats the octopus raw in accordance with his uncouth and primitive ways. It is impossible to tell whether the story was devised with hostile or with merely humorous intent; but the grotesque fate seems somehow appropriate for the eccentric sage, and this is one of the more memorable features of his legend.

Cercidas of Megalopolis: 3rd century BC, a poet with Cynic sympathies who also engaged in public affairs, and drew up a constitution for his Arcadian city.

Diogenes in very truth: his name means 'born of Zeus'. At least no translator can be accused of failing to convey an adequate impression of the virtues of Diogenes Laertius' poetry.

Antisthenes: not the supposed master of Diogenes of course, but a later author of books about philosophers, apparently a Peripatetic (Phlegon, *On Wonders* 3.5).

he had deliberately held his breath: this form of suicide was also ascribed to Metrocles, **459**, and Zeno, DL 7.28; it could be seen as a noble form of death, as one that is calm, involves no violence and causes no disfigurement, and demands exceptional will-power. Whether any such person actually killed himself in that way is another question; the main advantage of this form of suicide for creators of biographical legends seems to have been that, since it would leave no mark, it could be ascribed to a sage who was simply found lying dead.

398b *one sees among other memorials*: an eyewitness account by the travel-writer Pausanias, who visited Corinth in the 2nd century AD. That a memorial was shown to visitors there in later ages as being that of Diogenes does not prove, of course, that he did in fact die in Corinth, although that came to be the most favoured tradition.

399 *Ilissos*: a stream that flowed just outside Athens, its surroundings are evoked at the beginning of Plato's *Phaedrus*, 229a ff. The neighbouring gymnasium would have been the Cynosarges, which was evidently brought into the story because of its association with Antisthenes, who was said to have taught there (see **534** and note).

400a *he choked himself*: evidently by holding his breath, as in the tradition associated with Corinth.

401 *expired after being bitten in the leg by a dog*: it was poetic justice for the Dog to die from the bite of a dog (as was also recounted of his runaway slave: see **13c**); as Diogenes Laertius mentions in **398**, there was a secondary version of the octopus story in which he was said to have suffered this fate while dividing an octopus among some dogs, although it is possible that there was also another story (or stories) in which he was said to have been bitten in other circumstances.

402a *to remove the need for the use of fire*: since the eating of a raw octopus could be seen as an absurd or revolting act, or as one that was undertaken out of a vain desire for notoriety, authors who had Cynic sympathies tried to provide a favourable explanation for it, by claiming that Diogenes was setting out to test whether the belief that raw meat is unfit for human consumption is truly justified, or else no more than a conventional supposition. If that were so, he could be said to have been risking his life for the benefit of humanity. Writing long after our present author Plutarch, in the 4th century AD, the Emperor Julian defended Diogenes' action on such grounds (*Oration* 9.11, 191b–193c), although it is plain the idea had already been suggested by Plutarch's time, and indeed clothed in anecdotal form. Plutarch himself is unimpressed, and poor Diogenes is subjected to undeserved reproof.

Pelopidas . . . Harmodios and Aristogeiton: Pelopidas was a Theban who played a leading part in delivering his city from Spartan tyranny in 379; there is a life of him by Plutarch. For the Atheneian tyrannicides Harmodios and Aristogeiton see note to **235**.

403 *Sosicrates*: a historical writer of the 2nd century BC.

Xeniades . . . purchased Diogenes: see **254** ff.; Diogenes supposedly acted as pedagogue to Xeniades' children, this being a duty that was performed by trusted slaves.

convinced that he was mad: even if conversion stories of this kind did not generally need to be approached with some scepticism, there is specific reason to doubt that this one has any historical basis, namely because it presupposes that Diogenes really served as a domestic slave in Corinth, and that his supposed master Xeniades was a historical figure, which is open to serious doubt. It is quite possible that this story originated in one of the romances that were written about Diogenes' life as a slave in Corinth (see **266–7** and notes).

Menander, the writer of comedies: c.342–291, the leading author of Athenian

New Comedy; a younger contemporary of Monimos who was writing for an audience who would have had knowledge of him as a local character.

Not one but three: the suggestion presumably being that he was rather too fond of his food.

light poems leavened with a hidden seriousness: the fragments from the poems of Crates in 439 ff. will give an impression of their probable nature; Monimos was evidently one of the initiators of this Cynic genre of seriocomic moralizing verse.

404a *Xeniades of Corinth*: an obscure philosopher with sceptical views who apparently lived in the 5th century (at any rate not later than Democritos); not to be confused with the Xeniades who was supposed to have purchased Diogenes.

everything is illusion: he used the word *tuphos*, the favourite Cynic term for illusion or vanity. This report by Sextus Empiricus, a sceptical philosopher of the 2nd century AD, is confirmed by the verses from Menander cited in 403. By contrast to conventional Cynics, who were concerned only to criticize conventional value-judgements as consisting of no more than vain illusion, Monimos evidently developed sceptical views with regard to our experience of the world around us, which led him to deny that sense-impressions can provide us with knowledge of anything that lies beyond them, and so to denounce any assumption of such knowledge as being mere *tuphos* or illusion. So although he was making use of a Cynic catchword, he was applying it in a different context from the usual one. As is indicated in Menander's verses, his scepticism affected his moral outlook too, but we can only speculate as to exactly how.

404b *Metrodoros and Anaxarchos*: Metrodoros of Chios and Anaxarchos of Abdera, 4th century BC, two followers of Democritos who held sceptical views. Anaxarchos accompanied Alexander to the East, together with Pyrrho of Elis, who would become the most famous of the early sceptical thinkers; he was said to have achieved an extraordinary impassibility, *apatheia*, which enabled him to remain happy in any circumstances (see DL 58–60). In that respect, his scepticism seems to have brought him quite close to what the Cynics were aiming at, and this may enable us to form some idea of how the scepticism of Monimos harmonized with his Cynicism.

the criterion: i.e. criterion of truth, which would enable us to determine whether any assertion is true as against its opposite.

in sleep or madness: memorable imagery which is presumably intended to convey an epistemological argument. Stage-scenery is painted to deceive: it gives the impression of portraying a solid three-dimensional world, but is in fact a mere surface with nothing behind or beyond it. In everyday life we imagine similarly that our senses are bringing us into contact with solid reality, but all that we really experience is a flux of sensation which provides no reliable information about what lies beyond that; our sense-impressions can thus be compared to delusive mental states, in which we imagine that we are beholding things that are not really there. The Cyrenaics developed a similar scepticism with regard to sense-experience (see **621–4**), but Monimos seems to have been exceptional among the Cynics in showing an interest in such matters.

404c *the words that were addressed to the Cynic Monimos*: the point seems to be that his very words were turned against him; if it is true that everything is mere supposition, then this very claim is itself a mere supposition, and the assertion is self-refuting. Although Marcus, as a Stoic, could not have accepted his scepticism in any case, he sees some value in the thought if it is interpreted in the right way. We should not worry too much about external things but concentrate on forming right judgements within ourselves.

405 *vomit of fortune*: also ascribed to Diogenes, **139**, but more likely to have been transferred from the lesser-known figure to the more famous than vice versa.

406 *the ditch . . . the pit*: *borthron, barathron*; the two words were related and meant much the same, a pit or cleft, but *barathron* was also the name that was specifically applied to the cleft at Athens into which criminals were hurled, and was thus used figuratively as a term for ruin or perdition.

407 *Onesicritos*: as the following accounts of his life and activities would suggest, Onesicritos did not follow the full Cynic way of life even if he had sympathy for Cynic ideas. Of particular interest in this connection is his account of the 'gymnosophists' (naked sophists), Indian ascetics whom he encountered on his travels (Strabo 15.1.63–5); he confirmed in this account that he had been a pupil of Diogenes. He was chief pilot of Alexander's fleet during the voyage from the Indus to the Persian Gulf.

Cyrus . . . Alexander: Xenophon took part in the unsuccessful expedition that the younger Cyrus, son of Darius II of Persia, mounted against his brother Artaxerxes II; he wrote an account of this 'expedition of the ten thousand' in his *Anabasis*. There is no record of the nature of Onesicritos' services to Alexander until he was appointed to be pilot of his fleet on the way back from India.

Education of Cyrus: or *Cyropaedia*, which purported to be an account of the education of Cyrus the Great, the founder of the Achaemenid dynasty in Persia.

in praise of Cyrus: i.e. of the younger Cyrus, in the *Anabasis*.

408 *a certain Onesicritos of Aegina*: DL's use of language here would suggest that he regarded this Onesicritos as being a different man from the famous Onesicritos who became the pilot of Alexander's fleet. If the latter had adult sons, moreover, at the time when he set off with Alexander, he must have been a fair age when he left. So were there two men of that name who both became followers of Diogenes (unlikely though that may seem), one from Aegina and the other from Astypalaia? Opinions differ and there is too little evidence to enable a definitive conclusion to be reached.

already mentioned: in connection with the question of the authorship of Diogenes' writings, see following note. No anecdotes are recorded of Philiscos or indeed of his brother, apart from the present one.

drawn no less than his sons: it hardly needs saying that this tale, which follows a pattern familiar in folklore, should not be taken too seriously. It is indeed quite possible that the father, if he was in fact a different man from the famous Onesicritos, never really became a follower of Diogenes and the tale itself came to be invented because the two men of that name were wrongly identified. Philiscos at least seems to have been a figure of some significance in the early Cynic movement, since the tragedies ascribed to Diogenes were sometimes said to have been his work (see 218), and a *Philiscos* is named among the supposed writings of Diogenes (see 217 and 218). The *Suda* (s.v. Philiscos) claims that Philiscos of Aegina was the boyhood tutor of Alexander (cf. Aelian, *Miscellaneous History* 14.11, in which a Philiscos gives him some good advice), but that can be ruled out on chronological grounds alone, even if that role were not normally ascribed to Leonidas of Epirus; the story may well have been no more than an invention (although some have suggested that this was another Philiscos who was the father of Onesicritos rather than his son).

Phocion: 'the Good', a prominent Athenian statesman and general, *c*.402–*c*.318; the report here that he was a disciple of Diogenes cannot be taken seriously, although one can understand how that notion could have arisen, since he was famous for the austerity and frugality of his way of life.

Stilpo: *c*.360–280, and thus a contemporary of Crates, the third head of the Megarian school of philosophy. Although he, like other members of that school, diverged from the Cynics in the attention that he devoted to dialectic, he does seem to have had some affinity to them with regard to his moral ideas. Diogenes Laertius reports elsewhere (9.2.113) that he derived his philosophical education from followers of Eucleides, the founder of the Megarian school, and perhaps specifically from Thrasymachos of Corinth, a friend of Ichthyas, his predecessor as head of the school. The *Suda* (s.v. Stilpo) also mentions another Megarian, Pasicles, the brother of Crates, as a teacher of his. Any associations with the Cynics are likely to have been more informal. Whether or not he was directly influenced by Diogenes, he is shown in the company of Crates in the anecdotal tradition (see 446, 466, and 490) and also with the Cynic Metrocles (Plutarch, *On Tranquillity of Mind* 468a, in which Stilpo defends himself against the reproach that the loose morals of his daughter cast discredit on him); and one of the books ascribed to Stilpo is entitled the *Metrocles*.

410 *written precepts*: it is surely Diogenes' Cynic disciple (408) who makes this request, rather than the Cyrenaic of that name as is sometimes supposed. The saying is neater in the original Greek because *graphō* and related words can refer both to writing and painting.

411 *Bryson the Achaean*: an obscure 4th-century philosopher, apparently

belonging to the Megarian school; no importance should be attached to this divergent account. The verses of Crates which are inserted in DL's biography of him will be placed separately along with the other verse fragments.

411 *the 'Door-opener'*: *Thurepanoiktēs*; as a peace-maker of conciliatory character who was widely regarded with affection, Crates is presented as being of very different character from the acerbic Diogenes.

113th Olympiad: 328–324 BC.

Telephos, in a tragedy: in legend, the son of Heracles and Auge who became king of the Mysians in Asia Minor. When the Greeks landed in his kingdom by accident when they first tried to cross over to Troy, Achilles inflicted a wound on him which failed to heal. This anecdote plainly refers to a lost tragedy by Euripides, the *Telephos*, in which Telephos visited the Greek camp at Aulis disguised as a beggar to try to find out how his wound could be healed. Odysseus finally revealed the cure by working out the correct interpretation of an enigmatic response from the Delphic oracle. For distressed heroes from tragedy as an exemplar for Cynics, cf. **15** and note.

Philemon: of Athens, *c.*362–262, a leading playwright of the New Comedy and rival of Menander.

stayed in that of Hipparchia: the verb that governed both parts of the sentence has dropped out, but it seems most likely that the monarchs were said to have lodged in the respective houses, the only other possibility being that they destroyed those houses. Philip of Macedon captured Maroneia, the home-city of Crates' wife Hipparchia, in 355, most probably before Hipparchia's birth. The idea that he lodged in her family house at that time, whether or not that was true, could have inspired the corresponding idea that Alexander had stayed in that of her future husband Crates (even if he would never have had an opportunity to do so). People seem to have been determined to wind the Macedonian kings into the legends of the early Cynics; cf. also **424** and note for Crates.

if his sons turned out to be ordinary men: this account seems to imply that he already had children at the time of his conversion to philosophy, which appears not to be the case; it is otherwise reported that he had a single son as a result of his 'dog-marriage' to Hipparchia. Demetrios was a biographer and literary scholar of the 1st century BC.

Eratosthenes: of Cyrene, polymathic scholar of the 3rd century BC and director of the Alexandrian library.

took him to a brothel: cf. **165** and note, but more drastic in this context; the usual Cynic message that sex is mere biology and we should have no illusions about it.

Pasicles, who was a pupil of Eucleides: although Pasicles, as the brother of Crates, would have been born too late to be an immediate pupil of Eucleides, the friend of Socrates who founded the Megarian school, he apparently belonged to that school, and there was a tradition that Stilpo was a pupil of his (see note to **407**); the fact that Crates had a brother in that school may help to explain the close ties that developed between the Cynics and Megarians at this period. Diogenes Laertius has presumably confused Eucleides with a more obscure member of the Megarian school, Dioclides, who is stated elsewhere to have been a pupil of Eucleides who became the teacher of Pasicles (*Suda* s.v. Stilpon).

412a *left 30 talents to the Thebans*: as can be seen here, various conflicting stories were recounted about the way in which Crates was supposed to have disposed of his wealth, and it may be assumed that all of them were invented in accordance with conventional patterns.

413 *Epictetus*: AD *c.*55–*c.*135, a Stoic philosopher familiar from his surviving *Discourses*, which were recorded by one of his followers.

'Crates robs Crates of all that he owns': the two sayings in **413** and **414** are ultimately derived from verses by Crates himself, the one running 'Crates robs Crates of his goods,│lest they should come to hold sway over their master', and the other, 'Crates of Thebes sets Crates free', both probably forming part of the same poem.

416d *household god*: *lar familiaris*, protective spirit of the household; in this Latin source the comparison is drawn from Roman culture, but Apuleius was evidently following Greek sources in which Crates was described as a good spirit, *agathos daimon* (cf. Julian, *Oration* 9, 17, 200b).

large entrance-hall: i.e. to be able to receive many clients, properly a feature of Roman rather than of Greek culture.

good and happy life: the end of this passage is lost.

417a *Demetrios of Phaleron*: an Athenian orator (*c.*350–280) who held power in Athens from 317 to 307 after being installed as head of the government by Cassandros, king of Macedonia; a highly cultivated man who might well have taken a sympathetic interest in someone like Crates. Although Crates abstained from wine, Diogenes seems to have been happy to drink it, and this was a matter for individual choice among Cynics.

420 *all schemings of envy*: this passage reports something that Crates said about himself, evidently in some verses.

423 *as though he were at a festival*: cf. Diogenes in **112**, for the wise and good every day should be like a festival.

424 *native city to be rebuilt*: Alexander destroyed Thebes in 335 after the Thebans mounted an unsuccessful revolt against the Macedonian hegemony. W. W. Tarn once remarked that 'the only occasion on which Alexander and Crates could conceivably have met was when Alexander was actually destroying Thebes'. Be that as it may, the saying is a good one.

426 *monument of the courtesan Phryne*: see **169** and note.

432 *generals . . . no different from donkey-drivers*: the Greek word for a general, *strategos*, means 'army-leader' but could also be interpreted as meaning 'army-driver' (cf. *onegos*, donkey-driver); we should come to see that they are more like donkey-drivers, driving their men into battle like brute beasts. In the Cynic view, war was a pointless activity, provoked by covetousness aroused by the material excess in rival cities.

434 *the inscription 'Nicodromos did this'*: according to a story derived from an early Cynic source, Diogenes was said to have reacted in a similar manner when assaulted (see 188 and note). The inscription resembles that which a sculptor would mark on his statue ('X made this'), as is explicitly mentioned in an account of this story by Gregory of Nazianzen (*Oration* 4.72, where this action is ascribed to Antisthenes, doubtless by error).

435 *your knees*: to grasp someone by the knees was a standard gesture of supplication; the man objected to Crates' gesture because it could have sexual overtones.

436 *From heaven's threshold*: *Iliad* 1.591, Hephaistos describing how he was thrown down from heaven by Zeus.

Menedemos . . . Asclepiades: two leading members of the Eretrian school of philosophy, an offshoot of the Eleian school founded by Phaedo, a pupil of Socrates; the two men were famous for their close friendship, DL 2.137.

at home: *endon*, literally meaning inside; this is what one would ask if one were enquiring at the door to ask whether someone was at home.

437 *Demetrios . . . banished from his homeland*: the regime of Demetrios of Phaleron at Athens was overturned when Demetrios I of Macedonia sailed there in 307. He had to flee and was sentenced to death in his absence by his enemies in the city. This story may be compared with that in which Diogenes approaches Dionysios II of Syracuse during his exile in Thebes, 251, and really does give him a Cynic tongue-lashing. Any distress that Demetrios may have suffered was not long-lasting, since he found a comfortable berth at the court of Ptolemy I at Alexandria.

never came to know such a man as that: this is a quotation from a tragedy by Euripides fr. 962 Nauck.

438 *Exhortation to Philosophy*: or *Protreptic*, a famous early work of Aristotle from which only fragments have survived.

Philiscos: plainly not the early Cynic of that name in 408. Since this tale seems to have been inspired by the story of the cobbler Simon, who was supposed to have written Socratic dialogues after listening to the conversation of Socrates in his workshop (see 671-3 and notes), this Philiscos may well be an imaginary character.

439 *a city, Pera*: a pseudo-epic passage, describing the city of Pera ('Knapsack') as though it were some island encountered by Odysseus on his travels. Instead of being set in the 'wine-dark sea', it is set in the wine-dark 'vapour' (*tuphos*, a word also used in a figurative sense to mean vanity and illusion, see 137 and note; in the Cynic context specifically used to refer to the illusions that people become embroiled in because of the value that

they attach to wealth, sensual gratification, social repute, etc.); so in short, 'Knapsack', symbolizing the life of moderation and self-sufficiency, is an island of refuge in the midst of the world of illusion that most people inhabit. The first two lines are a direct parody of *Odyssey* 19.172–3, 'There is a land called Crete, in the midst of the wine-dark sea, fair and rich [literally, fat], girded round with water'; *perrirutos*, the word that was used to express the latter idea, is altered into *perirupos*, 'very filthy'.

thyme: there is evidently a play on words here between *thumos*, meaning thyme, and *thumos* (identical in sound except for the different accentuation) meaning courage or good heart.

do not fight or go to war: for the thought here, cf. **217**, the uselessness of weapons, and note.

'Account-book': that the price of things does not accord with their true value, and that the most valuable things are sold for a song, was a standard Cynic thought (cf. **24**) which Crates expressed anew in this versified account-book. There were 6 obols to the drachma, 100 drachmas to the mina, and 60 minas to the talent in the Athenian reckoning. One should make allowance here for hyperbole.

empty smoke: i.e. *tuphos* again, also meaning vanity, illusion; the riches of the soul are what really belong to us, it is an illusion to suppose that material wealth does. These verses parody an inscription that was supposed to have been found on the tomb of Saradanapalos (a legendary king of Assyria noted for his extreme self-indulgence), in which it was said that he had eaten and enjoyed the delights of love, but that all his great wealth was gone.

a noose: cf. **111** and note.

440 *my prayer*: this is a parody of a famous verse-prayer composed by the Athenian statesman Solon (*c*.638–558; fr. 13 Bergck); or, perhaps more accurately, it is a Cynic variation on that prayer. Whereas Solon starts by saying that he wants prosperity and reputation, Crates asks for just enough food to enable him to maintain his simple way of life.

Make me useful rather than sweet to my friends: Solon, ibid., line 5, asks to be sweet to his friends but sour to his foes, reflecting the traditional thought, rejected in the Socratic tradition, that one should strive to help one's friends and harm one's enemies. Crates asks, by contrast, not to be sweet even to his friends; for that might suggest complaisance and flattery to a Cynic—to be genuinely useful to one's friends, one might need to be harsh with them. Diogenes was said accordingly to have cast scorn on Plato as being a man who had never caused pain to anyone (**122**, and cf. **221–3**).

wealth: the possession of *olbos*, wealth and prosperity, righteously gained but then enduring, is the prime object of Solon's aspiration in his prayer, but Crates starts by stating his scorn of wealth, and points to righteousness as being his essential aim; only secondarily does he ask for a modicum of 'wealth', i.e. as much in the way of material things as may be

easily gained and conducive to virtue. One may compare the thought
here with that in Socrates' prayer at the end of Plato's *Phaedrus* (279bc).

442 *lentil soup*: as a form of cheap natural food, lentils came to be especially
associated with the Cynics (see e.g. Athenaeus 4, 156ce), in the same way
as lupin seeds, and lentil soup could be seen as symbolizing their simple
way of life.

443 *lentil soup*: *kogchos*, apparently referring to a form of lentil soup rather
than cockles.

for the rout of penury: since the verses have been wound into the prose
text, the original lines have had to be reconstructed, 'in a pot' and
'friend' being additions made for that purpose; after a battle, it was customary for the winning side to raise a trophy, by building up a tumulus
or setting up captured arms, either at the battlefield or an appropriate
religious sanctuary.

444 *a quart of lupins*: such a quantity of lupin seeds could be bought at negligible expense (see 24 and notes), and this was a food that was emblematic of the Cynics in the same way as lentils.

446 *a new coat and a change of mind*: in the original Greek the latter point is
not directly stated but, rather, indicated through a play on words (though
a gloss explaining the point later found its way into the text); for in the
phrase *himatiou kainou*, meaning new tunic, the second word could also
be interpreted as *kai nou*, 'and mind'. The same word-play is ascribed to
Antisthenes in DL 6.3; when a new pupil comes to attend his lectures
and asks what he will need, Antisthenes replies, 'Come with a new book,
and a new pen, and a new writing-tablet', the double meaning being
implied in each case. The moral ideas of the Megarian philosopher Stilpo
(see note to 407) were not so very different from those of the Cynics, but
he was also greatly interested in dialectic, which the Cynics regarded as
no more than useless logic-chopping and deceptive argument; and that is
the ground on which Crates launches his counter-attack.

Stilpo . . . suffering bitter woes: a parody of Odysseus' account of his visit
to the Underworld in book 11 of the *Odyssey*, during which that hero
sees (among other things) a succession of dead heroes suffering punishment (575 ff.). A typical posthumous punishment was some form of
never-ending labour, and here Stilpo is caught in never-ending disputes
about the nature of virtue, without ever drawing a step nearer to the
achievement of virtue. In the view of the Cynics the pursuit of virtue was
more a matter of strenuous action than of words and theories.

In Megara: Stilpo's home of course, but in the Greek this sounds very
similar to the common Homeric expression *en megaroisi* ('in the halls
of . . .').

bed of Typhoeus lies: Typhoeus, perhaps more familiar as Typhon, was a
fearsome primordial monster who was variously said to have been
consigned to Tartaros, or buried in the land of the Arimoi (wherever
that may have been), or buried under Mount Etna, hence that volcano's

occasional eruptions. The second alternative is stated in a line in the *Iliad* (2.783), which Crates reproduces here in altered form, replacing *ein Arimois* with *en Megarois*, 'in Megara', and so adapting the Homeric verse to suggest that *tuphos* or 'illusion' was firmly embedded in Megara. Another shaft aimed at the Megarian school—all their disputations are nothing more than hot air. The monster had no particular connection with Megara in myth.

argued: Crates uses the word *erizesken*, pointing to the sort of 'eristic' disputation that placed victory above truth.

with many a comrade around him: this second part of the line is drawn from Homer, *Iliad* 8.537; Hector says that he will leave one of his most valiant adversaries, Diomedes, dead on the ground with many of his comrades around him.

in word alone: i.e. through similitude, in verbal representations, rather than engaging directly with virtue itself (cf. 410); finally a line without any epic allusions.

447 *Asclepiades . . . Eretrian Bull*: this refers to Asclepiades and Menedemos, two leading members of the Eretrian school already mentioned in a previous anecdote; both studied with Stilpo, and Crates plainly included them too among the people whom he saw in the Underworld. The notion in 446 that he improvised the poem, or part of it, in response to a sally from Stilpo should not be taken seriously. Diogenes Laertius, 2.126, interprets Menedemos' nickname of the 'Eretrian Bull' as being a hit at his gravity or pomposity. There was a famous 'Eretrian bull' at Olympia, a magnificent bronze statue of a bull which the Eretrians had dedicated there as a votive offering, Pausanias 5.27.9.

448 *Micylos*: the reference is obscure, perhaps Micylos (meaning 'little') was simply a suitable name for an imaginary man of small means, as seems to be the case in Callimachus, *Epigram* 28; cf. the poor cobbler of that name in Lucian's *Cock*. The final line is altered from *Odyssey* 12.257, in which Odysseus describes how sailing companions of his who had been seized by the sea-monster Scylla 'reached out their hands toward me in their dreadful struggle'. The poverty-stricken Micylos and his wife are engaged in a death-struggle of their own kind.

453 *says Bion*: of Borysthenes: see Section XVI.

dropsy: see 479 and note.

Metrocles: a pupil of Crates (see 459), who had initially studied with Theophrastos and Xenocrates, who came to preside over the Peripatetic and Academic schools respectively.

454 *pedagogue*: *paidagogos*, a slave who would be entrusted with the care of young boys, and accompany them whenever they left the house.

cadet: at the age of 18 male Athenian citizens would be enrolled as *epheboi* or 'cadets', and undertake military training and garrison duty.

more heavily than Etna: lines from Euripides, *Heracles* 636–7; Mount

Etna was supposed to have been flung down on top of Typhon (according to one account of that monster's fate).

455 *Maroneia*: a coastal city in Thrace. It may be assumed that Hipparchia became acquainted with Crates through her brother Metrocles.

accompanying him to dinners: married women would not normally attend dinners with their husbands; the only female company that could be expected at male parties was that of *hetairai*, courtesans.

Lysimachos: a Macedonian officer who served under Alexander and, from 306 onward, ruled a kingdom on either side of the Hellespont.

Theodoros: see **633** ff. He made a famous visit to Lysimachos' court as an envoy for another king (see **634–8**), hence the setting for this story, but it is hardly probable that Hipparchia would ever have gone there. Theodoros was notorious for using sophistic arguments like the one that follows—see the examples in **633**—so it would seem that she is paying him back in his own coin. She could be reasonably supposed to have met him while he was living in Athens, and the *Suda* (s.v. Hipparchia) mentions some 'questions put to Theodoros the Atheist' among the works ascribed to her (the others being of unspecified content; Diogenes Laertius makes no reference to any such works).

shuttle and loom: Euripides, *Bacchae* 1326.

a great many others: all lost unfortunately, and we otherwise only have various apocryphal letters that are addressed to her: see **657** to **655**.

457 *Musonius*: Musonius Rufus, a Roman Stoic of the 1st century AD.

458a *Zeno . . . Cleanthes . . . Chrysippos*: three of the foremost early Stoics.

with regard to the philosopher Crates: plainly an exaggeration from the later tradition.

459 *Theophrastos the Peripatetic*: a pupil of Aristotle who became his successor as head of the Peripatetic school at Athens in 323/2.

deliberately ate a quantity of lupins: because lupins, rather like baked beans, were notorious for causing flatulence.

Hecaton: of Rhodes, a Stoic philosopher and author of the 2nd–1st century BC, a pupil of Panaetius.

infernal dreams: a tragic verse of unknown origin, adesp. 285 Nauck.

has need of you: *Iliad* 18.395; Hephaistos was the god of fire.

having choked himself: i.e. committed suicide by holding his breath, as Diogenes was also supposed to have done: see **398** and relevant note.

460 *his [Crates'] pupils*: these should be regarded as pupils of Crates, and not of Metrocles as is sometimes wrongly inferred from the position of this passage in Diogenes Laertius' text. Nothing more is recorded of Timarchos, Theombrotos, Echecles, and Demetrios. Cleomenes wrote a book describing the supposed activities of Diogenes as a pedagogue in Corinth (see **266**). On Menedemos see **461** and notes. Menippos of Sinope may be identified with the satirist Menippos: see **462** and note on his origins.

461   *Colotes of Lampsacos*: latter 4th to 3rd century BC, a leading pupil of
      Epicurus. Two papyri from Herculaneum (208, 1082) show him as argu-
      ing with Menedemos about the proper attitude to take to poetry. There
      seems no reason to doubt Diogenes Laertius' report that he also attended
      the lectures of the Cynic Theombrotos. This Menedemos should not be
      confused with Menedemos of Eretria who is mentioned above in con-
      nection with Crates.

      he went around in the guise of a Fury: Erinys, avenging spirit. It is assur-
      edly hard to believe that Menedemos should have claimed to have visited
      the Underworld, and to be acting as an agent for the infernal deities;
      fiction and reality have plainly become confused. Humorous accounts
      of supposed visits to the world of the dead were a feature of Cynic litera-
      ture. Crates presented himself as having seen a series of people in the
      Underworld, rather like a modern Odysseus (see 446–7), and Menippos
      developed the idea in his *Nekuia* (see 462 and note). Now it seems
      probable from Lucian that Menippos presented himself as a character
      in this work, as one who had visited Hades and seen the dead with his
      own eyes (just as Crates pretended to have done). So according to the
      usual view, first suggested by Walter Croenert a century ago, Menedemos
      has become confused with Menippos in the present passage, that is to
      say with Menippos as he portrayed himself in fictional guise in his
      Nekuia. Such errors could easily occur when compilers like Diogenes
      Laertius were making extracts from their sources, especially with regard
      to people who had similar names. As it happens, the *Suda* (s.v. *phaios*)
      quotes this same passage from Hippobotos, but as referring to Menippos
      the Cynic rather than to Menedemos. Hippobotos was writing in the late
      3rd century BC.

      tragic buskins: actors in tragedy wore distinctive knee-boots; one might
      say his entire garb is deliberately portrayed as being highly theatrical.

462   *his master was from Pontus*: Menippos was said to have come from Gadara
      in Hollow Syria (Strabo 16.759, Stephanos of Byzantium s.v. Gadara),
      and that is consistent with what Diogenes Laertius says about his
      Phoenician descent; if he was supposed to have been enslaved to a mas-
      ter from Pontus, i.e. the Black Sea area, it may have been by no mere
      error that DL should previously have referred to him as Menippos of
      Sinope. He lived in the 3rd century.

      his books are full of mockery: Menippos was remembered for his satirical
      writings rather than as a practitioner of the Cynic way of life. It should
      not be inferred from DL's remark about their lack of seriousness that
      they were lacking in all serious intent, since he wrote in the seriocomic
      (*spoudaiogeloion*) vein that was characteristic of Cynic authors.
      Unfortunately none of his works has survived, but we can gain some idea
      of their nature from Lucian, who sometimes imitated him quite closely.

      Meleager: Meleagros of Gadara; although best known for his surviving
      erotic epigrams, he also wrote Menippean satires. Even if he came from

the same city as Menippos, he was no contemporary of his, but in fact lived considerably later in the 1st century BC.

462 *usurer-by-the-day*: *hemerodaneistēs*, a word recorded nowhere else. According to this account, ascribed to Hermippos of Smyrna, late 3rd century BC, he made his fortune by lending money to shipping merchants, asking for a valuable security, and then making a handsome profit from that if their vessels were lost and they were unable to repay their loans. But this raises an obvious problem. Loans made for such a purpose are necessarily long-term loans, so why his name of lender-for-a-day? It has been suggested that a slight amendment should be made to the text, so that it would read that Menippos made his loans 'at nautical rates' (i.e. at very high rates, shipping being a risky business) rather than 'on the shipping'; but whatever the truth of that particular matter, no confidence can be placed in any of these biographical reports.

be a dog: a proper Cynic would have known that loss of money is no cause for despair.

not really his work: not to be taken too seriously; the supposed forgers are obscure figures.

A visit to the world below: *Nekuia*, a grave theme in Homer when Odysseus visits the Underworld in the 11th book of the *Odyssey*, but also one that lent itself to humorous or satirical treatment. The *Charon* and *Dialogues of the Dead* of Lucian give an idea of the approach that Menippos would have taken.

written by the gods: one may compare Lucian's *Letters of Cronos*.

honouring of the twentieth day: Epicurus asked in his will that his school should hold a special celebration on the twentieth day of every month in honour of himself and of his disciple and friend Metrodoros, DL 10.18. The practice was continued into the Roman period.

and some others: including the *Sale of Diogenes*, mentioned elsewhere by Diogenes Laertius (see 256a), a *Symposium* (Athenaeus 14, 629f) and an *Arcesilaos* (Athenaeus 14, 664c).

463 *Peiraeus*: the harbour of Athens.

cargo of purple: an expensive dye extracted from shellfish, especially the murex, which was one of the main export products of the Phoenicians.

Xenophon's Memorabilia: a collection of Socratic discourses; Antisthenes is one of the interlocutors in the second book (5.1–5), which also contains the little parable in which Heracles chooses the hard road to virtue (1.21 ff.), a theme that would become very important to the Cynics.

wanting to cure him of his bashfulness: compare the stories in 42 in which Diogenes imposes similar tasks on the prospective followers as a test.

Republic . . . on the dog's tail: this book took up some of the scandalous themes that had been developed in the *Republic* (and other works) ascribed to Diogenes (see 217). *Kunosoura* ('Dog's Tail') was a Greek name for the constellation of the Little Bear.

466 *Stilpo*: of Megara, a contemporary of Crates who was interested in logic and dialectic, but seems to have had some sympathy for Stoic moral ideas (see note to **407**). Zeno did in fact study under a variety of teachers, including two other dialecticians, Philo and Diodoros Chronos (DL 7.16), and developed a systematic philosophy in which logic, physics, and ethics formed three interlocked parts: see **96** and relevant note. So part of his mind could indeed be said to have remained with Stilpo.

467 *Borysthenes*: i.e. Olbia, a Milesian colony on the north coast of the Black Sea, often called Borysthenes after the river of that name that ran nearby. Bion was probably born in about 335 and lived until the late 240s.

Antigonos: Antigonos Gonatas (319–239), king of Macedonia; Bion spent some time at his court at Pella.

what parentage: *Odyssey* 10.325, a single line in the original; Circe asks this of Odysseus.

no face to show: there is a play in the Greek, not fully translatable, between the literal meaning and a figurative sense of the word *prosopon*, 'face'. After first stating figuratively that his father was a man of no consequence (or perhaps more technically that he had no legal personality, if that usage was not of later origin), Bion goes on to suggest that he had no face in a more literal sense, because it had been gravely disfigured.

branding: *sungraphē*, literally writing, but here most probably meaning branding, or else tattooing.

defrauded the customs: or acted dishonestly while working for the customs; the verb used here is otherwise unrecorded.

bought by a rhetorician: it seems to be suggested here that the man bought him because he found him sexually attractive.

I boast of having sprung: *Iliad* 6.211, 20.241, a proud declaration by heroes of noble descent; the irony of Bion's use of it in the present context hardly needs remarking.

Persaios and Philonides: Persaios of Citium (306–243) was a Stoic philosopher and pupil of Zeno who was invited to the Macedonian court; nothing is recorded about this Philonides. Evidently the people who had been primarily responsible for maligning Bion to the king.

provided detractors of philosophy with plenty of material: as will be seen, there were aspects of his way of life that might be seen as conflicting with his philosophical preaching.

sociable: reading *potimos* as in the manuscripts, although this is sometimes amended, e.g. to *pompikos*, to suggest that he could be pompous. After the end of this sentence, some paragraphs containing anecdotal material are omitted, until the end of 4.51, where the biographical narrative is resumed. The sayings and anecdotes have been separated out to be placed with others of a similar nature.

discourses of Crates: not Crates the Cynic but a rather obscure Academic philosopher of the same name, who presumably provided him with an introduction to moral thought.

467 *adopted the Cynic way of life*: it would seem from what follows, however, that he did not continue to live as a Cynic, but made a good living from his teaching and lectures as he travelled around the Greek world, and eventually came to benefit from the patronage of Antigonos Gonatas. As can be seen in this paragraph, he studied with philosophers from a variety of schools, as was not unusual at that period. His exact affinity is thus quite hard to pin down, although his preaching and mode of expression were distinctly Cynic in vein.

the lectures of Theodoros the Atheist: Theodoros was classed among the Cyrenaics (see 633 ff.), although he too was fairly eclectic in his views. His interest in sophistic argument, which is specifically mentioned here, was something that marked him off from more orthodox Cyrenaics; he had studied dialectic with a member of the Megarian school (see 633 and relevant note). Although there is nothing distinctively Theodorean or Cyrenaic in the sayings of Bion, he resembled the Cyrenaics in so far as he was happy to accept fees, associate with potentates, and apparently enjoy worldly pleasures when they were available to him. If he had ever been tempted to adopt a rigorously Cynic way of life, his association with Theodoros may have encouraged him to take a more relaxed attitude.

Theophrastos the Peripatetic: the successor of Aristotle as head of that school, an old man by the time that Bion was studying with him. As to what specific influence Theophrastos may have exerted on Bion, that is very hard to say. It has been observed, however, that in his portrayal of character-types (e.g. the superstitious man, the envious man, and the like), he does seem to have been influenced by Theophrastos' book of character-sketches.

a flowery dress: of the kind worn by courtesans. Eratosthenes of Cyrene (*c*.275–194) was a versatile scholar who became director of the Alexandrian library.

Archytas: the Archytas addressed here is presumably the famous Pythagorean, Archytas of Tarentum, 4th century BC. The parody plays around with Homeric expressions.

philosopher's dress: or scholar's dress, *scholastikas esthetas*; i.e. a simple cloak without a tunic.

'friends hold all things in common': naturally a helpful thought for a scrounger; this entire section is derived from a hostile source, containing malicious gossip and standard motifs of abuse.

Betion . . . Menedemos: the philosopher Menedemos of Eretria, who was also associated with Bion's patron Antigonos Gonatas, DL 2.141. This Betion or Bition is otherwise unknown.

wear an amulet: Bion had been exceedingly scornful of superstition (see 490 ff.).

468 *to blame for all these ills*: see **107** and note.

471 *moral wisdom*: *phronēsis*, as in the preceding apophthegm; Bion is specifically praising moral and practical wisdom, which was the supreme
virtue for the Cynics, rather than wisdom of a theoretical or contempla-
tive nature. The foolishness grounded in false opinion, which is the subject of the following apophthegms, is the opposite of this *phronēsis*, and
it is attacked accordingly as providing an obstacle to moral progress.

474 *all grief*: reading *aniōn*, to give a similar meaning to the two preceding
sayings; *areton* gives a meaning that is surely inappropriate to Bion,
'glory is the mother of all virtues'.

475 *suitors . . . Penelope*: the leading men of Ithaca tried to court Penelope
during the long absence of her husband Odysseus, but she managed to
fend them off until his return, a central theme of the *Odyssey*. This is a
figurative expression of the general Cynic attitude to 'useless culture',
cf. **96** ff. and notes. Aristippos is said to have remarked similarly that
those who studied the standard (encyclical) educational subjects but
stopped short of philosophy were like Penelope's suitors (DL 2.79), and
the comparison was also taken up by the Cynicizing Stoic Ariston of
Chios (Stobaeus 3.4.109).

476 *wanderings . . . gone astray*: there is a play here between two different
senses of the word *planē*, which can mean both 'wandering' and, in a
more metaphorical sense, 'wandering astray' or 'falling into error' (cf.
104 and note); Diogenes was said to have used a similar comparison to
make the same point, **97**.

477 *those in the heavens*: i.e. the constellations of the Fishes and the Southern
Fish; a rather strained elaboration of the old commonplace that those
who devote their attentions to the heavens (or more generally, study of
universal nature) fail to see what lies beneath their feet. The early sage
Thales was said to have fallen into a ditch while looking at the stars,
prompting an onlooker to ask, 'How can you expect to know what goes
on in the heavens, Thales, when you cannot even see what lies beneath
your feet?' (DL 1.34).

478 *mother-city of all evils*: also ascribed to Diogenes, **138**, and probably popular wisdom that was older than either.

479 *hydroptic*: for this comparison, also ascribed to Diogenes, see **146** and
note.

  good repute and superstitious: this saying can be seen in its original setting
in Teles' diatribe in **453**, in a passage which is largely concerned with
Crates.

487 *Amphiaraos*: a legendary Argive hero and seer who took part in the expedition of the Seven against Thebes; to save him from being killed as he
fled in his chariot after the failure of the attack, Zeus opened up a cleft
in the ground to enable him to disappear. Unfortunately English idiom
does not permit the use of the word 'earth' (*gē*) in both contexts.

489 *sinews of business*: neura pragmatōn, the sinews of affairs or business. The saying also appears in another version which comes over better in English and is now more familiar, that 'money is the sinews of war' (e.g. Cicero, *Philippics* 5.3.5; Plutarch surmises in his life of Cleomenes, 27, that this was the original version). In either form this saying has a proverbial ring and probably did not originate with Bion. According to Aeschines, *Against Ctesiphon* 166, Demosthenes used similar language in one of his speeches. The saying was presumably cited by Bion simply as an observation about the way of the world.

490 *Stilpo*: of Megara, who was quite close to the Cynics and Stoics in his moral teaching; it was probably Crates the Cynic who posed the question.

wretched old man: a line of verse of unknown origin, not from Homer.

491 *procure that for himself*: the two sons of his marriage to Hera were the vicious war-god Ares, whom he despised (*Iliad* 5.858 ff.), and the lame artisan-god Hephaistos, who was thrown down from heaven by him (or by Hera).

492 *mouse has gnawed through a sack*: to find that something was mouse-eaten was regarded as ominous. Theophrastos mocks this belief in his character of a superstitious man (16.7), who will consult an exegete if he finds that a mouse has gnawed through a meal-bag, and will make a sacrifice to avert the omen even if he is merely told to have the sack stitched up again. Augustine, *On Christian Doctrine* 2.77, ascribes the same joke to Cato, although this was doubtless an old saw by Cato's time.

Arcesilaos: an Academic philosopher (316/15–241/0) who succeeded Bion's teacher Crates (see **467** and relevant note) as head of that school.

493 *slaying the dead*: i.e. that educated people viewed diviners with scepticism anyhow, so he is flogging a dead horse.

494 *rolls naked in the mud*: this was a punishment in the Underworld (cf. **199** and note)—the superstitious man submits himself to it in this world to expiate his faults. Sackcloth and the like are familiar forms of penitential garb.

divine indication: his 'faults' are purely formal ones, he has failed to heed some taboo with regard to food or drink, perhaps by consuming something that might be classed as impure, or has not paid due attention to some ominous warning, such as an owl hooting or a weasel running across his path (cf. Theophrastos, *Characters* 16).

whatever they please: things that would serve as amulets to keep evil influences at bay.

495 *holes bored through them*: to fetch water in leaky pitchers was a form of punishment that was supposed to be inflicted on the people in the Underworld, as a never-ending futile labour; but Bion makes fun of the idea by suggesting that it would really be worse if the vessels had no holes in them, since the load would then be heavier to bear.

496 *if God punishes the children of the wicked*: that this would be absurd and unjust had been argued long before, e.g. Theognis 731–52.

497 *Tarpeian Rock*: a steep cliff on the Capitoline Hill at Rome from which criminals were thrown; the following argument would imply that everyone deserves such punishment because no one could avoid committing sacrilege.

498 *another's good: allotrion agathon*. This seems to have been an expression that was used primarily in connection with certain virtues. In Plato's *Republic* (1, 343c), Thrasymachus argues that justice is 'the other fellow's good', i.e. that it benefits other people but is against one's own interests, whilst Aristotle (*Nicomachean Ethics* 1130a ff.) uses the expression in a positive and descriptive sense, as characterizing the nature of justice as a (laudable) other-related virtue. Bion's saying can be seen as a humorous variation on the saying that 'justice is another's benefit'; personal beauty may be regarded as a good quality, but it is others who gain the pleasure and enjoyment of it. The expression *allotrion agathon* could also be applied humorously to beneficial things that we do not care to be on the receiving end of, such as a rebuke (see **223**).

499 *brought down by a hair*: the suggestion is that a beautiful youth will lose his sexual attractiveness at puberty when his beard begins to grow.

500 *Harmodioi and Aristogeitones*: Harmodios and Aritogeiton (whose names are given here in the plural) were famous Athenian tyrannicides (see **253** and note).

501 *his behaviour*: see Plato, *Symposium* 217a–219e, where Alcibiades describes how he tried to seduce Socrates, but met with no success although they slept under the same cloak all night.

503 *to bear . . . to share: hexeis poinēn . . . hexeis koinēn*, the former meaning 'you'll pay for it' or 'suffer for it'. In quoting this anecdote, Diogenes Laertius remarks parenthetically 'for it was ascribed to him [i.e. Bion] too', thus acknowledging that it was also credited to others, e.g. Antisthenes (DL 6.3, etc.); the expression was surely older than Bion and may have originated in comedy.

504 *win over a youth*: i.e. to philosophy and his teaching, the erotic dimension is secondary here; he is too soft and unformed to be caught on the hook of reason, cf. Epictetus 3.6.9.

508 *something very good to somebody else*: also ascribed to Democritus (e.g. *Gnomologium Vaticanum* 266), among others, and presumably a traditional joke.

510 *by their ears*: referring to the handles of the jugs; there is a corresponding expression in English, although it is not widely familiar nowadays.

513 *three races*: see Hesiod, *Theogony* 109–38; according to Hesiod's myth, there were four races prior to our own, three named after metals of decreasing worth, and then a race of heroes (representing the people of the age of legend), but Bion has no occasion to refer to the fourth.

514 *taught philosophy at Rhodes*: the humour of this lies in the fact than Rhodes was particularly associated with rhetoric and Athens with philosophy.

515 *tongue is tied*: Theognis 177–8; Theognis was a 6th-century nobleman at Megara who fell on hard times as a result of factional conflict.

516 *you're badly educated*: since conversation and exchange of wit was such an essential feature of a *symposion*, to fail to make a contribution would be thought ill-mannered; on the other hand, it is right and proper for the foolish to remain silent, hence the occasion for the present joke, which was primarily associated with Theophrastos (DL 5.40, *Gnomologium Vaticanum* 333, etc.).

517 *plead on your behalf*: the joke here seems to be that the man could not in fact pursue his court case unless he appeared in person, so Bion is in effect refusing to help him; the story would otherwise be rather banal.

519 *the other side*: Euripides, *Bacchae* 1129; in a frenzy inspired by the wine-god Dionysos, the Bacchants are tearing apart Pentheus, king of Thebes; after his mother Agave has made a start, his aunt Ino now sets to work on the other side. When applied to the way in which Bion is avidly laying into his piece of fish, this provides a vivid and unexpected comparison. This story is also recounted of Zeno (Athenaeus 5, 186d), but it seems less appropriate for him.

528 *shelter of the boat*: a verse-fragment of unknown origin, referring to Charon's boat in which the dead are ferried across the infernal boundary-river to their final home.

529 *Accius*: Lucius Accius (170–*c*.86), a tragic poet who based many of his works on the Greek originals. For the quoted line, cf. *Iliad* 10.15.

530 *many a tragedy*: as in Sophocles' *Antigone*, in which that heroine tries to give her brother Polyneices a token burial, even though that has been forbidden because he was a traitor to the city.

531 *the dead*: simply *anthropous*, but plainly referring to the burning of people's corpses after their death.

invoke them: reading *parakalountōn*, referring with critical intent to the cult of the dead; the text of this saying is uncertain.

533 *mother of the gods . . . a Phrygian*: Rhea, the consort of Kronos and mother of the Olympian gods of the first generation, was identified with Cybele, the great mother-goddess of Phrygia in Asia Minor. Antisthenes is using the term 'Phrygian' here in a vague sense to indicate that his mother, who was Thracian and thus born in Europe, was of barbarian birth.

battle of Tanagra: in 426, early in the Peloponnesian War, an Athenian army defeated an army of Thebans and Tanagrans at Tanagra in Boeotia.

hardly have turned out so brave: a joke, he is suggesting that Antisthenes fought like a savage, in reference to his mother's origin.

sprung from the earth: the Athenians claimed to be autochthonous, i.e. people who had always lived in their land rather than having come in from outside; in mythical terms, this was expressed through the idea that their first king Cecrops (and indeed three subsequent ones) had sprung from the earth.

Gorgias the rhetorician: Gorgias of Leontini (*c*.485–*c*.380) introduced Sicilian rhetoric into Athens, first arriving there in 427. Antisthenes became an accomplished writer, and clearly attached some importance to literary style, in marked contrast to Diogenes, who had nothing but contempt for rhetoric and graces of style.

Hermippos: of Smyrna, biographer, second half of 3rd century BC.

forty stades: the Peiraeus was the harbour of Athens; forty stades was about five miles.

hardship: *ponos*, toil, exertion, hardship, a central Cynic theme.

Heracles ... Cyrus: Cyrus the Great, died 529, founder of the Achaemenid Persian Empire, who came to be presented in the Greek tradition as an ideal ruler; Xenophon wrote a long and largely fictional account of his education in the *Cyropaedia*. Although Antisthenes wrote extensively about both Cyrus and Heracles, only Heracles was adopted as an exemplar in the Cynic tradition, as a hero who had lived a life of toil and hardship (*ponos*).

strength of a Socrates: i.e. one needs not only a knowledge of right and good to achieve happiness and self-fulfilment, but strength of mind and character, as shown in exemplary fashion by Socrates, to ensure that one consistently applies that knowledge.

Cynosarges: on the banks of the Ilissos just outside Athens; it was intended especially for those who were not of pure Athenian blood. Its name could be interpreted as meaning white or swift dog. Although philosophical schools could derive their name from the place where their teaching was carried out, as in the case of the Stoics and Academics, this attempt to derive the name of the Cynics from the Cynosarges shows a certain desperation. No Cynic is recorded as having any association with the Cynosarges, and Aristotle refers to the pupils of Antisthenes as *Antistheneioi* (e.g. *Metaphysics* 1043b24).

Haplokuon: plain dog, dog pure and simple. Since the origin of the name 'Dog' was so firmly connected with Diogenes (Aristotle refers to him as the Dog without even troubling to name him: see 189), this more elaborate form of the nickname had to be devised if it was to be suggested that Antisthenes had been the first to be called a dog; so this report is virtually self-refuting.

first to double his cloak: if Antisthenes was to be the first Cynic, he had to have invented the Cynic uniform. That he carried a staff and knapsack, as asserted by Diocles of Magnesia (2nd–1st century BC), may surely be ruled out; what use would they have been to a married man who had a home in the city? Neanthes of Cyzicus, an author who lived somewhat earlier in the 3rd century, seems to have claimed only that he doubled his cloak, which is doubtless untrue also, even if not totally implausible. There is no indication of any such thing in Xenophon's portrayal of Antisthenes in his *Symposium*.

533 *Diodoros of Aspendos*: a Pythagorean of the 4th century, he lived after the manner of the Cynics, letting his hair grow, being dirty, and walking barefoot (Athenaeus 4, 163c–f). The ascetic Pythagoreans ('Pythagorists') who are mocked in Middle Comedy are described in similar terms (the testimonies are collected in Diels-Kranz, *Fragmente der Vorsokratiker* 535). This may be taken as a case of convergent evolution: they and the Cynics both fitted themselves out like vagrants because they adopted a similar way of life.

 Theopompos: of Chios, 4th-century historian, noted for his rhetorical style.

534 *Autolycos here to dust himself with it*: Autolycus is a character in the dialogue, the young favourite of Callias, one of the wealthiest men in Athens, who is holding a symposium in his honour. He was a successful athlete who won a junior victory in the pancration at the Panathenaean Games in 421; before exercising or competing, athletes would oil their bodies and dust them with powdered clay or the like. Hermogenes, another character in the dialogue, was the brother of Callias.

 without ever being able to satisfy his hunger: a thought that was expressed in Cynic circles through the dropsy comparison: see 146 and 479.

 welcome me with the utmost joy: cf. DL 6.3, 'one should make love with such women as will be properly grateful'; although the approach is gentler and more humorous, this accords with the Cynic belief that sexual desires should be satisfied in the simplest and most direct way possible, which presents no difficulty if one is not too choosy. Antisthenes approved of marriage, however, for the procreation and rearing of children within the established social order, as has been seen in 533.

PART 2: ARISTIPPOS AND THE CYRENAICS

535 *Aeschines*: of Sphettos, a friend of Socrates who wrote Socratic dialogues.

 Phanias of Eresos: philosophical and historical writer, late 4th century, a friend and associate of Theophrastos, Aristotle's successor as head of the Peripatetic school.

 divine sign: a mysterious inner voice that sometimes warned Socrates against taking certain courses of action (e.g. Plato, *Apology* 31cd, 40a–c); here he seems merely to be using it as an excuse to avoid taking Aristippos' money. Socrates and his followers liked to draw a sharp distinction between people like themselves, who engaged in a joint investigation of moral and other philosophical matters as a group of friends, and the sophists who taught rhetoric and other skills that would help people to achieve success in public life in return for a fee. 80 minae was a substantial sum of money, and the amount is presumably exaggerated for effect.

 directed against him: Xenophon, *Memorabilia* 2.1; the section from that chapter which is most revealing about Aristippos' own attitudes is translated in 613. The treatment of Aristippos is not in fact hostile, even if Xenophon would not have sympathized with his views.

Theodoros: a Cyrenaic: see **633–40**.

in his work On the Soul: i.e. the *Phaedo*, 59c; Plato merely indicates that Aristippos was away at Aegina at the time of Socrates' death, without any direct criticism. For an elaborate explanation as to why this passage should supposedly be regarded as critical in intent, see Demetrius, *On Style* 288. Diogenes Laertius makes a similar remark about Plato's attitude in his life of Plato, 3.36 (which had evidently been written before this life of Aristippos since he refers back to it here), saying that Plato was 'ill-disposed toward' him. It is a notable fact that Plato never refers elsewhere to Aristippos (at least directly, since scholars have not failed to hunt for tacit references), even when discussing the nature of pleasure; if one bears in mind also that Aristotle never discusses his hedonistic ideas, although he does examine those of Eudoxos of Cnidos, this may taken as confirming the supposition that the elder Aristippos did not attempt to construct any theoretical system.

the favour of Dionysios: Dionysios I, who ruled over Syracuse as a tyrant from 405 until his death in 467; see also note on **578**.

Diogenes used to call him the royal dog: as a saying ascribed to Diogenes, this can hardly have been intended as a compliment; he was the wrong kind of dog, the king's lapdog, paying court to him so as to be able to enjoy the pleasures of the court. To interpret this saying as implying that Aristippos was some sort of 'Cynic' because he maintained his inner freedom at court is over-subtle; the whole point is that he is a dog of rather ignoble kind as opposed to a dog in the honourable Cynic sense.

who fondled error: Timon fr. 27 di Marco; Timon of Phlious, *c.*320–*c.*230, was a sceptic philosopher and author of satirical poems about philosophers, the *Silloi*. This line is aimed against the Cyrenaic belief that only sense-impressions (*pathē*) can be known, and that they alone can be said to be true (see **621–4**); by thinking that it is only possible to place reliance in what one can 'touch', the enjoyment of present sensations, Aristippos found only falsehood and error. Timon was hostile to Epicurus also.

ascribed to the Cyrenaic philosopher: it is impossible to say whether all or any of the works listed in these two paragraphs were actually written by Aristippos; as can be seen, there was already disagreement on the matter in the Hellenistic period.

the following works: quite a few of these correspond with constituent works of the collection of twenty-five dialogues mentioned previously. Sotion of Alexandria and the Stoic Panaitios both lived in the 2nd century BC.

three Treatises: *Chreiōn tria*, surely to be identified with the three works entitled *Chreia* in the preceding list; if that is so, these would not be collections of *chreiai* in the sense of sayings and anecdotes.

smooth movement resulting in sensation: i.e. pleasurable sensations. Aristippos undoubtedly believed that happiness is grounded in pleasures of the moment, but the idea that pleasure is aligned to a certain form of motion (see further in 618 and 619) seems to have been introduced at a later stage, in the time of his grandson, the younger Aristippos.

536 *Epicurus drew material*: he agreed with the Cyrenaics that pleasure is the end, but disagreed with them about almost everything else; see further in 619 and 620.

never lectured in public about the nature of the end: this passage should be read in conjunction with 618, in which the same author, Aristocles of Messene, a Peripatetic of the 1st century AD, states that it was the younger Aristippos who first defined the end, and introduced the theoretical framework which the Cyrenaics employed to explain their understanding of pleasure (especially by connecting it with a certain kind of movement).

538 *Lais*: see 569 and 574–7 and notes; she lived at Corinth.

539 *Isomachos*: in Xenophon's *Oeconomicus*, 6.17 ff., Socrates discusses household management with an Athenian gentleman of that name, who is sometimes identified with the Ischomachos mentioned by Andocides, *On the Mysteries* 124 ff.

540 *'What benefit did Socrates bring you?'*: to be unable to stand up for oneself in public could be seen as shameful, and might suggest that any instruction that he had received from Socrates had been useless; but he indicates that Socrates taught him something of greater importance, how to be a good man. Oratory and speech-writing is dismissed in the following apophthegm as a purely technical accomplishment, like cooking.

544a *Pharnabazos*: Persian regional governor of Phrygia from *c*.413 to 370, who supported Sparta against Athens in the Peloponnesian War. Diogenes Laertius in 545b names the satrap as Artaphernes, which would be anachronistic, but it seems probable that both sources are incorrect, since an *Artabazos* is named among the works attributed to Aristippos (535), which would suggest that the man in question was Artabazos II (*c*.390–*c*.325), satrap of Hellespontine Phrygia. The confusions could easily arise since this Artabazos was a son of Pharnabazos and his name was quite similar to that of Artaphernes. It is hard to imagine in what circumstances Aristippos could have fallen into the hands of the satrap. This may have formed part of a fictional story.

544b *Artaphernes*: evidently another version of the same story, with the name of the satrap erroneously and anachronistically given as Artaphernes.

545 *through fear of the law*: although also ascribed to Aristotle (DL 5.20), this saying seems to have been primarily associated with Xenocrates, the third head of Plato's Academy (*Gnomologium Vaticanum* 417, Plutarch, *On Moral Virtue* 7, 446e, Cicero, *Republic* 1.3, etc.), and one should not expect to find anything specifically Aristippean in it.

547 *'Our friend would never have spoken like that'*: since this is reported by Aristotle, it may be an authentic record of something that Aristippos actually said. Scorning the idea that moral insight could be passed on as ready-made knowledge, Socrates preferred that his followers should

regard him as their friend rather than as their master. Plato developed a more systematic philosophy than Socrates, although, significantly, he never committed it to writing in the form of theoretical treatises, sharing Socrates' conviction that true understanding could only be awakened through living discourse.

552 *so much bother*: the *Gnomologium Vaticanum* ascribes very similar sayings to both Aristotle (57) and Isocrates (355), and this was doubtless a commonplace that came to be attached to a variety of suitable people.

554a *two obols*: there were six obols to a drachma, which may be regarded as being roughly the daily wage of a skilled workman. As will be apparent from these anecdotes, good fish could be an expensive luxury.

556 *Polyxenos the sophist*: see 88 and note.

557 *at the festivals of the gods*: it is not only the pomp of the festivals that is envisaged but also, and above all, the feasting; since the meat from the sacrificial victims would be eaten by the participants, civic sacrifices offered citizens their prime opportunity for eating animal meat.

558b *Charondas . . . Phaedo*: Phaedo, properly Phaidon, of Elis, a friend of Socrates and the founder of the Elean school of philosophy; this Charondas is more obscure, certainly not the famous lawmaker.

561 *only as much as you can manage*: this story appears in an exaggerated form in one of Horace's *Satires* (2.3, 99–102), in which Aristippos is said to have ordered his slaves to throw away his gold in the middle of Libya because they were being slowed down by the weight of it.

563a *swim off with if they were shipwrecked*: this also appears as a detached saying ascribed to Antisthenes (e.g. DL 1.6), indicating that it is best to travel light, on a journey and doubtless through the course of life too. In all probability the story of Aristippos' shipwreck was built up around such a saying, whatever the true origin of that saying may have been. It should be noted that Aristippos was said to have written a work entitled *The Shipwrecked* or *To the Shipwrecked* (DL 2.85 and 84).

563b *even the meanest gifts*: Sophocles, *Oedipus in Colonus* 3–4.

564 *meeting him after a shipwreck*: since he was wrecked off Athens in one version of the preceding story, 563a, Plato could easily be imagined as having met him after a shipwreck.

565b *Straton*: if the Peripatetic philosopher Straton of Lampsacos is envisaged here, it is by error, since he lived at a later period than Aristippos.

569 *the courtesan Lais*: the traditions about the courtesan, or more likely courtesans, of that name are thoroughly confused. This Lais seems to have lived at the time of the Peloponnesian War and somewhat later, and to have resided at Corinth, where her memorial could be seen in the Craneion near that of Diogenes (Pausanias 2.2.4). There was apparently also a younger Lais, born at Hyccara in Sicily, who lived rather later. Athenaeus has much to say about Lais, 13.582 ff., etc., and Aelian recounts the tale of her thwarted love for the Cyrenaean athlete Eubatas (*Historical Miscellany* 10.2).

569 *'I possess Lais but am not possessed by her'*: although this is the only possible translation in English, it is perhaps slightly misleading, since he is not meaning to suggest any idea of ownership or possession; his literal words are that he 'has' her, but is not 'had' by her, i.e. she does not have any hold on him. Both maintain their freedom.

573 *It did Paris no good*: in myth Paris, son of Priam, king of Troy, was asked to judge whether Athena, Hera, or Aphrodite was the most beautiful, and this started the train of events that led to the outbreak of the Trojan War, which would bring disaster to his city and to himself.

576 *with Diogenes*: most unlikely of course! Diogenes belonged to a younger generation in any case.

578 *Dionysios*: it is possible that Aristippos visited Syracuse in the time of both the elder and the younger Dionysios, but if one keeps in mind that Socrates died in 399, and Dionysios I did not die until 367, over thirty years later, when Aristippos would probably have been almost seventy, we can reasonably imagine that Dionysios I is his interlocutor in these anecdotes.

579 *education . . . diversion*: *paideia . . . paidia* in Greek; both words were related to the noun *pais*, meaning 'child', in reference to education and play respectively.

580 *Hegesandros*: of Delphi, author of historical works, 2nd century BC.

Antiphon: a tragic poet who lived at Dionysios' court (sometimes confused in antiquity with the politician and rhetorician Antiphon of Rhamnous); it was said that Dionysios had him put to death either for making an approving remark about tyrannicides (see note to **253**) or for mocking the tragedies that had been written by the tyrant (Plutarch, *Lives of the Ten Orators* 833bc, Philostratus, *Lives of the Sophists* 1.15, Aristotle, *Rhetoric* 1385a 9–10).

581 *to take a blenny*: the wit of this reply rests on an untranslatable play on words: *blennos*, the name of the fish, bears a close resemblance to the word *blenna* meaning mucus or phlegm (the fish owed its name to its slimy surface).

583a *not be corrupted*: Euripides, *Bacchae* 317–18, in response to Plato's quotation from later in the play, 836; in that play Pentheus, king of Thebes, puts on women's clothing to spy on the local women as they perform Bacchic rites.

585 *free he come*: Dionysios quotes two lines from Sophocles (fr. 789 Nauck), to which Aristippos responds by offering an improvised correction. The invention of this correction is also ascribed to the Stoic Zeno (Plutarch, *How to Study Poets* 12, 33d).

586 *why philosophers come to rich men's doors*: a traditional theme. The following anecdote was told of the poet Simonides (*c.*556–468): 'In response to the wife of Hiero, when she asked him whether it is better to grow rich or wise, he said, "To grow rich, for I see the wise waiting at rich men's

doors" ' (Aristotle, *Rhetoric* 2, 1391a 9 ff.; Plato makes a critical allusion
to the saying in *Republic* 489bc). Simonides spent some time at the court
of Hiero, tyrant of Syracuse, as did Aristippos later at that of Dionysios,
who now raises this same matter with him. A similar saying is ascribed to
Antisthenes (*Gnomologium Vaticanum* 6): 'When asked by the tyrant why
it is that the wise approach the rich, and not vice versa, he replied,
"Because the wise know what they need for life, while the rich do not,
because they have devoted their concern to money rather than to wisdom." ' Since the question is posed by this unnamed tyrant, however, it
looks as if this latter version too may properly have belonged to
Aristippos.

588 *'Just as doctors are always with the sick'*: a commonplace in the Socratic
tradition; an almost identical story was told about Antisthenes (DL 6.6),
and cf. Diogenes in 63.

589 *was not at a loss*: the verb used here, *aporein*, can mean both to 'be in want'
and to 'be at a loss' about how to do something. Dionysios playfully rejects
Aristippos' request for money by saying that he has told him that the wise
man will never be in want. Aristippos contrives to get him to hand over
the money, and then says, using the word in the other sense, 'Now you can
see that I was not at a loss', i.e. as to how to obtain the money.

590 *Plato has need of books*: in view of the stories that claimed that Plato had
plagiarized from Pythagorean books that he had acquired from Sicily
(e.g. DL 8.15, 8.85), this apparently innocuous remark presumably contains the malicious suggestion that he has need of books to be able to
pilfer ideas from them.

593 *as though of a sacred disease*: an allusion to epilepsy, which was known as
the sacred disease because it was widely thought that epileptic seizures
were induced as a result of divine or daemonic influences.

594 *more suitable place*: this story was also told of Diogenes (see 145); such
drastic behaviour seems more appropriate to Diogenes than it does to
the urbane Aristippos.

596a *washing raw vegetables*: cf. the similar stories told of Diogenes and Plato,
125, and Theodoros and Metrocles, 633.

597 *to freeze rather than be seen in purple robes*: although this is one of the best
of these stories of joustings between philosophers, it is plainly a fiction
assembled from motifs in the prior tradition. That the adoption of
shabby dress is just another form of ostentation was a standard criticism;
the story goes, for instance, that when Antisthenes once turned a tear in
his cloak outwards so that it would be plainly visible, Socrates remarked
to him, 'I can see your love of fame peeping out through your cloak' (DL
6.8). Conversely, Aristippos was praised for being able to adjust to any
circumstances, and seeming as dignified and contented in rags as in
splendid robes (565). So the idea of him leaving his purple robes behind
for Diogenes while he happily emerged in the Cynic's robes could naturally suggest itself. The story has a serious point, that Aristippos could

be regarded as being freer than the Cynic, because he is happy to enjoy the pleasures of life when they are available while feeling no pain at their absence.

599a *Aeschines*: of Sphettos, a friend of Socrates. He was supposed to have spent some time at the Syracusan court after Socrates' death, and this story may have been set there. According to Diogenes Laertius (2.61), 'it is said that he went to the court of Dionysios in Syracuse for lack of money, and Plato paid no heed to him, but he received support from Aristippos; and in return for the gift of some dialogues, he received gifts from him [Dionysios].'

604 *ask them for any particular thing*: a Socratic thought; since we have no knowledge of the future and only an imperfect knowledge of what is good for ourselves, we cannot tell whether any specific thing will be good for us or not; cf. Xenophon, *Memorabilia* 1.3.2.

606 *humanity*: *anthropismos*, a word otherwise unattested, and perhaps to be regarded as being improvised for the occasion; only education can provide us with what we need to be properly human.

607 *one stone sitting on another*: stones were proverbially insensitive: cf. Aristotle, *Eudemian Ethics* 2, 1221a 22.

610 *through a clump of thistles*: in the original 'through club-rushes' (*Scirpus holoschoenus*), in reference to the spikelets on the flower-heads of that plant; but 'club-rushes' would hardly call up an appropriate image in the minds of most readers.

613 *Sinis, Sceiron, and Procrustes*: three mythical villains who preyed on the travellers on the Isthmus of Corinth, at Megara, and near Athens respectively; Theseus was supposed to have killed them while travelling from Troezen to Athens to claim his inheritance (see Plutarch, *Life of Theseus* 8–11).

614 *This is how things stand*: this is Diogenes Laertius' account of the Cyrenaic succession. The essential point is that Aristippos' teaching was passed on within his own family to his grandson of the same name, who seems to have been largely responsible for developing it into a consistent body of thought, while the two other main branches of the school were founded by Hegesias and Anniceris, who belonged to another line descended from Aristippos' pupil Antipatros. The teachings of each of these three branches of the school are outlined by Diogenes Laertius in 619, 625, and 630.

Arete: meaning 'Virtue'; it may be noted that Aristippos' patron Dionysios I named his daughters after virtues—Dikaiosyne, Sophrosyne, and Arete (Plutarch, *On the Fortune of Alexander* 5, 388c)—evidently as an indication of how he wanted his regime to be viewed.

Antipatros: only a single anecdote is recorded of Antipatros (see 632), and Epitimides and Paraibates are no more than names to us. It is not known whether any significant body of doctrine was developed within this line before the time of Hegesias and Anniceris.

616a *his son*: never named, if he indeed existed; in all probability this story was simply invented to explain why Aristippos' teaching was passed on through a daughter, which might seem strange and unexpected. The response ascribed to Aristippos may have been based on the very similar sentence in Xenophon's *Memorabilia* 1.2.54.

616b *grew dissolute*: Aristippos may have loved pleasure, but he believed in the maintenance of self-control and of a measure of detachment; so it would not have been hypocritical of him to react in this way to the dissolute behaviour of a son.

618 *clearly defined the end*: cf. 536, in which the same author, Aristocles of Messene, a Peripatetic of the 1st century AD, states that the elder Aristippos indicated through his way of life and manner of talking that pleasure is the end of life, but never explicitly defined the end. By further stating that the younger Aristippos introduced the idea that pleasure is connected with motion, our author makes it clear, if his report is correct, that it was only in his time that the Cyrenaic teaching was developed into the coherent philosophy which is outlined in the following doxography (619), as provided by Diogenes Laertius.

619 *Panaitios*: of Rhodes, a prominent Stoic philosopher of the 2nd century BC.

which Epicurus accepts: see 620, in which he states this in his own words, distinguishing his views from those of hedonists like the Cyrenaics.

621 *Ariston of Chios*: cf. 96 and note.

622 *affections: pathē*, sense-affections.

623 *a yellowish affection*: it was believed that people suffering from jaundice see everything tinted yellow, although that is apparently not the case.

ophthalmia: a general term for eye disease.

sees Thebes twice over: in Euripides' *Bacchae* 918–19, Pentheus, a legendary king of Thebes, sees his city and the sun twice over while under the influence of the god Dionysos.

625 *Hegesians: Hegesiakoi*. Hegesias would have been active from the late 4th to early 3rd century BC.

happiness cannot exist: since a preponderance of pleasure cannot be consistently assured for any length of time, happiness cannot properly be said to exist; the originality of this branch of the school lies in this depressing insight.

can both be desirable: according to the circumstances, depending on the current balance of pleasure and pain.

makes it his end to live without pain and distress: since we are so little able to ensure any continuous stay of pleasure and happiness, it is better to concentrate on avoiding distress; and this can best be achieved by a general cultivation of indifference, *adiaphoria*, toward pain, pleasure, and life itself. By a back-route the Hegesians thus arrived at a position that came surprisingly close to that of the Cynics.

626 *for the sage, death is*: it can be assumed that Hegesias merely argued that the sage will recognize that death, and thus suicide, is best in certain circumstances, and that, by contrast, it is foolish to regard life as being unequivocally good, or indeed as tending on the whole to be more good than bad.

the Death-persuader: *Peisithanatos*.

627a *Ptolemy*: Ptolemaios I Soter, king of Egypt from 323 to 283, who had annexed Cyrene; Hegesias would presumably have been lecturing in Alexandria.

630 *Annicerians*: *Annikeirioi*. Anniceris was a contemporary of Hegesias; according to the *Suda*, he lived at the same time as Alexander the Great (reigned 336–323), but he would presumably have died considerably later than Alexander.

nonetheless be happy: since they were less narrowly hedonistic than the Hegesians, thinking that satisfaction could also be found in human relationships and various aspects of social life, they were accordingly less pessimistic, supposing that there is more that can be added to the positive side of the balance.

out of a natural feeling of goodwill: it would seem that the Annicerians explicitly recognized other values in addition to pleasure. Epicurus attached notable importance to friendship, but it is doubtful whether (theoretically at least) he valued it as anything other than a source of pleasure. The Annicerians appear to have been less dogmatic, taking the common-sense view that altruistic sentiments and behaviour can be of value not merely in so far they are conducive to pleasure, but as a source of meaning and fulfilment in our lives.

632 *Antipatros*: the founder of the line to which Anniceris and Hegesias belonged (see **614**).

633 *Dionysios the dialectician*: Dionysios of Chalcedon, active in the latter part of the 4th century and associated with the Megarian school; Theodoros evidently studied with him because, exceptionally among the Cyrenaics, he had a taste for sophistic argument.

joy and grief . . . the supreme good and evil: this shows that Theodoros struck out on a path of his own, diverging quite sharply from Cyrenaic orthodoxy. Instead of locating the end (exclusively or primarily) in pleasurable sensations as enjoyed in the moment, he proposed instead that that ultimate good is *chara*, joy or delight, a settled state of the soul, which is founded in turn in practical wisdom. Correspondingly, pleasure is not unequivocally good, but can be good or bad according to the circumstances, whereas the wisdom that enables us to achieve that state of joy is good in itself.

nature . . . common opinion: in judging whether something is good or bad, we should consider solely whether it is in accordance with nature, without attaching any importance to the prescriptions of the law or to social and moral conventions. Here Theodoros comes close to the Cynics, deliberately setting out to shock people by advocating unholy actions and shameless behaviour. He was in fact more an eclectic than a Cyrenaic in any strict sense.

arguments based on question and answer: this was how he put into effect the training that he had received in dialectic. The sophistic arguments that he employed in this connection were rather different from the paradoxical arguments that the Cynics advanced in defence of their more scandalous ideas (although it may be noted that a similar argument is ascribed to Aristippos in **574–5**). One may hope that he did not take them too seriously.

called 'god': by humorous inversion of his name of 'atheist'.

the hierophant Eurycleides: high priest of the cult of Demeter at Eleusis, who initiated people into the Eleusinian Mysteries, providing them with the secret revelations that were supposed to assure them of a better lot in the afterlife. This involved not only verbal instruction, but also ritual and religious theatre. The exact content of the revelation is unknown because those who were due to be initiated had to swear a strict oath of secrecy.

hauled in front of the court of the Areiopagos: Theodoros was prosecuted, or at least came under danger of being prosecuted, in this ancient Athenian court on a charge of atheism, during the period when Demetrios of Phaleron held power in the city (i.e. from 317 to 307; probably during the latter part of that period). The present account by Diogenes Laertius suggests that Demetrios, a man who had wide intellectual interests, intervened to save him from being brought in front of the court, so enabling him to make a safe voluntary departure from Athens; but most other accounts state that he was actually convicted and banished. What may actually have happened is that Demetrios intervened to save him from being executed as a result of his conviction. Philo indicates in **635** that he was tried for atheism and corruption of the young, and it seems that his talk and writings would have provided ample evidence to support such a charge.

to drink hemlock: this claim may be confidently rejected because so much is recorded about his subsequent life. This Amphicrates may perhaps be identified with the Athenian sophist and rhetorician of that name from the 1st century BC.

Metrocles the Cynic: a follower of Crates, see **459**.

also told of Diogenes and Aristippos: see **596**; and Diogenes and Plato too, see **125**.

Megas: a stepson of Ptolemy I Soter, the founder of the Macedonian ruling dynasty in Egypt. After initially holding power in Cyrene as a governor, he seized power in his own right in 276 and ruled there until his death in 250.

expelled from Cyrene: probably during the disturbances in the late 320s that preceded Ptolemy's annexation of Cyrene, or possibly during the unsuccessful revolt against Ptolemy's rule in 313.

634 *Ptolemy, son of Lagos*: i.e. Ptolemy Soter; his court was an obvious destination for Theodoros because Cyrene was under his power.

Lysimachos: a Macedonian officer who established a kingdom on either side of the Hellespont, embracing Macedonia, Thrace, and Asia Minor. Since Lysimachos first assumed the title of king in 306 or somewhat later, Theodoros' visit must have fallen after that date if he was in fact king at the time.

Semele . . . to bear Dionysos: while Semele, a Theban princess, was pregnant with the god Dionysos, she persuaded her lover Zeus to visit her in his full divine form; this caused her death, but Zeus snatched out her unborn child and sewed him into his thigh, to enable him to be brought to birth at the proper time. So it was really Zeus who caused her death rather than any inability to bear her divine child.

hateful to the gods: cf. **214** and note.

635 *put off the ship by the Argonauts*: it was commonly thought that Heracles had been left behind at an early stage of the voyage of the Argonauts, and various explanations were offered, one being that he was simply too heavy for the ship (Apollodorus, *Library* 1.9.19, citing Pherecydes). The real explanation was that he was a late addition to the story, and so had no worthy role to play in the seizing of the golden fleece when the ship reached its destination.

636a *rots in the ground or in the air above*: this accords with a standard Cynic attitude about burial (see **395–7**); it need not be assumed that the phrase about rotting below or above originated with Theodoros, the humour lies in his bravado in applying it in this particular situation, when he has been threatened with a very painful death. This response is also ascribed to Anaxarchos, a philosopher who accompanied Alexander to the East (*Gnomologium Vaticanum* 64): 'When King Alexander said to the natural philosopher Anaxarchos, "I'll hang you", he replied, "Direct your threats against others, it makes no difference to me whether I rot above the ground or beneath it."' But it may be assumed that this is a secondary attribution.

637 *Telesphoros*: an officer in the service of Lysimachos (conceivably to be identified with the nephew of Antigonos the One-Eyed mentioned in other connections) who was supposed to have offended the king by joking at a banquet that his wife Arsinoe was much given to vomiting (Athenaeus 14, 616c). The king responded by enclosing him in a cage and inflicting picturesque punishments on him.

638a *poisonous fly*: cantharis, the 'Spanish fly', actually a kind of beetle; here we have variations on the preceding story, in which Theodoros responds with suitable impertinence to similar threats from the king.

640 *Phocion*: 'the Good', 402–318 BC, an Athenian statesman and general who was famous for his austere and upright character. Various tales are told about his disreputable son Phocos in Plutarch's biography of him.

a companion woman: hetaira, the Greek term for a courtesan; so this is one of the sophistic arguments that so appealed to Theodoros. A *hetaira*, who could be an accomplished woman, should be distinguished from a *pornē*, a prostitute in a brothel, like Phocos' inamorata.

PART 3: APOCRYPHAL LETTERS

641 *Hiketes*: the name that is given here to Diogenes' father, named elsewhere as Hicesias (see 2).

a pupil of Socrates: evidently Diogenes' supposed master Antisthenes; there is no need for the author of the letter to name him.

two paths that lead to happiness: the motif of the choice between difficult and easy paths originally goes back to a speech by the sophist Prodicos of Ceos (*c*.465–*c*.395), who recounted a little parable about the choice of Heracles, in which the hero had to decide whether to take the hard and strenuous path to virtue, or the short and easy path to pleasure and vice. Although Prodicos' work has not survived, the essential features of this tale are recorded in Xenophon's summary of it in *Memorabilia* 2.1.21–34. Since Heracles was adopted as an exemplar by Antisthenes, it is appropriate that Antisthenes should be presented as imposing a comparable choice on Diogenes. But both paths now lead to the same end, happiness and self-fulfilment, as approached through a harder or easier route, and the difficult path now specifically represents the Cynic way of life, as supposedly invented by Antisthenes.

led us into town: presumably we are meant to imagine them walking into Athens from the gymnasium of Cynosarges just outside the city, where Antisthenes used to teach (see 533 and relevant note).

oat-brew: trimma, a brew prepared from pounded groats and spices.

this equipment: the standard Cynic uniform and accoutrements, cf. 10 and 11.

to clear away the oil and dirt: although we might tend to think of Diogenes as being dirty, Diogenes Laertius, 6.81, quotes Athenodoros (perhaps the Stoic Athenodoros Cordylion, 1st century BC) as saying that he had a shining body because he oiled himself (cf. Epictetus 3.22.87–9, 4.11.21). That is the idea envisaged here, whether it goes back to the early tradition or is a result of later idealization.

to belabour scoundrels: or against the poets, the text is uncertain here.

642 *dog of heaven*: there is an implicit reference in this passage to the meaning of his name, 'born of Zeus', as in the poem of Cercidas cited in 398.

and miserable knapsack: much as in *Odyssey* 13.434–8, but the first line is more like *Odyssey* 3.467. The goddess disguised Odysseus as an old beggar when he arrived in his homeland, so as to enable him to make secret

preparations for his confrontation with the suitors, who had been court-
ing his wife Penelope and seeking to take over his kingdom during his
long absence.

644   *the Thebans will surround you again*: Crates came from a rich Theban
family, so his friends and relations would naturally have accused him of
perversely casting himself into misery; cf. in 411, 'Relations would often
visit and try to turn him aside from his course, but he would chase them
off with his stick, and remained steadfast.'

645   *Metrocles*: the early Cynic and pupil of Crates (see 459).

same things as Heracles: referring particularly to his twelve labours, in which
he could be seen as exerting himself to the benefit of the human race.

Socrates . . . for what is theirs: see 44 and note; the saying can be more
appropriately associated with Diogenes than with Socrates, who never
begged.

on these grounds: see 18 and note.

646   *the shepherd's hand*: referring to masturbation, as a practice specially
associated with shepherds because they live a solitary life while pasturing
their sheep.

Paris . . . once a cattle-herd: the Trojan prince was exposed at birth
because his mother had a sinister dream foretelling that he would bring
disaster to his homeland, but he was rescued by a herdsman, and herded
cattle outside the city during his earlier years; he later provoked the
Trojan War, and no end of suffering, by abducting the beautiful Helen,
hence the wish expressed here.

learned from Pan: the text is corrupt here, but this proposed reading
makes excellent sense, the rustic deity Pan being the patron-god of shepherds. In Dio Chrysostom, Speech 6.17–20, Diogenes recounts a little
myth in which it is claimed that Hermes taught the practice of masturbation to Pan during the time of his hopeless passion for Echo, and Pan
then passed it on to goatherds.

647   *he was beaten*: this story is not recorded among the surviving anecdotes
of Diogenes, and it is in fact more likely that this was a joke from the
popular tradition than a story specifically associated with Diogenes.

duly grateful: cf. 46.

house of a young man: Olympia was of course a festival site rather than a
town, so this story has been tacked on rather ineptly. Cf. 145 and 594.

648   *the pancratiast Cicermos*: the pancration was a form of wrestling in which
punching and kicking were also allowed; this Cicermos is a fictional
character. Nothing is recorded about the recipient of this letter.

crown . . . palm branch: a crown of wild olive, associated with Olympian
Zeus, was the official prize at the Olympic games, while the palm branch
was a standard token of victory.

picked by lot: in the combat sports, pairs of opponents would be picked out by lot in each round of the contest, and the victors would pass on to the next round; so the ultimate victor did not have to compete against all other contestants. If there were uneven numbers of contestants, furthermore, an athlete could gain a bye from one round into another without having to compete.

did you defeat Cicermos: a serious point lies behind this apparently frivolous question, since for a Cynic the real fight is the one that he fights with himself, to achieve self-mastery. When Cicermos is converted to the Cynic way, he will cease to compete against others.

from leather thongs and fists: before competing in the pancration and boxing, athletes would wind leather thongs around their hands. These would provide a measure of protection for their hands, and also render their punches more damaging.

strength to call off his journey: he would have been returning home to make a ceremonial entrance into his city (cf. 70), be greeted with adulation, and receive a civic reception; but he has now come to realize that none of this has any value.

649 *courtyard*: *aithrion*, the Greek equivalent for the Latin word *atrium*, presumably referring to a courtyard in the gymnasium in the Craneion (where this meeting with Alexander is usually placed, e.g. 236); cf. Lucian, *Anacharsis* 2.

the Aloadai: two gigantic brothers who wanted to storm Olympos by piling mountains on top of one another, but were killed by Apollo before they could do so (*Odyssey* 11.306–20). There is a corrupt passage before this.

650 *Dionysios, the tyrant of Syracuse*: i.e. Dionysios II, who was finally deposed in 344. This letter develops the well-known story of a supposed meeting with Diogenes during his exile (see 251), bringing in the tradition that he was obliged to work as a primary-school teacher (an ill-rewarded and poorly regarded occupation).

A pity that you're teaching: Diogenes means to suggest that he is a bad teacher, but Dionysios misinterprets his statement as an expression of sympathy; the Greek expression is more directly ambiguous.

652 *festival of Hermes*: since Hermes was the tutelary deity of the gymnasia, celebrations and contests would be held in gymnasia in his honour during the festival of the Hermaia. Diogenes refers to this festival in particular because it would often provide an occasion for rowdy behaviour among the young men. Plato's *Lysis* is set in a wrestling-school during the Hermaia (see 206d ff., although there is no reference here to any indecorous behaviour).

in a letter: evidently another apocryphal letter.

war against the barbarians: referring specifically to Alexander's campaigns in Asia.

653 *drive off any beasts that might cause me any harm*: cf. 397.

654 *Niobe . . . remembered to eat*: *Iliad* 24.602; see **255** and relevant note.

to bad masters moreover: i.e. to their uncontrolled desires; cf. **151–2**.

promised him his freedom: in all other accounts Diogenes is in fact sold by the pirates, and this version in which they themselves want to learn from him is exceptional. Otherwise this letter simply recounts a selection of the usual stories from the tale of his auction (see Section IX).

658 *Maron, a man who was a wine-seller*: when Odysseus sacked Maron's home-city on the north coast of the Aegean while returning from Troy, he spared Maron and his family because he was a priest of Apollo; and Maron showed his gratitude by giving Odysseus twelve jars of strong honey-sweet wine and other splendid gifts (*Odyssey* 9.196–205). So Maron was not exactly a wine-seller, and Diogenes' remark here is humorously intended. Maroneia was the home-city of Hipparchia and her brother Metrocles; its name was not actually changed to Hipparchia.

660 *at home*: it would seem that in this series of letters, Hipparchia is living apart from Crates, presumably in her family home in Maroneia because she is expecting the child mentioned in **665**. In the letter in which Crates responds to the news of the birth of the child, it is indicated that she has not told him about her pregnancy, so we should probably regard these letters as having been deliberately composed as a series to build up a little story, in which Crates is initially worried that she is simply falling back into an ordinary female way of life, and finds some confirmation for his worries when she sends him a garment that she has woven.

664 *a new tunic*: this is merely another version of the preceding letter, taken from a different source. One may suspect that some prose-narrative about Hipparchia provided the story which different authors used as a basis for composing apocryphal letters.

665 *given birth*: Crates and Hipparchia were said to have had a son called Pasicles (see **411**), but nothing is recorded about the circumstances of his birth and rearing.

Aithra gave to Theseus: Aigeus, king of Athens, was tricked into sleeping with Aithra, a princess of Troezen. Before leaving her, he hid a sword and pair of sandals under a heavy stone, and told Aithra that if she gave birth to a son, and he was able to raise the stone when he grew up, she should send him to Athens with the sword and sandals as tokens of his paternity. When Hipparchia's child grows up, she is to send him to Athens fitted out as a Cynic, since the Cynic way of life provides the surest security in life. This presupposes that she will remain apart from Crates for a long while.

rear him as a stork: referring to the popular belief that old storks are fed by their young (Aristotle, *History of Animals* 615b 23–4, cf. Aristophanes, *Birds* 1353–7). It is not clear whether he means just for his own old age (implying that Hipparchia would remain apart from him) or for the old age of the two of them.

666 *Diogenes 32, to Aristippos*: this comes from the collection of Cynic Letters, from which all the preceding letters have been drawn.

the tyrant: Dionysios of Syracuse.

washing chicory to eat with my bread: see **125** and note.

the stone-quarries: the notorious quarries to the north of the city where prisoners were confined and put to work.

in conflict with your reason: I have omitted the final part of this sentence because the text becomes too corrupt.

667 *Aristippos 27, to his daughter Arete*: this and the following letters are drawn from a different collection from the preceding, the Letters of Socrates and the Socratics. It should be remembered that the teaching of Aristippos was transmitted to his grandson of the same name through his daughter Arete. In this letter Aristippos is imagined as having fallen ill while trying to sail home to Cyrene in his old age, and is communicating his final wishes to his daughter, in what is in effect a sort of will; his true bequest lies not in material wealth, but in the wisdom that Arete will pass on to her son.

Lipari: one of the Aeolian Islands off the north coast of Sicily; since it does not lie on the route from Syracuse to North Africa, a story of separate origin has presumably been worked in here.

Berenice: in Cyrenaica, in the region of modern Benghazi.

Xanthippe and Myrto: Xanthippe is familiar as Socrates' wife in the works of Xenophon (e.g. *Symposium* 2.10) and Plato (*Phaedo* 60a), but later sources also refer to another wife or female companion of his named Myrto. Plutarch mentions a work by Aristotle, *On Nobility of Birth*, as a source for this, but doubts whether the work is genuine, and says that the Stoic philosopher Panaitios exposed the tradition about Myrto as being inauthentic (Plutarch, *Life of Aristides* 27.3–4). Diogenes Laertius, 2.26, who again refers to Aristotle, indicates that some people regarded Myrto as the first wife of Socrates, while others described her as living with him as an additional wife along with Xanthippe (no wonder Xanthippe was so ill-tempered). The whole story sounds like a fiction, perhaps originating in some Hellenistic biography, although it is not inconceivable that Socrates had been married to another woman before his marriage to Xanthippe.

the Mysteries: the Eleusinian Mysteries: see **199** and notes.

Lamprocles, son of Socrates: his eldest son (Xenophon, *Memorabilia* 2.2.1), no more than an adolescent at the time of his father's death (Plato, *Phaedo* 116b). Aristotle describes Socrates' descendants as being fatuous and torpid (*Rhetoric* 1390b 30–2), in evident contrast to Arete and the young Aristippos.

no longer wish to rear your daughter: the significance of this is unclear because the following passage is very corrupt.

668 *Antisthenes 8, to Aristippos*: the remaining letters form an interconnected group; Aristippos gains the upper hand in exchanges with members of the ascetic wing of the Socratic movement, through heavy use of irony and indeed sarcasm. The author of the letters was probably more interested in the presentation of character than in the philosophical content.

668 *Anticyra . . . hellebore*: black hellebore, *Helleborus niger*, was thought to provide a cure for madness (e.g. Aristophanes, *Wasps* 1489) and the mountains above Anticyra in Phocis were regarded as an especially good source for that drug (Pausanias 10.36.4).

669 *three Sicilian women*: a detail evidently suggested by the anecdote recounted in 573.

Nine Springs: *Enneakrounos*, a fountain-house in the Agora, built in the 6th century, which was a main source of water for the Athenians.

discourse on Heracles: in which Antisthenes would have been exhorting his listeners to adopt a simple and frugal life.

670 *the Locrian youths*: presumably a story invented by reference to a passage in a letter of Plato, which mentions, with little further detail, some Locrian youths who were being entertained at a banquet in Syracuse (*Letter* 13, to Dionysios, 360ab; the letter is probably inauthentic). Aeschines was a friend of Socrates who was supposed to have visited the Syracusan court after his death, where Plato proved less helpful to him than Aristippos, who is represented as being on good terms with him (see 599 and note). It is Aristippos who helps him out here too; but Aeschines is imagined here as writing to him from Athens, as is plainly indicated in Aristippos' reply.

671 *Scironian winds*: violent north-westerly winds that affected Athens.

Simon: Socratic discourses were circulated as the work of a cobbler called Simon, who was supposed to have written them on the basis of conversations that he heard when Socrates visited his workshop (DL 2.122, which includes a list of the writings ascribed to him). It is hard to know whether this Simon actually existed, although, remarkably enough, excavations have revealed that there was a shoemaker's workshop in a corner of the Agora which may have belonged to someone of that name.

673 *Prodicos . . . encomium of Heracles*: Prodicos of Ceos (*c*.460–*c*.395) was a sophist who made frequent visits to Athens, and seems to have been on good terms with Socrates, to judge by Plato's references to him. He was particularly interested in linguistic matters, above all the correct use of words. His eulogy of Heracles is mentioned by Plato (*Symposium* 177b). Its most famous feature, an allegorical tale in which Heracles had to make a choice between the arduous path to virtue and the easy path to pleasure and vice, can be appreciated from the summary of it in Xenophon's *Memorabilia*, 2.1.21–34. Phaedo, an associate of Socrates, is reported to have written a work called *Simon* or the *Cobbler's Tales* (DL 2.105), and it is to that work that the present letter is evidently referring when it says that Simon refuted Prodicos with regard to the encomium of Heracles. Now Simon, as a Socratic who was associated with the ascetic wing of the movement, could hardly have objected to the content of Prodicus' discourse; for, as we have seen, the choice between the hard and easy paths was a favourite theme with the Cynics. So presumably Phaedo suggested that Simon had 'refuted' Prodicos with regard to the encomium of Heracles by making plain that Prodicos did not live up to the ideals expressed in it, by contrast to the humble Simon. Prodicos was said to have charged high fees for his instruction, and to have lived in some luxury.

Alcibiades . . . Phaidros . . . Euthydemos: young men belonging to the gilded youth of Athens, all familiar from Plato's dialogues.

Epicrates the Shield-bearer: an Athenian who was active in public affairs after the Peloponnesian War, as a leading democrat. He was nicknamed the Shield-bearer because of his enormous beard, suffering mockery on that account in comedy, and he was presumably picked out for mention here because he had a beard like that of a philosopher (there is in fact a reference to philosophers' beards later in the letter).

even Pericles: the suggestion that the great Pericles, the leading states-man of Athens, might have frequented Simon's workshop if he had been less busy can surely be interpreted as sarcastic (even if Diogenes Laertius, 2.123, cites a story about Simon refusing an invitation from Pericles).

INDEX OF NAMES

This is an index of the historical figures who are explicitly mentioned in the main text; deities and mythical figures are not included. Further information about many of them can be found in the Explanatory Notes.

Accius, Latin poet and dramatist 117
Achaicos, philosophical author of unknown date 102
Aeschines, friend of Socrates, author of Socratic dialogues 123, 139, 179
Agesilaos, king of Sparta 45
Agesilaos of Cos, acquaintance of Diogenes 47
Aithiops of Ptolemais, Cyrenaic, pupil of Aristippos 143
Alcibiades, Athenian politician and general 113, 180
Alexander the Great, king of Macedon 10, 12, 53–6, 86, 88, 91, 165–6
Amphicrates, author of a book on famous men 154
Anaxarchos of Abdera, sceptical philosopher 85
Anaximenes, of Lampsacos, rhetorician 51–2
Androsthenes, son of Onesicritos, pupil of Diogenes 86
Anniceris, Cyrenaic philosopher 144, 152–3
Antigonos I, Macedonian general and ruler in Asia 44, 81
Antigonos II Gonatas, king of Macedon 81, 105–6
Antipater (*properly* Antipatros), Macedonian general 56
Antipatros, of Tarsos, Stoic philosopher 49
Antipatros, of Cyrene, pupil of Aristippos 143–4, 153
Antisthenes, friend of Socrates, philosophical writer, supposed teacher of Diogenes 7–8, 10, 27, 60, 80, 82, 87, 117–21, 159–60, 169, 172, 177–80
Antisthenes, author of book on the philosophical successions 153

Apollonios of Tyre, Stoic philosopher 104
Arcesilaos, Academic philosopher 111
Arete, daughter of Aristippos 123, 143–5, 176–7
Aristippos, founder of the Cyrenaic school 5–6, 12, 34, 37, 123–44, 154, 175–80
Aristippos, unnamed son of 144
Aristippos, 'the Mother-taught', son of Arete, Cyrenaic philosopher 143–50, 177
Aristogeiton, Athenian tyrannicide 57, 84, 112
Ariston of Chios, Stoic philosopher with Cynic sympathies 27, 34, 148
Aristotle, philosopher 34, 53, 94
Artaphernes, Persian satrap 126
Asclepiades of Phlious, philosopher of Eretrian school 93, 96
Athlias, a messenger 56
Autolycos, Athenian athlete 119

Baton, owner of Menippos 102
Betion, friend of Bion 106
Bion of Borysthenes, moral preacher with Cynic sympathies 97, 105–17
Bryson the Achaean, philosopher 87

Callias, wealthy Athenian politician 120
Callisthenes, of Olynthos, historian 55
Cercidas of Megalopolis, poet with Cynic sympathies 82
Charondas, otherwise unknown 129
Chrysippos, early Stoic philosopher 16, 49–50, 101
Cicermos, fictional athlete 164–5
Cleanthes, early Stoic philosopher 48–9, 100
Cleitomachos, Academic sceptic philosopher 147

Cleomenes, author of a book on pedagogues 61

Cleomenes, early Cynic, pupil of Crates 101–2

Crateros, Macedonian general 56

Crates, Academic philosopher, a teacher of Aristippos 105

Crates, Cynic, follower of Diogenes 85, 87–101, 103–4, 111, 161, 169–75

Croesus, king of Lydia 30

Cyrus, the Great, emperor of Persia 86, 118

Cyrus, the Younger, son of Darius II 86

Demetrios of Alexandria, Cynic philosopher 102

Demetrios of Magnesia, biographer and literary scholar 55, 86, 88

Demetrios of Phaleron, orator who held power at Athens 90, 93, 154

Demosthenes, Athenian orator and statesman 51

Diocles of Magnesia, author of books about philosophers 6, 17, 27, 87, 93, 102, 118–19, 136

Diodoros of Aspendos, ascetic Pythagorean 119

Diogenes of Sinope, founder of Cynic movement 3–91, 107, 123–5 130, 133–8, 154, 159–75

Dionsysios I, tyrant of Syracuse 33, 35, 123, 125, 130, 133–7, 139, 175–6, 178–9

Dionysios II, tyrant of Syracuse 56–7, 166–7

Dionysios of Chalcedon, philosopher of the Megarian school 103, 153

Dionysios of Colophon, credited with writing works of Menippos 103

Dionysios of Heraclea, Stoic philosopher 52

Diotimos of Carystos, acquaintance of Diogenes 19

Dioxippos, Athenian athletic champion 21–2

Echecles of Ephesos, early Cynic 102

Epaminondas, Theban general and statesman 45

Epicrates, Athenian politician 180

Epictetus, Stoic philosopher 88

Epicurus, founder of Epicureanism, a hedonistic philosophy 103, 124, 145–7, 152–3

Epitimides of Cyrene, Cyrenaic philosopher 144

Eratosthenes of Cyrene, polymathic scholar 88, 106

Euboulides, author of book on Diogenes, perhaps identifiable with Euboulos 6

Euboulos, author of a book on the enslavement of Diogenes 61

Eucleides, friend of Socrates, founder of Megarian school 36, 88

Eurycleides, hierophant at Eleusis 154

Eurysthenes, Athenian politician 180

Euthycrates, Corinthian acquaintance of Crates 93

Euthydemos, sophist, acquaintance of Socrates 180

Eutychides, slave of Aristippos, 127

Favorinos of Arelate, rhetorician and author 34, 48, 106

Gorgias, of Leontini, sophist and rhetorician 118

Harmodios, Athenian tyrannicide 57, 84, 112

Harpalos, a pirate 47

Hecaton of Rhodes, Stoic philosopher and author 101

Hegesandros of Delphi, author of historical works 134–5

Hegesias, 'Dog-collar', Cynic, pupil of Diogenes 87

Hegesias, 'the Death-Persuader', Cyrenaic philosopher 144, 150–2

Hipparchia, Cynic philosopher, wife of Crates 88, 99–101, 172–5

Hermippos of Smyrna, biographer 102, 118

Hesiod, early epic poet 77, 114

Hicesias of Sinope, father of Diogenes 6

Hiketes, alternative name for preceding 159

Hipparchia, a Cynic, wife of Crates 88, 99–101, 172–5

Hippobotos, author who wrote about philosophers 87, 102, 146

Homer, epic poet 13, 77–8, 117, 166

Isomamachos, an Athenian contemporary of Xenophon 125

Lais, a courtesan 123–5, 132, 134
Lamprocles, son of Socrates 177
Lysanias, son of Aischrion, author 10
Lysias, a pharmacist 48
Lysimachos, Macedonian officer and ruler 100, 154–6

Manes, supposed slave of Diogenes 11
Megas, governor and later ruler of Cyrene 154
Meidias, rich Athenian 74
Meleager (*properly* Meleagros), of Gadara, poet 102
Meleagros, author of work on the opinions of philosophers, 147
Menander (*properly* Menandros), author of comedies 85
Menandros, known as 'Oakwood', a Cynic 87
Menedemos, a Cynic 102
Menedemos, philosopher of the Eretrian school 93, 106, 111
Menippos, Cynic satirical author 58, 102–3
Metrocles, a Cynic, pupil of Crates 43, 98–101, 154, 161–2, 170–1
Metrodoros of Chios, Democritean philosopher 85
Micylos, a poor weaver, possibly fictional 96
Mithras, treasurer of Lysimachos 155
Monimos, Cynic with sceptical views 84–6
Musonius Rufus, Stoic philosopher 100
Myrto, supposed wife of Socrates 177

Nicodromos, a harpist 93

Olympiodoros, an Athenian magistrate 10
Onesicritos, historian, pilot of Alexander's fleet 36

Panaitios, Stoic philosopher 145
Paraibates of Cyrene, Cyrenaic philosopher 144
Pasicles, son of Crates and Hipparchia 88, 100

Pasiphon, credited with writing works attributed to Diogenes 48
Patakion, disreputable Athenian informer 45
Pelopidas, heroic Theban general 84
Perdiccas, general of Alexander and briefly regent of his empire 56
Pericles, Athenian general and statesman 180
Persaios, of Citium, Stoic philosopher 105
Phaedo (*properly* Phaidon), friend of Socrates, founder of Eleian school 129, 180
Phaidros, friend of Socrates 180
Phanias of Eresos, philosophical and historical writer 123
Pharnabazos, Persian satrap 126
Philemon, author of comedies 87
Philip II, King of Macedon, father of Alexander the Great 52–3, 88
Philiscos, son of Onesicritos, pupil of Diogenes 48, 50, 86–7
Philiscos, a cobbler, possibly fictional 94
Philonides, associate of Antigonos II, otherwise unknown 105
Phocion, Athenian general and statesman 86, 157
Phocos, disreputable son of Phocion 157
Phryne, a courtesan 40, 91
Plato, philosopher, friend of Socrates 26, 32–5, 56, 96, 123, 126–8, 131–2, 135–8, 179
Polyeuctos of Sphettos, Athenian orator 10
Polyxenos, philosopher of the Megarian school 24, 128
Prodicos, sophist, a contemporary of Socrates 180
Ptolemy I Soter, king of Egypt 97, 151, 154–5
Pythagoras, philosopher and mystic 100

Satyros, author of biographies 10, 50
Simon, cobbler and acquaintance of Socrates, possibly fictional 179–80
Simos, steward of Dionysios I 137
Skirpalos or Skirtalos, a pirate in time of Diogenes 57, 61
Socrates 35–6, 100, 108, 113, 117–18, 121, 123–7, 132, 134, 142–3, 162, 177–80
Sonicos, a friend of Aristippos 176

Sophocles, tragic poet 45
Sosicrates of Rhodes, historical
  writer 84, 90, 119, 124
Sotion of Alexandria, author of book on
  philosophical successions 35, 50, 124,
  132
Speusippos, Academic philosopher,
  nephew of Plato 80
Stilpo, philosopher of the Megarian
  school 87, 96, 104, 111, 154
Straton, of Lampsacos (?) 132

Telesphoros, an officer of King
  Lysimachos 156
Themison, king of Cyprus 94
Theodoros, 'the Atheist', Cyrenaic with
  eclectic views 100, 105–6, 123, 144,
  153–7
Theognis of Megara, elegiac poet 114
Theombrotos, Cynic, pupil of
  Crates 101–2

Theophrastos, Peripatetic philosopher, a
  pupil of Aristotle 9, 98, 101, 105
Timarchos of Alexandria, early
  Cynic 102

Xanthippe, wife of Socrates 177
Xeniades, sceptical philosopher 85
Xeniades, supposed purchaser and
  master of Diogenes 57–61, 85
Xenocrates, Academic philosopher 80,
  98
Xenophon, Athenian soldier and author,
  friend of Socrates 86, 103, 123

Zeno of Citium, founder of the Stoic
  movement 27, 48–9, 91, 94, 100,
  103–4
Zoilos of Perga, otherwise unknown 46
Zopyros of Colophon, credited with
  writing works of Menippos 103

INDEX OF THEMES

abuse, proper response to 23–4, 74, 140

accoutrements, Cynic, *see* cloak, cup, knapsack, stick

admonition 26, 51, 70–1

adultery, Diogenes on 41; Crates on 88; Theodoros that justifiable 153

affections, that sense-affections alone apprehensible, *see* scepticism

afterlife, *see* Hades, initiations

anger, Aristippos on the suppression of, 139–40

animal, as exemplar 9; cruelty to 115

assault, response to 74, 43, 93

astronomy, mocked as useless 28–9, 109, 163

atheism, of Theodoros, 153–5; *see also* gods

Athenians, criticized by Diogenes as self-indulgent 20, 44

athletes, criticism of 20–1, 73, 78, 84, 164–5

avarice, Diogenes on 378; Bion on 109–10

baths, as shelter for Cynic 98, 107; various references 20, 42, 66, 76, 78, 138

beauty, physical, 42–3, 72, 92, 112

beggar, Diogenes as 8, 10, 12, 17–19, 55, 161; does Plato beg? 34

benefits, should be proportional to worth of recipient 68

birth, high, of no value 27, 150; Antisthenes not of pure Athenian 117–18; Bion's low birth no cause for shame 105

black people, jokes about 72

books, Diogenes on the use of 65, 87

brothel, as revealing nature of love 40, 88; Bion's mother from 105; Diogenes seen leaving 76

bread, black versus white 15, 98

burial, Diogenes on 61, 81–3; Bion on 117; Theodoros on 170

cakes, should sage eat? 15

cannibalism, justifiable 48–9

cloak, rough doubled as Cynic uniform 4, 8, 10, 27, 49, 82, 87, 91, 98, 105, 159–62, 164, 175, 178; did Antisthenes wear one? 119; Aristippos exchanges with Diogenes 138, wears doubled cloak in emergency 131, 138

clothing, luxurious, Aristippos wears 125; but happy in any 131–3, 135–6, 138; mocked by Diogenes 43–4

cobblers, philosophical 94, 179–80

coinage, *see* restamping

contrarian, Diogenes as 21–4

cosmopolitanism, of Diogenes 3–4, 12; of Aristippos 143

courtesans, Diogenes on 40–1; Aristippos associates with 125, 132–4, 141; Crates on 88, 91; Theodorean sophism about 157

crowd, non-Cynics characterized as mere members of 19–20

cultivation and education, value of 37, 63, 69–70, 86, 101, 127, 141

culture, mocked as useless by Diogenes, 27–9; by Bion 108–9; *see also* astronomy, geometry, music, literature, nature

cup, as Cynic accoutrement, 10–11, 159–60

Cynic name, originated as term of abuse 24; supposedly originating with Antisthenes 119; *see also* dog

death, Diogenes on 80–2, 170; tales about his death 83–4; Aristippos fears 138–9; Bion on 116–17; Crates foresees 97, *see also* burial

demagogues, Athenian orators as 50–1

dialectic, mocked by Diogenes 31–2; practised by Theodoros 105, 153, cf. 100 and note

dispossession, Cynic, 4, 8–9, 12, 87–9

dissolute, sayings by Diogenes about the 39; Aristippos disowns his son as being 144; himself caricatured as being 6

divination, mocked, 46, 11, 163

dog, Diogenes as 3, 5, 24–6, 34–5, 49;
    disciple called Dog-collar 87; name
    supposedly connected with
    Antisthenes 119
doctor, philosopher likened to 20, 136–7
dream-reading 46–7
dress, *see* clothing, cloak
drink, Cynic attitudes to 14–17, 27, 90,
    98, 107; *see also* wine
dropsy, as analogy for insatiable
    greed 37, 97, 109

eating, *see* food
effeminacy, attacked by Diogenes 19, 25,
    42–3, 59
education, of young 61–3, 65, 114, 127,
    141; *see also* cultivation
Eleusinian Mysteries, *see* initiations
end, of life, for Cynics to live in
    accordance with virtue, 27; for
    Cyrenaics pleasure 125, 152; *see also*
    pleasure
enslavement, of Diogenes, *see* slavery
envy, Diogenes immune to 91; envious
    man mocked 113–14; sage will
    avoid 90, 146
Epicureanism, how it resembles and
    differs from Cyrenaic hedonism 124,
    145–7, 152–3
exercise, benefits of 29, 66, 92, 172;
    should aim at good of soul 21
exile, of Diogenes 6–8, 60; Bion consoles
    Demetrios for 93–4; no hardship to die
    in 81; of Theodoros 154–6
expense, *see* values
extravagance, of Aristippos 125, 128–9,
    138; source of strife 95; spendthrifts
    mocked for 18, 39–40

farting, no great offence 101
fees, Aristippos charges for teaching, *see*
    money
flattery 50, 69–70, 92, 114; *see also* plain
    speaking
food, Diogenes on the right approach to
    14–16; criticizes wrong approach
    38–40; other references by Diogenes 4,
    10, 58, 138, 161–2, 175; Aristippos
    justifies buying expensive 128–9;
    Antisthenes on simple diet 120; Bion
    on same 107; but greedily devours a fish
    115; Crates on simple diet 90, 95, 98

fortune, Cynic invulnerability to 30–1;
    should accept any role imposed by
    106–7; Aristippos admired for adapting
    to any 123, 131–2; thanked for
    imposing afflictions, 31, 104; wealth as
    vomit of 36, 86
freedom, destitution as beginning of
    88–9; Diogenes values above all else
    30; *see also* slavery
friendship 26, 57, 66–7, 69, 114, 139,
    146, 150, 152–3
Fury, Menedemos supposedly assumes
    guise of a 102

Games, Diogenes at Olympic 19–21,
    162–4; confronts victor on way back
    from 164–5; supposedly dies on way to
    80; Antisthenes plans to deliver speech
    at Isthmian 118; Aristippos learns
    about Socrates at Olympic 125; *see also*
    athletes, victor
geometry, rejected as useless 27, 106
gods, Diogenes on the existence of 47–8;
    Bion's attitude to 106, 111; Theodoros
    as atheist 153–5; wise are friends to 13,
    27–8, 162
gratitude 69, 150–2
greed, insatiable 52, 97, 109; *see also*
    avarice

Hades, fate of dead in 45, 112;
    Menedemos as spy from 102; road
    to 81, 97, 116
happiness, for Diogenes arises from
    dispossession 4–5, 159–62; lies in
    invulnerability to fortune 29–31; not to
    be judged by predominance of
    pleasures 98–9; Cyrenaic views about
    its source 124–5, 143, 145–6, 150
hedonism, of Cyrenaics, *see* pleasure
Heracles, as exemplar for Cynics 4, 30,
    90, 118, 161–2, 179–80
hetairai, *see* courtesans
homelessness, Cynic 4, 8, 10, 27, 96, 98;
    see also jar
hunchback, joke about 76; Crates as 97

ideas, Diogenes mocks Plato's theory
    of 32–3
illusion, as governing human action
    36–43; Bion on false opinion 108–9;
    sense-experience as source of,

according to Monimos 85; to Cyrenaics 148–9.

incest, supposedly favoured by Cynics and early Stoics 49

informers, as dangerous beasts 69

Initiation, into Eleusinian Mysteries 45, 154, 177

insults, *see* abuse

invulnerability, *see* fortune

jar, as home of Diogenes 4, 8, 10, 27, 52–3, 55; *see also* homelessness

jokes, of popular nature ascribed to Diogenes 72–8

kings, interchanges of Diogenes with 52–6, 165–6; Theodorus' boldness toward 154–7; *see also* tyrants

knapsack, as Cynic accoutrement 3–4, 10–11, 15, 85, 90–1, 94, 96, 106, 119, 159–61, 164, 175

knucklebones, as currency in Cynic state 49

letters of recommendation, rejected as pointless 64

literature, study of, rejected as useless 27–8, 109

love 40, 42, 95, 112–13, 118, 134, 146, 163; *see also* sex

lupin seeds, as favourite Cynic food 4, 14, 28, 96, 101, 161, 179

luxury, Cyrenaic 5, 123–5, 128–9

mad, Diogenes viewed as 22, 35; Monimos feigns madness 85

man, true, as against mere member of the crowd, scum or slave 19–22

marriage, Diogenes on 41, 48–50, 167; Antisthenes on 118; Bion on 113; Crates on 88; dog-marriage of Crates and Hipparchia 99–101, 172–5

masturbation, virtues of 16, 41, 49, 162

misanthrope, Diogenes represented as in apocryphal letters 167–70

misers, mocked by Diogenes 18, 38; Bion on 109–10

money, Diogenes scorns 13; begs for daily needs 10, 17–19; criticizes love of 38–9; Crates gives his away 87–9; proper attitude to 97–8; other Cynic reflections on 86, 101, 110; c.f.

Antisthenes 119–21; Aristippos charges much for teaching 123, 127–8; his attitude to 128–30, 134, 137, 141; *see also* poverty, wealth

mourning, Bion criticizes excessive 116

mouse, Diogenes draws lesson from 9; has one as scrounger 15

music, mocked as useless 27, 106; jokes directed at musicians 72, 78

nature, study of, rejected as useless 27–9, 147–8

non-attachment, Aristippos that should adopt a detached attitude toward pleasure and possessions 129–34

octopus, Diogenes dies from eating raw 82, 84

old age, Diogenes on 30, 68, 71, 79–80; Bion on 116; Crates on 97

orators, mocked by Diogenes 50–2; *see also* rhetoric

pain, philosophers should cause 33

parody, of Homeric verses by Diogenes 77–8; parodic tragedies ascribed to him 48–50; in verses of Crates 94–6; practised by Bion 106; seriocomic writings of Menippos 102

pedagogue, Diogenes supposedly served as during his enslavement 61; strikes one for misbehaviour of child 63

pederasty 42, 77, 106, 112–13, 154–5

perfume, Diogenes mocks use of 13, 43–4; expense of 14; favoured by Aristippos 6, 125, 129, 178

pessimism, hedonism as resulting in 150–2

pirates, Diogenes captured by 57–61; Aristippos threatened by 130; Bion threatened by 115; success of pirate evidence against divine providence 47

pleasure, Diogenes that should despise 4, 23, 29–30; Antisthenes on 126; Bion that should be derived from wisdom 108; Crates that happiness should not be judged by its predominance 98–9; the Cyrenaic regard it as end of life 124–5, 145–6, 150–2; interpret it in terms of motion 145–6

possessions, Crates gives away 88–9; overvaluation of 37, 52, 119–21

poverty, blessings of 4, 12, 38, 88–9, 91,
  95, 161, 166; Poverty's self-defence in
  Bion 107
praise, a bad sign to receive it 23;
  Diogenes praised but not followed
  25–6; Bion on the beneficial effects
  of 114
prayer, Diogenes criticizes conventional
  44–6; Aristippos that we should not
  pray for specific things 140; Bion
  on 111
prodigies, mockery of attitudes to 47,
  111
prostitutes, *see* courtesans
public, Diogenes carries out all activities
  in, *see* shamelessness
purifications 45–6, 111

quarrels, Crates as a counsellor who
  resolves 89–90; Aristippos resolves
  personal quarrel 139

religion, Diogenes on 44–50, 55; Bion on
  11–16; *see also* gods
reputation, should be viewed with
  contempt 23, 27, 46, 50
restamping the currency, literal and
  figurative, 6–7, 30
rhetoric, scorned by Diogenes 28, 50–2;
  by Bion 114; orator hired by Aristippos
  125; rhetorical style of
  Antisthenes 118
ridicule, *see* abuse
ruling, art of 58, 142–3

sacrifices, criticism of 44–5
sacrilege, can be justifiable, Bion 112;
  . Theodoros 153; sacrilegious act
  ascribed to Diogenes 46; *see also*
  temple-robbery
scepticism, Cyrenaic regarding
  sense-experience, 147–50; of
  Monimos 85–6
self-sufficiency 12, 118, 153; Bion's
  discourse on 106–8
sex 16, 40–2, 48–50, 88, 101, 106,
  112–13, 120, 125, 132–4, 147, 153–4,
  162, 169
shamelessness, Cynic, 5, 16–17, 25, 49,
  103–4
shipwreck, of Aristippos 130–2; of
  Zeno 103–4

short cut to happiness, Cynic, 5, 27,
  159–61, 172; caricatured as path to
  notoriety 5
silence, proper time for 62, 115
slavery and freedom, Diogenes happy to
  lose his slave 11; has no slave to bury
  him 81; most people slaves by nature
  21, 38, 160–1; freedom depends on
  knowledge of good 64, 108; Diogenes
  remains free when enslaved 57–62,
  170–2; Crates sets himself free by
  giving away his possessions 88–9, 95;
  Bion sold into slavery 105; *see also* for
  Aristippos 127, 136, 142–3
sophisms, Diogenes responds to 32;
  Hipparchia responds to 100; employed
  by Theodoros, 153–4, 157; *see also*
  dialectic
Spartans, praised by Diogenes for
  hardiness, 20, 31; interchanges with 77;
  vain about mean clothing 44
spitting, into face of uncultivated 37,
  137–8, 164; used as analogy by
  Aristippos 144
spy, Cynic as 52, 102
stick, Antisthenes threatens Diogenes
  with 8; as carried by Diogenes 3, 10,
  159–61; Diogenes strikes people
  with 20, 74, 163; to deter scavengers
  after death 82, 170; wielded by
  Crates 88, 103–4; did Antisthenes or
  Diodoros first adopt stick and
  knapsack? 119
suicide, Diogenes on 79–80; did he kill
  himself? 82–3; Metrocles said to have
  101; and Menippos 102; Hegesias
  encourages as 'Death-persuader'
  150–3; Theodoros that never
  justifiable 157
superstition, Diogenes mocks 44–7; Bion
  mocks 111–12; but finally yields to it
  106; sage will be free of 147

taverns and wine-shops, 17, 40, 44, 51, 81
tax-collectors, as dangerous beasts, 69
temple-robbery, may be justifiable, 48,
  112; custodians the worse thieves 46
tragedy, Diogenes has suffered all
  curses of 12; mocked by him 28;
  parodies of tragedy ascribed to him
  48–50; Crates inspired by a distressed
  hero from 87

training, Cynic life as form of 29–30, 161; procedures adopted to train for endurance 10, 77; of children 59, 61–3, 64–5

tyrants, Diogenes's attitude to 56–7, 166–7; mocks Plato for associating with 133–4; Aristippos at court of 6, 123, 125, 134–8, 175–8; Theodoros responds to threat from 156; *see also* kings

underworld, *see* Hades
universe, study of, *see* astronomy, nature

values, relative, the best things cheapest 13–14, 94
vanity, different kinds of 44; Diogenes accused of 35, 138

vegetable washing, anecdotes centring around 33, 138, 154, 175
victor, the Cynic as true 20–1, 164–5

wealth, true 12–14, 23, 95, 97–8, 119–20; conventional evaluation attacked 36–9, 70, 109–11; Aristippos that cannot have too much 129; productive of pleasure but not inherently valuable 147; *see also* money, poverty
wine, Diogenes on 14–15; Crates rejects 90; other references 98, 107, 120, 123, 134, 178
women, popular misogynistic jokes 71–2; suited to philosophy 100, 172–5; virtue same as man's 118
world, Diogenes citizen of, 3–4, 12

The Oxford World's Classics Website

www.worldsclassics.co.uk

- Browse the full range of Oxford World's Classics online

- Sign up for our monthly e-alert to receive information on new titles

- Read extracts from the Introductions

- Listen to our editors and translators talk about the world's greatest literature with our Oxford World's Classics audio guides

- Join the conversation, follow us on Twitter at OWC_Oxford

- Teachers and lecturers can order inspection copies quickly and simply via our website

www.worldsclassics.co.uk

American Literature

British and Irish Literature

Children's Literature

Classics and Ancient Literature

Colonial Literature

Eastern Literature

European Literature

Gothic Literature

History

Medieval Literature

Oxford English Drama

Poetry

Philosophy

Politics

Religion

The Oxford Shakespeare

A complete list of Oxford World's Classics, including Authors in Context, Oxford English Drama, and the Oxford Shakespeare, is available in the UK from the Marketing Services Department, Oxford University Press, Great Clarendon Street, Oxford OX2 6DP, or visit the website at www.oup.com/uk/worldsclassics.

In the USA, visit www.oup.com/us/owc for a complete title list.

Oxford World's Classics are available from all good bookshops. In case of difficulty, customers in the UK should contact Oxford University Press Bookshop, 116 High Street, Oxford OX1 4BR.

A SELECTION OF   **OXFORD WORLD'S CLASSICS**

Classical Literary Criticism

The First Philosophers: The Presocratics and the Sophists

Greek Lyric Poetry

Myths from Mesopotamia

APOLLODORUS   The Library of Greek Mythology

APOLLONIUS OF RHODES   Jason and the Golden Fleece

APULEIUS   The Golden Ass

ARISTOPHANES   Birds and Other Plays

ARISTOTLE   The Nicomachean Ethics
Physics
Politics

BOETHIUS   The Consolation of Philosophy

CAESAR   The Civil War
The Gallic War

CATULLUS   The Poems of Catullus

CICERO   Defence Speeches
The Nature of the Gods
On Obligations
Political Speeches
The Republic and The Laws

EURIPIDES   Bacchae and Other Plays
Heracles and Other Plays
Medea and Other Plays
Orestes and Other Plays
The Trojan Women and Other Plays

HERODOTUS   The Histories

HOMER   The Iliad
The Odyssey

A SELECTION OF OXFORD WORLD'S CLASSICS

HORACE	The Complete Odes and Epodes
JUVENAL	The Satires
LIVY	The Dawn of the Roman Empire
	Hannibal's War
	The Rise of Rome
MARCUS AURELIUS	The Meditations
OVID	The Love Poems
	Metamorphoses
PETRONIUS	The Satyricon
PLATO	Defence of Socrates, Euthyphro, and Crito
	Gorgias
	Meno and Other Dialogues
	Phaedo
	Republic
	Selected Myths
	Symposium
PLAUTUS	Four Comedies
PLUTARCH	Greek Lives
	Roman Lives
	Selected Essays and Dialogues
PROPERTIUS	The Poems
SOPHOCLES	Antigone, Oedipus the King, and Electra
STATIUS	Thebaid
SUETONIUS	Lives of the Caesars
TACITUS	Agricola and Germany
	The Histories
VIRGIL	The Aeneid
	The Eclogues and Georgics
XENOPHON	The Expedition of Cyrus

A SELECTION OF   **OXFORD WORLD'S CLASSICS**

THOMAS AQUINAS	Selected Philosophical Writings
FRANCIS BACON	The Essays
WALTER BAGEHOT	The English Constitution
GEORGE BERKELEY	Principles of Human Knowledge and Three Dialogues
EDMUND BURKE	A Philosophical Enquiry into the Origin of Our Ideas of the Sublime and Beautiful Reflections on the Revolution in France
CONFUCIUS	The Analects
DESCARTES	A Discourse on the Method
ÉMILE DURKHEIM	The Elementary Forms of Religious Life
FRIEDRICH ENGELS	The Condition of the Working Class in England
JAMES GEORGE FRAZER	The Golden Bough
SIGMUND FREUD	The Interpretation of Dreams
THOMAS HOBBES	Human Nature and De Corpore Politico Leviathan
DAVID HUME	Selected Essays
NICCOLÒ MACHIAVELLI	The Prince
THOMAS MALTHUS	An Essay on the Principle of Population
KARL MARX	Capital The Communist Manifesto
J. S. MILL	On Liberty and Other Essays Principles of Political Economy and Chapters on Socialism
FRIEDRICH NIETZSCHE	Beyond Good and Evil The Birth of Tragedy On the Genealogy of Morals Thus Spoke Zarathustra Twilight of the Idols

A SELECTION OF OXFORD WORLD'S CLASSICS

THOMAS PAINE — Rights of Man, Common Sense, and Other Political Writings

JEAN-JACQUES ROUSSEAU — The Social Contract
Discourse on the Origin of Inequality

ADAM SMITH — An Inquiry into the Nature and Causes of the Wealth of Nations

MARY WOLLSTONECRAFT — A Vindication of the Rights of Woman

Bhagavad Gita

The Bible Authorized King James Version
With Apocrypha

Dhammapada

Dharmasūtras

The Koran

The Pañcatantra

The Sauptikaparvan (from the
Mahabharata)

The Tale of Sinuhe and Other Ancient
Egyptian Poems

The Qur'an

Upaniṣads

ANSELM OF CANTERBURY   The Major Works

THOMAS AQUINAS   Selected Philosophical Writings

AUGUSTINE   The Confessions
On Christian Teaching

BEDE   The Ecclesiastical History

HEMACANDRA   The Lives of the Jain Elders

KĀLIDĀSA   The Recognition of Śakuntalā

MANJHAN   Madhumalati

ŚĀNTIDEVA   The Bodhicaryàvatàra

A SELECTION OF   **OXFORD WORLD'S CLASSICS**

The Anglo-Saxon World

Beowulf

Lancelot of the Lake

The Paston Letters

Sir Gawain and the Green Knight

Tales of the Elders of Ireland

York Mystery Plays

GEOFFREY CHAUCER   **The Canterbury Tales**
                          Troilus and Criseyde

HENRY OF HUNTINGDON   **The History of the English People**
                          1000–1154

JOCELIN OF BRAKELOND   **Chronicle of the Abbey of Bury**
                          St Edmunds

GUILLAUME DE LORRIS   **The Romance of the Rose**
and JEAN DE MEUN

WILLIAM LANGLAND   **Piers Plowman**

SIR THOMAS MALORY   **Le Morte Darthur**

An Anthology of Elizabethan Prose Fiction

An Anthology of Seventeenth-Century
Fiction

Early Modern Women's Writing

Three Early Modern Utopias (Utopia; New
Atlantis; The Isle of Pines)

FRANCIS BACON — Essays
The Major Works

APHRA BEHN — Oroonoko and Other Writings
The Rover and Other Plays

JOHN BUNYAN — Grace Abounding
The Pilgrim's Progress

JOHN DONNE — The Major Works
Selected Poetry

BEN JONSON — The Alchemist and Other Plays
The Devil is an Ass and Other Plays
Five Plays

JOHN MILTON — The Major Works
Paradise Lost
Selected Poetry

SIR PHILIP SIDNEY — The Old Arcadia
The Major Works

IZAAK WALTON — The Compleat Angler

Travel Writing 1700–1830

Women's Writing 1778–1838

WILLIAM BECKFORD   Vathek

JAMES BOSWELL   Life of Johnson

FRANCES BURNEY   Camilla
Cecilia
Evelina
The Wanderer

LORD CHESTERFIELD   Lord Chesterfield's Letters

JOHN CLELAND   Memoirs of a Woman of Pleasure

DANIEL DEFOE   A Journal of the Plague Year
Moll Flanders
Robinson Crusoe
Roxana

HENRY FIELDING   Jonathan Wild
Joseph Andrews and Shamela
Tom Jones

WILLIAM GODWIN   Caleb Williams

OLIVER GOLDSMITH   The Vicar of Wakefield

MARY HAYS   Memoirs of Emma Courtney

ELIZABETH INCHBALD   A Simple Story

SAMUEL JOHNSON   The History of Rasselas
The Major Works

CHARLOTTE LENNOX   The Female Quixote

MATTHEW LEWIS   Journal of a West India Proprietor
The Monk

HENRY MACKENZIE   The Man of Feeling

A SELECTION OF   OXFORD WORLD'S CLASSICS

ALEXANDER POPE	Selected Poetry
ANN RADCLIFFE	The Italian
	The Mysteries of Udolpho
	The Romance of the Forest
	A Sicilian Romance
CLARA REEVE	The Old English Baron
SAMUEL RICHARDSON	Pamela
RICHARD BRINSLEY SHERIDAN	The School for Scandal and Other Plays
TOBIAS SMOLLETT	The Adventures of Roderick Random
	The Expedition of Humphry Clinker
LAURENCE STERNE	The Life and Opinions of Tristram Shandy, Gentleman
	A Sentimental Journey
JONATHAN SWIFT	Gulliver's Travels
	Major Works
	A Tale of a Tub and Other Works
JOHN VANBRUGH	The Relapse and Other Plays
HORACE WALPOLE	The Castle of Otranto
MARY WOLLSTONECRAFT	Mary and The Wrongs of Woman
	A Vindication of the Rights of Woman

LUDOVICO ARIOSTO	Orlando Furioso
GIOVANNI BOCCACCIO	The Decameron
LUÍS VAZ DE CAMÕES	The Lusíads
MIGUEL DE CERVANTES	Don Quixote de la Mancha
	Exemplary Stories
CARLO COLLODI	The Adventures of Pinocchio
DANTE ALIGHIERI	The Divine Comedy
	Vita Nuova
LOPE DE VEGA	Three Major Plays
J. W. VON GOETHE	Faust: Part One and Part Two
LEONARDO DA VINCI	Selections from the Notebooks
FEDERICO GARCIA LORCA	Four Major Plays
NICCOLÒ MACHIAVELLI	Discourses on Livy
	The Prince
MICHELANGELO	Life, Letters, and Poetry
PETRARCH	Selections from the Canzoniere and
	Other Works
GIORGIO VASARI	The Lives of the Artists